Contextualization of Sufi Spirituality in Seventeenth- and Eighteenth-Century China

Contextualization of Sufi Spirituality in Seventeenth- and Eighteenth-Century China

The Role of Liu Zhi (c. 1662–c. 1730)

DAVID LEE

Foreword by Peter G. Riddell

◆PICKWICK *Publications* · Eugene, Oregon

CONTEXTUALIZATION OF SUFI SPIRITUALITY IN SEVENTEENTH- AND EIGHTEENTH-CENTURY CHINA
The Role of Liu Zhi (c. 1662–c. 1730)

Copyright © 2015 David Lee. All rights reserved. Except for brief quotations in critical publications or reviews, no part of this book may be reproduced in any manner without prior written permission from the publisher. Write: Permissions, Wipf and Stock Publishers, 199 W. 8th Ave., Suite 3, Eugene, OR 97401.

Pickwick Publications
An Imprint of Wipf and Stock Publishers
199 W. 8th Ave., Suite 3
Eugene, OR 97401

www.wipfandstock.com

ISBN 13: 978-1-61097-254-3

Cataloguing-in-Publication data:

Lee, David (1954–)

    Contextualization of Sufi spirituality in seventeenth- and eighteenth-century China : the role of Liu Zhi (c. 1662–c. 1730) / David Lee.

    xvi + 290 p. ; 23 cm. Includes bibliographical references and index.

    ISBN 13: 978-1-61097-254-3

    1. Liu Zhi, active 1670–1724. 2. Sufism—China. 3. Islam—China. 4. Islamic sects—China—History. 4. Muslims—China. I. Title.

BP173 C65 L45 2015

Manufactured in the U.S.A.   12/07/2015

To my dear mother
Mrs. Lee Wan Lai-ying (1924–2015)

Contents

List of Figures and Tables | ix
Foreword by Peter G. Riddell | xi
Acknowledgments | xv

1 Methodological Introduction | 1
2 The Historical, Philosophical, and Islamic Context in China | 19
3 An Examination of Liu Zhi's Writings | 66
4 Liu Zhi's Engagement with the Concept of the Unity of Existence of the Ibn 'Arabi Tradition | 90
5 Liu Zhi's Sufi Spirituality in Conversation with the Neo-Confucian Context in China | 123
6 Liu Zhi's Engagement with Islam and Neo-Confucian Culture in His *Rules and Proprieties of Islam*: An English Translation and Detailed Examination | 157
7 Model of Contextualization, Contemporary Relevance and Final Conclusion | 194

APPENDIX I
The Poem of the Five Sessions of the Moon in English | 205

APPENDIX II
Translation of Selected Texts of the *True Record of the Utmost Sage of Islam* | 210

APPENDIX III
Personal Narrative of *Tianfan Dianli*: (Selected Essential Explanations of the Proprieties of Islam) | 215

APPENDIX IV
The Rules and Proprieties of Islam | 218

Bibliography | 257
Index | 275

Figures and Tables

Figures

Figure 1.1 A Map of the Models of Contextual Theology | 10
Figure 1.2 The Translation Model | 12
Figure 1.3 The Conversation Model | 14
Figure 2.1 The Diagram of the Limitless or Infinite | 57
Figure 2.2 The Triad of Interconnected Relationships | 61
Figure 4.1 Liu Zhi's *Three-character Classic* | 98
Figure 5.1 *The Chinese Code of Success* | 125
Figure 5.2 Translation of the First Stanza of the First Session of the Moon | 132
Figure 6.1 Diagram of the True Practice of Sage Endeavor | 165

Tables

Table 2.1 Pointers of Liu Zhi's Contextualization | 64
Table 4.1 Grade of Disclosure between Ibn 'Arabi's Basic Scheme and Chinese Traditional Schemes | 92
Table 4.2 Continuation between the Ibn 'Arabi Tradition and Wang Daiyu's Concept of Divine Disclosure | 93
Table 4.3 Wang Daiyu's Concept of Existence in Terms of the Three Ones | 94
Table 4.4 Observations and Remarks of Liu Zhi's *Displaying the Concealment of the Real Realm* | 101

Table 4.5	Comparison between Wang Daiyu and Liu Zhi on the Three Sub-grades of the Embodied One	115
Table 5.1	Remarks and Comments of *The Poem of the Five Sessions of the Moon*	126
Table 7.1	Various Aspects of Liu Zhi's Contextualization	198

Foreword

When most people think of China and its massive population of 1.4 billion, few take account of Islam as a part of the Chinese multicultural landscape. Nevertheless, China's Islamic community numbers roughly twenty-five to thirty millions according to many estimates: a sizeable community by any measure. Ten of China's fifty-five recognized minority communities are majority Sunni Muslim.

Islam came early to western China thanks to the famous Silk Road. This route had been established during the Han dynasty (206 BC–AD 220) and stretched from the area covered by the present day city of Xi'an in the East to Rome in the West. It wound its way through the rugged terrain of Central Asia, to Persia, the Fertile Crescent, leading to the shores of Asia Minor and on to various points in the Roman Empire.

Early contacts via the Silk Road were made during the period of the Tang Dynasty (618–907). This period encompassed the Arab Umayyad dynasty (661–750), which sent seventeen envoys to the Tang Dynasty court. In all, there were more than thirty visits between 651 and 798 by Arab envoys.

Trade and diplomatic contacts inevitably led to the establishment of new communities. Indeed, Chinese cities witnessed the emergence over time of communities of Arabs and Persians. Relations were not always cordial; military clashes between Muslim armies from the Middle East and the Tang dynasty led to the defeat of the Tangs at Talas in 751 CE. Shortly after that, widespread destruction resulted from sectarian conflict between Chinese and the Arab and Persian communities in Guangdong in 758.

By the late Tang Dynasty, much of the overseas trade of China was in the hands of Muslim Persians and Arabs. There is evidence that Muslim merchants from the Southeast Asian Hindu-Buddhist kingdom of Srivijaya visited China in the tenth and eleventh centuries. By the time of the Mongol Yuan Dynasty (1279–1368), Islam had cemented its place in China and was in an important phase of consolidation, benefiting from the growth of religious establishments which were granted exemption from taxation by the authorities.

This important study by Dr. David Lee picks up the story of Islam in China from this point. He sets the scene with an overview of the Yuan Dynasty, the Ming Dynasty (1368–1644) and the Qing Dynasty (1644–1911), arguing for their key role in shaping Chinese Islam as we know it today. Dr. Lee then moves to his central focus: the figure of Liu Zhi and his contextualization during the early Qing period of Sufi spirituality in China.

There is an abundance of originality in this study as it opens fresh, new windows into understanding the story of Islam in China, applying principles taken from the broader study of contextualization to classical Islamic texts, thereby unearthing new information of some considerable significance.

Dr. Lee's research is important for a range of reasons. First, it adds to the extensive body of literature devoted to the study of contextualization. This literature is already rich in studies of contextualization by Christians, but there is a dearth of quality research available on the study of contextualization by Muslims. This has particular ramifications for the modern day when Muslim groups engaged in *da'wa* (mission) in China and, indeed, across the world, are becoming increasingly adept at contextualizing their missionary message. Dr. Lee's book shows that this contemporary process has deep roots.

Second, there has been much research into Christian mission in China, but the understanding of the history and methods of Muslim Mission in China is much less known, especially in terms of English-language scholarship. China is a dynamic country that will play a major role on the world stage in the twenty-first century, and the place of Islam in that nation will assume increasing importance in decades to come. David Lee's book fills an important gap for those who will increasingly study Islam in China.

Third, Dr. Lee's book has important things to say about the process of transmission from source texts to target texts. The writings of the scholar in focus, Liu Zhi, served as a bridge for Chinese Muslims to access the rich heritage of classical Islamic writings from other regions. This process of transmission represents an important piece in the puzzle of the history of Islam in China.

Fourth, Dr Lee's book considers in detail a set of writings by his chosen scholar which still have circulation among Chinese Muslims today. A visit to Islamic bookshops in China will reveal that Liu Zhi's writings are still stocked on shelves for sale. Therefore this study provides a direct window into the thoughts and teachings that shape Chinese Muslims today.

Dr David Lee's new book represents an important contribution to the study of Islam, both in China and beyond, and adds another piece to the puzzle of the history of Islamic thought in the world's most populous nation.

Professor Peter G. Riddell
Melbourne
May 2015

Acknowledgments

This book began as my doctoral thesis, which I undertook in London and Hong Kong. The writing of the thesis has been a fairly long process. I am greatly indebted to my supervisor, Professor Peter Riddell, for his patience and encouragement throughout. His guidance and advice during the course of my studies in London and Hong Kong have been tremendous. His perceptive criticisms are always made with sensitivity and kindness. Without his patience, I would not have been able to finish the thesis.

My study would not be possible without the support and prayers of the pastors and leaders of my home church, the Chinese Church in London. I am thankful for their prayer and support.

I am thankful to the board members of Evangel Seminary in Hong Kong to grant me a sabbatical leave to finish my thesis. Also, the faculty members, staff, and pupils have prayed continually for the completion of my research.

I am also thankful to family members who have waited long enough to see the completion of my study. Words cannot express my appreciation of their support. Finally, I am greatly grateful to my wife, Jessie, and our son, Cliff. Their love and support have made the completion of the thesis less difficult than expected.

1

Methodological Introduction

GENERAL AIMS

Liu Zhi (c. 1662–c. 1730) is known as one of the greatest Muslim scholars to have lived in China, and his teachings on Islam are still influential among Muslim people today.[1] The Qing dynasty in China with its dictatorial emperors in the seventeenth and eighteenth century allowed limited religious freedom to Muslims in China. Local rioting was not uncommon in the fight for religious autonomy. In such a historical context, Liu met his challenges by translating the Qur'anic materials, classical Persian and Arabic texts in medieval Islam into Chinese and simultaneously re-interpreting the source materials using Confucian language and religious concepts, making Islam more comprehensible and less threatening for the Chinese authorities; thus allowing greater freedom for Islamic teaching. Ibn 'Arabi and his followers have exerted great influence in Chinese Sufism. Ibn 'Arabi (1165–1240) was born in Murcia,[2] Al-Andalus, and his writings had an immense impact throughout the Islamic world and beyond. Liu Zhi's translation of the Ibn 'Arabi tradition was far from literal. Liu Zhi was both a neo-Confucian and Islamic scholar, well trained in both traditions. In order to reach out to more

---

1. Sun Zhenyu is the only scholar who attempts to date the time of Liu Zhi. He suggests the year of birth around 1662. Sun, *Critical Biography*, 211. No scholar is able to date precisely the year of Liu Zhi's death. Many Chinese scholars simply speculate around the year of 1730. Liu Zhi's last work is dated around 1724.

2. Stephen Hirtenstein gives an account of the spiritual life and thought of Ibn 'Arabi. See Hirtenstein, *Mercifer*.

Muslims who could not read any Qur'anic or Islamic text in Arabic or Persian, he insisted that the Chinese language should be used to propagate the Islamic faith. A general aim of this study is to analyze Liu Zhi's contextualization of Islam using Confucian concepts.

The general research questions of this study are: firstly, while Liu Zhi attempts to reach out to a majority of the Muslim people using Confucianism, what is his model of contextualization? How is he affected by the cultural, political, religious and philosophical contexts? Secondly, Liu Zhi adheres to the rich resources of traditional materials. Are there any successes and dangers in his use and interpretation of sources and traditions? Critical analysis needs to be made and evaluation is required. Thirdly, the question of getting Islam to be acceptable means that Liu Zhi has to integrate doctrine, religious spirituality and culture. What sort of integration? Is it adaptation, accommodation or Confucianization? These issues will be revisited in the final concluding chapter of this work.

SPECIFIC OBJECTIVES

Liu Zhi transmitted the ancient texts in Arabic and Persian into Chinese, a language that was inaccessible to most Chinese Muslims. The first objective of this study is to examine the major and minor works of Liu Zhi including his translation work.

Liu encouraged Muslims to pursue personal virtue in a form of Islamic spirituality known as Sufism or mysticism. Is Sufism mystical rather than spiritual? Anthony Johns argues that there is no need to equate spirituality with mysticism. Undoubtedly, mysticism has many negative connotations and may give a misleading impression to many.[3] The mystics had great passion in their quest for spiritual rigors. For Liu Zhi, such pursuit of closeness with God was grounded on the concept of the unity of existence of God. The second specific aim is to examine critically Liu Zhi's contextualization of Sufi spirituality by using a Confucian concept of self-realization.

It should be noted that the two specific objectives are inter-related. Liu Zhi's translation makes extensive use of Confucian terms and his teaching of Islamic spirituality is articulated using the Confucian wisdom of self-realization. Liu Zhi's goal is to persuade Muslims in China that Islam is a living faith. For a living faith to grow, develop and persevere, people of faith must understand the divine revelation through the ancient text and the tradition. This is the primary task of Liu Zhi as the transmitter of tradition. Then, the people of faith must draw close to God by embodying the

---

3. Johns, "Perspectives," 9.

practical wisdom inspired by the written text. Sufi spirituality provided the way for practical wisdom in seventeenth to eighteenth-century China. This is the secondary task of Liu Zhi and other similar transmitters to explain how doctrines would be expressed in Islamic spirituality.

Previous Relevant Studies

Many contemporary scholars, especially those in China, agree that Liu's Islamic works have made a valuable contribution to Chinese philosophy, especially the later Confucian, namely Neo-Confucian tradition. Through Liu Zhi and other Islamic activities, the Chinese philosophical and cultural tradition has been enriched to become a diverse, multi-ethnic Chinese philosophy, integrating Islamic thought in Chinese into Neo-Confucian culture. Against this common consensus, there are recent and differing voices that should be taken seriously. A Malaysian Chinese, Zheng Wenquan, has disagreed in his dissertation with the concept of the so called "sinicized Islam" in China.[4] Furthermore, he asserts that seventeenth-century Chinese Islam belonged to Ibn 'Arabi's Sufism, which had existed in China, i.e. Sufism *in* China (emphasis on the word "in") rather than *sinicized* Islam in China (emphasis on the word "sinicized").

Sachiko Murata gives a modern English translation of Jami's *Lawa'ih* and argues that while Liu's translation of *Lawa'ih* was far from literal, Liu Zhi did not overtly betray its Islamic origin.[5] Later, Murata further published a very significant and substantial treatment of Liu Zhi's *Nature and Principle in Islam*.[6] Her recent works continue and build on her previous scholarship on Liu Zhi. However, this present research study examines another important work of Liu Zhi, namely *The Rules and Proprieties of Islam*, which has been acknowledged as one of the most contextualized or Confucianized works of Liu Zhi. While *The Nature and Principle in Islam* is concerned with the nature of God, cosmogony, humanity and Islamic philosophy, *The Rules and Proprieties of Islam* concerns the way of life for Muslims living in China.

Two scholars have written substantial studies on *The Rules and Proprieties of Islam*. Liang Xiangming writes in Chinese and James Frankel in English.[7] They have offered their own accounts of Liu Zhi's contextualization. This present study will determine a model of Liu Zhi's contextualization that is more convincing than the two accounts offered by Liang and Frankel.

---

4. See Zheng, "Islamic Nature."
5. Murata, *Gleams*, 121.
6. See Murata et al., *Sage*.
7. See Liang, *Study of Liu Zhi*. Frankel, *Rectifying*.

METHOD OF STUDY: ENGAGING ISLAMIC TEXTS WITH CHINESE CULTURE

Contextualizing the Religious Message

As a religion, Islam has a religious message and theology to communicate. The Islamic message needs to be contextualized in China. What is contextual theology? In a general sense, theologians realize that all theology is contextual. A classic example is the emerging Christian liberation theology in Africa in the 1960s. Theologians in post colonial Africa and Latin America have usually focused their study on justice-seeking theologies that express very clearly their political, cultural and social stances. Thus, "theologians have always been influenced by their context and to varying degrees some have demonstrated an awareness of the influence that their own specific context and experiences have had on the theologies they develop."[8] In a specific sense, contextual theology means more than merely "all theology is contextual."[9] Angie Pears asserts that theology is contextual when a theologian "explicitly places the recognition of the contextual nature of theology at the forefront of the theological process."[10] That is, theology is contextual when it "is explicitly shaped, if not driven, by the recognition of the contextual nature of theology with all of its potentially controversial and problematic implications."[11]

This present study aims to show that Liu Zhi's contextualization of Islam in China is not merely contextual in the general sense. He consciously and explicitly shaped his works by using Chinese philosophical and cultural concepts. He was aware of potential controversial and problematic implications. However, such contextualization was common among Hui literati in the early Qing dynasty. Practitioners include Wang Daiyu (c. 1580–c. 1660), Ma Zhu (c. 1640–c. 1711), and others in sixteenth to eighteenth-century China. When they engaged with Islamic texts in Persian and Arabic, they needed to translate and equally important to interpret the texts.

---

8. Pears, *Contextual Theology*, 9.

9. Several authors understand contextual theology not merely as methodology but as a distinct theology, contemporary and effective in its own right. See Schreiter, *Constructing*. Pattison, 'Some Straw," 135–45. See also Bergmann, *God in Context*.

10. Pears, *Contextual Theology*, 1.

11. Ibid.

Engaging with Islamic Texts: Exoteric and Esoteric Interpretation of Islamic Text

According to Alexander Knysh, philologists face a difficult task in translating Qur'anic technical words and philosophical concepts. Part of the reason is the notion that the Arabic language is the repository of God's final revelation and this makes the interpretation of that revealed text highly sensitive and contested. In their philosophical reconstruction, Ibn 'Arabi and his followers often used Qur'anic verses to support their concept of the unity of existence. That is, the Qur'an is the foundational source of their understanding of the unity of existence. However, verses taken out of their context may yield themselves to widely different or even diametrically opposed interpretations.[12] A well-known Islamic theologian and philosopher al-Ghazali (1057–1111) argued that interpretation created new meaning.

Martin Whittingham, in his study of al-Ghazali's hermeneutics, observes that on the one hand, al-Ghazali affirmed the idea of an authoritative text and authorial intention. On the other, he "could be said [to be] a prime example of an interpreter producing meaning."[13] Whittingham argues that it is not the context and preconditioning that al-Ghazali identifies; rather it is al-Ghazali's preconceived worldview that uncovers meanings in the Qur'an. It is the interdependence of the visible and invisible realms of the cosmos and this leads to his affirmation that "both exoteric and esoteric interpretations are necessary and that esoteric interpretations supplement and build on exoteric exegesis, rather than replacing it."[14] He did not favor one above the other. Rather, he insisted on the connection between the two meanings, that is, between the pearl and the shell. In addition, al-Ghazali gave two sets of rules for the understanding of the meaning of the revealed text, namely, external and internal rules. External rules are concerned with the physical condition of the reader and the internal rules the mental condition of the reader.[15] Furthermore, according to Muhammad Kamal, al-Ghazali notes that the degrees of textual interpretation are parallel to five degrees of existence.

1. Essential existence, as the highest degree of existence, corresponds to the entities beyond the domain of sensory experience and human understanding.

---

12. Intra-Islamic debate is not uncommon in the history of Islam. See Knysh, "Multiple Areas," 219.
13. Whittingham, *Al-Ghazali*, 129.
14. Ibid., *Al-Ghazali*, 64.
15. Kamal, "Al-Ghazali," 83–85.

2. Sensory existence, which includes all sorts of images produced by the mind while dreaming or daydreaming.

3. Imaginative existence, which is the image of an object when it is absent from the senses or when it is not perceived directly by sense experience.

4. Mental or intellectual existence, which is able to represent the essence of an object.

5. Analogical existence, which is something that does not exist in the senses, imagination or intellect but exists as a property or attribute of something, such as mercy or anger, which are used in relation to God.[16]

Kamal concludes by stating two contributions of al-Ghazali's hermeneutics. Firstly, the priority of tradition or certain schools of thought to get access to the essence of the Qur'an is rejected. The reader needs to have a presuppositionless mindset before reading the revealed text. Secondly, the readers are encouraged to apprehend the meaning of the Qur'an on their own and arrive at an independent understanding.[17] According to Knysh, al-Ghazali's method is classified as a moderate or *shari'a*-oriented approach to Qur'anic exegesis.[18] For Knysh, "al-Ghazali is convinced that the depth of one's understanding of the Qur'an is directly linked to one's level of spiritual purity, righteousness and intellectual progress."[19] It should be noted that al-Ghazali was the teacher of Ibn 'Arabi when he was in Baghdad.

Ibn 'Arabi's exegetical skill can be shown in his comment on Sura 42:11: "there is nothing like unto Him." This verse is often understood as underscoring God's transcendence and being the fact that He is beyond any comparison with the world. However, Ibn 'Arabi noted that there were two "likening" words in Sura 42:11. "It literally says: 'There is nothing like (*ka*) His likeness (*mithlihi*).' The expression thus actually affirms God's likeness, but denies that that likeness is any way commensurable with anything else."[20] For Ibn 'Arabi, God's likeness referred to the perfect man in Sufi cosmology.[21] Toby Mayer asserts that according to Ibn 'Arabi, "the revealed scripture ... must be respected as a text, not used as a *pretext*. Correspondingly, Ibn 'Arabi's intensely esoteric hermeneutic of the Qur'an is often strictly in line

16. Kamal, 'Al-Ghazali's Hermeneutics,' 86–7.
17. Ibid., 88.
18. Knysh, "Sufism and the Qur'an," 143.
19. Ibid., 151.
20. Mayer, "Theology and Sufism," 282–83.
21. See Chodkiewicz, *Seal,* 60–73.

with the literal sense of the text."²² Thus, the key feature of Ibn ʿArabi's hermeneutic may be called esoteric literalism. However, in the view of Knysh, Ibn ʿArabi's exegesis aimed to bring out the spiritual quintessence. When he expounded Sura 24:35 of the Qur'an, there were three levels of understanding of its meaning: "the metaphysical and cosmological, the analogical (built around the implicit correspondences between the universe and the human individual) and the existential-experiential based on the notion"²³ of unity of God, humankind and the universe.

It is clear that both al-Ghazali and Ibn ʿArabi emphasized both exoteric and esoteric interpretation of the Qur'an and did not play esoteric interpretation against exoteric, always seeking the unveiling of the text with orthodoxy and orthopraxis. They could both be considered "moderate" Sufis because their exegesis was not characterized by a visionary and ecstatic approach to Qur'an interpretation. As asserted by Chittick, Sufis "stress inwardness over outwardness, contemplation over action, development over legalism, and cultivation of the soul over social interaction."²⁴

Liu Zhi did not belong to any Chinese Sufi sect. However, Sufi thought influenced Liu Zhi and he took seriously both exoteric and esoteric meanings of Islamic texts. He paid careful attention to the full range of meanings of the sacred texts. In his translation of text and conversation with the Chinese culture, he might create or expand new meaning with the goal to make these Islamic texts in Chinese comprehensible to the Muslim and non-Muslim readers. Not only did Liu Zhi interpret the text, he also interpreted his Neo-Confucian culture.

Engaging with Chinese Culture: Interpreting and Conversing with the Neo-Confucian Culture

Liu Zhi translated and interpreted the Islamic texts using Confucian terms. Also, he engaged with the Neo-Confucian context. His contextualization moved from text to context. However, it is debatable whether Neo-Confucianism is theistic. Does Neo-Confucianism provide a theistic worldview and monistic lexicon for Liu Zhi to translate the Islamic texts into Chinese?

Julia Ching, a Neo-Confucian scholar, gives an affirmative answer. Firstly, the debate whether Neo-Confucianism is theistic or not is ongoing.²⁵ However, the more important point is that the philosophical system

22. Mayer, "Theology and Sufism," 282.
23. Knysh, "Sufism and the Qur'an," 155.
24. Chittick, *Sufism*, 19.
25. Fung Yulan argued that Confucianism could not be considered as a religion

of Neo-Confucianism is religious or religio-cultural enough to enable Liu Zhi to carry out his program of contextualization. In her study of Zhu Xi (1130–1200), who developed Confucianism into Neo-Confucianism in twelfth-century China, Ching avoids the excessive use of terms like monist and dualist while admitting that Zhu Xi's concept of *li* (principle) and *qi* (vital energy) seems to suggest dualism. Ching asserts that the concept of Great Ultimate with many manifestations can exclude Neo-Confucianism from strict dualism. For Ching, Zhu Xi's system of thought was architectonic. That is, it contains many parts that are held together by certain main concepts. Ching believes that in Chinese thought, the question of whether Zhu Xi is a theist or atheist is not important. Rather, "the quest for an ultimate or absolute remains the strong motivation for his religio-philosophical pursuit."[26] It is to be shown that Liu Zhi contextualized Zhu Xi's Great Ultimate of Neo-Confucianism as the Real Ruler of Islam.

Secondly, Neo-Confucian thought began in eleventh-century China, peaked in the thirteenth century and began to decline in the sixteenth century. By the time of Liu Zhi, Neo-Confucianism had a long and flourishing tradition. At the same time, it was highly diverse and dynamic. Liu Zhi could selectively use Confucian terms to interpret the religious message of Islam.

Thirdly, at the time of Liu Zhi, there were not many Chinese translated Islamic works. Murata notes that the Islamic languages have numerous theological and philosophical terms that "translating these called for a good knowledge not only of Islamic thought but also of the Chinese intellectual tradition."[27] This academic capability almost perfectly fits the credentials of Liu Zhi. He did not make a literal translation of the Islamic texts. Rather, he made use of the opportunity to define, delineate and invest intensively Islamic terms with Neo-Confucian meanings.

MODELS OF CONTEXTUALIZATION

David Hesselgrave simply defines contextualization as "the attempt to communicate the message of the person, works, word, and will of God in a way that is faithful to God's revelation . . . and that is meaningful to respondents

---

within the traditional understanding of the word religion. See Fung, *Short History*, 4. Huston Smith argues that from a broader perspective, the distinctive character of Chinese religion is its social emphasis. Leaning on Paul Tillich's definition of religion as ultimate concern, Smith then justifies that Confucianism is theistic because it is 'social as it is religious. Smith, "Chinese Religion," 6. The contemporary Neo-Confucian scholar Tu Weiming also argues that Neo-Confucianism is theistic.

26. Ching, *Religious Thought*, viii.
27. Murata, *Gleams*, 19.

in their respective cultural and existential contexts."²⁸ Stephen Bevans prefers the term contextualization to inculturation or indigenization because it emphasizes the need "to interact and dialogue not only with traditional cultural values, but with social change, new ethnic identities and the conflicts that are present as the contemporary phenomenon of globalization encounters the various peoples of the world."²⁹ This present study of the concept of Liu Zhi's contextualization owes much to Bevans's works. Bevans's published work *Models of Contextual Theology* has been so popular that his book has been the standard textbook of contextualization in the Roman Catholic tradition. More importantly, Matteo Ricci (1552–1610) and other Jesuits had a successful period of Christian mission in seventeenth and eighteenth-century China. Thus, such a method of contextualization as developed in China during that period can offer an insight into Liu Zhi's works. Bevans delineates six models of contextual theology. They are the translation, anthropological, praxis, synthetic (or conversation), transcendent and countercultural models. Bevans asserts that "models are *constructions*, either theoretical positions without any concrete expression or abstraction from actual concrete positions . . . The process of contextualization is a complex one, and must take into account all four factors of Scripture, tradition, culture and social change."³⁰ Bevans's model of contextualization is not rigid. It is a tool of theological reflection and analysis. Each of his six models has different emphases. Bevans also says that since the process of contextualization is a complex one, it is common for a combination of models to be operative in such a process.³¹

---

28. Hesselgrave and Rommen, *Contextualization*, 200.
29. Bevans, *Models*, 27.
30. Bevans, "Models of Contextual Theology," 187.
31. Bevans uses 'synthetic' but this study prefers conversation or dialogical model.

Bevans provides a diagram of his models as follows:[32]

Figure 1.1: A Map of the Models of Contextual Theology

Transcendental					
Model					
*					
*					
*					
Anthropological	Praxis	Conversation	Translation	Countercultural	
Model	*	Model	Model	Model	Model
*	*	*	*	*	*
*	*	*	*	*	*

Experience of the Present	Experience of the Past
(Context)	
←——————— ———————→	
Human experience (personal, communal)	Scripture
Culture (secular, religious)	Tradition
Social location	
Social change	

On the right side of the diagram is the countercultural model, which emphasizes the experience of the past. However, it takes seriously the present local culture. It is not anticultural. It emphasizes true encounter and engagement with the context through respectful yet critical analysis. For any imported religion to take root within a people's context, the workers of that faith feel the need to challenge that context. Bevans says that the fundamental tenet of faith "is used as a lens through which to interpret, engage, unmask, and challenge the experience of the present, the context of the individual and social experience, secular and/or religious culture, social location, and social change."[33] Generally speaking, this model is often associated with religious exclusivism.

On the left side of the diagram above, the transcendental, praxis and anthropological models do not emphasize tradition or scripture in the past. Rather, these models emphasize the present context or the subjective experience.

32. Ibid., 32.
33. Ibid., 123–24.

The transcendental method was pioneered by Immanuel Kant who emphasized that religion was a reality beyond the realm of human knowledge. The transcendental approach asserts that the process of coming to know reality is the present authentic experience of the subject. Bevans explains that this model works "through a model of both sympathy and antipathy—sympathy in that a person of integrity might learn much from another person of integrity from another context; antipathy in that if a person analyses why he or she is repulsed by or not attracted to a particular way of doing theology, he or she has already taken a first step to doing contextual theology as such."[34]

The praxis model has been closely associated with many liberation theologians in Latin America in the past. The present experience and future possibilities are their paramount concern of this model. The inspiration is neither from classic texts nor classic behavior. The model does not follow the process of faith seeking understanding. Rather, it is a process of faith seeking intelligent action. Bevans explicates that by "first acting and then reflecting on that action in faith, practitioners of the praxis model believe that one can develop a theology that is truly relevant to a particular context."[35]

The anthropological model emphasizes the good, holy and valuable human context. Even divine revelation is embedded and conditioned at all times by the various cultures. The practitioner of this model "looks for God's revelation and self-manifestation as it is hidden within the values, relational patterns, and concerns of a context." Generally speaking, this model is often associated with religious pluralism.

The above four models do not fit into Liu Zhi's model of contextualization. His method is neither outright exclusivism nor pluralism. A more detailed discussion is provided on two more models, namely, translation and conversation.

The translation model is a conservative approach: the basic tenets of a belief system are understood as an unchanging message that is supracultural. Bevans stresses that translation incorporates not only form but also meaning. Thus, the meaning of the basic tenet of belief is translated into culturally appropriate terms.[36] While culture is important, culture is subordinate to the basic tenet of the belief system. In this model, the basic tenet is clearly prioritized over culture. Bevans emphasizes the basic and undifferentiated message of the belief system that is sought to be translated and thus it is a reduced minimal message. It is short and cannot be questioned.

---

34. Ibid., 106.
35. Ibid., 74.
36. Ibid., 37–38.

During the process of translation, culture is encountered. However, its role is neutral and not valued for its difference or uniqueness.[37]

The following diagram summarizes the major contents of the translation model.[38]

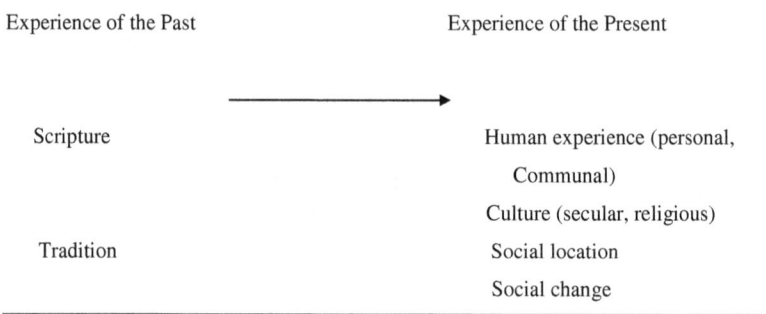

Figure 1.2: The Translation Model

Experience of the Past	Experience of the Present
Scripture	Human experience (personal, Communal)
	Culture (secular, religious)
Tradition	Social location
	Social change

Alternative titles: *accommodation; adaptation*
Basis in Tradition: *Matteo Ricci; Pope John XXIII*
Revelation: *tends to be interpreted as propositional, content-oriented*
Scripture/Tradition: *supracontextual; complete*
Context: *basically good and trustworthy*
Method: *know the context so as to effectively insert the doctrinal message*
Analogy: *bring seeds, plant in native ground*
Critique: *Positive: takes doctrinal message seriously; recognize contextual ambiguity; can be used by participants and nonparticipants in a culture*
  Negative: naive notions of culture and doctrine; propositional notion of revelation

Bevans describes the conversation approach as a middle-of-the-road model.[39] This model maintains the value of the translation approach in emphasizing the truth and unquestioned basic tenets of a belief system. Simultaneously, it values the significance of culture and the role culture may play during the process of contextualization. The practitioner of contextualization is always conscious of this model's dialogical nature and the changing nature of experience, and culture. Thus, this model should be regarded as an ongoing theological movement. There are two closely related elements in the practice of this model. Firstly, a careful balance must be made between

---

37. Ibid., 37–53.
38. Ibid., 42, 44.
39. Ibid., 88.

commitment to tradition, scripture and to the contemporary local context. Secondly, synthesis is the goal. It is developed between the practitioner's own cultural point of view and the points of view of others "in the Hegelian sense of not just attempting to put things together in a kind of compromise but of developing, in a creative dialectic, something that is acceptable to all standpoints."[40] Bevans also avers that the process is very complex and the practitioner may need to juggle several cultural values sensitively and smoothly. "One needs, rather, to place emphasis on message at one point, while at another point one needs to emphasize cultural identity. At one point traditional practices might need to be cultivated. Perhaps in another set of circumstances they need to be resisted."[41] Thus, one always needs to keep in creative tension between the scripture, tradition in the past and the cultural and religious experience in the present. Bevans is fully aware of the built-in weakness of this model. The "model is always in danger of 'selling out' to the other culture, tradition, or social location . . . the theologian must always be aware of the power and subtle manipulations of a dominant culture as well."[42]

The word conversation is preferred to Bevans's use of synthesis. It is a better word in the case of Liu Zhi's contextualization. While conversation emphasizes the broad basis and nature of dialogue, synthesis emphasizes more the resulting interaction between cultures. Moreover, the conversation model can easily accommodate more than two dialogical partners. Secondly, conversation is preferred because the encounter may be carried out in a formal or informal way. Synthesis or dialogue may seem too academic or formal for ordinary Muslims. Finally, conversation "does not imply an equality of status of the participants that might be implied by 'dialogue.' Mutual respect between conversation partners may be highly desirable, but a conversation may still take place where the balance of power is very much tilted toward one partner."[43] In the context of Liu Zhi, he contextualized his Islam by extensive conversation with the all-powerful Neo-Confucian culture, which had the support of the imperial ruler.

The following diagram summarizes the major contents of the conversation model:[44]

---

40. Ibid., 90.
41. Ibid., 92.
42. Ibid., 94.
43. Kim, "Missiology," 49.
44. This is a revised and composite diagram of two diagrams in Bevans, *Models*, 93, 95.

Figure 1.3: The Conversation Model

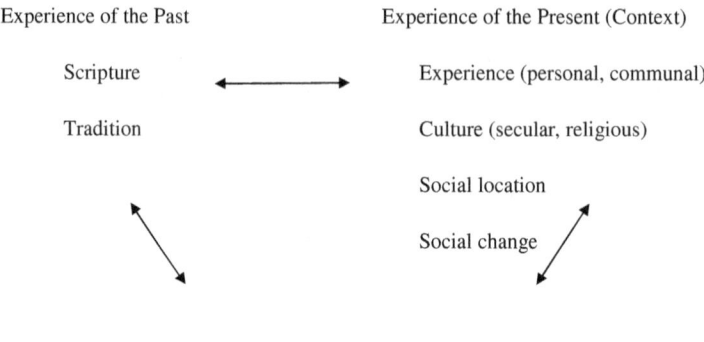

Alternative Titles: *dialogical model; analogical model*

Basis in Tradition: *development of doctrine*

Revelation: *elements of (1) propositional (2) tends to be understood as personal presence (3) envisioned as God at work in the world, calling men and women as partners*

Scripture/Tradition: *culturally conditioned; incomplete*

Context: *ambiguous and incomplete*

Method: *conversation with all partners*

Analogy: *cross-pollination*

Critique: *Positive: attitude of dialogue; emphasis on ongoing progress; witness to universality; easy to dialogue with other religions*
Negative: danger of 'selling out'; might seem 'wishy-washy'

This study has found the works of Bevans helpful in formulating a model of Liu Zhi's contextualization for the following reasons. Firstly, part of his study involves cross-cultural contextualization in Asia, in particular his discussion of the conversation (or synthetic according to Bevans) model. Bevans uses Kosuke Koyama's contextualization in Asia to explain the details of the conversation model. Thus, it has regional relevance. Secondly, while Bevans writes from the Christian tradition, his model is valid for the contextualization of Islam cross-culturally also. Both religious traditions are monotheistic in nature and have their own sacred and authoritative scripture. Finally, there is no substantial examination of cross-cultural contextualization of Islam in China. The contextualization model of Bevans is a helpful idea to start with. Moreover, Bevans is well aware of the limitation of his model in studying contextual theology. He gives six models of contextualization. He asserts that his model is not fixed or beyond development or change. "Though each model is distinct, each can be used in conjunction with others . . . In the same way, it is my contention that no one model can be used exclusively and an exclusive use will distort the theological enterprise."[45]

There are possible pitfalls with both translation and conversation models. With regards to the translation model, the translators tend to emphasize the supracultural or supracontextual nature of the basic tenets of belief. They attempt to keep the basic doctrine and try to get rid of the cultural context. "The problem, however, is to know the exact difference between the two."[46] It is impossible to access the key doctrine without any human formulation. . . Another possible problem of the translation model is the over-emphasis of the inspired and revealed text, the Qur'an, at the expense of the Islamic tradition. The Qur'an is not merely a list of doctrines and propositions. Tradition plays an important and valid part in wrestling with faith and religious practice. With regard to the conversation model, Bevans asserts that proponents of this model may also encounter built-in dangers because the basic tenets of belief have the danger of being inculturated. "Openness is a good thing, and it cannot be discarded, but the theologians must always be aware of the power and subtle manipulations of a dominant culture as well."[47]

ORIGINAL CONTRIBUTION TO KNOWLEDGE

Beginning from the late seventeenth century, the imperial rulers of China increasingly became less tolerant of Islam. Politically, Muslims had to struggle for survival under such a government. Religiously, they were not pietistic and had only a basic knowledge of Islam. Faced with the threat of acculturation and sinicization, Liu Zhi determined to confront the challenge of his times by translating and paraphrasing the ancient Persian and Arabic Islamic texts. His writings were to re-establish the Islamic tradition in Neo-Confucian contexts.

The original contributions of this study to the present knowledge of Liu Zhi and his works may be listed as follows:

1. This present study determines Liu Zhi's method of contextualization of Islam. It is argued that his method is translation-conversation.

---

45. Ibid., 32.
46. Ibid., 43.
47. Ibid., 94.

2. This study investigates Liu Zhi's application of his contextualization method in his works. After examining some specific texts, the translation-conversation model gives a more convincing account of his contextualization than contemporary scholars have offered so far.
3. This is the first ever full English translation of Liu Zhi's poem, *Five Sessions of the Moon* which is still commonly taught and memorized by many Hui Muslims.
4. This is the first ever full English translation of the first five chapters of Liu Zhi's *Rules and Proprieties of Islam*.
5. This is the first ever English translation of selected sections of Liu Zhi's *The Explanation of the Five Endeavors*.
6. A modern translation of selected sections of Liu Zhi's *True Record of the Utmost Sage of Islam* is provided, taking more seriously into consideration Liu Zhi's Islamic background.

The study is important for the following reasons:

1. While Chinese scholars in China have published extensively on Liu Zhi's work in Chinese, they have not engaged with Western scholarships. So far, only a few English research essays have been translated into Chinese. Thus, this present study makes available Chinese language scholarship to an English readership.
2. The present study is the most extensive examination of Liu Zhi's works in English, examining his trilogy especially *The Rules and Proprieties of Islam* in greater detail. It also captures present scholarly debate about the nature of *The Rules and Proprieties of Islam*.
3. This study examines his long treatises as well as short Confucianized works, like *Three Character Classics* and philosophical works for teachers of Islam as well as popular works for the general public.
4. A critical assessment of both contemporary Western and Chinese key scholars of Liu Zhi is provided. This work chooses substantial published works by both Western and Chinese contemporary scholars and engages with them critically. Other minor works in academic journals are also consulted when appropriate.
5. This present study provides an up to date account of the state of research and scholarship on Liu Zhi by Chinese scholars who have written so far in Chinese only.

SUMMARY OF EACH CHAPTER

Chapter 1 outlines the methodology and research questions of this study. Examination and discussion are primarily based on the major and some minor works of Liu Zhi. The aim of this research is to determine Liu Zhi's model of conextualization.

Chapter 2 provides a historical background of Islam in seventeenth-eighteenth-century China. This chapter discusses the historical, philosophical and Islamic contexts that Liu Zhi experienced. This is important background material to understand the works of Liu Zhi.

Chapter 3 gives a comprehensive survey and examination of Liu Zhi's writings, followed by a critical assessment of recent scholarly discussions of Liu Zhi's contextualization. This chapter gives a broad perspective of the overall writings of Liu Zhi.

Chapter 4 investigates the first aspect of Liu Zhi's contextualization, namely his engagement with the concept of unity of existence of the Ibn 'Arabi tradition. Two of Liu Zhi's works will be examined. Firstly, the relevant parts of his short and concise *Three Character Classic* will be translated into modern English. It demonstrates that Liu Zhi's Islam followed the concept of unity of existence in that the Real Ruler began the great transformation in the innate heaven and eventually in the acquired heaven. Muslims are encouraged to return to the Real Ruler by following the way of Islam. Liu Zhi's *Displaying the Concealment of the Real Realm* is a paraphrased translation of Abd al-Rahman Jami's *Lawa'ih*. This demonstrates Liu Zhi's contextualized translation of Islamic text. He added explanation, re-interpreted and edited *Lawa'ih* freely using Neo-Confucian terms in order that his readers may understand the teaching of *Lawa'ih*.

Chapter 5 examines the second and more important aspect of Liu Zhi's contextualization, namely, his Sufi spirituality in conversation with the Neo-Confucian culture in China. Two of Liu Zhi's works will be translated. Firstly, his complete poem of *The Five Sessions of the Moon* will be translated into English for the first time. Examination of this poem demonstrates that Liu Zhi's Islam is influenced by the theoretical Sufi tradition in his times in accordance with the Ibn 'Arabi tradition. Secondly, a relevant section of Liu Zhi's *True Record of the Utmost Sage of Islam* is translated into English. This is a modern translation that improves on an old translation of a century ago. In this, on the one hand, Liu Zhi's Islam emphasized the concept of unity of existence. On the other hand, he emphasized that seekers on the way of return to the Real Ruler must follow the five endeavors of Islam. These endeavors are not interpreted legalistically. Rather, he contextualized them by using Neo-Confucian wisdom, which was understood as self-cultivation.

Chapter 6 gives a more specific perspective of Liu Zhi's works with the main focus on his interpretation and teachings of the rites of Islam. It provides for the first time an English translation of the first five chapters of Liu Zhi's *Rules and Proprieties of Islam*. While his shorter *The Explanation of the Five Endeavors* gives only concise teaching of the rites of Islam, this longer work provides a more thorough and deeper discussion in terms of Neo-Confucianism. It is to demonstrate unmistakably that he used Neo-Confucian self-cultivation to explain the rites of Islam, in particular, the five pillars of Islam. The chapter will end by critically examining two recent scholars who have studied this particular work. The translation-conversation approach is argued to be a more convincing model than other options suggested by the two scholars.

The final chapter 7 concludes with a discussion and summary of Liu Zhi's model of contextualization. It also provides a contemporary relevance of this study.

2

The Historical, Philosophical and Islamic Context in China

Muslims in China were marginalized and often persecuted by the imperial Qing dynasty in eighteenth- to nineteenth-century China. However, they have survived and grown with little imperial or state support for the two last centuries. The most conservative estimates of numbers of Muslims in China vary from eighteen to twenty-three millions[1] and yet Islam in China has been considered to be at the periphery of the Islamic world. This chapter considers historical, philosophical and Islamic context at the time of Liu Zhi.[2]

HISTORICAL CONTEXT

Islam in Pre-Modern and Modern China

There are Chinese sources that show both trading and diplomatic relations between China and Persia from 455 to 651 AD. Thus, there was

---

1. It is very difficult to give an accurate number and the number of Muslims is increasing. Alles, "Chinese Islam," 7, 32. The ten Chinese Muslim ethnic nationalities are Hui, Uyghur, Kazakh, Kyrgyz, Tatar, Bonan, Dongxiang, Tajik, Uzbek and Salar. The Hui comprise at least 9 millions. Many western and Chinese studies mainly focus on the Hui and secondarily on the Uyghurs.

2. The Chinese name convention is surname first followed by other names. This rule applies throughout our study. Also, Liu Zhi has been known by other names. They are Liu Yizhai, Liu Jielian, Lieo Kai Lien and Liu Chih.

communication between the Far and Near East prior to the founding of Islam.[3] Arab-Chinese contacts started around 651 AD.[4] Islam came to China not long after the death of the prophet Muhammad. Arabic sources strongly support the presence of Muslims in the province of Guangzhou, Southeast China in 916.[5] The evidence of the early spread of Islam was fragmentary but it seems clear that Middle Eastern and Central Asian Muslim traders introduced the new faith to the Chinese. The traders came through the well-known old Silk trade routes and also by sea routes via the South China Sea. Through the Silk routes, the traders brought Islam to the Northwest region, i.e. Xinjiang province and then to other main trading cities, including the capital city. Later, northwest China was occupied by Muslims of Turkic descent, comprising mainly the Uyghurs. Through the sea routes via the Malacca strait, the traders brought Islam to Southeast China, first to various port cities and later gradually further inland. The main group of Muslims was known as the Hui from the Yuan dynasty onwards, occupying mainly the Northwest province of Gansu (east of Xinjiang) and the southwestern province of Yunnan.

The founding of the Mongol Yuan dynasty (1279–1368) ushered in a golden age for the growth of Islam in China. The emperors did not have the administrative and financial skills to rule the expanding territory. They did not rely upon the Han Chinese. The emperor Khuilai Khan imported Muslims from various parts to help govern China. He gave them senior positions as the financial ministers of the government. As the Mongols continued to expand and invade, they turned to the Muslims to raise the required revenue. Eventually, mosques were built and Muslim communities with hospitals were established all over China. Muslims were speaking in Arabic and Persian. In the southwestern region and under the leadership of Sayyid 'Ajall Shams al-Din, a government minister, Muslims intermarried with natives and became the ancestors of the modern Muslim community of Yunnan.[6] They were allowed to recite the Qur'an, fast during Ramadan and circumcise male infants.[7] In 1345, a Muslim trader named Ibu Battutah visited a Southeast China seaport and recorded that Muslim musicians were able to perform songs in Arabic and Persian. Islamic representatives, *Shaykh* (Shaikh) and a *Qadi* (judge) were allowed to judge and rule the local admin-

---

3. See Leslie, *Integration*. This work by Leslie is the most informed, supported by historical sources and yet suitable for general readership.
4. Li et al, *History of Islam*, 4.
5. Leslie, *Integration*, 15.
6. See Armijo-Hussein, "Sayyid 'Ajall Shams al-Din."
7. Ding, "Anatta," 68–76.

istration with an indirect power over religion.⁸ Yang Zhijiu's careful study is a detailed examination of the Hui's contribution to the Yuan dynasty.⁹ Yang asserts that the Hui originated from diverse backgrounds in Central Asia speaking in Persian and Arabic. They were traders and travelers who immigrated into China long before the Yuan dynasty and settled down. By the time of the Yuan dynasty, Hui became an ethnic nationality in China, comprising only Muslims. For Yang, then, the Hui were not a homogeneous group but all were Muslims. Hui were distinguished from other Chinese Muslims by their competence in the Han Chinese language.¹⁰ The Mongols exploited the Hui who assisted the Mongols to rule the empire.¹¹ It is during the Yung dynasty (1271–1366) that foreign Muslims who had settled in China no longer considered themselves as overseas nationals. Sinicization officially began from this era.¹² However, from the later Mongol rule about 1320, the Muslim position deteriorated as new laws cancelled the special privileges and tax exemptions of all religions including Islam. These anti-Muslim laws and subsequent popular sentiment against Muslims led to a reaction.¹³ Mongols and also the Han Chinese disliked the food law of the Muslims.¹⁴

After the fall of the Yuan dynasty, the native Ming dynasty (1369–1644) did not mistreat the Muslims but wanted Muslims to be acculturated. The founding emperor of the Ming dynasty, Zhu Yuanzhang, had three well-known army generals who were Hui Muslims.¹⁵ The Ming emperors recruited the Hui as envoys, translators and interpreters. Muslims were renowned as explorers, philosophers and military leaders. The well known Hui imperial fleet admiral was Zheng He.¹⁶ Mosques were built with imperial approval. In general, Muslims sought peaceful co-existence with the ordinary Han Chinese people during the Ming dynasty. Muslims were not

8. Berlie, *Islam in China*, 1.

9. See Yang, *Study of the Hui*.

10. Morris Rossabi believes that the Hui are Chinese Han men who married with wealthy Muslim women and subsequently converted to Islam. Such a narrow view of Hui identity is not too uncommon in western historical accounts. Rossabi, "Islam in China," 382.

11. Yang, *Study of the Hui*, 59–72.

12. Leslie would not call these Muslims Chinese Muslims. He prefers the term 'Muslim settlers in China.' See Leslie, *Integration*, 19.

13. Leslie, "Living," 182.

14. Leslie, *Integration*, 23.

15. Leslie, "Living," 185.

16. Tan argues that Zheng's desire and mission was to propagate Islam. See Tan, "New Exploration," 95–103.

aggressive in their religious duties and generally did not attempt to convert the Han Chinese. However, the number of Hui gradually dropped because fewer Arabs and Persians arrived by sea and more Turkic speaking Muslims arrived from Central Asia. These Uyghurs and similar ethnic groups began to form a larger percentage in the northwest of China. The Ming emperors gradually began to compel the Muslims to accept some Chinese ways. Muslims, especially the Hui, adopted Chinese dress and started to learn the Chinese language. They even had to assume Chinese names. However, these attempts had limited success because Muslims united themselves behind local leaders and the mosque served to reinforce a separate identity. In the late Ming dynasty, some Hui *ulama* became both Islamic and Confucian scholars/literati. They began to transmit, paraphrase and interpret Persian and Arabic Islamic texts using the terminology and vocabulary of traditional neo-Confucian thought. Donald Leslie argues that it "is only with the Ming (1369–1644) that we can talk confidently of integration into Chinese society and use the term 'Chinese Muslims' or 'Muslim Chinese' rather than 'Muslims in China.'"[17] The late Ming and early Qing dynasty saw the first of several waves of Chinese Islamic scholars who propagated the Islamic texts translating them into meaningful religious spirituality for ordinary Muslims who could no longer read the ancient text in Arabic or Persian. As argued by Ben-Dor Benite, these Hui scholars "were at once fully Muslim and fully Chinese... That is to say, these individuals used textual production as a way to create for themselves a space that overlapped Chinese culture and Islamic tradition."[18] Notably, the first mention of the Qur'an was about 1368.

The last imperial dynasty was ruled by the Manchus and was known as the Qing dynasty (1644–1911). By 1758, the Qing government also ruled the Uyghurs and other Muslim ethnic minorities in Xinjiang. The Manchus made policies that were difficult for the Muslims and compelled the Muslims to assimilate. The government sometimes imposed heavy taxes and other obligations on the Muslims and contravened the regulations of the court to impede the Muslims' practice of their religion. Starting from the late eighteenth and the nineteenth century, the Muslims in both northwest and southwest China rebelled against the Qing government. However, the early Qing rulers were more tolerant. The seventeenth-century Muslim scholars like Wang Daiyu and Liu Zhi were able to anticipate the threat of the Qing emperors. They made use of Neo-Confucian thoughts in their Islamic teaching but later eighteenth-century Chinese *ulama* were more radical. One such leader named Ma Mingxin (1718–1781) in Gansu, North

17. Leslie, *Integration*, 27.
18. Benite, *Dao*, 14.

China was hostile to Neo-Confucianism. He studied in the Middle East and returned to China to introduce the new teaching, advocating a different form of the Sufi teachings. Ma's view was to establish a Muslim state along China's borders. Ma led revolts against the imperial ruler in 1781 and was killed. Sporadic ongoing revolts continued into the next century. The most devastating rebellion erupted in Gansu in 1862. The leader was Ma Hualung and he also advocated the new and untainted pure teaching. The whole rebellion was defeated by the Qing army in 1877.[19] Another equally severe rebellion took place in southwest China, Yunnan province between 1855 and 1873. These revolts led to an erosion of trust in the Muslims among the Chinese public and the imperial Qing government.

Today, the largest Muslim ethnic group is the Hui, commonly found in Gansu and Yunnan provinces.[20] The second largest Muslim ethnic group is the Uyghurs in Xinjiang province. There are tensions due to conflict between Chinese cultural practices and Islamic ideals. The history of Muslims in China during the last two centuries from the beginning of the Qing dynasty has shown that there were various ways of dealing with the conflict. They ranged from integration with traditional Chinese society to isolation in the form of a return to an Arabicised pure Islam.[21] After Tang Xiaoping's reforms in the nineties, the government of the People Republic of China has taken positive steps to help the Muslims in China. Qur'ans have been printed, mosques rebuilt and monuments repaired and preserved. The government has avoided heightening the conflict and tried to work at reconciliation. Today, while most Hui are not highly conversant with the tenets of Islam, they still perceive themselves to be different from the Chinese Hans after centuries of living in China.[22] They are not totally sinicized and readily identify themselves with the larger Islamic world community. Two scholars have demonstrated this unusual phenomenon. After extensive field research in the eighties under the watchful eyes of the Chinese authority, Dru Glad-

---

19. An excellent historical study for this period in northwest China based on various sources from Russian, Chinese and Western scholars has been done by Hodong Kim. His work is highly praised for his meticulous research on sources. See Kim, *Holy War*.

20. Compared to other Muslim nationalities in China, most Hui are closer to the Han Chinese in terms of demographic proximity and cultural accommodation. The Uyghurs are the least integrated Muslim minority. Uyghurs believe firmly that their ancestors were indigenous people in the Tarim Basin occupying most of the present province of Xinjiang. Another small ethnic group living in Xinjiang is the Tajiks whose language distantly relates to old Persian. Gladney, 'Islam in China," 453–5.

21. Ibid., 466.

22. A fairly accurate and concise account for general readership, supported by field-research, of contemporary Hui and Uyghurs in China is given by J. Berlie. See Berlie, *Islam in China*.

ney developed a more nuanced conclusion that while there is remarkable diversity among the Hui, they regard themselves as one family and one united nationality.[23] After examining a century (1850–1950) of Christian–Chinese Muslim interaction, Raphael Israeli concludes that not only Christian missionaries were aliens, the Chinese Muslims, too, felt alienated from the Chinese mainstream and at times even rebelled against it.[24] Needless to say, the Uyghur Muslims and other smaller Muslim ethnic nationalities in the Xinjiang province of Northwest China have found it difficult to identify themselves as Chinese Muslims since their native languages are not Chinese.

In the early twentieth century, studies of Chinese Islam were carried out by western scholar missionaries with the aim of converting Chinese Muslims to Christianity. Marshall Broomhall carried out research among the Muslims in China in 1910.[25] Other studies by Rudolf Loewenthal[26] and Isaac Mason[27] were more interested in the sociological data on Muslims in China. Very little work was done between 1949 and 1960 when China closed the door to any western interest in Chinese study. Scholarly studies on Islam in China resumed around 1970 and have been carried out by Jonathan Lipman[28], Françoise Aubin[29], Raphael Israeli[30] and David Leslie[31], followed recently by Dru Gladney.[32] Scholarship from the Chinese, mostly Hui Muslims, began from the early nineties; this has made rapid progress.[33] Chinese Islamic studies have covered a very broad area including sociological, theosophical, Sufi, political and historical themes. Substantial works on Liu and his contemporaries in both journals and book-length studies have been published during the last twenty years by Han and Hui scholars alike.

---

23. Gladney, *Muslim Chinese*, 325. This unity is particularly relevant in the modern context after Tang Xiaoping's economic reforms.

24. Israeli, "Cross," 217.

25. See Broomhall, *Islam in China*.

26. See Loewenthal, "Russian Materials," 449–79. Also, "Sino-Islamica," 209–12.

27. Mason, "Mohammedans," 1–54; also, see Mason, *Arabian Prophet*.

28. See Lipman, "Border World."

29. Aubin, "Chinese Islam," 73–80.

30. See Israeli, *Muslims in China*.

31. During this period, only two studies by western scholars focus on Liu and his contemporaries. One of them is a very scholarly historical study by Leslie and Wassel. See Leslie and Wassel, "Arabic and Persian Sources," 78–104; Ford, "Some Chinese Muslims," 144–56.

32. See Gladney, *Muslim Chinese*.

33. The most well known and prolific Hui scholar is Jin Yijiu who has written many articles as early as the eighties and a book-length study on Liu Zhi.

The Scripture Hall Education System

The early Muslims came from the West through the ancient Silk Road to Northwestern China and also by sea to the Eastern part of China as long ago as the time soon after the death of the prophet Muhammad.[34] In the Yuan dynasty (1279-1368), the status of Muslims was elevated and this brought a new wave of immigrant Muslims into China.[35] While Muslims were scattered, there was in Nanjing (including the greater region Jiangnan) a more concentrated and localized Muslim group in the seventeenth century. Nanjing in the Ming dynasty was an important city, centrally located with fertile conditions for agriculture including silk cultivation. This was also the capital city of the Ming founding emperor Zhu Yuanzhang (1328-1398). This brief historical context will not cover the major area in Northwestern China of Xinjiang province especially the Uyghur Muslims because of the nature of this study focusing on the Hui Muslims. The historical background will focus on the Hui Muslims near Nanjing and the Eastern more prosperous part of China. This school of Chinese Muslims is called the Nanjing school.[36] Under the Ming rule, the city of Nanjing and the region of Jiangnan became a principal centre for various religious institutions and philosophical traditions. However, in 1424, emperor Yongle (1403-1424) moved the capital to Beijing. By the seventeenth century, Nanjing remained prosperous. It was estimated that Muslims accounted for about one hundred thousand people. In addition, educated Hui Muslims were trained in both Chinese and Islamic philosophy.

The Scripture Hall Education System was the key institution that contributed to the growth of Muslim education in various subjects of Islamic knowledge. It was started by Hu Dengzhou (c. 1522-c. 1597) in Shan Xi, northern China as early as the mid-sixteenth century.[37] During the Ming dynasty, Shan Xi was a prosperous region and had fertile agricultural land. Muslims were farmers, tea growers and established their financial resources. Hu learnt Chinese when he was young. He was taught Islam by an overseas Arabic master when he was grown up. Hu was disappointed that few Islamic materials were available and Muslims did not understand Islamic works. Hu began teaching in his home and later set up teaching centers in

---

34. The most authoritative history of the Hui is a two-volume edited work by Bai Shouyi. See Bai, *History*.

35. Yang, *Study of the Hui Nationality*, 143-287.

36. For a brief and concise summary of the history of the Nanjing school, see Mi and Ma, "Islamic Jinling School," 268-75.

37. Michael Dillon gives a comprehensive survey of Sufi orders and the Xi Dao Tang education system. See Dillon, *China's Muslim*, 91-152.

the mosque. Pupils could learn for free or partially subsidized. This was the prototype of the later Scripture Hall Education System. The education was divided into primary, secondary and university level. Children studied in the primary level. Adults without education or beginning in Islam studied in the secondary level. University level was to train future Islamic teachers, namely *Ahong*.

By the time of Liu Zhi, there were at least two school networks among the Scripture Hall Educational System. One school network was based around Shan Xi and the other in Shandong, Northeastern China. Owing to the fact that there were few standard textbooks, transmission of tradition was heavily dependent on the experience and charisma of each Islamic teacher (*Ahong*). It should be noted that Liu Zhi belonged to the Shan Xi School[38] and yet he made contact with the Shandong school.[39] This demonstrated the effort made by Muslim literati eager to establish networking between different places and school networks.

The key feature of sixteenth and seventeenth-century Chinese Islam was vigorous activity by the Hui Muslim literati producing scholarly Muslim literature in Chinese and in parallel with it an impressive development of the Scripture Hall Education System.[40] The need of Islamic literature in Chinese and the Scripture Hall Education System was due to firstly a desire for a better understanding of Muslim faith and secondly for clearing any misunderstanding from the Hans and ruling Manchu imperial court, who were increasingly suspicious of Muslims' rites, with regard to their loyalty to the ruling imperial power. With such cultural and political pressure, the Hui Muslim literati stood up to the cultural and political challenge. They translated their received Islamic tradition into Chinese texts and encouraged further development of various networks of the scriptural hall educational system into the eastern part of prosperous China. Wang Daiyu and Liu Zhi in the seventeenth and eighteenth– century China were Hui Muslim literati who were competent in both Neo-Confucianism and Arabic/Persian Islamic traditions in China. To understand the translated and edited Islamic works in Chinese was no easy task for the common Hui people, let alone to read the source materials in Arabic or Persian. For the sake of Muslim education, the task of translation was the necessary first step to facilitate the propagation of the Islamic faith. Hui Muslims in general needed to be taught. Translating the Islamic text and educating the ordinary Hui Muslims

---

38. Jin, *Exploring Chinese Islam*, 3.

39. Sha, *Chinese Islam*, 62.

40. For a short history of the scripture hall educational system, see Li et al., *History of Islam*.

to understand the texts by the learned teachers or *Ahong* were two different tasks. Yet, they were to be done simultaneously in seventeenth-century Islamic scholars in China.

One should not think that the Hui Muslim literati could succeed in the task effortlessly. Firstly, traditionalists would always concern themselves with, and sometimes actively resist, translating sacred received Islamic traditions in Persian or Arabic into local languages. Secondly, compared to the majority Hans, most Hui were not good readers of written work in Chinese. The literary competences of Hui Muslims living in less developed areas like North and South-western China were even worse.[41] Nevertheless, Muslim literati like Liu Zhi wrote, and edited scholarly Islamic works and translated them into Chinese. Liu also wrote Sufi poem and popular Islamic short tracts that could be rhymed for quick memorization even among children. It was and still is today common among Hui children that they can memorize Liu Zhi's poems and tracts even before they can understand the meaning of the poems and tracts. The rise of the education system in the mosque was a native development among the Chinese Muslims. The Chinese language has been the educational language in addition to being a social language.[42] Hui people could have the opportunity to learn Arabic or Persian should they desire to do so and be taught by the master, *Ahong*.

Islamic Text Transmission in Chinese

The translation of Arabic and Persian Islamic works into Chinese began in the sixteenth century and continued through to the nineteenth century. These few centuries of Islamic activities laid the philosophical and theological foundation of modern Chinese Islam. This foundational period may be further divided into two stages. The first stage is represented by Wang Daiyu (c. 1580–c. 1660), Ma Zhu (c. 1640–c. 1711) and Liu Zhi in Nanjing and the second stage is led by Ma Dexin (1794–1874) and Ma Qixi (1857–1914) in Yunnan, in the southwestern region of China. The first stage took place in Nanjiang city and the greater Jiangsu region. Islamic work in Chinese primarily focused on philosophy, religious rituals, creeds, Islamic histories, *Hadith* and Sufi materials. The second stage, which took place mainly in

---

41. This might contribute partly to the fact that Uyghurs in North-western China are not much influenced by the seventeenth-century Islamic reform. For the Uyghurs, Han Chinese is not their native language.

42. In addition to the social Han Chinese language, Hui have developed a modified Chinese scripture language that is primarily used within the education system in the mosque.

Yunnan, encompassed Islamic work in both Chinese and Arabic covering other areas, including linguistic usage, astronomy, geography and the Qur'an in Chinese.

Wang Daiyu (c. 1580–c. 1660)[43]

Wang Daiyu claimed to have Arabic ancestry, whether in Central Asia or the Middle East was not certain.[44] His ancestors came to China to pay respect to the emperor and eventually settled down in Nanjing in the fourteenth century. During Wang Daiyu's time, *Ahong* might be trained to read Arabic and Persian and not necessarily Chinese. Wang Daiyu grew up under the mosque training educational system and learnt Arabic but hardly any Chinese. At the age of twenty, he began to study Chinese. By the age of 30, he was reading Chinese history, philosophy and also Buddhist and Daoist books. He often used Islamic truth to criticize non-Islamic philosophies. He lived in Beijing in his later life. His three famous works have been recently collected and published together in one single volume.[45] The goal of Wang Daiyu was to use Neo-Confucianism to explicate and propagate the Islamic faith. He defended his approach by arguing that words and languages were merely earth and wood. These were part of the building materials to build the mosque. Thus, contemporary Chinese scholar Liu Yihong labels Wang Daiyu's methodology as "using Neo-Confucianism to explain Islam."[46]

While Ma Zhu was born in Yunnan, he traveled widely in China because of political uprisings in Yunnan. He grew up in a poor family and was eager to learn and write. At the age of twenty he began to write. At thirty years of age he left for Beijing and his stay there was a turning point in his life. At forty-three years of age, he left Beijing and travelled all over the country, networking with other Islamic scholars and teachers in various parts of China. Liu Zhi's father wrote a preface for his book.[47] He tried three times to submit his book to the imperial court and hoped to win imperial approval. His motive was to raise Islam to legitimate status. His book was popular and being read by more people than Wang Daiyu's works. Liu Yihong asserts that Ma Zhu's main goal was to illustrate that both Neo-Confucianism and

---

43. The year is approximate and few scholars have argued for a definite year.

44. A recent thesis-length study of Wang Daiyu in English is Kristian Petersen. See Petersen, "The Heart."

45. See Wang, *Collected Classical Writings*.

46. Liu, *Dialogue*, 115.

47. See Ma, *Compass*.

Islam are mutually illuminating traditions.[48] While Liu Zhi spoke highly of Ma Zhu's writings, he did not adopt his methodology. Rather, he borrowed from Wang Daiyu and further developed his concept of divine Ruler.

One of the earliest Islamic texts in Chinese was written by Wang Daiyu.[49] The Muslim literati began to propagate the basic tenets of the Islamic faith by translating and commenting on Islamic texts in Chinese. These early Muslim writers sought to use Neo-Confucian, Daoist and even Buddhist ideas and terms in their writings. Wang Daiyu was one of the two Chinese Muslim writers who were prominent in the seventeenth and eighteenth-century, the other being Liu Zhi.

Wang Daiyu was the first well-known scholar who wrote important texts in Chinese on Islam using Confucian terms and concepts. Most of his Muslim contemporaries had only a scant knowledge of Islam. He argued that both Islam and Neo-Confucianism had similar views of personal virtue, brotherly love, social and filial relationships. He prepared to adopt the dualistic concept of yin and yang from Daoism. The five Confucian virtues of benevolence and wisdom were appropriated with the five cardinal responsibilities of a Muslim. However, he was critical that Neo-Confucianism was unwilling to accept monotheism. Undoubtedly, Wang did not disclaim Neo-Confucianism. Rather, he used it for the sake of clarifying and championing Islamic belief. In addition to those of Liu Zhi, the works of Wang have been studied enthusiastically in recent years by both contemporary Western and Chinese scholars.[50]

Wang Daiyu wrote three main works. The longer work is known as *The Real Commentary on the True Teaching* and two shorter treatises, *The True Answers of the Very Real* and *The Great Learning of the Pure and Real*.[51] These works cover the essential teachings of the basic tenets of Islamic belief in terms of Neo-Confucianism and are intended for an elementary level of learning. In term of length and details, they are comparatively shorter than the works of Liu Zhi and more basic than Liu Zhi's work. *The True Answers of the Very Real* is written in a question and answer format. It is a collection of dialogues in which Wang answers questions put to him by a variety of enquirers. It also provides a quick and easy reference to basic teachings of Islam for beginners.

---

48. Liu, *Dialogue*, 117–21.

49. Jin, *Exploring Chinese Islam*, 5.

50. Murata has translated some of Wang's *Great Learning of the Pure and Real* into English. See Murata, *Gleams*.

51. These three works are often combined together and published as one book.

The Great Learning of the Pure and Real is the shortest of the three main works and explains the basic concepts of the Real One, Numerical One and the Embodied One.[52] The Real One is God in himself and the Numerical One is the first principle of creation. Murata asserts that "Wang's discussion employs terminology drawn largely from Neo-Confucianism showing that he felt it to be the most adequate of the Chinese traditions to explain the nature of things."[53] In Liu Zhi's influential work, *The Nature and Principle in Islam*, Liu Zhi continued what Wang had begun. Not only did he explain in greater details the beginning of the world by using Wang's terms of Real One, Numerical One and the Embodied One, he added diagrams to make clear what he wrote in the text. Liu Zhi's work is longer, more comprehensive and intended not primarily for an elementary level of teaching and learning.

The Real Commentary on the True Teaching is divided into two parts. The first part begins with the explanation of the Real One, continues with the Utmost Sage and ends with the five endeavors. The second part begins with human relationships, continues with filial piety and ends with the afterworld. Thus, Wang firstly discussed the essential doctrines of Islamic beliefs and secondly he contextualized his teachings in a Neo-Confucian context. He explained what the ways of Muslim living should be in a Chinese society in terms of human relationship, diet, Islamic endeavors and so on for a Muslim living in a non-Muslim country. Liu Zhi again continued what Wang had begun. Liu Zhi's *Rules and Proprieties of Islam* followed a similar format to that of Wang's work. Again, *The Rules and Proprieties of Islam* is longer, more comprehensive and contextualized even more thoroughly with Neo-Confucian ethical teachings. The first five chapters follow similarly the content of part one of *The Real Commentary on the True Teaching*. Chapters 6 to 20 cover similar content to Wang's part two. Liu Zhi continued and further contextualized Wang's Islamic teaching into his Chinese contexts.

Liu Zhi (c. 1662–c. 1730)

Liu Zhi was a prolific writer and was able to leave a significant legacy for the later generations of Chinese Muslims. He pursued studies in Islam, Neo-Confucianism, Daoism and Buddhism. Like Wang, he borrowed religious concepts from these ideologies and applied them to his Islamic writings. While he borrowed religious and philosophical terms available to

---

52. Murata has translated the text and commented briefly on the Islamic concepts. Murata, *Gleams*, 69–79.

53. Ibid., 72.

him, his writings presented Islam as a unique religion and different from other ideologies. While he was interested in Sufism, his main views were in accordance with the *Hanafi* School of law within Sunni Islam.[54] After a careful analysis of the Arabic and Persian sources used by Liu Zhi, Donald D. Leslie and Mohamed Wassel give the following summarized comments. Firstly, two key Arabic texts, namely *Wiqaya* and *'Aqaid*, used by Liu Zhi are standard Sunni Hanafite texts of law and ritual, influential in the nineteenth and twentieth centuries. Secondly, very few, if any, are *Shi'a*. Thirdly, most works, especially those in Persian, are Sufi. Finally, Leslie and Wassel postulate that the geographic sources of Liu's work are Central Asian, Persian and the original Arabic.[55] It should be noted that both the teaching of Wang and Liu were popular in Nanjing during the seventeenth and eighteenth centuries. Their works have gone through various re-printings through the last two centuries.

The legacy of Wang and Liu is unquestionable. Often, their publications have been bound together and used as a standard textbook for basic Islamic materials. Suffice to mention at this moment three scholars indebted to Liu's legacy. Firstly, Ma Lianyuan, 馬聯元 (1840–1903) in Yunnan, eagerly promoted Islamic education in that province. He was fluent in both Arabic and Chinese and encouraged bilingual Islamic teaching in both languages. Ma translated Zhi's *Nature and Principle in Islam* into Arabic. His translation of Liu's text was very free and should be regarded as a paraphrase of Liu's own work. This indicated the popularity of Liu's writing. Secondly, another Chinese Muslim scholar, named, Ma Qixi 馬啟西 (1857–1914) championed Islamic learning in the province of Gansu, North China. He initially set up tents in his house for the sake of easier access to Islamic learning. This setup later became a community centre. He used Liu's writings as his teaching materials. His students came from far and near, even sacrificing their livelihood in order to learn from Ma. Not only was Ma well acquainted with Liu's writings, he also advocated the *Jahriyya* Sufi order which was the largest among the four Chinese Sufi movements (*menhuan* 門宦).[56] With his emphasis on Islamic education, Ma established a unique and rapidly expanding Muslim community, called Xi Dao Tang西道堂 with teaching staff and learning centers. This community was not merely a *madrasa*. The community centre also operated commercial activities in order to fund all the Islamic teaching activities. Ma extended branches into

---

54. Joseph. F. Ford notes that while Liu was indebted to the *Hanafi* school, he also used at least four works which were definitely Sufi. See Ford, "Some Chinese Muslims," 151.

55. Leslie and Wassel, "Arabic and Persian Sources," 104.

56. Ma and Ding, "Preliminary Analysis," 18.

other big cities including the Chinese capital.⁵⁷ The Xi Dao Tang began to decline by the mid-twentieth century. However, Xi Dao Tang still exists today and has contributed towards the modernization of China.⁵⁸ Finally, not only Liu's writings were translated into Arabic by Ma; Liu's teaching on the life of the prophet Muhammad was translated into English by Isaac Mason in 1921.⁵⁹ While Liu began his career in Nanjian, his teaching and writings live on both in the provinces of Yunnan and Gansu, both areas densely populated by the Hui today. There is a clear resurgence of interest in Liu's writings. Research theses on his writings have been published recently in book length as well as in many academic journals. Some earlier copies of Liu Zhi's works are on public display in Beijing Niujie mosque today.

Ma Dexin (1794–1874)

Ma Dexin was born in the southwestern province of Yunnan in the late Qing dynasty and led a group of Hui Muslims into political rebellion in Kunming city against the Qing government in 1857. He acquired a thorough and comprehensive education in Arabic and Persian both in Yunnan and Shan Xi province. He made a pilgrimage to Mecca at the age of fifty and made use of the opportunity of seven years of pilgrimage to search, copy, and collect important Islamic manuscripts. Ma's works are in both Chinese and Arabic. His Chinese works are significant in that they intentionally complement the Islamic activities of Wang Daiyu and Liu Zhi.⁶⁰

His two well-known Chinese works are *An Explanation of Four Classics* and *The Final Return of the Great Transformation*. In the preface, Ma lamented that both the works of Wang and Liu did not give adequate exposition of the doctrine of return to the Real.⁶¹ So, his works sought to supplement both of their works. In particular, he wrote a commentary on Liu Zhi's *Nature and Principle in Islam*. One of his followers, Ma Lianyuan wrote a commentary of *The Nature and Principle in Islam* in Arabic.

Ma Dexin's Islamic works represent the second and final stage of intensive Islamic activity in the Ming and Qing dynasties. Ma continued

57. Ma, *Short History*, 113–51.

58. Gao, "Problem," 93–98.

59. See Mason, *Arabian Prophet*. Liu Chia-lien is another name of Liu Zhi.

60. See for details, Yang, *Ma Dexin's Thoughts*. Yang argues that Ma's works sought to identify Islamic culture and thoughts with the Confucian culture. Ma attempted to persuade the Hui people to obey their traditional Islamic principles and simultaneously they should recognize and respect the dominant Chinese culture. Yang, *Ma Dexin's Thoughts*, 2.

61. Yang and Yu, *Islam and Chinese Culture*, 414.

Historical, Philosophical and Islamic Context 33

the translation and interpretation of Islamic texts using Confucian terms. Two of Ma's distinctive contributions are his emphases on the concept of return to the Real and enthusiastic support of the unique role of the Prophet Muhammad as the Utmost Sage. He translated *The Poem of Eulogizing the Prophet Muhammad* in Chinese with clear divisions of pre-existed life, present life and afterlife of the Prophet Muhammad. This poem originally was written by an Egyptian Sufi poet, al-Busiri (c. 1212–c. 1294) and the work is known as *Qasida al-Burda* (Poem of the Mantle). Ma got the copy during his pilgrimage and then under his supervision, he and his pupils translated the poem. In comparison with Liu Zhi's works, Ma's translated poem included a clear and more detailed explanation of the significant role of the Prophet Muhammad.[62] The original poem has one hundred and sixty two lines. Ma reorganized them into ten chapters and a total of one hundred and one lines.

The intense Islamic activities of the above three Islamic scholars in seventeenth- to nineteenth-century China are consistent in their methodologies. They use Confucian terms to explain Islamic teaching. Their teachings of the unity of existence and the role of the prophet Muhammad are within the Sufi tradition in accordance with the tradition of Ibn 'Arabi.

PHILOSOPHICAL CONTEXT

Daoism, Buddhism and Neo-Confucianism are commonly regarded as the Three Teachings in China. The Ming and early Qing dynasties (fourteenth to eighteenth centuries) were a golden era for both Neo-Confucianism and Daoism because the ruling classes encouraged literature studies and literati were able to earn ministerial offices through various government-arranged examinations. The form of Confucianism in the Ming and Qing dynasties is known as Neo-Confucianism. It is not easy to define Daoism because it has assumed different aspects within its philosophical and religious system. Fung Yulan asserts that Neo-Daoism comprised both rationalists and sentimentalists.[63] During the Yuan and Ming dynasties, occasionally the emperors would favor Neo-Daoism for various pragmatic reasons. However, Neo-Confucianism dominated Chinese culture at the time of Liu Zhi.

---

62. See Zhou, "Ideologies."
63. Fung, *Short History*, 356–95.

Daoism

Daoism is the most ancient of the Three Teachings. The founder of Daoism is Lao Zi (c. 571–c. 471 BCE.). His work is called the book of *Lao Zi* or *Daodejing* (*Classic of the Way and Power*). It may be divided into two section, the teaching of *dao* (way) and *de* (power). The school of classical Daoism was further developed by Zhuang Zi (c. 369–c. 286 BCE) and his representative work is called the book *Zhuang Zi*.

The formative concepts of Daoism consist of some general principles of governing the world and man, the antithesis of yin and yang, the complementary aspects of the *dao* as natural order, mysticism and finally emphasis on afterlife. Several aspects of Daoism resonate with Liu Zhi's contextualization of Islamic thought. The most important philosophical teaching of Lao Zi is *dao* or the way. In Western philosophy, universals lie beyond shapes and features. It is a philosophical concept that represents the property of visible things. Red and green apples are visible things. However, red or green color or the colorless itself is called a universal which is invisible. Lao's *dao* is similar to the concept of universal but unlike universal, the *dao* cannot even be named. "The *Dao* that can be comprised in words is not the eternal *Dao*; the name that can be named is not the abiding name. The unnamable is the beginning of heaven and earth; the namable is the mother of all things."[64] In Lao's observation of the existence of things, the *dao* belongs to non-being which is unnamable and by which all things come to be. Thus, the *dao* is an ontological and yet not a static concept. "From Dao there comes one. From one there comes two. From two there comes three. From three there comes all things."[65] It is clear that from non-being comes being.

Zhuang Zi continued the teaching of Lao's *dao* and asserted that at "the beginning there was Non-Being. It had neither being nor name and was that from which came the One. When the One came into existence, there was the One but still no form. When things obtained that by which they came into existence, it was called the *De* [power or ability]." *De* is what makes us what we are. It may be interpreted as the ability of human nature. Zhuang Zi explained the moral teaching of the *dao* and *de*. In chapter 1 of *Zhuang Zi* called *The Happy Excursion*, Zhuang outlined the way of achieving absolute and relative happiness. Relative happiness could be achieved by the free development of our human nature. When humans allowed their natural ability to be fully and freely exercised, they are in a state of happiness. However, absolute happiness could only be achieved through higher

---

64. *Daodejing*, chapter 1.
65. *Daodejing*, chapter 42.

understanding of the nature of things. Zhuang distinguished between what is of nature and what is of man. Chinese philosopher Fung Yulan explains the distinction that

> "What is of nature," [Zhuang] says, "is internal. What is of man is external ... That oxen and horses should have four feet is what is of nature. That a halter should be put on a horse's head, or a string through an ox's nose, is what is of man."
>
> Things are different in their nature and their natural ability is also not the same. What they share in common, however, is that they are all equally happy when they have a full and free exercise of their natural ability.[66]

It should be noted that both Lao and Zhuang did not give clear systematic exposition of the concept of *dao*. Lao did not equate *dao* with the mind. The *dao* is regarded as mystery of mysteries. This present work is to show later that Liu Zhi's contextualization occasionally made use of some Daoist concepts in particular the concept of *dao* and the moral implication of *dao* and *de* (the way and natural ability). Furthermore, within the mysticism of Daoism, there is a concept of the perfect man in later Daoism.[67]

Buddhism

Buddhism first entered China via Central Asia in the first century and continued to expand in influence. The most influential period is in the sixth to tenth century. Its growth is due to the effort of non-Chinese missionaries from India into China and the gradual collection of imported Buddhist texts or *sutras* and later translation of these sacred texts into Chinese. Buddhism grew because it effectively absorbed other Chinese religious and philosophical concepts including Confucianism and Daoism.

Inculturation in late Ming dynasty was not the monopoly of any religious group including the successful Jesuit missionaries in the Ming imperial court. A Buddhist monk, Zhixu Ouyi (1599-1655) contextualized the Daoist classic *Yijing* (Classic of Change) by writing numerous works, including a Buddhist commentary of *Yijing*, namely a *Chanist Explanation of the Changes*.[68] While a Buddhist usually emphasized release by emptiness

---

66. Fung, *Short History*, 170.
67. Fung, *History*, 231-6.
68. Ouyi Zhixu is considered one of the four great Buddhist masters of the Ming dynasty. In his youth, he engaged in Confucian studies. At twenty four years old, he became a Buddhist after he had had a great insight. He was famous for his *Collected Essays Refuting Heterodoxy*. In this work, he vehemently criticized the teaching of the Jesuits.

of the mind, Zhixu was attracted to *Yijing* by the concept of *Shen* (wonder or god). "Shen is the efficient cause that translates the knowing capacity of the mind into actual understanding."[69] Yuet Keung Lo offers an insightful analysis of Zhixu and his contextualized commentary. Lo labels Zhixu as an eclecticist rather than a syncretist. In his commentary of *Yijing*, Zhixu began to realize the multifarious nature of Change in the teaching of *Yijing*. "The ultimate truth is dynamic, revealing itself in changes. Ultimate transformation in personal terms lies in understanding the revelation of Change by virtue of the inscrutable power of the shen inspired by the mind in a uniquely and idiosyncratically personal way."[70] Thus, his adaptation was ethically based and for the sake of personal transformation which was fundamentally the Buddhist goal. Therefore, the late Ming dynasty was clearly a period of religious openness as illustrated by the successful inculturation of Catholicism and adaptation of the Buddhist's emptiness of mind into the Daoist's ultimate truth.

By the early Qing dynasty, the trend of ecumenical and syncretic openness to various religio-cultural traditions began to stifle. The Qing emperor Yongzheng (1678–1735) acknowledged that Buddhism, Daoism and Islam derived from the same source and he asserted that each had its own specialties, strengths, and areas of inadequacy. However, his tolerance was merely pragmatic and political motivated. His aim was to discourage any rivalry between religious aristocrats or court officials taking sides. By the early eighteenth century, any creative interaction between religions was effectively stifled among the elites and other intellectuals.[71]

There are different schools of Buddhist teaching in different parts of Asia. Sacred texts that are translated into Chinese belong to the Mahayana (Great Vehicle) school which had major impact of Buddhism in China. Within Mahayana Buddhism, there exist different schools of thought. In general terms, two major philosophical concepts of Buddhism in China are oneness of reality and enlightenment. The concept of oneness of reality is a theory expounded by Daosheng (d. 434) who advanced many revolutionary theories. This oneness means an individual could identify with what is called the Buddha-nature. It is the self-consciousness of the individual's original identification with the universal mind. Humans could achieve Buddhahood by means of enlightenment. Fung Yulan explains this concept succinctly:

He argued that there was a clear difference between Christianity and Confucianism. See Zhixu, "Pi Xie Ji," 351–407.

69. Lo, "Change Beyond Syncretism," 286.

70. Ibid., 290.

71. Brook, "Rethinking Syncretism," 24.

> Every sentient being has the Buddha-nature; only he does not realize that he has it. This Ignorance (Avidya) is what binds him to the Wheel of Birth and Death. The necessity, therefore, is for him first to realize that he has the Buddha-nature originally within him, and then, by learning and practice, to "see" his own Buddha-nature. This "seeing" comes as a Sudden Enlightenment, because the Buddha-nature cannot be divided; therefore he either sees it as a whole or does not see it at all. Such "seeing" also means to be one with the Buddha-nature, because the Buddha-nature is not something that can be seen from outside.[72]

The Buddhist enlightenment has moral and practical aspects. It is more than merely an acquisition of merits through good works. It is a transcending understanding that can see through this world of illusion and perceive the reality behind this world. Enlightenment consists "of the intuitive experiencing of truth with one's whole being—an act through which the experience becomes merged with that Truth."[73] It should be noted that at this period of Chinese philosophy, the universal mind or Buddha-nature remains at the level of psychological understanding.

Neo-Confucianism

The foundation of Neo-Confucianism was laid in the Tang dynasty (618–907) and took on a significant importance beginning from the twelfth century. Buddhism cross-pollinated with Confucianism from the early period. By the time of the Song Dynasty in the eleventh century, Daoism as religion and philosophical thought began its influence upon Confucianism. Thus, there was considerable intermingling of ideas between the three major philosophical thoughts. One of the most conspicuous Confucians who adopted religious Daoism was Zhou Dunyi (1017–1073). In his diagram of the Great Ultimate, Zhou explained the beginning and end of all things. His diagram and explanation of *yin* and *yang* were inspired by the *Book of Changes*.

Neo-Confucianism comprised two main schools of thought, the School of Principle and the School of Mind. Zhu Xi (1130–1200) belonged to the School of Principle. He is sometimes known as a synthesizer of early Song dynasty Neo-Confucianism. He did not merely gather, organize and harmonize his tradition. Rather, he developed a coherent metaphysical system by selecting and introducing his own innovative elements into such concepts as the Great Ultimate which Zhu called *chi*, the ultimate. He defined

---

72. Fung, *Short History*, 412.
73. Fung, *History*, 238.

tai chi or Great Ultimate as the sum both of the principles of all discrete phenomena and the highest principle within each of them. It was beyond the realm of human affairs and included all affairs within the universe. The whole universe was one universal whole. At the same time, he emphasized that each phenomenon was endowed with its own defining principle, i.e. the principle was one but its manifestations were many. This emphasized the organic nature between phenomena and also the generative and creative ability of the Great Ultimate. The Great Ultimate embodied principles of activity and tranquility. It was out of these principles that the material forces of *yin* and *yang* naturally ensued. Zhu's philosophy of principle was opposed by another school of Neo-Confucianism, namely, the School of the Mind.[74]

A key proponent of the School of the Mind was Wang Yangming (1472–1529).[75] This school conceived the mind (literal: heart) as morally self-sufficient, endowed with the innate knowledge of good and the innate ability to do good. For Wang, then, the universal was a spiritual whole, in which there was only one world, the concrete actual world that we ourselves experience. Thus there was no place for that other world of abstract ultimate principle. "According to [Zhu's] system, all the *Li* [ultimate principles] are eternally there, no matter whether there is mind or not. But according to Wang's system, if there was no mind, there would be no *Li*. Thus the mind was the legislator of the universe and was that by which the *Li* are legislated."[76] The most significant contribution made by Wang was that he asserted a doctrine of the unity of knowledge and action. That is, knowledge was limited to moral knowledge and must have its logical expression in action. Action must be firmly based in knowledge. He tied moral knowledge to action and upheld the paramount importance of mind rather than metaphysical principle called *li* by Zhu. Modern scholars do not see the two schools as opponents but both of them were continuations of the great Neo-Confucian tradition of the Chinese history of philosophy.[77] It should be noted that Liu Zhi's emphasis on the role of heart is likely influenced by the School of Mind.

During the late Ming and early Qing dynasties, Zhu's philosophy always dominated Wang's. In 1644, the Qing imperial rulers reaffirmed the philosophy of Zhu and the school of ultimate principle as the orthodox teaching. Zhu's commentaries on Confucius were upheld and formed the

---

74. The literal word of mind is heart (*xing*). Scholars usually call this school as the School of Mind and not the School of Heart.

75. Ching, *To Acquire Wisdom*.

76. Fung, *Short History*, 508.

77. This includes Fung Yulan and other contemporary Neo-Confucian scholars.

basis for the civil service examinations. In the late seventeenth century, Neo-Confucian scholars tended to compromise between the perceived rationalism of Zhu and the idealism of Wang.

ISLAMIC CONTEXT

The Scripture Hall Education System began in Shan Xi in the sixteenth century. It gradually developed and established a teaching syllabus of about thirteen approved textbooks.[78] Only a few of these textbooks belong to the Sufi tradition. In Liu Zhi's *Nature and Principle in Islam* and *Rules and Proprieties of Islam*, he gave a list of about sixty books that he had referred to. However, Murata asserts that about six books were influential for Liu Zhi.[79] Four of them are Sufi writings. The fifth book in Arabic, *al-Mawaqif fi'ilm al-kalam* (The Standpoints in the Science of Theology) is quoted nine times and the sixth book is a well-known commentary of the Qur'an by Baydawi (d. c. 1300). The most frequently quoted Sufi text by Liu Zhi is Razi's *Mirsad al-'ibad* (cited thirty times). The second Sufi text is Jami's *al-Lama'at* (cited fifteen times). Jami is a supporter and follower of Ibn 'Arabi's teachings. The third Sufi text is Nasafi's *Maqsad-i aqsa* (cited fourteen times). The fourth Sufi text is Jami's *Lawa'ih* (cited eleven times). Liu Zhi translated *Lawa'ih* into Chinese and interpreted this short Sufi work.

Early Islamic Texts in Chinese

Najm al-Din Razi[80] *(1177–1256) and Mirsad al-'ibad (The Path of God's Bondsmen from Origin to Return)*

Mirsad al-'ibad is a required and approved Sufi textbook in the Scripture Hall Education System in sixteenth- to eighteenth-century China. Najm al-Din Razi lived in turbulent times. Threats came from the Crusaders in the West and the Mongols from the East. Razi's writings focused on the exploration and analysis of the visionary states experienced by the seekers in the course of their mystical journey. His work *Mirsad al-'ibad* in 1223 was intended as a gift to seekers and lovers of truth from a particular Sufi view. Razi's Sufism took a middle course between the mystics who concentrated on ecstasy and raptures and made light of religious rituals and the

---

78. Li et al., *History,* 419–23.
79. Murata et al., *Sage,* 11.
80. The work that Liu Zhi drew upon is Razi's *The Path of God's Bondsmen from Origin to Return.*

ascetic mystics who emphasized worship through meticulous or excessive performance of religious duties. *Mirsad al-'ibad* is divided into five parts and is written in a systematic and comprehensive manner. It begins with the origins and orders of creation, prophethood, the ritual practices and institutions of Sufi thought. The main discussion concerns different classes of people and different professions and trades who should follow the path and arrive at their destinations. In following the path, they reap spiritual benefit and heavenly rewards.

Mirsad al-'ibad describes spiritual ascent through meditation upon various Qur'anic images of stars, moon and sun and also relates it to the condition of the heart. The heart becomes mirror-like and is able to reflect knowledge that has come from the spiritual world.[81]

> As for those lights that are seen in the form of heavenly bodies,—stars, moons and suns—they derive from the lights of spirituality that appear in the sky of the heart, in accordance with its degree of purity . . . It sometimes happens that the soul attains such purity that it appears to be like the sky, and the heart is seen in it like the moon. If the full moon is seen, the heart has become completely pure; if it is less than full, a degree of impurity remains in the heart. When the mirror of the heart attains perfect purity and begins receiving the light of the spirit, that light will be witnessed in the likeness of the sun. The brightness of the sun is in proportion to the degree of the heart's purity, until a point is reached in which the heart is a thousand times brighter than the external sun. If the moon and the sun are witnessed together, then the moon is the heart, illuminated with the reflection of the light of the spirit, and the sun is the spirit.[82]

Akiro Matsumoto opines that *Mirsad al-'ibad* is preferred over other Sufi works of a similar genre in China because "in the last chapter of the book there is a call for people to fit into a society governed by temporary rulers in order to secure their religious life."[83] *Mirsad al-'ibad* advocates a peaceful and harmonious way of life with the ruling class and other people of different cultures. For Matsumoto, this explains to a large extent its popularity. Thus, it is not coincidence that in his *Five Sessions of the Moon* Sufi poem, Liu Zhi consciously uses the images of the moon, heart, purity and others as found in *Mirsad al-'ibad* to expound his teaching of the Sufi path

---

81. Ibn 'Arabi emphasized the role of heart in the knowledge of reality. Singh, "Heart," 20–40. Also, Singh, *Sainthood*, 62–101.

82. Razi, *Path*, 296.

83. Matsumoto, "Sufi Intellectual Tradition," 107.

in Neo-Confucian terms. For Liu, heart means the locus of human awareness and consciousness.[84] Also, Liu Zhi's *Rules and Proprieties of Islam* supports the legitimate rule of the Qing government and encourages Muslims to be obedient both the Qing emperor as well as the Real Ruler of Islam.

Abd al-Rahman Jami's Ashi'at al-Lama'at (Rays of the Flashes) and Lawa'ih (Gleams)

The contributions of Abd al-Rahman Jami (1414–1492) have been well known in Islam. He was a follower of the Naqshbandi Sufi order and was recognized by his contemporaries as a major authority in science, philosophy, astronomy, music, art, and most important of all poetry. He was a great admirer of the teachings of Ibn 'Arabi. He greatly enriched, analyzed and also developed the school of Ibn 'Arabi. He "has the ability to bring new life to the material by means of a style that is fresh, graceful, supple and highly distinguished . . ."[85] One of the important concepts in his Sufism is the unity of the existence of God. Jami stated that "we and Thou are not separate from each other, but we need Thee, whereas Thou doest not need us." For Jami, love for the Prophet Muhammad was the fundamental stepping-stone for starting on the journey. Two of his works explain the unity of existence and are translated into Chinese. These works were used as part of the teaching syllabus in the Scripture Hall Education System.

Jami's *Ashi'at al-Lama'at* is another required and approved Sufi textbook in the Scripture Hall Education System. It was translated into Chinese by She Yunshan (c. 1638–c. 1703). A most recent translation in Chinese was published in 2001 and translated by Ruan Bin with commentaries.[86] The work may be divided into two parts. The first part is shorter. It is the preface and gives not just the reason for the work. Jami gave over twenty different explanations of the concept of being in the preface. It explains the process of emanation from the beginning. These explanations become the foundation of understanding the flashes in the later major part of the work. The second part is Jami's teaching about flashes which consists of twenty nine discussions. Thus, Jami wrote in order to make clearer the teaching of the unity of existence. The emanation begins in the innate heaven and later moves into

---

84. Murata says that the Sufis prefer "heart" to the philosophers' "intellect" when the subject concerned is self-realization. Murata et al., *Sage*, 57. Liu is aware that *The Poem of the Five Sessions of the Moon* should address the heart rather than the intellect as this poem is meant for general readership.

85. Huart, "Djami," 422.

86. Jami, *Rays of Flashes*.

the acquired heaven. This process is known as descent. The process continues from the acquired heaven back to the Real which is known as the ascent. These understanding of the cosmogony, descent into acquired heaven and ascent into the Real are common themes in Liu Zhi's theosophy of Islam.

The second work is Jami's *Lawa'ih*. It is a reference textbook in the Scripture Hall Education System. Liu Zhi translated it into Chinese. This work will be discussed in detail in chapter 4 of this book.

Aziz al-Din Nasafi's (d. c. 1300) and Maqsad-i aqsa (The Furthest Goal)

Aziz Nasafi's *Maqsad-i aqsa* is a reference textbook of the Scripture Hall Education System. Nasafi was born in Central Asia and had followers in Iran. Nasafi's work *Maqsad-i aqsa* was produced probably before 1281, during the latter part of his life.[87] It was a theological treatise on God's essence, attributes and acts. It also discussed views of God as taught by other philosophers, *ulama* and Sufis. His own worldview entailed an image of the four seas. Extant manuscripts are also found in India, Pakistan and China.[88] *Maqsad-i aqsa* had a coherent writing style. The teaching of God's essence and attributes had a striking resemblance to Ibn 'Arabi's vision of God, in particular, understanding God as both incomparable (*tanzih*) and similar (*tashbih*) with the world. That is, God is both He/not He.[89] The emphasis of this particular work by Nasafi is a detailed discussion of the levels of existence in the image of four seas, with an interpretation similar to Ibn 'Arabi's school. In *Maqsad-i aqsa*, Nasafi also discussed the perfect man as the divine presence. Clearly, his worldview was an ontological hierarchy of the four seas (levels of existence) and the perfect man who comprehended all the four seas. His last two chapters in *Maqsad-i aqsa* explain the four seas.

Liu Zhi's works have been influenced primarily but not exclusively by Sufi thoughts. The main source of Sufi thoughts comes from primarily the Ibn 'Arabi's tradition through the works of Jami and Nasafi. Liu Zhi's works contribute towards the Islamic teachings in the Scripture Hall Education System and they continue the moderate or *shari'a*-minded Sufism.[90]

---

87. *Maqsad-i aqsa* was translated into Chinese in the seventeenth century by She Yunshan. It was summarized by Ma Fuchu in the eighteenth century. Matsumoto, "Sufi Intellectual Tradition," 107.

88. Ridgeon, *Nasafi*, 210–11.

89. Ridgeon, *Nasafi*, 17–19.

90. Wang Daiyu, Ma Zhu and Ma Dexin explicitly condemned *non-shari'a*-minded

The Ibn ʿArabi Tradition and the Concept of Unity of Existence

Some Foundational Principles of Ibn ʿArabi's Writings

The overarching principle of Ibn ʿArabi's Islamic thought is *tawhid* (unity of God) which can be understood by considering various complementary pair of ideas.[91] Only two of Ibn ʿArabi's key thoughts will be discussed because they are more relevant to this study. The first pair is represented by bringing together (*kurʾan*) and separation or differentiation (*furkan*). The second pair is incomparability (*tanzih*) and similarity (*tashbih*). Bringing together means that God brings all things together under his unitary creativity. Differentiation means that God has the knowledge and wisdom in all the differentiations of reality. Thus, God is one through his essence and many through his differentiated knowledge. This twin principle of the oneness of God and manyness of his knowledge gives existence to this cosmos. From the human perspective, the soul manifests the manyness of knowledge and the spirit the oneness of existence (*wujud*). Both the bringing together and differentiation "signify the two basic principles in terms of which God creates the universe and reveals himself in the 'sign' (*ayat*) that are found in the three fundamental domains of manifestation: the universe, the soul and the Book."[92]

The second complementary pair in Ibn ʿArabi's key thought is based on two interrelated and yet balanced concepts: God's incomparability (*tanzih*) and his similarity (*tashbih*). *Tanzih* "is to assert that God is pure and free of all the defects and imperfections of the creatures . . . [*Tashbih*] is to assert that God must have some sort of similarity with his creatures."[93] The twin perspectives of incomparability and similarity must be kept in view and balanced. God is far and he is also near. God is beautiful and stirs up love in the human heart and yet this beauty is not like any created thing.[94] Thus, in the midst of his nearness he is far. In the midst of his similarity, he is incomparable. According to Chittick, Ibn ʿArabi's insistence on the connection between *tanzih* and *tashbih* has great bearing upon his epistemology. "In brief, reason is innately constituted to set up distinctions and differentiations and thus to think abstractly . . . True knowledge depends upon seeing all things with both the eye of imagination and the eye of reason."[95]

Sufism in their writings. Yin, *Sufism in China*, 185–92.
   91. Chittick, "Tasawwuf," 317–24.
   92. Ibid., 318.
   93. Murata and Chittick, *Vision*, 71.
   94. Singh, "Possibility," 295–306.
   95. Chittick, "Ibn ʿArabi," 126–27.

Based on these two key thoughts, Ibn ʿArabi's understanding of reality and existence should not be considered as a strict philosophical system of epistemology. It is an emblem (according to Chittick) or may be understood as a Sufi vision of existence. Such a vision is governed by his concept of God's unity and affirms the necessity of both modes of knowing. God is one in his essence and many in his knowledge. He has the unity of his essence and the multiplicity of his names. He embraces incomparability and similarity, and "He" and "not He." Ibn ʿArabi criticized others who emphasized or over-emphasized just one mode of knowledge.[96] One should envision God with both eyes. Any single-eyed vision will suffer and distort the view of reality and is insufficient as a guide to God and as a judge of other viewpoints. It is important to keep both modes of knowing in healthy balance, both in the soul and in rational interactions. For Ibn ʿArabi then, to say merely "All is He" is short-sightedness. It is not considered as the highest stage on the path to God because it is seeing with one eye.[97] With the other eye also, the true Sufi can see that all is not He. Ibn ʿArabi's Sufi vision of God's existence is both "He/not He."

History and Development of the Concept of Unity of Existence in the Ibn ʿArabi Tradition

According to William Chittick, oneness of existence is not the highest expression of Ibn ʿArabi's teaching. The term *wahdat al-wujud* was not used explicitly by Ibn ʿArabi.[98] Furthermore, Ibn ʿArabi's understanding of the concept of *wahdat al-wujud* was gradually developed in his late literature and should be not based on a single or a few scattered sayings.[99] Chittick also insists that there is no doctrine of *wahdat al-wujud* as such in Ibn ʿArabi. Rather, *wahdat al-wujud* was an emblem for Ibn ʿArabi and "if al-ʿArabi was considered its founder, this simply indicates that his writings mark Sufism's massive entry into the theological discussion of *wujud* that before him had been the almost exclusive preserve of the philosophers and

---

96. One well-known example in Islamic history is Al-Hallaj (c. 858–922). See Massingnon, *Passion*.

97. Chittick, "*Wahdat al-Shuhud*," 38.

98. M. Asin Palacios suggested that Dante's Divine Comedy had its source in Ibn ʿArabi's concept of *wahdat al-wujud*. See Asin Palacios, *Islam*, 160.

99. Chittick, "Rumi," 73. Owing to a lack of careful reading of Ibn ʿArabi's works, Chittick argues that one may misinterpret and classify Ibn ʿArabi's teachings as pantheism, panentheism, existential monism, pantheistic monism or the like, not only in a Middle Eastern, but also in a Malay-Indonesian context.

Historical, Philosophical and Islamic Context 45

the *mutakallimun*."¹⁰⁰ The actual term *wahdat al-wujud* was developed by certain followers of Ibn 'Arabi, including his pupil and stepson Sadr al-Din Qunawi (d. 1274). It is Sa'id al-Din Farghani (d. 1300) who gave *wahdat al-wujud* a technical and specific meaning.¹⁰¹ The meaning of the term eventually was established by the time of Ibn al-Rahman Jami (d. 1492), a propagator of Ibn 'Arabi's metaphysical teachings.¹⁰² Two works of Jami are included as reference texts in the Scripture Hall Education System in sixteenth- to eighteenth-century China. The history of the term *wahdat al-wujud* is summarized by Chittick:

> The term is not found in the writings of Ibn al-'Arabi. For Qunawi, it has no specific technical sense . . . In Farghani's writing, *wahdat al-wujud* is well on its way to becoming a technical term, but it does not stand on its own, since it needs to be complemented by *kathrat al-'ilm*, the manyness of knowledge . . . other figures like Ibn Sab'in and Nasafi were employing the term as a kind of shorthand to allude to the fundamental nature of things. Ibn Taymiyya seized upon the expression as a synonym for the great heresies of unificationism and incarnationism. By the time of Jami, and perhaps much before, *wahdat al-wujud* became the designation for an expression of *tawhid* that was typified by the writings of Ibn al-'Arabi and his followers.¹⁰³

Chittick helpfully summarizes several possible meanings of the term *wahdat al-wujud* from both supporters and opponents of *wahdat al-wujud*.¹⁰⁴ The meanings offered by supporters are:

1. Qunawi and Farghani would use *wahdat al-wujud* as a straightforward statement about *wujud* (existence or being) and make no reference to the complicated thoughts behind this term. For them, the

---

100. Chittick, "*Wahdat al-Shuhud*," 37.

101. Chittick, "Spectrums," 208–9.

102. Caner K. Dagli studies the concept of the oneness of being from a historical development of the meaning of *wujud* and *wahdat al-wujud* for four generations from Ibn 'Arabi to Damud al-Qaysari (c. 1260–c. 1350). He notes that there has been gradual adoption and sophistication of the technical language of the study of being i.e. ontology. This increased level of sophistication is due to Sufism's effort to incorporate the prevailing philosophical and theological language of Islam. Thus, Dagli adopts a dynamic approach to the understanding of the oneness of being. While Ibn 'Arabi uses *wahdat al-wujud* as a fundamental vision of reality or as an intellectual key to Sufi treading the spiritual path, his later Sufi disciples and Ibn 'Arabi supporters interwove philosophy, theology and mysticism. See Dagli, "Mysticism," vi–ix.

103. Chittick, "Rumi," 87.

104. Ibid., 88–90.

divine being had manyness and plurality in his self-manifestation and such emanation or self-disclosure was affirmed by *wahdat al-wujud*.

2. In the later tradition of Ibn 'Arabi, for followers like Ibn Sab'in (d. 1270) and Aziz al-Din Nasafi (d. before 1300), *wahdat al-wujud* was a sufficient statement about the nature of things. Things in their multiplicity possessed a certain reality.

3. In the later tradition of Sufism and Islamic philosophy, the term meant *tawhid* and was used primarily by Sufis to express the unity of God.

While Chittick supports a distinction between *wahdat al-shuhud* and *wahdat al-wujud*, he disagrees with Massignon because he gave a simplistic dichotomy, namely static and dynamic, to these two terms. In addition, he failed to appreciate the highly complex doctrinal synthesis of oneness of existence and manyness of knowledge behind the concept of *wahdat al-wujud*. Chittick pleads for caution when people use the term *wahdat al-wujud*.

> In general, sympathizers see *wahdat al-wujud* as a restatement of *tawhid* in the language of the advanced and refined intellectuality of later Islamic history, while detractors consider it a deviation from the supposedly clear distinctions drawn between God and cosmos by the early and relatively unsophisticated schools of theology. Nevertheless, the term *wahdat al-wujud* carries a good deal of baggage because of the long debate over its use. Thus all sorts of complications can arise that obscure what is at issue.[105]

Mulla Sadra (c. 1571–1650) is a significant figure in the history and development of the concept of unity of existence in the Ibn 'Arabi tradition. He transformed and developed Ibn 'Arabi's Sufi vision into a theosophical and philosophical system. Sadra made several important contributions to the Ibn 'Arabi tradition and grounded his vision on more mature Peripatetic philosophical arguments.[106]

Sajjad H. Rizvi clarifies Sadra's teaching of divine self-disclosure. While God is the processual type of cause, he is also the processual sustainer. Divine self-disclosure indicates that God is both a transcendent, incomparable creator and immanent, participatory sustainer. That is, God is the one who participates in things and causes things to participate in him mutually. In

---

105. Chittick, "Rumi," 91.
106. Dagli, "Mysticism," 31.

addition, Rizvi explicates that rather than emphasizing God as the first cause, Sadra prefers to speak of the participatory immanence of God who introduces the one into all levels of the world-process. For Rizvi, Sadra is cautious to point out that it is not an equal mutual interpenetrated relation between two entities. Rather, "all that is other than God does not exist in reality. Things exist not because God causes them to exist but because He exists."[107] Thus, Sadra has provided a creative synthesis between the priority of existence and gradations of the reality of being to explain the relation between God and the world in the Ibn 'Arabi tradition based on his theosophical system. While Rizvi describes Ibn 'Arabi as a rationalizing mystic, he calls Sadra the mystical philosopher because Sadra uses experience as a means of understanding, the grounds for explaining, the truth.[108] That is, "experience is the ground for philosophy and philosophical discourse is a means for making sense of that experience."[109]

The philosophical contribution of Sadra to the Ibn 'Arabi tradition has been confirmed by various contemporary scholars of Sadra in addition to Rizvi. According to Chittick, Sadra's achievement is "an intellectual synthesis within which rational, philosophical speculation is combined with the mystical intuitions of the Sufis, the Koranic exegesis of the theologians, and a thorough familiarity with the Shi'ite hadith literature, which discusses the Divine Unity in technical terms peculiar to itself."[110] In addition, Ibraham Kalin argues that the concept *wahdat al-wujud* itself becomes a dynamic concept in Sadra's realist ontology. Kalin asserts that Sadra's central thought is ultimately God's face turned to the world. Sadra's ontology "is a step towards uncovering an aspect of the Divine, which, for Sadra, is the ultimate source of all being and knowledge."[111] Kalin asserts that Sadra's principle of gradation has a hierarchical order of being in which substances move either upward or downward in accordance with their ontological state. A being intensifies its potential and attains perfection in terms of its properties and qualities. Kalin illustrates such intensification with an apple which turns redder when it ripens. Redness is not an existential property of the apple for Sadra who argues that the ripened apple is another mode of existence of apple itself. Thus, Sadra "construes [things] as various modes and states of being in which a subject intensifies or diminishes."[112]

107. Rizvi, "Mulla Sadra,") 575.
108. Rizvi, "Mysticism and Philosophy," 231.
109. Ibid.
110. Chittick, "Mysticism," 88.
111. Kalin, "Mulla," 81.
112. Ibid., 93.

Rizvi summarizes succinctly Sadra's creative appropriation of Ibn 'Arabi's *wahdat al-wujud*. "Mulla Sadra is thus not caught between monism and pluralism, but rather seeks to escape the paradigms offered by Ibn 'Arabi by attempting to produce a synthesis based on the notion of grades of intensity of content in our experience of things, corresponding to greater and lesser degrees of the manifestation of Being."[113]

The Ibn 'Arabi Tradition and Sufi Spirituality

Sufi thought, in particular Sufi spirituality, in the seventeenth and eighteenth centuries has been widely studied in western scholarship.[114] In sixteenth- to eighteenth-century China, Sufism was common. However, Sufism today in China is no longer regarded as one of the mainstream branches of Islamic thought and is now being sidelined.[115] In China, the political turmoil in the early twentieth century and lack of religious freedom until the mid-twentieth century have stifled any scholarly study on Islam in general, let alone Sufi thought. Despite these setbacks, studies on Sufi thought in China have not been completely stagnant. Jin Yijiu in China has written scholarly works on Wang Daiyu and Liu Zhi and for the last twenty years also published works on theoretical Sufism in China.[116] It should be pointed out that Sufi spirituality is an expression of and also an interrelation with Liu Zhi's understanding of Ibn 'Arabi's tradition of the unity of existence. Sufi thought in China should be understood broadly and not limited to mystical practices. Spirituality as understood by William Chittick, Annemarie Schimmel and others embraces a broader dimension including the culture, literature, and arts of the Islamic world.[117]

---

113. Rizvi, "Mysticism," 239.

114. Sufism is usually regarded as the inner dimension of Islam and concerned with both the theoretical and practical aspects of that dimension. See Nasr, *Islamic Spirituality I and II*. Spiritual manifestations include various Sufi orders, Islamic literature, art, dance and music.

115. Elizabeth Siriyeh says that the major factor in anti-Sufism after the second World War is the state because of some politically activist Sufis. Despite various pressures from the state and other leading anti-Sufi reformers, both political and apolitical resurgent Sufism continue to flourish in many areas of the Islamic world. See Sirriyeh, *Sufi*, 140–53.

116. Jin, "Sufism and the Islamic Writings,"100–109. Jin, *Mysticism*. Jin, *Sufism*.

117. Annemarie Schimmel in her well known work, *Deciphering the Signs of God*, discusses Islamic mysticism from a perspective of signs, ranging from natural environment like plants and animals, to less obvious signs such as sacred time and space and eventually to ritual actions, worship and the order of the community. Schimmel, *Deciphering*.

Historical, Philosophical and Islamic Context   49

The Ibn 'Arabi Tradition and Sufi Thought

Scholarship is plentiful on Ibn 'Arabi's Sufism. A substantial monograph translated into English was written by the French philosopher-Islamist, Henry Corbin (1903–1978).[118] He wrote from a phenomenological standpoint. At the end of the twentieth century, two important scholars of Ibn 'Arabi are well known for their acclaimed scholarship. They are Knysh and Chittick. Only Knysh's work is to be outlined here as Chittick's works have been discussed. Knysh has written historical studies on Sufism in general[119] and Ibn 'Arabi and his school in particular. Knysh's work on Sufism takes its cue from the historical and socio-political contexts within which Sufism developed.[120] In his study, he notes that in general, the Sufi tradition "contained vastly disparate if not diametrically opposed views and principles."[121] Knysh also discusses the relationship between Sufism and the Qur'an. "From the outset, the Qur'an was the principal source of contemplation and inspiration for every serious Muslim ascetic and mystic, whether formally Sufi or not."[122] However, their interpretations have always faced oppositions from Muslim leaders. From the start to the pre-modern period, Sufi teachings have gradually grown and become distinctive practices and beliefs. Sufis have a distinctive life-style and a system of rituals. While Knysh acknowledges that Ibn 'Arabi's uses of the Qur'an are rich and varied, he argues that Ibn 'Arabi's spiritual exegesis of the Qur'an is preconditioned by his concept of the ultimate realities of existence. It is customary for the Sufi masters to exercise their imaginative faculties in order to decipher God's revelation through symbols and images.[123]

Summarizing the discussion of Ibn 'Arabi, Knysh's historical study of Ibn 'Arabi affirms that the teachings of Ibn 'Arabi have been gradually developed into a tradition, a process which has been both supported and opposed. Chittick's study of Ibn 'Arabi's overall writing affirms that the concept of the unity of existence is interrelated closely with Sufi spirituality, both in theory and practice.[124]

118. See Corbin, *Creative Imagination*.

119. See Knysh, *Islamic Mysticism*.

120. Ibid., 3. Chittick calls this book the best historical survey of the Sufi tradition in English. Unlike Knysh who finds Sufism difficult to define, William Chittick prefers to give a simple working definition of Sufism. 'Sufism can be described as the interiorization and intensification of Islamic faith and practice.' Chittick, *Sufism*, 18.

121. Knysh, *Islamic Mysticism*, 326–27.

122. Knysh, "Sufism and Qur'an," 137.

123. Ibid., 154.

124. It should be noted that often essays that are written on Ibn 'Arabi are based

Discussion of Sufi thought and the way in which Ibn ʿArabi influences Chinese Muslims have not been investigated in detail. This is due to a lack of interest by contemporary scholars who treat Sufism as a mystical and irrational pursuit of personal virtue. It should be noted that Sufi thought in China means traditionally *shariʿa*-minded Sufism. According to Jin Yijiu, two of fourteen approved textbooks in the Scripture Hall System are clearly Sufi literature.[125] One of them is Jami's *Lawaʾih*. Jin also discusses in depth Liu Zhi's Sufi thought as well as the contributions made by Sufi thought to Chinese Islam.[126] Jin is fully convinced that Liu was greatly influenced by Islamic mysticism.[127] Wang Junrong 王俊榮 studies the ontology of Ibn ʿArabi and discusses various similarities between Liu Zhi and Ibn ʿArabi.[128] Wang's work is the only book-length monograph investigating the teaching of Ibn ʿArabi and his influence upon Chinese Islam.

The Ibn ʿArabi Tradition: The Concept of the Perfect Man and Muhammadan Reality

Before Ibn ʿArabi, the teaching of Muhammad as light, the Muhammadan reality and its complement concept of the perfect man were a common theme among the Sufis. An Iraqi Sufi, Sahl al-Tustari (d. 896) interpreted Sura 33:46, 53:13–14. His commentary reads as follows:

> That is, in the beginning when God, Gloried and Exalted is He, created him as a light within a column of light, a million years before creation, with the essential characteristics of faith, in a witnessing of the unseen within the unseen. He stood before Him in servanthood, by the lote tree of the Ultimate Boundary (53:14), this being a tree at which the knowledge of every person reaches its limit.[129]

---

on just one chapter or one written work of Ibn ʿArabi. An undisputed contribution by Chittick is his effort to translate many passages of Ibn ʿArabi's works into English. His thematic study of Ibn ʿArabi is often based on the overall writings of Ibn ʿArabi.

125. Jin, "Sufism and Scripture Hall," 66.
126. Jin, "Sufism and the Islamic Writings in Chinese," 100–109; Jin, "Idea," 1–11.
127. Jin, *Exploring Chinese Islam*, 283–324.
128. Wang, *Unity*, 73–121.
129. Al-Tustari, *Tafsir al-Tustari*, 213.

Muhammad belonged to the sphere of light which pre-existed the creation of the world.[130] God created Adam from the light of Muhammad. Ibn 'Arabi is largely responsible for the central role of this light in later Sufism.[131]

Also, Michel Chodkiewicz explains the distinction between the Muhammadan reality and the perfect man. The two terms

> [e]xpress different views of man, the first seeing him in terms of his primordiality and the second in terms of his finality. The *kamal* or perfection of the *insan kamil* [perfect man] should not be understood in a "moral" sense (so as to correspond with the 'heroic virtues') but as meaning "fulfillment" or "completion." Properly speaking, this perfection is possessed only by Muhammad, the ultimate and total manifestation of the *haqiqa muhammadiyya* [the reality of Muhammad]. Yet, on the other hand, it is equally the goal of all spiritual life and the very definition of *walaya* [sainthood]. Hence, the *walaya* of the *wali* [saint] can only be participation in the *walaya* of the Prophet.[132]

Muhammad was the manifested principle, the messenger was the manifesting principle and the divine name Allah was the principle. Not only did the prophet Muhammad reveal God, he also implemented the divine will in this world.[133] He was active in divine self-disclosure and yet he was also the last prophet to appear in the flesh.[134] While he might look like any other human person outwardly, he was also unique in humankind because "he carried the Divine Light, whose rays became increasingly visible as time passed."[135]

According to Chittick, Jami asserted three aspects of significance in the concept of the perfect man. Firstly, according to Jami, "the name Allah is a unity in which was comprised all the divine Names. Therefore any heart which knows it knows all the Names. This is in contrast to the other Names, for the knowledge of not one of them entails the knowledge of the Name Allah."[136] The manifestation of the name Allah was equivalent to the manifestation of the universe as a whole.

130. Schimmel, *And Muhammad*, 125–6.
131. Ibid., 127.
132. Chodkiewicz, *Seal*, 71.
133. Schimmel, *And Muhammad*, 134.
134. David Singh avers that both Adam and Muhammad existed prior to the creation of the world in Ibn 'Arabi's epistemological model. Singh, "Onto-Epistemological Model," 277–86.
135. Schimmel, *And Muhammad*, 135.
136. Chittick, "Perfect Man," 143.

Secondly, the perfect man was the goal of creation. It was through the perfect man that God created the world. All other creatures depended upon him. According to Chittick, the implication is that through the perfect man, God sees unity in multiplicity. "In Himself He sees nothing but Unity, and in the world nothing but multiplicity. But in man Unity and multiplicity are combined in such a way that all of God's Attributes are manifested within one unitary locus of theophany in the midst of the plurality of the world."[137]

Finally, the perfect man was God's vicegerent. He was the vicegerent of "Allah" and of no other names of God. The perfect man contained the principles of all creatures. All that the world or the macrocosm contained, he or the microcosm also contained. The perfect man was the intermediate or *barzahkh* between God and the world.[138] Not only did he maintain the existence of the world, he also possessed the attributes of both. Chittick asserts that the perfect man is an isthmus who comprises the attributes of lordship and servanthood. "Through his attribute of lordship—i.e. his divine nature—he takes from God what the creatures demand. And through his attribute of servanthood he is able to establish contact with the other creatures and to see that they receive what they need from God."[139]

Furthermore, David Thomas succinctly avers that the prophet Muhammad is firstly "the channel of moral and ethical truth that enabled humans to live constructively and harmoniously together."[140] Secondly,

> Muhammad pre-eminently came to be seen as a source of wisdom that not only extended and supplemented the Qur'an, as for the legalists, or acted as a channel of revelation, but embodied esoteric wisdom in his very self, to the extent that knowledge of his ways and reflection upon his teachings opened possibilities of explaining the nature of reality and gaining proximity to God.[141]

The concept of the perfect man has taken on a multi-faceted significance in Ibn 'Arabi and his tradition.[142] For Sufis, the prophet Muhammad

---

137. Ibid., 151.
138. Little, "Al-Insan al-Kamil," 49.
139. Chittick, "Perfect Man," 153.
140. Thomas, "Receiving," 442.
141. Ibid., 443.
142. Chittick argues that the 'underlying theme of Ibn 'Arabi's writings is not, as many would have it, *wahdat al-wujud*, "the Oneness of Being," but rather the achievement of human perfection.' That is, the overarching principle of Ibn 'Arabi's writings should be the concept of the Perfect Man. Chittick, *Ibn 'Arabi*, 49–50. Alexander Knysh admits that since Ibn 'Arabi's writing has an open-ended and elusive discursive strategy, it is difficult to identify one single motif. Only several constantly re-emerging motifs can

who has embodied the concept has become the supreme example and channel of Sufi spirituality in gaining proximity to God.

For Liu Zhi, the prophet Muhammad embodied the Confucian idea of self-realization and transformation. Liu Zhi contextualized the perfect man of the Ibn 'Arabi tradition as the Utmost Sage. It is in the final part of his trilogy, namely *The True Record of the Utmost Sage of Islam* that the superiority of the Utmost Sage is expounded by using carefully selected and edited narratives and discourses.

The Twentieth-Century Understanding of Sufi Thought and Islamic Knowledge

In 1975, Annemarie Schimmel wrote a substantial work on the mystical dimensions of Islam.[143] Her work focused on some features of Sufism, both historically and phenomenologically. While her work was scholarly, it did not intentionally relate theory to practice, doctrine to religious rites, and orthodoxy to orthopraxis. In the present work the Sufi work of Chittick is to be discussed because he approaches Sufi thought from doctrinal and metaphysical perspectives. He also integrates theory with practice. Such an approach enables one to connect the doctrine of the unity of existence with Sufi spirituality.

Chittick asserts that Islam is a religion that teaches people how to understand the world and themselves. Moreover, Islam also teaches people how to transform themselves so that they may come into harmony with the ground of all being.[144] While a Sufi supports a theologian's claim that the basis of faith must be the Qur'an and *Hadith*, he also asserts that a true understanding of the Qur'an is achieved by unveiling. Without unveiling, the view of the theologian is purely academic or based on rational explanation. Chittick gives the following succinct summary:

> The theologians held that man must believe in the Koran, then follow its directives. The Sufis said that before one can attain personal and direct understanding of the Divine Truth through unveiling, he must "polish the mirror of the heart," which meant both practising the *Shari'ah* or exoteric Law and following the

be identified by experienced readers. "Paradoxically, the discursive windows through which Ibn 'Arabi sought to highlight the various facets of his monistic world-view leave their peculiar imprint on the ideas and experiences Ibn 'Arabi endeavours to convey." Knysh, *Islamic Mysticism*, 167.

143. See Schimmel, *Mystical*.
144. Chittick, *Sufism*, 5.

> *Tariqah* or spiritual Way. As for the philosophers, they did not find it necessary to speak of practice in their purely philosophical expositions, although they often did in other works.[145]

Sajjad Rizvi asserts that what Ibn 'Arabi "proposed most explicitly was a Gnostic practice that would lead the seeker to an experience of the Truth . . . there is little sense of a philosophical system or method in his articulation either of rational knowledge or mystical experience."[146] Thus, the unity of existence is a metaphysical and intellectual principle to assist the seeker to tread the spiritual path.[147] Both Ibn 'Arabi and his well-known disciple Qunawi hardly used the term unity of existence but their Sufi vision of reality and knowledge was clear enough. It is the later followers and supporters of Ibn 'Arabi who developed and established the more mature and sophisticated concept of the unity of existence.[148] The effort of these transmitters of the Ibn 'Arabi school, namely Farghani, Jami, Nasafi and others did not merely regurgitate Ibn 'Arabi's teaching but interpreted and articulated the concept as a pre-modern Islamic theosophy. In addition, they contextualized it to their audiences according to their cultural and ideological settings.

Chittick asserts that Sufi spirituality is concerned primarily with right unveiling.[149] It is right unveiling from the core of the Sufi's heart and concerns the perfection of the innermost self. Right unveiling begins from the heart which is the centre of intelligence, consciousness and self-awareness and radiates forth to the whole self. It determines the Sufi's thought and activity. The goal of the Sufis is inner awareness of the reality of things and they respond spontaneously before mental articulation to do the most wonderful thing in the depths of their souls. Thus, Sufis strive towards aesthetic and spiritual perfection. Chittick explains the theoretical and practical levels of Sufi spirituality.

> In order to reach human perfection, it is not enough to imitate others and follow religion blindly (*taqlid*). Rather, one must

---

145. Chittick, "Mysticism," 90.

146. Rizvi, "Mysticism," 227.

147. Abu Affifi said that Ibn 'Arabi had a definite philosophical doctrine and a formal dialectic which dominated the whole of his thought. Affifi, *Mystical Philosophy*, i. Also, Landau, "Philosophy of Ibn 'Arabi I," 46–61; Landau, "Philosophy of Ibn 'Arabi II," 146–61. See Corbin, *Creative Imagination*.

148. Chittick, "School of Ibn 'Arabi," 510–23.

149. Seyyed Hossein Nasr explains that veils are deep rooted in human nature. Veils are human forgetfulness and imperfections. Only with God's help may these veils be removed. Nasr, *Garden*, 54. In order to unveil, Nasr asserts that human intellect, different from reason, is central. He calls his esoterism 'sapiental esoterism that is based thoroughly upon the intellect and intellectual intuition.' Nasr, "Reply," 163.

achieve a total awareness of the principles and the spirit that animate the religion, or, as the Sufis express it, one must realize the Reality itself (*tahaqqua*). On the theoretical level, the Shahadah[150] becomes a concrete expression of the absolute reality of God, a sword that cuts away the illusory from the Real. On the practical level, the guidelines set down by the Sharia perform the same function, but here Sufis do not accept these guidelines "because they must," but because of their awareness that these play a basic role in allowing human beings to act in accordance with revealed truth and avoid error.[151]

The Sufi spirituality emphasizes right thinking, right doing and above all right unveiling which is achieved by following the Sufi mystical path. Furthermore, the concept of bearing witness (*Shahadah*) with its realization of the absolute reality of God is closely linked and rooted in Ibn 'Arabi's tradition of the unity of existence.

This present work has found Chittick's understanding of Sufi spirituality most helpful in interpreting Liu Zhi's Sufi thought in his writings. Sufi thought in Liu Zhi's works aims firstly to understand the Islamic texts better (right thinking). Secondly, rules and proprieties of Islam are carried out properly in compliance with *shari'a* and yet expressed primarily in Confucian terms (right doing). Finally, right unveiling is understood as the return to the Real Ruler with great emphasis on the role of the prophet Muhammad who can empower Muslims in their right thinking and doing. Also, Liu Zhi consistently emphasized the important role of the heart in the return to the Real Ruler.

Liu Zhi's Sufi Spirituality as Contextualized Neo-Confucian Wisdom

Neo-Confucianism and Zhu Xi (1130–1200)

The philosophical thought in seventeenth-century China approved by the imperial court was that of Zhu Xi (1130–1200) and his School of Principle. Zhu Xi was a consummate scholar and superbly brought to completion the ideas of many previous Confucian thinkers.[152] He also edited and annotated

---

150. *Shahadah* means the testimony of faith or to bear witness. This testifies that firstly there is no god but God and secondly, Muhammad is his messenger. It is a key to understanding the Islamic perspectives in all domains of faith.

151. Chittick, *Sufism*, 15.

152. Chan Wing-Tsit asserted that Zhu Xi was able to give Neo-Confucianism a new character and a new completion. Chan, *Chu Hsi*, 104.

essential Confucian texts, namely the *Analects of Confucius*.[153] He worked out a lasting renewal of the Confucian project and launched thirteenth-century China into Neo-Confucianism. Zhu Xi's thought and his influence gradually diminished with the rise of Chinese scholars like Wang Fuzhi (1619–1692) who rejected both the Zhu Xi and Wang Yangming schools of Neo-Confucianism. In the early Qing dynasty, Wang Fuzhi attacked both principle (Zhu Xi) and mind (Wang Yangming) schools and asserted that these schools were mainly responsible for the downfall of the Ming dynasty into the hands of the Manchu invaders.

Zhu Xi's religious, cosmological and ethical teachings require exposition because many of Liu Zhi's modern interpreters have argued that Liu's teachings resonated with Zhu Xi's writings. Interpreters also have asserted that Liu Zhi's works borrowed heavily from Neo-Confucianism in general and Zhu Xi in particular. The key concepts of Zhu Xi's teachings that bear religious connotations are *taiji* (the Great Ultimate), *li* (principle) and *qi* (matter-energy or energizing field). Although it is still debatable whether Zhu Xi is a theist,[154] we assert that he is not within the boundary of the monotheistic Semitic faiths. Zhu Xi's concept of the Great Ultimate was indebted to Zhou Dunyi (1017–1073) who had written and explained the diagram of the Great Ultimate or Infinite.[155] Zhou supplied Zhu Xi with ideas, concepts, philosophical vocabulary and metaphysical formulations. As noted by the modern Chinese scholar Julia Ching, the "concept of the Great Ultimate (T'ai-chi [Taiji]) marks the climax of Chu's [Zhu Xi] philosophical system . . . The concept became famous especially with his own contributions, which transformed its meaning by relating it to *li* and *ch'i* [*qi* matter energy]."[156]

---

153. Zhu Xi who is a key scholar of Neo-Confucianism wrote his commentary of Confucius's *Analects* and interpreted Confucius in his own way. See Gardner, *Zhu*

154. Under the concept of God's creativity, John Berthrong takes the cue from Zhu Xi's thoughts to defend the object–event creative view of Alfred N. Whitehead and against Richard Neville's *creatio ex nihilo* view of God. See Berthrong, *Concerning Creativity*.

155. See Liang, *Critical Biography*.

156. Ching, *Religious Thought*, 33.

Figure 2.1: The Diagram of the Limitless or Infinite

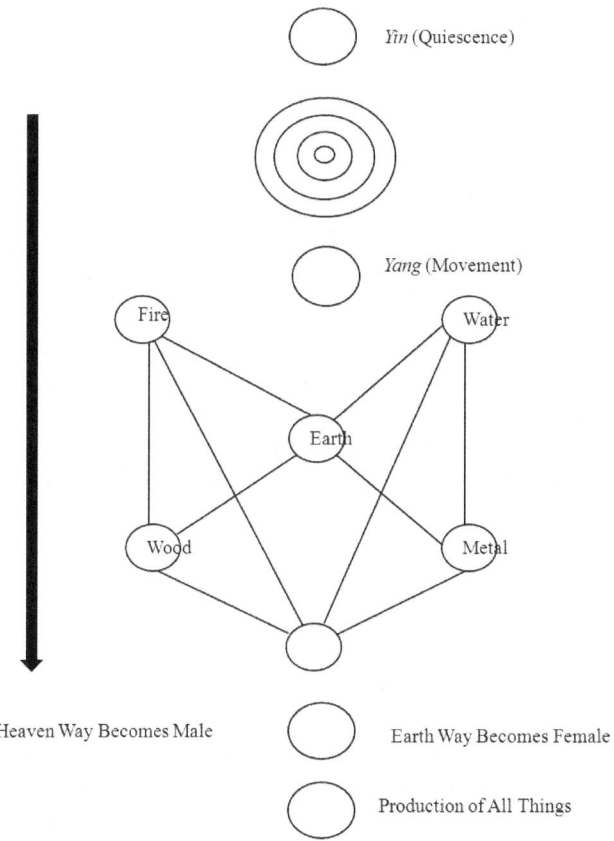

Zhou Dunyi expounded the concept of Ultimate Non-being or Infinite in his diagram, namely, the "Diagram of the Limitless or Infinite."[157] The diagram is to be interpreted from *top* to *bottom*. This diagram consists of a series of circles descending. The Ultimate Non-being transforms downward into interlocking, semicircular areas of light and darkness. This is Yin (quiescence) and Yang (movement). The movement and quiescence of the two bipolar sides further transmit downward to a network of five small circles, identified by water, fire, metal, wood and the centre as earth. Beneath this network is the creation of male and female and then at the bottom of the diagram is the production and transformation of all things.[158] Zhou Dunyi

---

157. This is also known as the diagram of Non Ultimate (*Wuji Tu*). The alleged source of this diagram was from the Daoist hermit Chen Tuan (c. 906–c. 989).

158. Ching, *Religious Thought*, 20–21.

did not explain the diagram as to how and why the Great Ultimate effused in such a manner.

Prior to the Great Ultimate, Zhu Xi posits the Ultimate of Nonbeing (*Wuji*) which is explicated as "the operations of Heaven have neither sound nor smell." The Ultimate of Nonbeing has neither physical form nor spatial restriction. It exists prior to creation and yet is not absent after the creation of all things. It is omniscient without any smell or sound. The subtlety of Zhu Xi as compared with his source "the Diagram of the Infinite" was noted by a well-known Neo-Confucian scholar, Chan Wing-tsit:

> He [Zhu Xi] also said, 'What is called 'Wu-chi erh T'ai-chi' [Great Ultimate as the ultimate non-being] does not mean that on top of the Great Ultimate there is separately an Ultimate of Nonbeing. It merely says that the Great Ultimate is not a thing, as in the saying, 'The operations of Heaven have neither sound nor smell.' Again, he said, 'What is called wu-chi [ultimate of nonbeing] is to bring out the wonder of its being soundless and odorless.'[159]

Thus, the Great Ultimate is the first principle which is both a creative principle as well as an explanatory principle that leads to an ordering of creation. Julia Ching helpfully explains that

> [b]y analogy, we might say the Great Ultimate is like God or necessary being in Thomas Aquinas's system, that which subsists, in and of itself, without depending on others, while all other exists, in and of the Great Ultimate. But the analogy is imperfect, as the Great Ultimate is, on another level, immanent as well as transcendent. It is above all things and yet present in all things. It is above motion and rest and yet involved in a cyclical cosmic process. The dialectic goes on.[160]

Zhu took insight from Zhou's explanation and elaborated that the Great Ultimate existed as opposed to others and in dialectical relationship with the *li* (principle) and *qi* (vital energy). The basic dynamic is that there is no mixing and yet no separation of *li* principle and *qi* vital energy in that they are mutually transcendent and interpenetrated without fusion or reduction. While *li* and *qi* are dialectically related, Zhu Xi gives ontological and logical priority to *li* over *qi* in his philosophy.[161]

---

159. Chan, *Chu Hsi New Studies*, 145.
160. Ching, *Religious Thought*, 52.
161. Ching, *Religious Thought*, 41.

This is a significant emphasis by Zhu. That is, *li* as a metaphysical concept serves as an organizing principle while *qi* serves as an actualizing principle. Chan Wing-Tsit expounds Zhu Xi's understanding and asserts that while *li* and *qi* are never separated, "Chu Hsi [Zhu Xi] repeatedly said that there must be the principle [*li*] of thing before that thing can come into being."[162] For Zhu Xi, the Great Ultimate is the most perfect *li* which may be defined as the excellent and supremely good normative principle (*tao-li*).[163]

What is the relationship between the Great Ultimate and *li*? While the summation of the *li* of the universe as a whole is the Great Ultimate, the Great Ultimate is also immanent in the individual examples of each category of things. Zhu Xi said, "with regard to heaven and earth in general, the Great Ultimate is in heaven and earth. And with regard to the myriad things in particular, the Great Ultimate is in every one of them too."[164] In addition to cosmogony, the Great Ultimate also relates to humanity.

Julia Ching explains concisely the subtle relationship between *li* and the Great Ultimate in terms of human cultivation. "I think it may be useful to see the immanent Great Ultimate as the *fullness* of *li* in the nature of sages. In other words, the identity between the Great Ultimate and *li* in the nature of sages is not true of ordinary humans. It can, however, be made so by a process of cultivation. Therefore, its manifestation is also in terms of degrees, depending on the person's nearness to sagehood."[165] That is to say, there is one principle with many manifestations. This immanence appears latent in many people but can be manifested and actualized by self-cultivation.

In almost all recent studies of Liu Zhi, especially the contributions by the Chinese scholars, it has been argued that Neo-Confucianism in general and Zhu Xi in particular have influenced Liu Zhi. Later, we will argue that while this Neo-Confucian background is important, Liu Zhi's Islamic work does not Confucianize or sinicize his Islamic message.

The Relationship between Religion, Chinese Culture and Self-Cultivation

Confucianism and Buddhism are sometimes regarded as philosophical systems rather than religions. However, Christianity and Islam have always been regarded as religions. How is Chinese religion defined? It is often

---

162. Chan, *Chu Hsi*, 112–3.
163. Ching, *Religious Thought*, 44.
164. Fung, *Short History*, 488.
165. Ching, *Religious Thought*, 98.

defined in broad and inclusive terms. Yao and Zhao define Chinese religion as referring "to religious ideas, belief and practices of the Chinese people, which developed in history, are continually pursued and practiced in today's personal and communal life, and have therefore become an important part of the Chinese way of life."[166] Like many other Chinese scholars, Yao and Zhao assert that "religion is part of culture and must be understood in its cultural context. Many Chinese beliefs and practices are phenomenologically meaningful only in relation to their cultural background and expectation."[167] For Yao and Zhao, there is no need for a clear distinction between religious and cultural studies. "In fact religion is part of culture, and culture is itself consolidated through religion . . . place Chinese religion in its cultural contexts, and examine Chinese culture against its religious orientations."[168] Thus, cultural religion means a religious system that is "deeply woven into the broad fabric of individual, family and social life, and is an integral part of Chinese culture."[169] Religious culture means that "religion has influenced all aspects of daily life such as food, clothing, shelter, travel, marriage, birth, death, and life crises. Historiography and philosophy are under the influence of religious interpretation."[170] It should be noted that Liu Zhi's method of contextualization is to interpret Islamic spirituality creatively as a legitimate Chinese cultural religion because it fully complies with the spirit of Neo-Confucian culture and yet without any compromise with the basic tenets of Islamic belief.

The Three Teachings, namely Neo-Confucianism, Daoism, and Buddhism, have had far reaching practical implications in Chinese culture for many centuries. Paracka Jr. gives a simple diagram of the inter-related or triangulating relationships between the three philosophical systems.[171] The diagram below also shows moral concerns and emphases of each of the Three Teachings.

---

166. Yao and Zhao, *Chinese Religion*, ix.
167. Ibid., x.
168. Ibid., 22.
169. Ibid., 79.
170. Ibid., 83.
171. Paracka Jr., "China's Three Teachings," 77.

Figure 2.2: The Triad of Interconnected Relationships

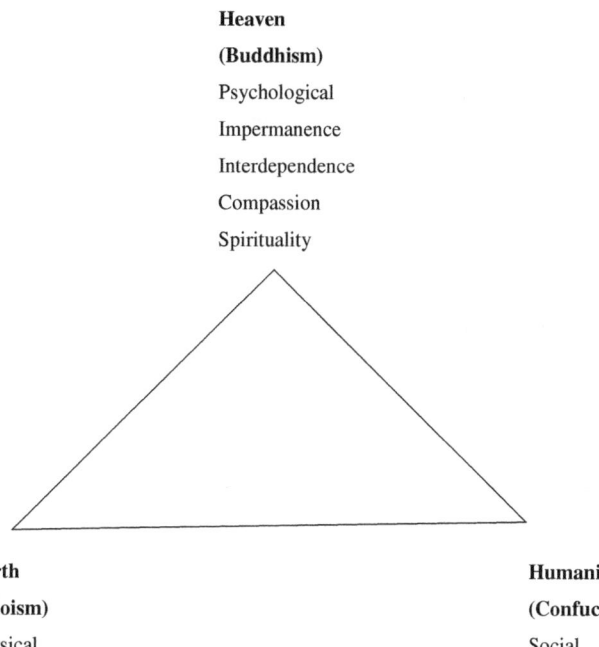

Heaven
(Buddhism)
Psychological
Impermanence
Interdependence
Compassion
Spirituality

Earth   **Humanity**
(Daoism)   **(Confucianism)**
Physical   Social
Ecological   Political
Medicinal   Family
Balance   Community
Longevity   Prosperity

Generally speaking, "Daoism focuses on living in harmony with the natural rhythms, flows and forces of life. Through careful observation, Daoists seek balance among alternating complementary and contrasting ideas such as night and day, masculine and feminine, yin and yang."[172] For practicing Daoists, longevity is about immortality or avoidance of the death-event. It "was to attain an exalted state of existence through diligent cultivation of the world's deeper realities. Such attainments were generally predicated upon a process of personal purification and an enhanced awareness of reality."[173] . . . "Buddhism focuses on how ignorance, greed and craving produce suffering in an interdependent world. It calls for compassion

172. Ibid., 75.
173. Kirkland, *Taoism*, 188.

and understanding in order to build up *karma*,¹⁷⁴ which may eventually lead to an end to one's participation in the cycle of rebirth and suffering."¹⁷⁵

On a practical level, Neo-Confucianism focuses on harmonious relationships among people, in the state and even with the environment. Social order reinforced by rites and merits is understood to be the vital prerequisite for peace and prosperity. Both Daoism and Buddhism encourage self-cultivation and the exemplar of moral cultivation is known as the perfect man¹⁷⁶ and holy sage respectively.

Sufi Spirituality as Contextualized Neo-Confucian Wisdom

Neo-Confucian self-realization is occasionally known as practical wisdom. Wisdom and religion are closely related terms, but they do not mean the same thing. Religion is a loaded word often associated with powerful, greedy totalitarian regimes; sterile observance of rigid rules; and obsolete creeds filled with archaic terms that lack contemporary relevance. While wisdom may sound mystical to some, it is a word associated with the practice of human self-cultivation and transformation according to Confucian thought. As Kirill Thompson puts it, Confucius understood wisdom to be knowledge of the actual state of affairs. Thus, the wise person is able to penetrate obscurity and change to comprehend the hidden, true state of affairs. Thompson asserts that while Zhu Xi's notions of knowledge and wisdom were to inform life practice, Zhu's purpose in seeking and exercising wisdom was "to cultivate a nuanced, holistic, responsive sensitivity to the immanent patterns of change and transformation."¹⁷⁷ Yao Xinzhong also asserts that Confucian wisdom is a "progress from 'what is below' to 'what is above' and the interrelationship between knowing human nature, human destiny, and heaven . . . "higher realms" that are initially beyond the reach of ordinary people but can be fully realized in their effort to know, understand, and appreciate."¹⁷⁸ Furthermore, after exploring the concept of *Yi* (righteousness) in Confucius's *Analects*, Yu Jiyuan concludes that

> While appropriateness [righteousness] is about practical affairs, wisdom seems to be both theoretical and practical. It is

---

174. Buddhism adopts the theory of reincarnation. 'The deeds or *karma* of each sentient being in successive past existences determine what he is to be in existences still to come.' Fung, *History*, 237.

175. Paracka Jr, 'China's Three Teachings,' 75.

176. Fung, *History*, 231–36.

177. Thompson, "Archery," 336.

178. Yao, "From What is Below," 359–60.

theoretical because it is knowledge of the *ming* [destiny] of heaven, the ontological premise of the good life; it is practical because at *A*, 12:22 . . . wisdom is to "know one's fellow human beings" . . . Wisdom is about what is appropriate [righteous] in human affairs . . . to have wisdom is to know the social rites and their ontological grounds, while appropriateness [righteousness] is more closely associated with the agent's choosing and determining.[179]

Clearly, wisdom in Neo-Confucian contexts has a minimal religious connotation but an extensive ethical-moral character. It can be acquired by practice and becomes a habitual attitude. Liu Zhi creatively contextualized Islamic proprieties as Neo-Confucian wisdom. The Qing emperor was convinced that Islam, like Buddhism and Daoism, had made contributions to the life of people in his country. So, Liu Zhi's Islam did not alienate itself from the imperial ruler.[180] Liu Zhi's task of contextualization was not easy because he argued that one could be both a Muslim and a Chinese under an increasingly oppressive Qing imperial rule. On the one hand, he distinguished Islam and the Chinese culture by stating that Islam belonged to the wisdom of the west, founded by a western sage, the prophet Muhammad who received direct revelation from God. Thus, he separated Islam as a religion from Chinese social culture. On the other hand, he argued that Islamic belief and Chinese socio-religious culture were compatible.[181] Thus, Islam witnessed to the richness of Chinese cultural traditions, especially self-realization and transformation. That is to say, the cultural religion of Islam as contextualized by Liu Zhi in the form of Confucian wisdom has enriched Neo-Confucianism into a multi-ethnic tradition.

Liu Zhi encouraged Muslims to be faithful witnesses of their faith and obedient to imperial rulers in their civil duty. They practiced their Islamic faith in the midst of Han communities. They should express their Islamic faith in both Islamic and Chinese communities. Liu Zhi rejected totally the mentality of "us vs. them." In addition, he also emphasized Sufi spirituality and taught Muslims to seek Sufi masters and follow the Sufi path. Sufi thought revitalized the faith of the individual beyond mere ritualistic observation of the proprieties of Islam. The strategy of Liu Zhi's contextualization

179. Yu, "Yi," 342.

180. Liu Zhi clearly taught that civilians and court officials should obey the imperial rule and be faithful to the emperor. The emperor should seek the well-being of the citizens because they are the basic units of the country. Liu Zhi, *Rules* (1988), 130–34.

181. Any conflict between Islamic and traditional Neo-Confucian teachings is due to deviations and cults within Neo-Confucianism. See Appendix III.

is ultimately to raise the legitimacy of Islam as a cultural religion in China in continuation with the Neo-Confucian tradition.

SUMMARY AND CONCLUSION

This chapter provides the contexts in which Liu Zhi's works can be better understood. He contextualized his Islamic message by triangulating the text, Chinese culture and wisdom. This means that Liu Zhi took the revealed texts and interpreted them in Neo-Confucian terms so that Hui Muslims would understand them meaningfully in their context. From that existential context, he encouraged all Hui Muslims to continue to live in the *dao* of Muhammad and eventually ascend or return to where the Real Ruler wants them in terms of Neo-Confucian wisdom. The table below provides a pointer to the following chapters in order to demonstrate the contextualization of Liu Zhi.

Table 2.1: Pointers of Liu Zhi's Contextualization

Liu Zhi's Theme/ Philosophical Thoughts	Neo-Confucianism	Buddhism	Daoism
The Unity of Existence	The concept of Great Ultimate and cosmogony by using yin/yang thought	Attachment to permanence	Oneness of reality
Sufi Spirituality	Self-cultivation and the concept of holy sage	The escape from the wheel of rebirth and death and the concept of Buddhahood	Exalted state of existence and the concept of perfect man

The spread of Islam in the history of China is possibly due to a dynamic process of cultural, commercial, political, philosophical, and religious factors. There is ample historical evidence to show that the seventeenth to eighteenth century was a period of intense Islamic activity in China. This particular era was a period of vigorous Islamic activity of teaching, writings and translation. The leadership of some *ulama* determined to transmit the Islamic traditions which they had received. This chapter has examined the historical and religious context of Liu Zhi. He faced political, philosophical, and religious challenges. His teachings and writings have brought forth the growth of Islam and had long-lasting effects in later generations.

This chapter of Liu Zhi's contexts has provided several pointers for the arguments in the following chapters:

1. In the concept of the unity of existence, Liu Zhi's interpretation and contextualization of Islam has been aided by Daoism's oneness of reality and Neo-Confucianism's combination of Yin/Yang thought and the concept of Great Ultimate. Several previous studies have asserted Liu Zhi's contextualization is eclectic. However, this present work aims to show that Liu Zhi's concept of the unity of existence is primarily influenced by Neo-Confucian and secondarily Daoist and Buddhist influence. He selectively employed Confucian, Daoist, and Buddhist terms.

2. In the concept of Sufi thought, Liu Zhi's exposition of *shari'a*-minded Sufism is to be proposed as right understanding, right thinking and right unveiling. Previous works have asserted that Liu Zhi's thoughts are influenced by Sufism. We would like to point out that his Islamic rules and proprieties are understood as Sufi spirituality in terms of primarily Neo-Confucian self-cultivation and secondarily a Buddhist escape from impermanence and a Daoist exalted state of existence.

3. The role of the prophet Muhammad is vitally important for Muslims to return to the Real Ruler. Previous studies of Liu Zhi have said little about the role of the prophet Muhammad in Liu Zhi's Sufi thought. The role of the prophet is understood in accordance with the Ibn 'Arabi tradition and is contextualized as the Utmost Sage of the Neo-Confucian tradition.

3

An Examination of Liu Zhi's Writings

This chapter provides an overview of the major and some minor works of Liu Zhi. The second part of this chapter introduces the contemporary discussion of Liu Zhi's works in Chinese and English. Finally, a brief discussion will be provided of contemporary scholarship on Liu Zhi's contextualization.

LIU ZHI'S TRILOGY: A BRIEF OVERVIEW

Jin asserts that the majority of Liu Zhi's writing is expositional and commentary work rather than translated work.[1] Liu Zhi used Arabic or Persian source materials available in his time. Then, he translated these source materials into Chinese and explained them. He also composed Islamic poems in Chinese and tracts for easier memorization. While he wrote, he freely used and selectively edited his source materials. The literary structure and topic divisions were Liu Zhi's own creation. In addition, his commentary on each topic was his own exposition. More precisely, then, Liu Zhi's work should be described as a fairly free exposition of or commentary of selected Islamic traditions in China at the time of his writing. Undoubtedly, Liu Zhi's trilogy is by far the most significant. His trilogy is listed as follows:

- *The Nature and Principle in Islam*
- *The Rules and Proprieties of Islam*[2]

---

1. Jin, *Exploring Chinese Islam*, 16–17.

2. Liu, *Rules*. The first five chapters of this work (reprinted 1988) have been translated into English in Appendix IV.

- *The True Record of the Utmost Sage of Islam*[3]

Liu Zhi explained the close relationship between his three books. *The Nature and Principle in Islam* explains the nature and principle of the Islamic *dao* i.e. the concept of God, the divine disclosure and the Islamic worldview. The *Rules and Proprieties of Islam* explains the meaning of Islamic rituals. The *True Record of the Utmost Sage of Islam* explains the origin of Islam. He emphasized that these three works should actually constitute one whole grand meta-concept of Chinese Islam.

Other works include:

- Sufi works: *The Poem of the Five Sessions of the Moon* and *An Explanation of the Arabic Alphabets*
- Translated work: *Displaying the Concealment of the True Realm*

His writings on the popular level are as follows:

- *The Three-character Classic* similar to *The Nature and Principle in Islam* in content but shorter and easier to read
- *The Explanation of the Five Endeavors* similar to *The Rules and Proprieties of Islam* in content but shorter and easier to read.

Liu Zhi's trilogy has often been re-printed with increasing prefaces by well known supporters/admirers throughout the past several centuries. The latest printing is published in modern and simplified Chinese for the contemporary readers. The more popular shorter works of Liu Zhi are often accessible on the Internet.

The Nature and Principle in Islam

The Nature and Principle in Islam[4] is the first of the trilogy by Liu Zhi. He stated that the aim of this work was to show the whole world the evidence of the way in its totality. Literally, the way is the *dao*. Liu Zhi discussed the metaphysical concept of the *dao* of Chinese Islam. The work is broadly divided into two sections. The first section has just one volume with five chapters and is known as the root classic.[5] This comprises the solid and complicated concepts including the Great Ultimate, transformation of one into many, the innate and the acquired heaven, and return to the Real One.

---

3. Liu, *True Record*. Selected sections of this work (reprinted in 1984) have been translated into English in Appendix II.

4. Murata has translated this work into English. Murata et al., *Sage*, 102–580.

5. This is the foundational section of the whole work and known as the 'root classic' (*Benjing*). The first chapter summarizes the whole root classic. The subsequent section serves to expound the meaning of the root classic. Murata et al., *Sage*, 82–84.

The second section takes up the major bulk of the book. This section has five volumes. Each volume in the second section explains in detail each corresponding chapter in the first section. In total, sixty diagrams are added into the second section to aid the explanation. Readers are expected to examine the diagram while reading the text to assist their understanding.

The core teaching of the work is the multiplicity and unity of God. From this foundational concept, Liu Zhi expounded various doctrines of ontology, epistemology, cosmology, and anthropology. Liu Zhi also briefly mentioned the uniqueness of the prophet Muhammad. Muhammad had a pre-creation metaphysical existence. He was the archetypal human example that all Chinese Muslims should follow. Liu Zhi's contemporary, Wang Daiyu regarded Muhammad embracing "in unitary fashion all the realities and principles that give rise to the infinitely diverse universe. Thus the Muhammadan Reality is God inasmuch as human beings are created in his image."[6] This work has been extensively studied and many essays in journals and a few book-length studies have been published in both English and Chinese. Murata also gives a reliable and full English-Chinese translation of the first five volumes or the root classic which is the foundational material of this work.[7]

The Rules and Proprieties of Islam[8]

The second work in the trilogy is *The Rules and Proprieties of Islam* that teaches the rationale and various religious practices of Islam. It consists of twenty volumes. The first four volumes recapitulate the Islamic philosophy including the concept of God, knowing God, and Islamic worldview. These few chapters recapitulate the main teaching of root classic in *The Nature and Principle in Islam*. The fifth to the tenth volumes give an account of the five meritorious works or endeavors. The rest of the book is concerned with religious and ethical practices and rites. This book was selected and collected into the *Annotated General Catalogue of the Compendium of the Four Treasuries, Authorized by the Emperor*.[9] Such inclusion into the imperial catalogue has raised Liu Zhi's literary work to national status beyond the ethnic status of the *Han Kitab* .It is the only work in the *Han Kitab* to have achieved such imperial status. The first five volumes or more commonly

---

6. Murata, *Gleams*, 75–76.
7. Murata et al., *Sage*, 93–580.
8. Liu, *Rules*. The reprinted edition in 1988 has been used in this work.
9. Chi et al., *Annotated General Catalogue*.

known chapters will be translated and discussed in greater detail in chapter 6 later.

The True Record of the Utmost Sage of Islam

The third and last major work is *The True Record of the Utmost Sage of Islam*[10] in which Liu Zhi gave a fairly comprehensive account of the life history of the prophet Muhammad.[11] Liu Zhi's purpose in writing is to explain the profound origins of Islam and its teaching. Liu Zhi's portrayal of the prophet came close to divinizing the prophet. This biographical work of Muhammad has been the most popular work by Liu Zhi. These three works form the trilogy and can be regarded as the *magnum opus* of his writings. *The True Record of the Utmost Sage of Islam* was translated into English in the early twentieth century. In the first half of the twentieth century, the English version was translated into Russian and French. In 1941, the Chinese version was translated into Japanese.

In Isaac Mason's edited translation of Liu Zhi's *True Record of the Utmost Sage of Islam,* Mason translated only sixteen volumes. He followed closely the original Chinese text in the beginning. By the seventh volume, he became increasingly selective because he found the account tedious and "omitted somewhat irrelevant portions to keep the book within moderate limits."[12]

A typical version of *The True Record of the Utmost Sage of Islam* in traditional Chinese contains sixteen volumes with four additional volumes which are really appendixes. In 1984, a simplified Chinese version was printed. It also has twenty volumes. The preface gives an account of different ways of presenting the prophet, namely portraits, books, and others. The first volume narrates the ancestral records of Muhammad, namely fifty generations in total from Adam the first human being to the prophet Muhammad. The second volume explains the various traditions that Muhammad inherited from or belonged to, namely the tradition of human ancestry, nation, prophet, and human nature. The third volume gives a concise

---

10. Liu, *True Record*. Selected texts of this reprinted work in 1984 have been translated into English in Appendix II.

11. Both Murata and Leslie have discussed briefly the source of this work. Leslie asserts that the original work is the fourteenth-century Persian work, *Tarjama-yi mawlud-i Mustafa* by 'Afif ibn Muhammad Kaziruni. Murata says that Liu Zhi's work 'retells many of the stories in 'Afif's work and follows the same general order, he also condenses the text drastically and adds material from other sources.' Murata, *Gleams*, 34.

12. Mason, *Arabian Prophet,* viii.

summary of major events in the life of the prophet. These few introductory volumes are important because Liu Zhi put the prophet and Islam at the centre of human existence including history and religion. In addition, he could also claim legitimacy for Islam in the Chinese culture and orthodoxy in all other religions.

From the fourth volume to the sixteenth volume, Liu Zhi gave a fairly comprehensive record of the life of the prophet Muhammad from his birth to death. The seventeenth volume was originally written by Ma Zhu in accordance with the Chinese Sufi tradition. Liu Zhi's comments keenly supported Ma's understanding of the role of the prophet. The commentary is about the eulogizing of Muhammad and Liu Zhi added this extra volume to complete his account of the life and role of the prophet in Islam. The eighteenth volume gives a record of the appearance, worship, fasting, and other aspects of the prophet's life and his way of dealing with various human relationships. Extra information about the land of the origin of Islam is provided in the nineteenth volume.

While some Western scholars showed keen interest in this work in the first half of the twentieth century, recent research of Liu Zhi in both China and the West has paid little attention to this last work of Liu Zhi's trilogy. In 1995, a paraphrased version was printed in modern simplified Chinese in China. Interestingly, this latest version deletes all the beginning prefaces, three introductory volumes and additional four volumes of appendixes at the end and solely narrates the life history of the Utmost Sage according to Liu Zhi.

OTHER WORKS OF LIU ZHI: AN OVERVIEW

The Explanation of the Five Endeavors

This is not a long work, about fourteen thousand Chinese words. It is also known as *The Book of Propriety: The Explanation of the Five Endeavors*. It explains the five pillars of Islam in Neo-Confucian terms. It consists of sixty-three short chapters, equivalent to sixty three years of the age of the prophet Muhammad. It is divided into three sections. The first seven chapters explicate the origin, basics and goals of the five endeavors. The second section covers from chapters 8 to 32 and explains the meanings and the regulations of such endeavors. The final section covers chapters from the 33 to 63. It explains in details the meanings of endeavor from a religious and ethical perspective. The length of such chapters may vary from a short chapter under twenty Chinese words (for example, chapter 43) to the longest chapter 33 about four hundred and twenty words. Each chapter begins with a chapter title. This work is a valuable, easy-to-read and concise summary of Liu Zhi's understanding and contextualization of the proprieties of Islam in Neo-Confucian terms.

In the first section, chapter 1 affirms that the origin of the five endeavors is based on the unity of existence and Islamic worldview in accordance with Liu Zhi's received Islamic tradition. The goal of Muslims is to recover the mandate and return to the Real. Return is the end of the spiritual way. Chapter 2 covers more basic doctrines of the proprieties. This is followed consecutively by chapters of love and hatred, external sensory organs, inner virtues, nature of the heart, and lastly chapter 7 of uprightness and distortion.

The second section teaches the rite, method, meaning, principle, and ultimate goal of the five endeavors, namely bearing witness (*shahadah*), ritual prayer (*salat*), fasting, alms tax, and pilgrimage.

The last section provides more detailed meaning and explanation from religious and ethical perspectives. It should be noted that Liu Zhi's *Rules and Proprieties of Islam* covers similar teachings to the *Explanation of the Five Endeavors*. Compared to his *Rules and Proprieties of Islam*, three particular points are more explicit in the third section of this shorter work. Firstly, this third section emphasizes that the five endeavors are spiritual progress (in chapter 58) and yet this progress is ongoing in a cyclic manner and never coming to an end (in chapter 44). Secondly, the benefits of the five endeavors (in chapters 42, 43, 45 and 51) have both real physical and spiritual well being. Lastly in chapter 50, the Utmost Sage, namely the prophet Muhammad, is unique. His endeavors are most subtle and he can see through the principle and image of things.

Other Works: *The Three-character Classic*, *Displaying the Concealment of the Real Realm*, *Explanation of the Meaning of Arabic Alphabets*, and *Poem of the Five Sessions of the Moon*

The teaching on the unity of existence and divine disclosure is clearly found in *The Three-character Classic* and *Displaying the Concealment of the Real Realm*. Both of these works will be discussed in the next chapter.

There is no reason to doubt Liu Zhi's competence to understand the Qur'an in Arabic. His knowledge of Arabic could be partly demonstrated by his work, *An Explanation of the Meaning of Islamic Letters*.[13] It should be

---

13. Liu, *Explanation of the Meaning*.

noted that this is not a grammatical introduction to the Arabic language. In this work, Liu Zhi explained the theological meaning of the Arabic alphabets within the framework of his cosmogony as expounded in his *Nature and Principle in Islam* from the perspective of Sufi mysticism. With regard to the explanation of the Arabic alphabets, Liu Zhi acknowledged his indebtedness to previous sources, namely, *Subtle Analogy Classic* and *Alphabet Classic*. According to Jin, Liu Zhi employed more Neo-Confucian concepts than any other Muslim literati.[14] Jin asserts that Liu Zhi's contemporary Xu Lan in his work *The Proper Meaning of Islam* also explained the meaning of the Arabic alphabets. While Liu Zhi was indebted to his sources, he differed from Xu Lan's interpretation. Xu Lan affirmed that the dot of the Arabic alphabet was identical to the Real One. However, Liu Zhi asserted that the dot represented the substance (*ti*).[15]

Liu Zhi explained that the dot was the origin of all Arabic alphabets. These alphabets come into existence by the disclosure of the dot. The process of disclosure is understood mystically in accordance with mystical Sufism.[16] He argued that from each dot of the alphabet, emanated something similar to the self-disclosure of the Real Being. The shape of the alphabet was the beginning of the word. The word was the manifestation of both dot and shape. Thus, Liu Zhi argued that an essay was a multiple manifestation of words and the word was a multiple manifestation of both dot and shape of each alphabet.[17] Jin Yijiu notes that for Liu Zhi, the Arabic word for Muhammad could be analyzed and deduced that he was the perfect man in the disclosure.[18] This work clearly demonstrates Liu Zhi's Sufi thoughts.

The other Sufi work is *The Poem of the Five Sessions of the Moon*. It will be fully translated into English and discussed in chapter 5 of this book.[19] The poem is still very popular among Hui Muslims and easily accessible on the internet.[20] While many scholars are able to point out that *The Rules and Proprieties of Islam* is quite Confucianized, only Jin briefly states that *The Poem of the Five Sessions of the Moon* is very eclectic with frequent use of Buddhist, Daoist and Confucian terms.[21]

14. Jin, "Liu Zhi's Explanation of the Meaning," 28–29.
15. Jin, *Exploring Chinese Islam*, 302.
16. Ibid., 314.
17. Jin, "Liu Zhi's Explanation of the Meaning,'" 26–27.
18. Jin, "Liu Zhi's Explanation of the Meaning," 27.
19. The full English translation is found in Appendix I.
20. http://www.douban.com/group/topic/24083421/
21. Jin gives a brief note of various Buddhist, Daoist and Confucian terms in *Poem of the Five Sessions of the Moon*. Jin, *Exploring Chinese Islam*, 298.

CONTEMPORARY SCHOLARSHIP ON LIU ZHI'S WORKS AND A CRITICAL ASSESSMENT

An Overview

Works in English

Before the critical assessment of contemporary scholarship, it is appropriate to give a historical survey of research by both English and Chinese scholars. The last few decades have witnessed intense scholarly study of seventeenth and eighteenth-century Chinese Islam in general and Liu Zhi in particular. Certainly, the scholarly interest will continue throughout this century as China continues to seek political friendship and trading opportunities with the Western and especially Middle Eastern Arabic countries. However, the relationship between China and other countries a century ago was totally different. Owing to missionary endeavors at the beginning of the twentieth century, missionaries anticipated an open door opportunity to Muslims in China. To facilitate such Christian mission, Marshall Broomhall wrote a scholarly work on Islam in China.[22] In addition to a book-length work, other essays were published promoting a better understanding of the neglected people, Hui and Uyghurs, and other Muslims in China. Isaac Mason wrote several important essays. Relevant to this book is his abridged translation of Liu Zhi's *True Record of the Utmost Sage of Islam*.[23]

Interest in Chinese Islam went through a quiet period from 1949, when the communists came to power, with the founding of the People Republic of China. Then, most of the research, translation and publication work of Chinese Islam continued outside the Peoples' Republic of China, namely, in Taiwan,[24] Australia,[25] Japan and other Southeast Asian countries, Europe[26] and America. In 1974, Joseph Ford's historical study of Chinese Islam focused on the Chinese Muslim literati including Liu Zhi in the seventeenth and eighteenth centuries.[27] In the eighties, fuelled by the open-door policy of the Chinese government, study of Chinese Islam

22. See Broomhall, *Islam*.

23. See Mason, *Arabian Prophet*. Also, Mason, "Notes," 172–215.

24. During this period, some classics of seventeenth-century Islamic literature in Chinese were published in more modern Chinese in Taiwan.

25. The Australian National University has made tremendous advances in historical Chinese studies of both Jews and Islam, under the leadership of Donald Leslie.

26. Russians have occasionally shown their interest in historical study on Chinese Islam. Loewenthal, "Russian Materials," 449–79. Also Loewenthal, "Sino-Islamica," 209–12.

27. Ford, "Some Chinese Muslims," 144–56.

in general and seventeenth-century Chinese Islam in particular resumed momentum. Francis Cotter and Karl L. Reichelt translated into English in the early twentieth century Liu Zhi's *The Three-character Classic*.[28] Donald Leslie began his life-long work in the late seventies on historical study of Chinese Islam, often paying particular attention to seventeenth-century *Han Kitab* work by the Chinese Muslim literati.[29] Most relevant to us is his joint work with M. Wassel. They trace the various Islamic sources that Liu Zhi used and are able to identify most of the sources as Arabic and Persian. They conclude that Liu Zhi had diverse Islamic sources.

1. Most of the texts in Arabic are standard Sunni Hanafite texts of law and ritual.
2. Many works in Persian are Sufi. The influence of the Naqshabandiyya and Kubrawiyya orders is significant.
3. There are more works in Persian than in Arabic. Most of the works are extant in the West.
4. Possibly, the sources are primarily from Central Asian Muslim sources and secondarily Persians and lastly original Arabic sources.[30]

A ground-breaking study on seventeenth and eighteenth-century Chinese Muslims comes from a Japanese scholar who studied Persian Islam, now teaching in America, Sachiko Murata. Her work on Wang Daiyu's *Great Learning of the Pure and Real* and Liu Zhi's *Displaying the Concealment of the Real Realm* is the first ever English language book-length study and is recognized as the standard work for all subsequent historical study.[31] She is undertaking more translation of Liu Zhi's writings.[32] Admittedly, she is the most able contemporary interpreter of Liu Zhi's Islamic philosophy and Sufism in the West. Her most recent work on Liu Zhi is *The Sage Learning of*

---

28. Cotter and Reichelt, "The Three Character Classic," 10–15. Liu Zhi's original work was a tract which can be rhymed for easy and quick grasp of Islam. Each phrase of the tract consisted of three Chinese characters, covering a very broad spectrum of subjects from creation, the Qur'an, the five virtues, and worship to the unique position of the prophet Muhammad. Liu Zhi's work in Chinese was published in 1704.

29. Leslie, "Islam in China," 16–48; Leslie and Panskaya, *Introduction*; Leslie, *Islamic Literature*; Leslie, *Islam in Traditional China*; Leslie, *Integration*; Leslie et al, "Arabic Works," 7–27; Leslie et al., *Islam in Traditional China*.

30. Leslie and Wassel, "Arabic and Persian Sources," 78–104.

31. Murata, *Gleams*. All book reviewers conclude that Murata has provided the Western world with a foundational work in English on Wang Daiyu and Liu Zhi.

32. Murata, "Unity." Murata, "Creative Transformation," 141–48.

Liu Zhi: Islamic Thought in Confucian Terms.[33] Another book-length study was published in America by Zvi Ben-Dor Benite in 2005.[34] Benite admirably notes the cultural history of Islam within the educational network in late imperial China, paying attention to the Chinese Muslim literati and the Chinese Islamic school in Nanjing. A recent PhD thesis focusing solely on Liu Zhi was done by another American, James Frankel, in 2005.[35] He has studied Liu Zhi's *Rules and Proprieties of Islam*. Later, Frankel published his research.[36] In America, a recent thesis has been done on Wang Daiyu by Kristian Petersen.[37] Apart from the Americans, a few works on Liu Zhi's Chinese Islam come from Western Europe. One notable inclusion is the German, Barbara Stöcker-Parnian, who studied the Scripture Hall Education System in seventeenth to nineteenth-century China, paying brief attention to various Chinese Muslim literati including Liu Zhi.[38] It should be noted that Europeans, Americans, Australian and Japanese have made great advances in academic scholarship in the fields of historical, cultural, ethnic, comparative, and social science study on the Hui and Uyghurs.[39] However, these studies have only indirect relevance to this present research apart from the works of Murata and Frankel.

Works in Chinese

While the scholarship of Islam in China in the West has made gradual progress throughout the last century, the scholarship of Islam in China by Chinese scholars in Chinese has made rapid progress especially during the last few decades. From the People's Republic of China, the last twenty years have witnessed a flood of book-length studies and numerous essays on Islam in China and also on general comparative study between seventeenth- and eighteenth-century Islam and Neo-Confucianism in Chinese. Sadly, the Chinese scholars do not usually interact with the published works of Western scholars and there has been little sign of constructive dialogues. Only a few of Murata's formerly published essays in English are translated and published in Chinese and have appeared in a few Chinese journals. This

33. Murata et al., *Sage*.
34. Benite, *Dao*.
35. Frankel, *Liu's Journey*.
36. Frankel, *Rectifying*.
37. Petersen, "Heart."
38. Stöcker-Parnian, *Jingtang Jiaoyu*.
39. A few prominent names may be mentioned. Joseph Fletcher, Dru Gladney, Jonathan Lipman, Michael Dillon, Élisabeth Allès, and David Atwill.

present work makes contributions by introducing recent scholarship of Liu Zhi's works in Chinese into the English world.

The most substantial overview on Liu Zhi's Islam is carried out by the prolific writer Jin Yijiu in Chinese. In 1999, he published a book-length study on Liu Zhi's overall Islamic faith and practice, including an introductory study on Liu Zhi's Sufi teaching.[40] This is a classic and has become a foundational textbook for all subsequent study of Liu Zhi in Chinese. The second book-length study was written by Sha Zhongpin in 2004. He differs from Jin by narrowing his study to Liu Zhi's doctrine of God and humanity.[41] The third book-length study was done by Liang Xiangming and he wrote a general study on Liu Zhi's Islamic teachings in 2004.[42] His account of Liu Zhi follows Jin's textbook but he is not as articulate and comprehensive as Jin Yijiu. While Jin focuses more on Liu Zhi's philosophy, Liang focuses more on Liu Zhi's Islamic rules and proprieties. While Jin has continued to publish works on Liu Zhi, both Sha and Liang have diversified their research interests into other aspects of Islam in China.

Apart from research works which focus on Liu Zhi alone, there have been other works that discuss several Muslim literati during that period of Islam in China. Two more book-length studies were published in 2006, namely by Sun Zhenyu and Liu Yihong. Sun's work covers only three Muslim literati. They are the well-known Wang Daiyu, Liu Zhi, and Ma Dexin. While Sun's work is descriptive of each Muslim literatus, Liu Yihong examines the dialogue between Neo-Confucianism and Islam in the work of each Muslim literatus. Liu's work selects five Muslim literati. They are Wang Daiyu, Wu Zunqi (c. 1598–c. 1698), Ma Zhu, Liu Zhi, and Ma Dexin. Both studies have focused on some key thinkers during this important period of Islam in China.

Other recent and substantial book-length works related to this present study were carried out by Wang Junrong in 2006 and the prolific Liu Zhi scholar Jin in 2012. Wang's work discusses the ontology of Ibn 'Arabi.[43] Her work makes occasional references to Sufi thought in China and the works of Jin on Liu Zhi. She also introduces briefly the dialogue on Ibn 'Arabi's ontology between the Ibn 'Arabi tradition and the Islam in China. The prolific writer Jin continues to make unique contribution to Islam in China by publishing a substantial work on Sufism in China, giving a very comprehensive account of its history and teaching including the development of the

---

40. Jin, *Exploring Chinese Islam*, 283–324.
41. Sha, *Chinese Islam*.
42. Liang, *Study of Liu Zhi*.
43. Wang, *Unity*.

Scripture Hall Education System.[44] He discusses various aspects of Chinese Sufism within the context of the Scripture Hall Education System and the emergent development of *Han Kitab* from the sixteenth-century China.

In addition, many academic essays in Chinese on Liu Zhi's works have appeared in periodicals and journals in different parts of China during the last twenty years. The key scholars are Jin, Sha and Liang. In addition, other Chinese scholars have written on various aspects of Liu Zhi's works. One can safely say that academic study on Liu Zhi's works has come to a new stage of research. The recent secondary literature of the work of Liu Zhi in Chinese can be grouped under the study of sources, various influences, ontology and worldview, rites of Islam, and the most popular topic, namely the relationship between Liu Zhi's Islam and Neo-Confucianism. This may be broadly classified as follows:

- The identification of the Persian and Arabic sources of Liu Zhi's works.[45]
- Greek and other philosophical influences upon Liu Zhi.[46]
- Comparison between Zhu Xi's Neo-Confucianism and Liu Zhi's Neo-Confucianism.[47]
- Comparison of the Islamic concepts used by Wang Daiyu and Liu Zhi and of their use of Confucian terms.[48]
- Comparison of the ethical and moral teachings between Liu Zhi's rites of Islam and Neo-Confucian self-cultivation and spiritual wisdom.[49]
- The Confucianization or sinicization[50] of Liu Zhi's Islam and Chinese culture.[51]

It can be noted from the above brief historical account of the study of Liu Zhi that firstly, compared to the recent study of the works of Liu Zhi in English, the study of Liu Zhi in Chinese has covered a wider scope of interests. Secondly, the Chinese scholars have a keen interest in comparative study between Liu Zhi's Islam and Chinese culture. Finally, little study

---

44. Jin, *Sufism in China*.
45. One example of such a study is by Wang Genping. Wang, "Explanation," 37–47.
46. The most common influence is Neo-Platonism upon Chinese Sufi teaching. See Jin, "Idea," 1–11.
47. Tuoheti, "Study," 105–8.
48. Sun, *Critical Biography*.
49. Ji, "Comparative Study," 134–42.
50. Sinicization of Chinese Muslims may be defined simply as "the acculturation, the penetration of Han culture into the Hui's everyday life." Berlie, *Islam in China*, 8.
51. Cai, "Adaptation," 108–15.

has been made by scholars in both English and Chinese on Liu Zhi's Sufi thought and in particular the role of the prophet Muhammad in Liu Zhi's overall teaching. Part of the reason may be due to the fact that Liu Zhi's *True Record of the Utmost Sage of Islam* has not recently received much serious academic interest.

Discussion of Liu Zhi's Works by Scholars in English and Chinese

Works in English

The three main scholars of the works of Liu Zhi in English are Sachiko Murata, James Frankel and Zvi Ben-Dor Benite. However, their research on Liu Zhi's works is diverse and there is little room for debate between them in their published works. Benite's work is a cultural study and he has not studied any of Liu Zhi's works specifically in detail but he pays sufficient attention to Liu Zhi. Frankel studies specifically a part of Liu Zhi's *Rules and Proprieties of Islam* from the perspective of comparative religion. Murata's main focus is on Liu Zhi's theosophy, cosmogony, and worldview in *The Nature and Principle in Islam*. She gives great insight in explaining the Islamic concept behind Liu Zhi's Confucian terms.

Zvi Ben-Dor Benite[52] produces an admirable study based on a primary source[53] on the cultural history of Muslims in late imperial China. His study is firstly to establish various networks, based on Islamic educational movements involving thousands of people between the mid-sixteenth and eighteenth century. Benite also links the network of Ma Zhu, born in Yunnan (c. 1620) with Liu Zhi's father, Liu Sanjie who wrote the preface in Ma Zhu's work. It should be noted that Liu Sanjie was a teacher in the Yuan school in Nanjing, led by Yuan Ruqi.[54] Benite believes that the emerging and flourishing Hui Muslim literary work was not due to accommodation of Islam to

---

52. Benite, *Dao*.

53. The primary source is known as the *Register of Lineage and Transmission of Classical Learning*. It is noted by Benite as a genealogy, authored by Zhao Can before 1697, consisting of 26 chapters and three appendixes, covering one hundred and fifty years between 1550 and 1700. It is a study of various networks with biographical details for some teachers and scholars. Benite, *Dao*, 30–31. Another source is Yuan Guozuo's (b. 1717) bibliography, namely, *An Introduction of Collected Islamic Books in 1780*. See Benite, *Dao of Muhammad*, 155. Yuan also published Liu Zhi's books. Yuan undertook the task of compiling a bibliography of Muslim Chinese books written up to his time. In addition, he also provided biographical information on these authors and the network, i.e. teachers and students or intellectual relationships. See Benite, *Dao*, 27, 154–59. Both Liu Zhi and his father Sanjie belonged to the Yuan's network.

54. Benite, *Dao*, 145.

Chinese culture. Rather, these scholars presented their scholarship out of the context of their educational networks. Thus, Benite argues that Chinese Muslim scholarship in the seventeenth century must be studied and understood "against the backdrop of broad Chinese intellectual trends and within the context of their intellectual networks, educational system, lineage, and pedagogy . . ."[55] He also insists that the Muslim school "has as its starting point a filiation in Islam but insists that Islam be viewed through the lenses of dominant Chinese cultural categories."[56] Benite's work has established the significance of any seventeenth-century Hui Muslim literary work within the well-established intellectual networks and education system. Secondly, Benite's study establishes that the Chinese Muslims have understood themselves formally to be simultaneously Chinese and Muslim, i.e. Chineseness is as central as Muslimness. For Benite, then, one cannot assert that Liu Zhi's works diminish the Muslimness of Chinese Islam.

It should be noted that Benite has also studied the uniqueness of Muhammad in Liu Zhi's work.[57] According to Benite, Liu did not just write a mere biography of the prophet. Benite asserts the content and the purpose of Liu's writing as

> a characterization of the Islamic world, and Chinese historical documents pertaining to Chinese Islam, . . . Liu Zhi's perception of the Huihui people as a group who had contributed to the stability and strength of several Chinese dynasties and as a group who in the Qing were to make their most significant contribution to Chinese greatness through scholarship . . . By embracing the very cultural categories that stood as markers of Confucian literati dominance, Chinese Muslim intellectuals were able discursively to create a space for themselves and their tradition at the very centre of Chinese society . . . Paradoxically, through the adoption of the specific ingredients most essential to 'Chineseness' (the preservation of tradition, the study of Dao [real being], the veneration of the sages, and loyalty to the state), Chinese Muslims solidified their identity as Muslims as well.[58]

Thus, Benite argues that Liu's effort is to affirm his readers' Muslim identity and they should seek to be fully Muslims as well as fully Chinese. They should also be loyal subjects to serve the imperial Qing government though this government might not be tolerant to Muslim practices. The

55. Ibid., 123. Certainly, the religious and political contexts should not be ignored.
56. Ibid., 125.
57. Ibid., 208–13. Benite examines Liu's *True Record*.
58. Benite, *Dao*, 210–13.

principal argument in Benite's work is sound and he puts forward his case convincingly based on primary sources. To summarize, it is necessary to appreciate the importance of the Scripture Hall Education System and the intellectual networks in the eighteenth century. Benite gives support to the idea that the Muslim literati, including Liu Zhi, did not attempt to accommodate their Islamic works into Chinese cultures. Primarily, they attempted to establish the Hui identity, namely as both Muslims and Chinese.

In 2005, James D. Frankel examined the metaphysics and contextualized theology of Liu Zhi's *Rules and Proprieties of Islam* and finished with a PhD thesis from Columbia University. Frankel argues that Liu Zhi and his contemporary Chinese Muslim literati in late imperial China created a viable expression of Chinese Islamic ideology and identity, forming a *Han Kitab* genre, or canon. Such a canon is widely acknowledged as authoritative by many Hui Muslims. Frankel agrees with the common consensus that Liu Zhi was "an epitomic figure in this history, contributed significantly to the refinement, legitimization and popularization of this aspect of Chinese Islamic culture, residing rather comfortably in the space where two civilizations meet."[59] Frankel's argument about Liu Zhi's contextualization is nuanced and will be critically examined in chapter 6 later.

The best-known interpreter of Liu Zhi's Islamic teaching in English is Sachiko Murata. She has made substantial contributions to Liu Zhi's works in English for the last two decades. Murata would not agree that Liu Zhi's works sinicize Islam into Chinese culture. While Liu Zhi's doctrine belongs to the Sufi tradition, Murata notes that "clearly the Sufi works along with Neo-Confucianism that form the basis for Liu Chih's explanation of Islamic teachings."[60] Also, Murata argues that Liu Zhi's *Displaying the Concealment of the Real Realm* would not "overtly betray its Islamic origin."[61] Furthermore, Murata explains that "Liu Chih's constant mention of the term 'Real' is perhaps the major indication of the book's Islamic provenance. He speaks repeatedly of the 'Real Being' (*chen-yu*), an expression that is not employed in the Chinese classics."[62] When Murata examines Liu Zhi's translation of eighteenth Gleam of *Lawa'ih*, she notes that Liu Zhi added a long paragraph to introduce the Gleam using Neo-Confucian terms. According to Murata, the addition is not mutual dialogue or integration of Chinese philosophy with Islamic philosophy. While Liu Zhi added an extra introductory paragraph, he also removed Jami's Greek philosophy in the eighteenth Gleam.

59. Frankel, "Liu Zhi's Journey," 12–13.
60. Murata, *Gleams*, 26.
61. Ibid., 121.
62. Ibid., 123.

Liu Zhi used Neo-Confucian terms like substance, function, principle, and vital-energy to make clear to the Chinese readers very much the same philosophical scheme as written by Jami.[63] That is, Liu Zhi's translation is the dynamic equivalent meaning of the text achieved by using Neo-Confucian terms and concepts as a linguistic tool. In her most recent work, Murata competently demonstrates that in order to explicate Liu Zhi's work thoroughly and its continuity with Middle Eastern medieval Islam, it is important to be informed of Liu Zhi's Arabic and Persian source materials, in particular the Ibn 'Arabi tradition.[64]

It can be seen that works in English generally agree that Liu Zhi's works do not deliberately adapt or sinicize the Islamic tradition that he received into Neo-Confucian culture. Liu Zhi's contextualization is to use Confucian terms to communicate the Islamic message so that the Muslims may have the right understanding, thinking, and unveiling in their return to the Real.

Works in Chinese

Although works in English are not as plentiful and there is limited debate among scholars in their understanding of Liu Zhi, works in Chinese are more numerous and there is a spectrum of different opinions among scholars in China. One of the most common discussions is Liu Zhi's contextualization. As this topic is relevant to us, it is singled out in our discussion here.

Many Chinese scholars advocate that Liu Zhi's works have adapted Islam in China into a Confucianized Islam. The majority of scholars support the idea that Liu Zhi's Islam is not the traditional Islam but an adapted or Confucianized version of Islam. Some scholars can put the argument in a nuanced manner and others may not be so articulate. One such attempt by using a sociological approach is not convincing. Na Qi asserts that when two civilizations meet, namely Islam and Neo-Confucianism, the three natural steps of interaction are difference, conflict and integration.[65] Na Qi believes that the seventeenth-century sinicization of Hui Muslims was the inevitable end product and the final step of all encounters between two civilizations. Really, Na argues that Hui Muslims are justified sociologically to be classified as one of the Chinese ethnic minorities. His argument is far from convincing because of limited historical evidences.

---

63. Ibid., 125–26.
64. Murata et al., *Sage*.
65. Na, "Difference," 136–41.

A thoughtful approach is undertaken by Ding Kejia. Rather than examining Liu Zhi's trilogy, Ding examines his Sufism.⁶⁶ Ding compares Liu Zhi's own translation of Jami's *Lawa'ih*, namely *Displaying the Concealment of the Real Realm* with Jami's original work. Ding argues that while Liu Zhi was faithful to Jami's work, he creatively transformed it in his free translation by using Neo-Confucianism, Buddhism and Daoism. Not only was Liu Zhi able to explain the concept of unity of existence, he transformed the Persian Jami's Sufi teaching into the Chinese language context and made Sufism attractive as a very practical and yet transcending, self-exalting and ideal religious practice. Thus, Liu Zhi's *Displaying the Concealment of the Real Realm* was able to provide both intellectual and practical meanings within the Chinese language context for Sufism. When the Persian Sufi concept was freely translated and used in explaining the Hui Islamic rites within the Chinese language context, the two cultural contexts then had mutual learning, understanding, and dialogue. The result is fusion and exchanges. For Ding Kejia, then, Persian Sufism was sinicized by Liu Zhi's editing work. Ding's analysis is better than Na because Ding has examined the translated text of Liu Zhi and they both agree with the majority view.

Other Chinese scholars are more articulate than Na and Ding. They have written substantial monographs on Liu Zhi. They are Liang Xiangming, Liu Yihong and Sha Zhongping. While Liang accepts there are minor different emphases in ethics between Hui Muslims and Neo-Confucians, he asserts that Hui Muslim literati virtually adopted almost all the moral self-cultivating ethical principles of Neo-Confucianism as expressed by Zhu Xi.⁶⁷ In his book study of Liu Zhi, Liang argues that Liu Zhi absorbed and adapted Confucian, Buddhist and Daoist philosophy so that Islamic philosophy was enriched. The resulting effort of Liu Zhi's contextualization was that while Islam was different to other religions, Islamic truth was not separable from other religions. In addition, Liu Zhi used Buddhist and Daoist theosophical concepts to explain divine transformation, effusion of the oneness, and multiplicity of the real being.⁶⁸ Liang's thesis is that broadly speaking, Liu Zhi's works succeeded by integrating Hui Islam into Neo-Confucianism. However, he admits that Liu Zhi's teachings still retained some of the basic tenets of Islam like the existence of one supreme God.

Liu Yihong's comparative study between Chinese Islam and Neo-Confucianism provides a methodological analysis of the works by Wang

---

66. Ding, "Cultures," 25–30.
67. Liang, "Brief Discussion," 27.
68. Liang, *Study of Liu*, 46–48.

Daiyu, Liu Zhi, and Ma Dexin.[69] She argues that three models of dialogue can be identified. Firstly, Wang Daiyu used Neo-Confucianism to explicate Islam, i.e. explaining the doctrine of Islam through Neo-Confucianism. Wang Daiyu still maintained Islam was unique. Secondly, Liu Zhi perceived Neo-Confucianism and Islam as mutually complementing each other. In addition, fading Neo-Confucianism could experience revival when it was combined with Islamic philosophy. Thirdly, Ma Dexin believed that Islam could enhance Neo-Confucianism. It enriched certain aspects of Neo-Confucianism especially Islamic teaching on afterlife.[70] That is as a model of explication, mutual complement and enhancement. While Liu Yihong's model is perceptive, the conclusion of her study at the end of her book seems one-sided and contrary to her data, especially concerning Liu Zhi's work.

> While it is necessary [for the Chinese Muslim literati] to integrate Islamic and traditional Chinese philosophy, certain unsolvable problems of Islamic philosophy can be better explained by borrowing the wisdom of Chinese thoughts. Mystery is then solved and propagation of Islam is then enabled. This lays the foundation for Chinese Islam to spread and develop. The creative element of Chinese Islamic thought is due to the result of dialogue between cultures and civilizations.[71]

On one level, Liu Yihong argues that Chinese Islam is enhanced and enriched by Confucian thoughts. On another level, the articulate and architectonic system of Neo-Confucianism provides not merely the linguistic and conceptual tools to infuse rigorously the meaning of difficult Islamic terms. It also enables Arabic and Persian Islamic metaphysical terms to be imbued with creative and fresh meanings. When adaptation applies to Hui Islam, Liu Yihong interprets it as sinicization. Her view belongs to the majority view that Liu Zhi's Islam was Confucianized. Such a process began from the seventeenth century, has continued to the present and made Chinese Islam different from the Middle Eastern Islamic tradition. Such localized Islam with Chinese characteristics[72] is understood as sinicized Islam. Chinese Islam is adapted and different qualitatively from its Middle Eastern origin.

Sha Zhongping investigates Liu Zhi's doctrine of real being and humanity in *The Nature and Principle in Islam*. He focuses on the latter part of this work and analyzes Liu Zhi's diagrams. Liu Zhi used these diagrams to

---

69. Liu, *Dialogue*.
70. Ibid., 11–12.
71. Liu, *Dialogue*, 178.

72. This phrase is commonly found in popular Chinese religious literature. That is Islam with Chinese characteristics.

explain the teachings in the former part of his work. Sha asserts that Liu Zhi's Islam has been Confucianized. Firstly, he explains generally that the spirit of the age is expressed by philosophy. The linguistic terms are tools like cloth that clothes the spirit. Secondly, he avers that Liu Zhi used Neo-Confucian lexemes and concepts as his cloth, following the spirit of his age. Cloth covers the content. Sha then argues that Liu Zhi used Neo-Confucianism as the cloth that covered the content which was Persian Islamic philosophy, especially the Sufi teaching of Jami.[73]

The subtlety of Sha's argument can be demonstrated in his explication of Liu Zhi's doctrine of divine being. The Qur'anic divine name Allah was converted by Liu Zhi to "Real Ruler or Lord." For Sha, the first step is that the object of Islamic faith transformed from Allah to Real Ruler. This step is a contextualizing of naming. The second step is a transformation of the content. The Real Ruler becomes Real One. Again, the concept of Real One is initiated by Liu Zhi's predecessor Wang Daiyu who has taught the great transformation in terms of the Real One, Numerical One and the Embodied One. The concept of the Real One expresses the content of Confucianized Islam.[74] Then, Sha concludes that Liu Zhi combined medieval Arabic Islam with the school of principle (*li*) of Neo-Confucianism under the archetypal principle of "Real One." "Eventually, the concept of Real One forms the intellectual basis of Chinese Islamic philosophy."[75] The proof of sinicization of Chinese Islam is Liu Zhi's concept of Real One that takes over the Arabic divine name Allah.

Liang, Liu and Sha build up articulate and nuanced arguments in different ways that Hui Islam was sinicized by Liu Zhi's works. Other Chinese scholars have also attempted in other ways to support the thesis that Neo-Confucianism enriched Hui Islam and that Liu Zhi succeeded to a large extent in the sinicization of Chinese Islam.[76]

The minority camp disagrees with the common consensus about the sinicization of Hui Islam in seventeenth-century China by the Hui Muslim literati. There are not many of them and they have published short essays in Chinese journals. A few of them are discussed to present an overview of the minority view.

---

73. Sha, *Chinese Islam*, 281–82.
74. Sha, "Confucianism," 58–59.
75. Ibid., 58.
76. The following essays are some samples: Sun and Su, "Introductory Exploration," 63–66; Cai, "Fusion," 108–15; Ji "Comparison," 134–42; Tuohuti, "On Wang Daiyu's and Liu Zhi's Contributions," 104–7.

A critical work in Taiwan was done in Chinese by Zheng Wenquan.[77] He argues that Liu Zhi's philosophy of Islam is not a sinicized Chinese Islam. He asserts that the philosophical system of Liu Zhi was still Islamic and it is a mistake to claim that Islam has been sinicized by Liu Zhi. From a philosophical methodology, Zheng Wenquan emphatically disagrees with the majority view. His main argument is that the concept of Real One does not originate from Neo-Confucianism which the other side of the debate often takes for granted. Zheng asserts that such a concept already existed among Sufis in thirteenth-century Asia. Secondly, it is not so much that Islamic philosophy has been sinicized by Neo-Confucianism, Liu Zhi's work really re-interpreted Ibn 'Arabi's cosmology and humanity. Thirdly, while Liu Zhi used many Neo-Confucian terms, the dynamic meaning of the translated terms remains Islamic and not Chinese. It is just natural for Liu Zhi to use Neo-Confucian linguistic tools because there was no other available. Furthermore, Zheng argues that the Hui Muslim literati in the sixteenth and seventeenth century achieved the beginning of a new age of Chinese Islamic philosophy for the Hui. It was an existential Islamic philosophy in the Chinese language context that included primarily a re-presentation of Ibn 'Arabi-like philosophy and secondarily a dialogue with non Ibn 'Arabi philosophy current at that time.[78]

The second writer is Min Wenjie.[79] It is often argued that Liu Zhi's Islamic teaching of five endeavors is so closely related with the Confucian five relationships that Liu Zhi's Islamic ethic was again sinicized. Min is able to identify at least five differences between Liu Zhi's Islamic five endeavors and the Confucian five relationships i.e. basis, order, content, goal, and afterlife. He cautions the need for care and more thorough research and avoids reading Liu Zhi's works as simple resonance and parallels with Neo-Confucianism.[80]

The third writer is Yang Huaizhong who provides the Ming dynasty Islamic context of the Hui and the attitude of the Hui towards contextualization. Owing to stricter imperial control, forcing the Muslims to adopt Han names and dress, Yang argues that the Hui became more open minded, willing to study Neo-Confucianism. The eventual attitude of Hui intellectuals at the end of the Ming dynasty was "do not betray Islam and do not be tied down by Islam."[81] That is a sound judgment by Yang who provides a con-

77. Zheng, "Study on the Islamic Nature."
78. Zheng, "Islamic Philosophy."
79. Min, "Comparison," 32–36.
80. Ibid., 36.
81. Yang, "Do not Betray," 5–8.

text that fits best the effort of the Chinese Muslim literati. The revival spirit of Wang Daiyu and Liu Zhi that reflects in their work is more than mere survival and strengthening of the Hui Muslim identity. It is also to make exoteric aspects of Islam into esoteric spiritual discipline, namely, reform by inner transformation.

The last and most persistent opponent to a superficial reading of Liu Zhi's work is a Chinese scholar in China, Yang Zhongdong. He examines the comparative study between Zhu Xi and Liu Zhi and also studies Liu Zhi's Sufism. Yang Zhongdong emphatically asserts that Liu Zhi commonly used the Confucian terms but he infused such terms with Islamic meanings. While Liu Zhi's teachings of the return of humanity and reunion with the divine being by a/the Sufi path might have parallels with Zhu Xi's union with the principle *li*, Liu Zhi clearly had a specific goal of union with the divine being. Thus, Yang Zhongdong asserts that familiar Confucian terms did not carry the same meaning after Liu Zhi's redefinition.[82] Yang Zhongdong argues that Liu Zhi's Islam was firmly rooted in Sufi mysticism. He traces the Sufi source of Liu Zhi's concept of divine transformation. The source was Nasafi's *The Furthest Goal* and definitely not Neo-Confucianism's concepts of *li* and *qi* or the concept of yin and yang.[83]

Yang identifies that various Islamic concepts in Liu Zhi's *Nature and Principle in Islam* can be traced to six Sufi works available at the time of Liu Zhi. Yang Zhongdong asserts two implications. Firstly, Sufism in China was widespread in seventeenth-century China. It was not limited to several institutions or schools of Sufi thought. Certainly, it was common in Northwest China and also among Uyghurs. Secondly, Liu Zhi's Sufi Islam was fundamentally different from Neo-Confucianism. Sufi Islam was not merely mystical ritual. Seventeenth-century Chinese Sufi Islam was grounded profoundly in Ibn 'Arabi's philosophy. Yang Zhongdong's conclusion is very similar to Zheng Wenquan's. Yang argues that Liu Zhi's Islam is existential Sufi Islam because Liu Zhi used selectively and edited freely his Sufi source materials. This formed his core materials and philosophical framework. To express the Islamic philosophical framework, Liu Zhi used Neo-Confucianism as his tool. Then, he edited his core materials and philosophical framework to fit into the usage of Chinese language.[84] For Yang Zhongdong, then, it is permissible to say that the Chinese language context affected Liu Zhi's choice of Sufi and philosophical core Islamic materials. Nothing more can be said beyond that about Liu Zhi's contextualization of

---

82. Yang, 'Pilot," 55–56; Yang, "Similarity," 48–51.

83. Yang, "Mirsad," 26.

84. Yang,"Arabian Principles," 86–90.

Hui Islam. At this moment, the minority camp is not gaining any ground in this debate because more substantial research is needed to make this view more convincing.

Remark and Comment

Firstly, while the Chinese scholars contribute numerous essays on Liu Zhi's contextualization, the few English scholars have not written much and yet it is sufficient to see the emergent point of view. Murata has not paid much attention to Liu Zhi's contextualization. She supports the view that Liu Zhi's interpretation of Islam in Confucian terms is sophisticated and articulate. Frankel has studied Liu Zhi's *Rules and Proprieties of Islam*. Frankel says that Liu Zhi's trilogy reflects "an acceptance of the essential ethical and metaphysical harmony of Islam and Confucianism, and thus represents the heights of Muslim intellectual accommodation to the Chinese cultural paradigm."[85] Frankel further opines that "Liu Zhi downplayed the role of revelation, rather expounding theological concepts with frequent reference to natural law."[86] Frankel supports the view that syncretism "in the realm of ideas is then the obvious, logical product of the evolution of a genuine simultaneity of identity and consciousness. Such is the case of Chinese Muslims generally, and of Liu Zhi more specifically, whose heritage of accommodation and assimilation produced a simultaneity that resulted in the sophisticated syncretic thought found in the *Han Kitab* literature."[87] While there is little dialogue between Western and Chinese scholars on Liu Zhi's contextualization of Islam into Confucianism, it would be simplistic to divide scholarly opinions into mere Western and Chinese camps.[88]

Secondly, it should also be noted that while Liu Zhi's works are often studied and analyzed, Wang Daiyu's works are likewise earnestly studied by both Chinese and English contemporary scholars. Both Wang Daiyu and Liu Zhi initiated the first important stage of translating and interpreting Islamic texts into Chinese using Confucian terms and concepts in sixteenth to eighteenth-century China. Thus, Wang Daiyu and Liu Zhi are occasionally studied comparatively. While Murata studies the two scholars comparatively in one single monograph, Jin publishes two monographs, firstly on

---

85. Frankel, *Liu's Journey*, 10.
86. Ibid., 11.
87. Frankel, *Rectifying*, xvii.
88. It should be noted that even within the Chinese works in Chinese, scholars are not accustomed to interacting with opposing views and examining critically various points of view.

Liu Zhi and secondly on Wang Daiyu.[89] They are studied together to enforce the argument that both of them attempted to expound the fundamental tenets of Islam using Confucian concepts and terms. Wang is known for his three works on Islam.[90] Various research works on Wang have been done by Chinese scholars and they share a broadly similar point of view.[91] The common consensus or the majority view among recent Chinese scholars is that Wang was a highly educated sinicized Muslim and great expositor of Islamic doctrines, in particular the doctrine of divine unity. He made great efforts to write and preach to his fellow Muslims who were fast acculturated into Chinese culture. Wang's endeavors were to enable his fellow Muslims to continue and hold fast to their religious theory and practice. Thus, both the works of Wang and Liu are interpreted similarly by the Chinese scholars in the majority camp.

Thirdly, the Chinese scholars in the majority camp are over-confident that Hui Islam was unavoidably integrated both into the Chinese language context and the architectonic philosophy of Zhu Xi of Neo-Confucianism during the translation of the Islamic texts. They prejudge that the overpowering sinicization of Buddhism, Daoism and the almighty Chinese syncretism in the form of Neo-Confucianism can do the same to Liu Zhi's and other Muslim literati's works. However, Liu Zhi set his heart not to betray Islam and simultaneously not be tied down by it. This was the context in which Liu Zhi and others operated.

Finally, a preliminary study of Liu Zhi's *Poem of the Five Sessions of the Moon* later in greater detail can demonstrate that while Liu Zhi employed Daoist, Buddhist and Confucian terms, his concern was to integrate Islamic doctrines with Sufism. He used these concepts as linguistic tools. Thus, his work was in the spirit of Hui Islamic reform using the Chinese language context as a God-sent opportunity to modernize Islam and the traditional Chinese Sufism using Neo-Confucian concepts. After critically examining the contemporary scholarship on Liu Zhi, the most likely theory is that in the spirit of reform, Liu Zhi worked to reformulate and construct a pre-modern and existential Hui Islamic philosophy and Sufism within the Chinese language context.

---

89. Murata, *Gleams*; Jin, *Exploring Chinese Islam*; Jin, *Study on Wang Daiyu's Thoughts*.

90. Wang Daiyu, *Collected Classical Writings*.

91. Li, "Wang Daiyu," 58–62; Jin, "Ideological Structure," 14–19; Sun, *Critical Biography*.

CONCLUSION

This chapter has provided an overview of almost all Liu Zhi's works including both long and short treatises. It has given a brief account of Chinese scholarship on his works especially the debate of Confucianization of Liu Zhi's work into Chinese culture. In addition, this chapter has introduced recent scholarship of Liu Zhi by Chinese scholars to the English speaking world.

This chapter begins by introducing almost all extant works by Liu Zhi, not only his trilogy but also easy-to-read shorter tracts and treatises. Although research work in English and Chinese often focuses on his trilogy, this chapter provides an overview of Liu Zhi's theosophical and Sufi works. The final section of this chapter gives an account of recent scholarship in English and Chinese in Liu Zhi's work. There has been intense research interest in the works of Liu Zhi in recent years. It is hoped that the following chapters can make a significant contribution.

4

Liu Zhi's Engagement with the Concept of the Unity of Existence of the Ibn 'Arabi Tradition

The chapter will give an account of Liu Zhi's concept of the unity of existence in his short work, namely *The Three-character Classic* and longer work, namely his trilogy. It will then discuss this concept in his translated work, namely *Displaying the Concealment of the Real Realm*. His translated work complies with Jami's scheme of the unity of existence in accordance with the Ibn 'Arabi tradition and yet Liu Zhi gave a contextualized translation and made the work easier to understand for his Chinese readers. This chapter will end by giving a new perspective of the thematic analysis of the unity of existence in Liu Zhi's *Nature and Principle in Islam* and *Rules and Proprieties of Islam*.

LIU ZHI AND THE IBN 'ARABI TRADITION OF THE UNITY OF EXISTENCE

Wang Daiyu and the Ibn 'Arabi Tradition in China

The foundational principles of Ibn 'Arabi's teachings are the unity of existence, the perfect human being, microcosmic, and macrocosmic worldview. These principles form the basics of Islamic teachings in sixteenth- to eighteenth-century China. Wang Daiyu's works were influenced by Ibn 'Arabi and his Sufi thought. In Wang Daiyu's famous work, *The Real Commentary*, Wang said that his ancestors had lived in Arabia and come to China three hundred years earlier.[1] Wang did not know any Chinese when he was young and later he was able to master the intellectual ideas and even have dialogues and debates with other Chinese scholars on their own terms. Wang began to write Islamic texts in Chinese in the tradition of Ibn 'Arabi and use various eclectic Neo-Confucian concepts to convey Islamic teachings.

Wang's core teaching was concerned with *tawhid*. "Tawhid demands that all of existence be governed by a single, supreme Reality."[2] Wang conceived God in terms of three basic grades or levels, namely, the Real One, the Numerical One and the Embodied One.[3] Three such Ones served an explanation of *tawhid*. God is one and nothing is like God. The three Ones express oneness in manyness. Murata provides a succinct summary of Wang's concept of the three Ones.

> "Real One" knows in itself the principle of all manyness. This principle of manyness is called the "Numerical One," because it gives rise to the multiplicity of the universe just as the number one gives rise to all the numbers. But the universe can only reach the fullness of its possibilities through being brought back to the One from which it arose. This is the function of human beings, who, among all creatures, are uniquely qualified to be the "Embodied One."[4]

Murata argues that one should interpret Wang's concept in the light of the Ibn 'Arabi tradition. Most of Murata's explications of Wang's writings are based on probable parallel concepts between Wang and Ibn 'Arabi. Her argument is persuasive as Sufi thought has been deeply influential on Islam in China.[5]

As pointed out by Jin Yijiu, Wang is influenced by Ibn 'Arabi's concept of the perfect human being.[6] One of the common Ibn 'Arabi schemes of divine disclosures has five grades. The fifth grade is the perfect human being, "the full manifestation of the human reality, which brings together,

---

1. Wang, *Collected Classical Writings*.

2. Murata, *Gleams*, 8.

3. Tu Weiming says that "technical terms such as 'embodied one,' 'numerical one,' and 'real one' are perplexing to Confucian moral and religious reasoning, but the implicit anthropocosmic vision is Confucian to the core." Murata et al., *Sage*, 615.

4. Murata, *Gleams*, 75.

5. Sufi teachings have been popular since the founding of the Madrasah education system in the late sixteenth century in various parts of China. Persian works on Sufi ethics and the philosophy of the unity of being are adopted as the text books in the Madrasah. Matsumoto, 'Sufi Intellectual Tradition,' 111. Also, Jin, *Sufism in China*.

6. Jin, *Study on Wang Daiyu's Thoughts*, 152.

actualizes, integrates, and synthesizes all realms of being."[7] Wang often called the perfect human being the human ultimate.[8] Thus, Wang and others including Liu Zhi are set firmly in the tradition of Ibn 'Arabi.[9]

The following tables analyse and summarize the tradition of Ibn 'Arabi's understandings of the unity of existence and divine disclosure by Murata and Wang Junrong. Murata outlines a very basic scheme common among all the followers of Ibn 'Arabi. Wang Junrong presents a scheme that is common among Chinese Muslim literati. The table below illustrates the various grades of existence and the continuity between the Ibn 'Arabi tradition and the Chinese tradition supported by the Chinese Muslim literati.

Table 4.1: Grade of Disclosure between Ibn 'Arabi's Basic Scheme and Chinese Traditional Schemes

Grade of Disclosure	Ibn 'Arabi's Basic Scheme (Murata)[A]	Chinese Traditional Scheme (Wang Junrong)[B]
First grade: God in itself	God is unknown to anything other than itself	The substance of Real Ruler
Second grade: God and the creator of universe	God is known by a diversity of names; grade of divinity	The names and attributes of the Real Ruler
Third grade	God brings the many into existence based on its own knowledge of its infinite reality	The will and power of the Real Ruler
Fourth grade		The world of images and imaginations
Fifth grade		The world of thoughts or spiritual beings
Sixth grade		The visible world of humans and ten thousand things

A. Murata, *Gleams*, 74.
B. Wang, *Unity*, 53.

Murata further elaborates and explains the continuity between the Ibn 'Arabi tradition and Wang Daiyu's concept. The basic concept of Wang's divine being is expressed by three grades, namely the Real One, Numerical

7. Murata et al., *Sage*, 47.

8. Jin, *Study on Wang Daiyu's Thoughts*, 153.

9. Liu Zhi's concept of the human ultimate has been researched by Murata. See Murata, "Liu Zhi's View," 16–18.

Liu Zhi's Engagement with the Concept of the Unity of Existence

One and Embodied One. Murata demonstrates the similarities in structural framework between Wang and the Ibn 'Arabi tradition. The following table shows the continuity between the Ibn 'Arabi tradition and Wang Daiyu's concept of divine disclosures.

Table 4.2: Continuation between the Ibn 'Arabi Tradition and Wang Daiyu's Concept of Divine Disclosure

Unity and Multiplicity of the Divine Being	Wang Daiyu's Interpretation in Confucian terms	Wang Daiyu's Reconciliation with the Ibn 'Arabi Tradition (Murata)
God in himself (oneness)	*Real One*: root origin of the non-Ultimate; the unique One	The divine essence (*dhat*) is not to be properly designated by any name or attribute
At the level of the origin of universe (still at the grade of oneness)	*Numerical One*: If this existence is perceived in negative terms, it is the non-Ultimate; in positive term, it is the Great Ultimate. This is the principle of multiplicity	The divinity (*uluhiyya*) can be discussed in terms of names and attributes. The divinity embraces all principles[A] and it is the pattern or logos for all of creation[B]
At the grade of multiplicity	*Embodied One*: humans alone are able to bring the many back to the One	The human perfect being (*al-insan al-kamil*)

A. It is called the Reality of Realities (*haqiqat al-haqa'iq*). Murata, Gleams, 49.
B. It is called the Muhammadan Reality. Murata asserts that Wang refers to both the Reality of Realities and Muhammadan Reality as the Utmost Sage. Murata, Gleams, 75.

The following table illustrates further the content of Wang's *Great Learning of the Pure and Real*, which primarily teaches the concept of existence in terms of the three Ones.[10] It shows Wang Daiyu's concept in greater detail.[11]

---

10. Wang, *Collected Classical Writing*, 232–49.

11. The table is composed after consulting both the work of Murata and Jin. Murata, Gleams, 81–100; Jin, *Study on Wang Daiyu's Thoughts*, 256–61.

Table 4.3: *Wang Daiyu's Concept of Existence in Terms of the Three Ones*

The doctrine of the three Ones: the *Real One*, the *Numerical One*, and the *Embodied One*	*The Real One*: the unique and independent One; the Real Lord; at root the Real has nothing to do with the ten thousand things	Root nature (*substance*): the Beginningless Original Being Root allotment (*function*): attribute ; movement and quietude of the root nature Root act (*act*): the surplus of the unique and independent One, possessing all the subtlety of the formless
	The Numerical One: the one root of ten thousand things and the chief summit of the Powerful Being; this root origin is called the Non-Ultimate	Original honored (*substance*): the Utmost Sage; great fountain of nature and mandate Representative (*function*): opening and issuing forth of ten thousand spirituals Scribe (*act*): surplus of the Pure Essence; and it is the naturally issuing disclosure to the outside or the Great Ultimate.
	The Embodied One: at the human level of the oneness of recognition with body	Recognition with knowledge (*substance*): to inquire about and to imitate the sages and worthies Recognition with seeing (*function*): while with the body, humans recognized the Real Ruler with the body. Recognition with continuity (*act*): to conquer entirely both selfishness and opinions of self, returning completely to the fountainhead and recognizing the Real Ruler with body while depending on no-self.

The above table contains additional information that the previous two tables have not shown. While Murata has provided a helpful English translation of Wang's text and a few comments on Wang's Islamic concepts, she has not analyzed in details the scheme of the three Ones. The following comments should be noted.

Firstly, it gives a clear description of existence in accordance with Wang Daiyu's work and also an account of human existence. Contrary to the usual five or seven grades of divine disclosures in the Malay-Indonesian world in the sixteenth and seventeenth century,[12] Wang's scheme of three

---

12. Hamzah Fansuri in the sixteenth century supported five grades and Shams al-Din al-Samatra'i in the seventeenth century supported seven grades. Riddell, *Islam,*

Ones seems to be simpler. However, each grade of the One is further divided into sub-grades, namely substance, function and act. Wang's scheme is in fact still complex.

Secondly, Wang's concept of the three Ones at the second grade includes not only the divine disclosure of the Real but even at the first sub-grade of the Embodied One, humanity or rather the perfect human being can recognize this grade and return to the Real Ruler from this grade. Each grade of the One has three further sub-grades. These grades are in descending order. However, humanity can ascend and return to the Real. Wang specified a process of ascent which emphasized the "recognition with continuity" (the act) at the third sub-grade of the Embodied One. It shall be explained later in chapter 6 later that Liu Zhi asserted that the prophet Muhammad had a very unique nature of continuity. He is indeed the perfect human being. Liu Zhi contextualized the prophet as the Utmost Sage in the Neo-Confucian context.

Finally and in addition to the above tables, in Wang's *Real Commentary of the True Teaching*, it says that there are three types of heart, namely real, human and animal. "According to the *Hadith*, heaven and earth encompasses Me not, but the heart of the true believer does encompass Me."[13] People have seven grades which are desire, wisdom, humanity, seeing, enjoying, mystery, and the utmost grade. Only Muslim people have all these grades. Worldly people have only three grades: desire, wisdom and benevolence. Animal people have only one grade, namely desire. While Wang did not give great emphasis to the role of heart, Liu Zhi made use of Wang's scheme of three Ones and revised it with greater emphasis on the role of the heart.

The next section will examine Liu Zhi's shorter tract, *The Three-character Classic*, his translated work *Displaying the Concealment of the Real Realm* and his longer works, the trilogy. By making a more comprehensible examination of both short and long works, one can present and demonstrate a more convincing case of Liu Zhi's contextualization than previous studies have made.

Liu Zhi's Theological Conversation with a Neo-Confucian Classic: *The Three-character Classic*

The Three-character Classic is a short tract for general readership by Liu Zhi and the text has over one thousand and three hundred Chinese words; each

---

103–15.

13. Wang, *Collected Classical Writings*, 58–59. A good analytical study of Wang's understanding of the role of heart is by K. Petersen. See Petersen, "Heart."

phrase in three Chinese characters and total four hundred and forty phrases of three characters. It should be noted that from the time of the Song dynasty (960–1279), Chinese literature work for educating beginners often was structured into three characters to help easier memorization. It was a common type of pedagogy in primary education. Not only did each phrase have three characters and taught a simple idea, but the tone might also vary. Some had rhymed arrangement and might have continuous meaning.[14] They were purely designed for easy understanding and memorization. The three-character style began in the late Song dynasty and became a fundamental element of literacy throughout the Qing period.

Liu Zhi wrote *The Three-character Classic* not only for easier memorization; it was intended primarily for beginners and novices of Islam. He adopted the Neo-Confucian three-character literary style into his Islamic work. It should be noted that this work was very popular and repeatedly copied in the Qing dynasty. It is divided into four sections.

The first section begins with the knowledge of the Ruler. It is the foundational teaching of this work. The Ruler is the creator and the origin of the heaven and earth. In addition, the Ruler does not occupy space, without any form and nothing resembles the Ruler. Liu Zhi also described his attributes as omnipresent, omniscient and almighty. The Ruler created humankind who was the pinnacle of creation. Only humankind had a soul. Humankind through himself could understand the subtle function and the existence of the Ruler. "The self serves as a reflector of God and a mirror of life."

The second section gives an account of the origin and history of Islam. The transmission is through the holy sages and eventually to the Utmost Sage who is the seal of the sages.

In the third section, Liu Zhi explained Islamic rules and proprieties in terms of Neo-Confucian ethics. These included obedience to teachers, respect to the elderly, watchfulness of speech and action and many others. Clearly, Liu Zhi contextualized Neo-Confucian ethics with Islamic rules and rites. However, there are two distinctive differences. Firstly, the coming of the Utmost Sage, the prophet Muhammad is highlighted. On his arrival, Islam is complete. It is in contrast with Confucianism which is not a completed tradition. Confucianism has been developed into Neo-Confucianism and there would be further development. Secondly, the Ruler is invisible and nothing is like the Ruler. To bear witness to the Ruler means that the Ruler is one and Muhammad is the messenger. Islam is unique in its monotheism and with its emphasis on the role of the prophet Muhammad.

---

14. Liu, "Classical Chinese Primer," 191.

In the final section, Liu Zhi reminded Muslims that they needed to hold firm to the way of Islam. He also gave warnings that they should persevere in learning and practicing the five endeavors. Continuous learning and practicing could bring nobility of character and blessedness.

Any careful reader can note one of the main characteristics of this work, namely Liu Zhi's pedagogical technique. He used discourses in the first half of the work to expound the knowledge of the Real Ruler, the importance of the prophet Muhammad, and the teaching of the way. In the second half, Liu Zhi turned to the teaching of the rites and proprieties of Islam using Neo-Confucian ideas. His teaching technique changed to question and answer once in a while. He anticipated a number of commonly encountered queries from both beginners and outsiders of Islam. Questions like "why are you a Muslim?" He gave a very direct and short answer without any deliberation. According to Liu Zhi, "I am a Muslim by the grace of God."[15] Similarly, the five endeavors are simply clearly listed and each endeavor is supported with one reason only. Thus, Liu Zhi's sole purpose in this work is for the general public to get a good idea of the basic tenets of Islamic belief and the foundational principle of the rites and proprieties of Islam. The belief in one God of Islam leads to obedience to that God in rules and proprieties of Islam.

The complete *Three-character Classic* was translated into English by Francis Cotter and Karl L. Reichelt in 1918 without any comments on Liu Zhi's Islamic background.[16] There was no analysis provided by Cotter and Reichelt. Part of Liu Zhi's *Three-character Classic* is now translated below and this selected translation is provided in parallel format to illustrate the three-character Chinese literary format. The three-character format is clearly shown on the right hand side of the following parallel translation.

---

15. Cotter and Reichelt, "Three Character," 12.
16. Ibid., 10–15.

Figure 4.1: Liu Zhi's Three-character Classic

At the beginning of the heaven and earth, ten thousand things were to be formed. The supreme being had existed and was called the Real Ruler.	天地初,萬物始,有至尊,曰真主!
It governed the innate heaven, ordered the principle and vital energy. It divided light from darkness; transformed heaven and earth.	統乾元,運理氣,分陰陽,化天地,
It set the foundations of mountains and rivers; called into life grass and trees; foreordained calamity and fortune; gave brightness to the sun and moon. . . .	奠山川,茁草木,定災祥,彰日月。...
The first of the way is to bear witness. There is no god but the Real Ruler.	道之首,念真言:物非主,惟真主。
Muhammad was sent by the Ruler to be the messenger. The essence of the way is to read the Qur'an.	穆罕默,主差使。道之心,念真經,
The teaching of the *Hadith* is very clear. Everything has its essence and the essence of Qur'an is the 36th Sura. . . .	有聖渝,理分明。凡萬物,皆有心,真經心,雅西音。
The Qur'an says, 'watchfulness leads to realization of the way to eternity. Be watchful not to lose it.'	真經雲:慎得遂,後世途,慎作費。
The core of the way is to know the will of return. When it is clear, other endeavors can begin.	道之髓,識歸旨。歸旨明,萬功啟。
The foundation of the way is sincerity. If you have sincere thoughts, other endeavors can succeed.	道之根,在誠意,意既誠,百為濟。
The way resides in the heart. It is inside the Muslims' heart. The heart is the dwelling place of the Lord.	道之宅,穆民心。穆民心,主之闕。

The above selected translation of *The Three-character Classic* can illustrate some general and specific aspects of Liu Zhi's work. From a general perspective, firstly Liu Zhi's understanding of Islam adheres closely to the basic tenets of Islam. The divine being is a pre-existent being and the creator of all existents. All creatures are created by the divine being and humankind is an exceptional creature because only humans have the heart. Secondly, he also held to the unique status of the Utmost Sage, Muhammad who is

Liu Zhi's Engagement with the Concept of the Unity of Existence 99

the accomplisher of the way of the Real. The Qur'an also has a unique status because it is divinely revealed through Muhammad. Thirdly, Liu Zhi's contextualization is based on his use of contemporary literary structure to convey directly the teachings of Islam. These general teachings of Islam according to Liu Zhi are: the Real is supreme; the prophet Muhammad is unique, and humanity has a heart which is indwelt by the way and able to return to the Real.

From a specific perspective, Liu Zhi clearly upheld the Real Ruler as the creator of all things, including humankind. The Utmost Sage, Qur'an, *Hadith* and the five endeavors point to the way of Islam. For Muslims, the way begins with a sincere and watchful heart. Then Muslims can begin with a firm foundation and seek the way of return to the Real. The role of the heart is repeatedly emphasized in all short and long works of Liu Zhi.[17] He used question and answer format: "Are you in the way? Is the way in you? If one asks you, you should say, I am in the way and the way is in me! Your answer should be without any doubt or uncertainty." Questions are used to sharpen the reader's thinking and understanding of Islam. All these questions can find detailed answers in Liu Zhi's trilogy and translated work.

Liu Zhi's Translation: Abd al-Rahman Jami's *Lawa'ih*[18] (1414– 1492) and Liu Zhi's *Displaying the Concealment of the Real Realm*

The fact that Liu Zhi translated Jami's work further suggests that he supported the Ibn 'Arabi tradition. Jami's *Lawa'ih* was translated by Liu Zhi into *Displaying the Concealment of the Real Realm*.[19] Abd al-Rahman Jami was a famous Sufi, a follower of the Naqshbandi Sufi order and a poet-theologian of the school of Ibn 'Arabi. He popularized Ibn 'Arabi's tradition of *wahdat al-wujud* (the unity or oneness of existence) and played an important role in the spreading of his teaching. He expounded a number of teachings about the Sufi path. Jami emphasized that love for the prophet Muhammad was the prerequisite stepping-stone to starting the spiritual journey. In Jami's

---

17. A detailed discussion of the role of heart according to Liu Zhi is given in chapter 6 of this present work. Liu Zhi is influenced by the School of Mind of Neo-Confucianism.

18. Heer, "Al-Jami's Treatise," 223–56. See also, Arberry, *Classical Persian Literature*; also, Rizvi, "Existential Breath," 58–87.

19. Matsumoto says that both Jami's *Lawa'ih* and *Ashi''at al-lama'at* (Rays of the "Flashes") have been popular in Madrasah education. He also says that the Persian version of *Ashi''at al-lama'at* has exerted great influence than its Chinese version. Matsumoto, "Sufi Intellectual Tradition," 107.

Lawa'ih, he expounded the teaching of Ibn 'Arabi in an attractive style and balance of poetry and prose. Murata comments that

> [t]he practical issue is the devotional imperative of turning one's full attention towards the One. The theoretical issue is discerning between the One and the many, or God and the world. In practical terms, Jami is telling his readers that it is necessary to see things correctly in order to be able to remember God as he should be remembered. In theoretical terms, he is differentiating between existence (*wujud*) per se, or the reality of God, and the existence that is ascribed to the cosmos.[20]

This work consists of thirty six Gleams in total.[21] The major theme from the thirteenth Gleam to the end of the treatise is to explain the self-disclosure of God into the external and sensual world. In the fourteenth Gleam, Jami distinguished two meanings of existence. Firstly, existence could mean a concept or a mental assertion. However, Jami supported the second meaning. That is, existence is "a Reality that has being through Its own Essence, while the rest of the existents have being through It. In reality, there is no existent other than It in the eternal world."[22] Thus, to say that God is existence or God is being really means that God is the ultimate reality that undergirds all of reality. In the twenty-fourth Gleam, Jami said that there were six levels of self-disclosure by the true existent which was not more than one. The first level was the level of unboundedness or nonentification. The last level was "the engendered level's differentiation, which was the level of the cosmos."[23] Murata concludes her analysis of Jami's *Lawa'ih* by saying that

> Jami addresses three basic theoretical issues. One is Being per se, the second is Being's self-disclosure, and the third is the nature of the things that appear through self-disclosure. Being is the utterly undifferentiated original reality that brings forth all secondary reality, self-disclosure is the bringing forth, and the things are what has been brought forth . . . The text speaks of the movement from the absolute unity of God to the infinite multiplicity of the universe, a movement that has stages and can be conceptualized.[24]

---

20. Murata, *Gleams*, 116.
21. Gleam means flash. It is Jami's reflections on Qur'anic wisdom and spirituality.
22. Murata, *Gleams*, 154.
23. Ibid., 182.
24. Murata, *Gleams*, 118,

Liu Zhi's Engagement with the Concept of the Unity of Existence

Liu Zhi's *Displaying the Concealment of the Real Realm* in Chinese is a free translation of Jami's *Lawa'ih* and is far from literal. At the end of each Gleam, Jami provided quatrains which served to clarify the philosophical discussion of the gleam by the use of poetry. Liu Zhi simply deleted all Jami's poetries in *Lawa'ih*, usually situated at the end of each Gleam. Thus, Liu Zhi was only interested in the philosophical discourse and did not want any poetry to digress from his explication. Liu Zhi called each of Jami's Gleams a chapter and thus his translated work has thirty six chapters.

The following table is a brief and selected summary of *Displaying the Concealment of the Real Realm*.[25] Observations and remarks demonstrate Liu Zhi's edition, revision and interpretation of Jami's work. A more detailed analysis of the translated work will be given after this table.

Table 4.4: Observations and Remarks of Liu Zhi's
Displaying the Concealment of the Real Realm

No. of Chapter or Gleam	Title of Liu Zhi's Chapter	Observations and Remarks of Liu Zhi's Displaying the Concealment of the Real Realm
1	One heart	From chapter 1 to 13, this part of the work emphasizes the practical aspect of the unity of existence or 'the endeavor of seeking and cultivating the *dao*.' Liu Zhi put Jami's affirmative statement into a question, namely 'Why do you not have one heart and one bearing, reject the things, and run to the Lord?' Liu Zhi wanted to challenge his readers to be single-minded in their practice of Islam. The reason for single-mindedness is due to Jami's prior statement that the Lord entrusted humanity with one heart only.
2	Collectedness and division	Collectedness 'means to return from the image to the One with clear seeing.' In Jami's Gleam, the text reads: 'they stayed in endless dispersion.' Murata translates Liu Zhi's text as 'their hearts were finally drifting into division.'[A] Although Liu Zhi's text does not have the word 'heart,' Murata's paraphrased translation with the word 'heart' is appropriate and justified because the prose at the end of this Gleam specifies explicitly the spiritual condition of the heart.[B]
3	Seeing the *dao*	Humanity needs to see what the Real sees.

---

25. The English translation of the text is found in Murata, *Gleams*, 136–209. The Chinese text can be found in Zhou Xiefan, "Great Classics," 1–20.

4	Alteration and perishing	The Real Lord is hidden and other existents are illusory in the sense of being transient. In contrast to Jami, Liu Zhi emphasized the role of the heart in two aspects. With a pure heart, let go with all material things. With a dedicated heart, care for and be united with the Real Lord.
5	Completion and beauty	The surplus light emanates and gives rise to the completion and beauty of the ten thousand levels.
6	Search and examination	The practice is to guard the *dao*. One needs to forget oneself and all things. While Jami used 'soul,' Liu Zhi translated this into heart. The practice of *dao* is to transform the heart. Jami used 'the bounded becomes the Unbounded, and "I am the Real" turns into "He is the Real."' Liu Zhi interpreted as 'preserving self is preserving the Lord, and portraying self is portraying the Lord.'
7	Storing and piling up	While Jami's text emphasizes constant and unceasing relationship with the Real Lord, Liu Zhi emphasizes preserving 'the heart' and self-awaking.
8	Conquering Self	The existent has substance, nature and form. One needs to forget the form, examine the nature and substance. The way of *dao* is conquering self and leaving selfishness.
9	Conquering the conquering	While Jami discussed annihilation, Liu translated and interpreted it as conquering awareness of external things. The heart should dismiss any awareness of external things.
10	Returning to the One	The unity of existence means the heart to be united with the One.
11	Uplifting the awareness	While Jami did not mention the word 'heart,' Liu Zhi explained that the uplifting of awareness is by the purification of the heart.
12	Real guarding	While Jami emphasized the guarding of relationship with the Real, Liu Zhi focused on the guarding of the heart.
13	Real Being	From chapter 13 to the last, it clarifies the theoretical aspect of the unity of existence or 'the hidden and manifest meaning of the Real Principle.'

14	Being	Liu Zhi edited and simplified several difficult concepts in Jami. He just asserted that being had two meanings. They are illusory being and the Real Being. 'Illusory' is defined as transient existence and does not go beyond human rational understanding and manifested images.
15	Substance and function	Liu Zhi replaced Jami's essence and attributes with substance and function respectively.
16	Names and similatives	Liu Zhi replaced Jami's first, second and third grade of self-disclosure with first, second and third movement. Jami emphasized the role of light which revealed the hidden into manifested. Liu Zhi simplified Jami's scheme of disclosure.
17	The origin of transformation	Liu Zhi selectively translated and simplified the process of transformation or disclosure according to Jami.
18	The total order	Liu Zhi added an extra beginning paragraph to explain the total order of the visible and invisible world. Plentiful Confucian terms are used, namely substance, principle, power, vital-energy and others. He edited the second and other following paragraphs of Jami extensively and deleted all Neo-Platonic concepts. He emphasized that the ultimate existence was the principle and nature of the Real. Other existents depended on the Real for their existence.
19	The subtle container	Liu Zhi explained the relation between oneness and manyness similarly to Jami but with easier to understand examples from daily living. He followed closely Jami's concept of oneness.
25	The grade of the Real	Liu Zhi followed closely Jami's work in his translation from the twentieth to the twenty-fourth Gleams. Jami gave an account of six grades of divine disclosure and Liu Zhi complied with the six grades and translated them quite closely. Liu Zhi translated closely Jami's work from the twenty-sixth to thirty-sixth Gleams in Confucian terms.

A. Murata, *Gleams*, 137.
B. See also Murata, *Gleams*, 136.

Jin, the Chinese scholar of Liu Zhi, has studied briefly Liu Zhi's *Displaying the Concealment of the Real Realm*.[26] While Murata has translated Liu Zhi's *Displaying the Concealment of the Real Realm* into English and

26. Jin, *Sufism in China*, 87–100.

made a few helpful comments on Islamic concepts,[27] the following comments from the above table are additional new analyses that Murata and Jin have not noted. By observing and analyzing the way Liu Zhi translated and interpreted Jami's *Lawa'ih*, one can deduce some characteristics of Liu Zhi's concept of the unity of existence and his contextualization of this concept in Confucian terms. Our analysis will be made from both a general and a specific perspective.

Firstly, generally speaking, *Displaying the Concealment of the Real Realm* is definitely not for beginners or novices. It is intended for readership at the intermediate level between the *Three-character Classic* and *Nature and Principle in Islam*. It is longer than the *Three-character Classic* and less difficult to read than *The Nature and Principle in Islam*. Some Chinese literati might be able to benefit and find similarities between Islam and Neo-Confucianism because Liu Zhi used many Confucian terms in his explanation.

Secondly, one of the official Chinese textbooks of Sufism in the Scripture Hall Education System at the time of Liu Zhi is Jami's *al-Lama'at*. The Chinese translator of *al-Lama'at* did not use Confucian terms.[28] The preface in the 1927 edition described the book as articulate. Even Confucian literati in academic institutions might not be able to comprehend. Jin asserts that Jami's *al-Lama'at* and the Chinese translator used the difficult Neo-Platonic concept of divine emanation.[29] However, the primary goal of Liu Zhi's translation of Jami's *Lawa'ih* into *Displaying the Concealment of the Real Realm* can be seen by his free and occasional selective translation of this work and his plentiful use of Confucian terms. Thus, Liu Zhi was aiming to provide an easy-to-read reference book on Jami's Islamic thought in the Scripture Hall Education System. Liu Zhi's work in Chinese soon became a reference book. Both Jami's works presented a fairly comprehensible understanding of the Ibn 'Arabi tradition through Jami, including both the theory and practice of the unity of existence. Jami explicitly acknowledged his Ibn 'Arabi source in the original twenty-sixth Gleam but Liu Zhi simply identified Ibn 'Arabi as a former worthy.[30]

27. Murata, *Gleams*, 74–77.

28. A recent edition of Jami's *al-Lama'at* with brief comments in modern Chinese was published in 2001 in Beijing. The style of the translator, Bin Ruan, is very different from Liu Zhi. Ruan's approach is fairly literal. Ruan follows the modern style of verse-by-verse brief commentary, in addition to his own translation. He even comments on Jami's poems that Liu Zhi totally ignored in *Displaying the Concealment of the Real Realm*. When Ruan comes across difficult philosophical concepts, he will explain them in greater detail. Compared to Liu Zhi's translation, Ruan's work is easier to read for modern Hui Muslims but some Sufi ideas are still difficult to understand. Jami.

29. Jin, "Reading," 8.

30. Murata, *Gleams*, 186–87.

Liu Zhi's Engagement with the Concept of the Unity of Existence 105

From the specific perspective, one can deduce some characteristics of Liu Zhi's concept of the unity of existence. Firstly, the concept of the unity of existence includes the integration of both practical and theoretical aspects, namely the first twelve Gleams and the remaining twenty four Gleams respectively. While Liu Zhi translated and interpreted the exposition of the divine disclosure, he was eager to point out the ethical aspects of Sufi thought. He translated and interpolated the Sufi text with a clear emphasis on *shar'ia*. The first twelve Gleams of his translation emphasize the practical aspects of *tawhid*. Liu Zhi calls such practical aspects "the endeavor of seeking the Tao [Dao] and cultivating the Tao."[31] For Liu Zhi, then, right thinking (orthodoxy) and doing (orthopraxis) are interwoven within the concept of *tawhid*.

Secondly, in the practical aspect of the unity of existence, Liu Zhi had greater emphasis than Jami on the role of heart. The teaching of the first Gleam has to do with one heart. There are detailed teachings on the heart in subsequent Gleams. The meaning of oneness of heart (emphasis of the first Gleam) gradually develops. It expands to mean single-mindedness, purity, dedication, and others as illustrated in the above table. Above all in the tenth Gleam, Jami's asserting unity (*tawhid*) is to make the heart one. In Liu Zhi's translation, the unity means the heart is in union with the One.[32] The condition of the heart is vital for any successful unity. This may partly explain the wisdom of Liu Zhi in the ninth Gleam when he translated Jami's annihilation as conquering awareness of the external things. Some Sufis might interpret annihilation as the total absence of self and real union in the sense of fusion with the Real. However, Liu Zhi was able to avoid any misunderstanding by emphasizing the meaning of overcoming any desire or need for visible things.

Thirdly, in the sixth Gleam Liu Zhi made a clear and easy to understand interpretation of an ambiguous sentence in Jami's text. Jami used "the bounded becomes the Unbounded," and "I am the Real." Liu Zhi did not give the literal translation. He interpreted as "preserving self is preserving the Lord, and portraying self is portraying the Lord."[33] Sentences like "the bounded becomes the Unbounded" and "I am the Real or He" have been problematic in the history of Sufism because this way of speaking may blur the distinction between the creature and the creator.[34]

31. Ibid., 153.

32. Ibid., 150–51.

33. Murata has competently translated Liu Zhi's text which clarifies the ambiguity in Jami's version.

34. One of the most famous sayings of Al-Hallaj: "I am the Truth," which can be interpreted as "my 'I' is God." Massignon, *Passion*, abridged ed., 65. Other problematic saying is: "Now 'You' are 'me' in everything." Massignon, *Passion*, Vol. III, 41.

The two words that Liu Zhi chose to translate are "preserving (*cun* 存) and portraying (yu 喻)." The word *cun* in classical usage can have a variety of similar meanings, namely accumulate, deposit, keep and others. A paraphrased translation of Liu Zhi's "preserving" may be "taking the Lord into the heart." The word *yu* in classical usage can mean simply to explain, inform or understand. A paraphrased translation of portraying may be witnessing the Lord. Liu Zhi's translation may be understood as "you take the Lord into the heart" and "you become the Lord's true witnesses." Thus, Liu Zhi's translated text gives no possibility of blurring the distinction between creature and the creator. Clearly, Liu Zhi's edition and interpretation is to ensure that his Hui Muslims can have right understanding in the sense of orthodoxy which then leads to orthopraxis which is right doing.

Fourthly, the eighteenth Gleam is of special interest because it illustrates the purpose of Liu Zhi's revision and modification of Jami's work.[35] Liu Zhi added a single paragraph at the beginning with over one hundred and forty Chinese characters. It explains the movement from the oneness to manyness and then from manyness into oneness in Neo-Confucian terms.[36] Rather than using the Real One, he now used substance. Substance is limited to two functions, namely knowledge and power "Knowledge and power are the function of the Substance, and they put forth acting and making."[37] Various grades of movements are due to movement initiating from the substance and then the dual relation between knowledge and power that gives rise to further movements. The dual relation of two functions, namely knowledge and power, finds a parallel in the Confucian teaching of yin yang. The definition and description of substance is clearer in his *Rules and Proprieties of Islam* and is explained later in this chapter.

Acting and making eventually became external things. External things did not exist on their own, rather ultimately "depend on the Principle, and the Principle is the subtle container of the Real Being's knowledge and power."[38] Liu Zhi interpolated Jami's divine disclosure and eventual return by using Confucian terms. Liu Zhi gave an additional explanation of the relation between the one and the manifested many by using the analogy of fire.[39] "This is also like the power of giving light, keeping warm, cooking food that are contained in the fire. The fire possesses from beforehand

---

35. This additional paragraph has often been noted by modern scholar including Murata. Murata, *Gleams*, 165. However, Yin is silent and just discusses the content of the eighteenth Gleam. Jin, *Sufism in China*, 94.
36. In the eighteenth Gleam.
37. Murata, *Gleams*, 165.
38. Ibid.
39. In the nineteenth Gleam.

Liu Zhi's Engagement with the Concept of the Unity of Existence 107

all these powers, but as long as it does not encounter various things, these do not become manifest."[40] Liu Zhi made great effort to help his readers to understand Jami's detailed concept of transformation.

Finally, in the twenty-first Gleam, Liu Zhi again freely made use of contextualized terms in his translation. "Obstruction necessarily seeks penetration, whereas penetration does not seek obstruction. Thus, the demand is from both sides, but the seeking is from one side ..."[41] While Jami used "Unbounded and bounded," Liu Zhi used easy to understand words or phrase, namely, "penetration and obstruction" respectively.[42] The Unbounded is without boundary and thus can interpenetrate. The bounded with boundary may obstruct anything within its boundary. For beginner of Islam, Jami's words like "Bounded and Unbounded" are ambiguous. Again, the goal of Liu Zhi's interpretation is that his readers may understand Jami's text. Murata states that given "the general skill with which he translates the text and his wide reading in Arabic and Persian sources, it is difficult to believe that this modification could have been anything but intentional."[43]

So far, our above discussion of Liu Zhi's works may be summarized as follows:

- In his short and translated Sufi work, Liu Zhi's method of contextualization remains unchanged although the shorter work is too concise to make any definitive statement. However, his longer translated Sufi work, *Displaying the Concealment of the Real Realm,* begins to give a good account of his strategy. His works show intentional effort to help his Chinese readers to understand difficult philosophical concepts. He is in conversation or dialogue with his own Confucian context.

- Generally speaking, Liu Zhi concurred with Jami's concept of the unity of existence and also the Ibn 'Arabi tradition.

- Liu Zhi is a skillful translator and interpreter. In his works, he does not deviate from the original meaning of his source although he makes modifications and adds explanatory text. While he may modify certain words, these modifications retain the logic and the meaning of the text.

- In his contextualization, his works uphold the basic tenets of Islam and edit ambiguous sentences that may have the tendency to mislead

---

40. Murata, *Gleams*, 169.
41. Ibid., 173.
42. Ibid.
43. Ibid., 126.

his readers. In addition, his work emphasizes the role of the heart with respect to the practice of the unity of existence.

KEY THEMES OF THE CONCEPT OF UNITY OF EXISTENCE IN *THE NATURE AND PRINCIPLE IN ISLAM* AND *RULES AND PROPRIETIES OF ISLAM*

The second section of this chapter will focus on two major works of Liu Zhi, namely *The Nature and Principle in Islam* and *Rules and Proprieties of Islam*. Liu Zhi hardly discussed the unity of existence in the third part of his trilogy, namely *The True Record of the Utmost Sage of Islam*. Only the first three chapters of *The Rules and Proprieties of Islam* primarily deal with the unity of existence and return to the Real but *The Nature and Principle in Islam* discusses extensively such concepts. The detailed discussion of Islamic sciences in *The Nature and Principle in Islam* is often summarized and reiterated in the early chapters of *The Rules and Proprieties of Islam*. An English translation of these chapters is provided in Appendix IV at the end.

Murata has translated and examined Liu Zhi's *Nature and Principle in Islam*. She excels in explicating Liu Zhi's Islamic sciences of Sufi thought and philosophical terms like root suchness, nonbeing, and others based on his Persian and Arabic sources. In addition she also consults Ma Lianyuan's *Subtleties*.[44] Ma's work is a rather free translation of *The Nature and Principle in Islam*. Based on Liu Zhi's sources and Ma's Arabic translation, Murata is able to find the quoted sources and Ma's Arabic translation "helpful in clarifying some of Liu's discussions and testing our [Murata et al.] conjectures concerning the Arabic/Persian terms that Liu might have had in mind."[45] Murata finds Ma's commentary most helpful when she tries to interpret Liu's ideas in *The Nature and Principle in Islam*.

While Murata's study is based on the translation of each chapter and explanation of the Islamic concepts, Jin's study is a general thematic study based primarily on Liu Zhi's trilogy. The following analysis will focus on the details of Liu Zhi's concept of unity of existence which Murata, Jin and others have not noted or discussed.

---

44. Murata et al., *Sage*, 15.
45. Ibid., 18.

The Real Ruler: Transcendence and Immanence

Wang Daiyu often used the Real One. Liu Zhi's *Rules and Proprieties of Islam* prefers the term the Real Ruler. It is the real being and primordial existence. What is the Real Ruler?

Firstly, Liu Zhi stated that the Real Ruler was non-designated. Murata explains that the non-designation of the very beginning has parallels with Jami's *Lawa'ih* concept of nonentification[46] which is understood as the unknown essence that cannot be properly designated by any name.[47] "In the very beginning, there is only the Real Ruler's root suchness,[48] supremely pure and quiet, without limit and form, not controlled by light and darkness, not belonging to the creative transformation. The Real Ruler is really the root and source of heaven and earth, humans and things."[49]

Secondly, unlike the universe that has numerous and multi-faceted existences, the Real Ruler is one. Unlike the universe that has blossoming and withering lives and seasonal change, the Real Ruler takes no part in such change.[50]

Thirdly, while the Real Ruler does not change, it is the fount and source of the cosmic existence.

Fourthly, the Real Ruler can express the divine essence through the Numerical and Embodied One.[51] This concept of the One or the Real Ruler is the usual explanation given by Murata, Jin and others. However, these scholars have not noted further explanations of the Real Ruler in Liu Zhi's *Rules and Proprieties of Islam*.

---

46. According to Murata, 'nonentification' is the essence understood as an absolute unity in which no 'entity' or thing can be differentiated from any other.' Murata, *Gleam*, 119.

47. Murata asserts that the non-designation of the Very Beginning has parallels also with the Daoist classic text, 'The name that can be named is not the name.' Murata, "Unity."

48. Root suchness (*ren*) is a fundamental concept of Liu Zhi. The literal meaning of suchness (*ren*) is certainly, verily or yes. An alternative possible meaning is 'in existence.' The modern Chinese usage of '*ren*' means already exists and 'yet to *ren*' means yet to exist. Root is usually translated as 'original' and may mean 'without beginning. Root suchness can thus be paraphrased as 'without beginning and already in existence.' Murata uses the literal word 'suchness' and parallels it with the Arabic word *inniyya*, that-it-is-ness. 'In Islamic philosophy, *inniyya* is used as a synonym for existence (*wujud*). Murata further explicates root suchness as root substance which is the Real Being. Murata et al., *Sage*, 184.

49. See *Rules and Proprieties of Islam*, first chapter. Appendix IV.

50. See chapter 5 of his work, *Nature*. Also, Murata et al., *Sage*, 144.

51. Liu, *Nature and Principle*, chapter 5. Also, Murata et al., *Sage*, 144.

Not noted by Murata, Jin and other scholars, Liu Zhi further distinguished the Real Ruler into transcendent Ruler and inclusive Ruler in chapter 2 of *The Rules and Proprieties of Islam*. "The One is unique and this uniqueness has two meanings. The first meaning of the unique one is that it transcends all things. The second meaning of the unique One is that it embraces all things."[52]

> The transcendent One is beyond manifestations. Unlike the transcendent One, the heaven, earth and all things have manifestations. The vital energy then transforms to give out their forms. This is the number [function] of the acquired heaven. The root suchness of the Real Ruler does not have any manifestation. It does not participate in the vital energy's transformation and is not determined by the number [function] of the acquired heaven. The Real Ruler does not have any boundary and physical form, it is most pure and subtle, and is difficult to describe. The unique One means it is transcendent to heaven, earth and all things.
>
> With regard to the unique immanent One, it is unique because this One is not to be separated from manifestation and thus becomes 'unique.' It is not to separate from the many. It creates all matters from beginning to now, both visible and invisible and governs their activities with its real principle. The substance is not separated from its function and it is undifferentiated from all materials. This One is unique because outside the One, there is no manifestation. Outside this One, there is no boundary. This is the meaning of the immanent One.[53]

The Real Ruler has two senses of uniqueness: transcendence and immanence. The Chinese word for immanence is *bao*. In classical Chinese usage, it can take various meanings, namely wrap, bundle, pack and others. Liu Zhi's concept of the Real Ruler did not support pantheism. The meaning of immanence really has the connotation of panentheism.[54] When Liu Zhi discussed the disclosure of the Real Ruler, he really explained the origin of cosmos and relationship between a really unique panentheistic being and the cosmos. The Real Ruler in the sense of immanence is understood to be a panentheistic being that can interpenetrate and include all visible and invisible things. The Real Ruler in the sense of transcendence is understood to

---

52. Liu, *Rules*, chapter 2. Appendix IV.

53. Ibid.

54. Panentheism may simply be defined as the belief that God is greater than the universe and includes and interpenetrates it. A sophisticated version of it is argued by a twentieth-century prominent Christian theologian, Paul Tillich.

be a radically unique being that is beyond any human God-talk and outside the disclosure. The Real Ruler is in itself. Both aspects of the uniqueness of the Real Ruler must be held together. They are inseparable and yet they also must be distinguished.

The Rules and Proprieties of Islam makes it easier to understand Liu Zhi's concept of the unity of existence. With respect to the macrocosmic worldview, the panentheistic being is in eternal unity with the cosmos because it interpenetrates and embraces all things. With respect to the microcosmic worldview, humans in particular the perfect human being can return and eventually have a heart union with the panentheistic being. It is not a union of two different bodies to form a single entity which should be called fusion. In simple terms, the practical concept of Liu Zhi's unity of existence means that by removing all forms of visible and invisible obstructions, humankind may return to the substance or essence of the panentheistic being and eventually actualize a heart union. This understanding of the unity of existence forms the basis of Liu Zhi's idea of Sufi spirituality. This also explains his emphasis on the role of the heart.

The Second Grade of Disclosure

Murata takes great effort to explain the Islamic concepts of Liu Zhi's disclosure. Jin, Sha and others explain insightfully the intricate meanings of various Confucian terms in the disclosure. To our knowledge, no contemporary scholar has noted or attempted to explain the logic of Liu Zhi's argument of disclosure from the perspective of panentheism. Such a discussion is found not in his *Nature and Principle in Islam* but primarily in *The Rules and Proprieties of Islam* and *Displaying the Concealment of the Real Realm*.

The three major works of Wang Daiyu discuss the concept of the three Ones. However, these works do not explain the immanence and the logical argument of immanence in the divine disclosure. While Liu Zhi continued to use Wang's three Ones in his *Nature and Principle in Islam*, he also attempted to explain the immanence of the Real Ruler. Most probably, he derived such insight from Jami and in accordance with the Ibn 'Arabi tradition. In the nineteenth Gleam of *Lawa'ih*, Jami explained the inclusion of the manyness in the oneness of the essence or alternatively in the language of Liu Zhi the inclusion of multiplicity in the only One Real Ruler. According to Jami, inclusion does not mean the inclusion of the contained in the container.

> Rather, what is meant is the inclusion of the descriptions and the requirements in the described thing and the requirer, like

> the inclusion of one-halfness, one-thirdness, one-fourthness, one-fifthness, ad infinitum, in the essence of the numerical one. After all, these relations are included within it and have no manifestation whatsoever so long as it does not become part of two, three, four, and five through repetition of manifestation in the levels.[55]

Liu Zhi gave a simplified and easy to understand translation with interpretation. Inclusion does not mean the One Substance is a part contained in a whole.

> Rather, it is the substance's containment of the function and the requirer's containment of the required. For example, one is one-half of two, one-third of three, one-fourth of four, and so on, to one part of one hundred thousand billion. All these are contained in the root nature of "one," and "one" has beforehand the power to be the principle of one part of all numbers. However, as long as the various numbers are not added, its power will never become manifest.[56]

The basic argument of Liu Zhi is that the panentheistic being embraces all things. The panentheistic being is not a container that contains various parts. Strictly speaking, it does not contain, carry and divide all things. Rather, such inclusion means that it embraces and interpenetrates them. This insight came from Jami and Liu Zhi adopted it enthusiastically. Similarly, the Great Ultimate that is the most perfect *li* as propagated by Zhu Xi, the Neo-Confucian master, might also influence Liu Zhi's adoption.

Such understanding of immanence is further developed and seen clearly in chapter 2 of *The Rules and Proprieties of Islam* using similar easy to understand numerical examples. In chapter 2, Liu Zhi explained the fact that the Real Ruler did not beget or reproduce a son, unlike the Christian God in the gospel. As a monotheistic religion, Muslims believe in one and only Real Ruler. Liu Zhi expressed this unique panentheistic being by using the Confucian term, namely root substance. The following quotation comes from one single section in chapter 2.

> From one, it gives rise to and completes the ten thousand. One penetrates the beginning and end of ten thousand. The ten thousand comes from one, completes by one. The ten thousand needs one but the one does not need the ten thousand . . .

---

55. Murata, *Gleams*, 168. Murata asserts that Jami's source is Farghani's *Muntaha'l-madarik*. However, Farghani's scheme is much more complicated. Murata, *Gleams*, 231.

56. Ibid., 169.

> The root substance of one is all-inclusive and penetrating. Nothing is beyond it. It gives rise to number but it is not equal to number...
>
> The root substance of one is eternally unchanging and unmoving. It generates countless other numbers. The root substance of one is without increase and decrease. It increases and decreases the ten thousand numbers. The root substance of one has no beginning and attachment; it becomes the beginning of ten thousand and the attachment of ten thousand...
>
> Therefore, ten, hundred, thousand, ten thousand and countless other numbers have their source and foundation in one...
>
> The root substance of one is unparallel and nothing is like one. Any number is formed by addition, subtraction, multiplication, and division. If you take away this way of thinking, there is no existence of number. The result remains to be the same: one.[57]

What is the meaning of root substance? Root means source and origin. Murata says that in the common usage of Chinese philosophy, root substance is the unique general term for ultimate reality.[58] She also notes that substance is often paired with function in both Buddhist and Confucian thought. Substance refers to the essence and function refers to the names and attributes. "Generally, substance is the thing in itself, function its movement or activity; substance is a thing's fundamental reality, function its expression; the two are typically discussed together and designate a relationship."[59]

With such understanding of the root substance and function, several brief comments can be made from the above quotation about the relationship between the root substance and the existence of only one being. Firstly, the root substance simply refers to the second grade of disclosure, namely the Real One and may equally refer to the substance of the first sub-grade of the Real One, namely "quietness without manifestation." It should be noted that the term Real One does not derive from Confucianism. However, Liu Zhi used Confucian term, namely root substance, to explain the relationship between the Real One and the concept of one unique being. Secondly, it should be emphasized that the order of disclosure or the structure of emanation is a *logical* order and has no bearing or reference to the time line and status of each entity. It should be interpreted solely in terms of the logical sequence of hiddenness and manifestation. As an illustration,

57. Liu, *Rules*, chapter 2. See Appendix IV.
58. Murata et al., *Sage*, 77.
59. Ibid., 69.

substance is inherently hidden. While function can manifest substance, substance simply is manifested as a body-less substance. It does not have any embodiment at all even at the state of manifestation of function. Finally, the above quotation adequately illustrates the oneness and manyness of Liu Zhi's understanding of the panentheistic being. The "one" is the function and it is embraced by the root substance of the one. Thus, it is an interpretation of the divine disclosure in Jami's *Lawa'ih* in Confucian terms.

The Unity of Existence and Return to the Real

Many contemporary scholars are able to note that Liu Zhi's works have emphasized both theoretical and practical aspects of Islam. One obvious reason to support this argument is the inner structure of Liu Zhi's trilogy. The first work, *The Nature and Principle in Islam,* discusses the Islamic sciences including theosophy, cosmogony and nature of things. The second work, *The Rules and Proprieties of Islam,* discusses the rationale and rites of Islam. His work starts from Islamic theory and moves to practice. The final work ends with the origin of Islam and many extraordinary stories of the prophet Muhammad.

The following discussion can provide a fresh perspective of Liu Zhi's integration of theory and practice. Liu Zhi's Islam integrates both the theoretical and practical aspects of Islam using the concept of the unity of existence. The logical order of the various grades of divine disclosure in terms of descent and ascent integrates the two aspects into one single entity, as asserted by Liu Zhi.

The unifying theme of Jami's *Lawa'ih* is *tawhid* (the assertion of God's unity: there is no god but God). The work deals with *tawhid* as practice and *tawhid* as theory. The first twelve Gleams focus on the "devotional imperative of turning one's full attention toward the One."[60] The remaining Gleams "discuss various ways in which the relationship between the true Being of the Real and the existence of the world and things can be conceptualized."[61] It is in this second section, from the thirteenth Gleam to the end, that this work expounds the understanding of the unity of existence.

At the time of Liu Zhi, another work of Jami, namely the *al-Lama'at*, was a standard Sufi textbook in the Scripture Hall Education System. This work primarily deals with the philosophical explanation of the unity of existence and is a challenging work for many students. In Liu Zhi's translation of Jami's *Lawa'ih*, Liu Zhi did not alter Jami's structure, retaining the practical

60. Murata, *Gleams*, 116.
61. Ibid.

Liu Zhi's Engagement with the Concept of the Unity of Existence   115

aspect in the first twelve Gleams and followed by the theoretical aspect in all subsequent chapters. Probably, Liu Zhi's concern is not so much to put forth his revised view of the unity of existence which is similar to Wang Daiyu. Rather, his concern is to give an easy-to-read translation of Jami's concepts. This is confirmed by his additional paragraph of explanation in the beginning of the eighteenth Gleam as explained before.

In Liu Zhi's understanding of the unity of existence, he consulted the six grades of disclosure in Jami's work but continued with Wang Daiyu's simpler concept of the three Ones. While substance, function, act, yin/yang and others are Confucian terms, the three Ones, namely the Real, Numerical and Embodied One are not familiar Confucian terms. In his translated work of Jami, Liu Zhi generally followed Jami. In his own works, he chose to continue Wang Daiyu's scheme of disclosure. However, Liu Zhi also finetuned Wang Daiyu's concept of three Ones at the sub-grade of the second grade of disclosure. At the sub-grade of Embodied One, the following table summarizes the difference in understanding between Wang Daiyu and Liu Zhi:

Table 4.5: *Comparison between Wang Daiyu and Liu Zhi on the Three Sub-grades of the Embodied One*

Three Sub-grades of the Embodied One by Wang Daiyu[A]	Three Sub-grades of the Embodied One by Liu Zhi[B]
Recognition with knowledge: to inquire about and to imitate what the sages and worthies reflected upon and witnessed.	*Recognition with body knowing*: our endeavor is to comply and follow. It is to know what ought to be done without being able to know why it is so. At this level we know the name, but we do not know the reality.[C]
Recognition with seeing: to transcend all the conditions so that humans recognize the Real with the body.	*Recognition with heart seeing*: our endeavor is to understand. To understand is to see why it is so but not to be able to obtain why it is so. At this level we see the differentiation, but we do not see the union.
Recognition with continuity: to conquer entirely both selfishness and opinions of self, returning completely to the fountainhead and recognizing the Real with body while depending on no-self	*Recognition with nature, continual knowing*: our endeavor is to be without interval. To be without interval is to be rooted in why it is so and to be undifferentiated from why it is so; this is the utmost.

a. Murata, *Gleams*, 97–100.
b. Murata et al., *Sage*, 518–19. Murata describes the three grades as knowing, seeing and continuity.
c. Murata et al., *Sage*, 518.

The above table illustrates the subtle differences between Wang Daiyu and Liu Zhi. When Liu Zhi translated Jami's work, he added the role of the heart in the practical aspect of Islam. Similarly, Liu Zhi's concept of the three Ones emphasizes the role of the heart again at the sub-level of the Embodied One. The heart can acquire understanding at the differentiated level. The *heart* seeing is to understand the world of the acquired heaven. The goal of Liu Zhi's minor revision is to integrate the unity of existence with the return to the Real with the emphasis on the role of the heart. While Wang discussed the heart which has different grades, Liu Zhi put greater emphasis on the role of the heart with respect to the return to the Real.

Liu Zhi used the concept of the unity of existence to integrate his understanding of God's disclosure, anthropology and eschatology together. "In other words, it sets down the principle of what may be called *wahda al-wujud*, which is to say that it expresses the first principle of Islamic thought, *tawhid* or the unity of God in terms of *wujud*."[62] The return is a closed system of circular movement, beginning from and returning to the Real One. It begins from a spontaneous movement of the "heart"[63] that triggers the movement through invisible and visible matters in returning to the Real One, similar to Ibn 'Arabi's *Wahdat al-wujud* concept, namely existence and unity.

Neo-Confucianism had a similar concept of movement but in terms of a humanist aspect emphasizing self-cultivation and moral transformation through the teachings of the sage as established by many ancient sacred texts. Since the fourteenth century and the great work of Zhu Xi, a powerful linguistic and philosophical system with ethical concerns was in place to allow foreign ideas and concepts to be contextualized. Instead of glorifying Neo-Confucianism in the manner of Ma Zhu, Liu Zhi followed the strategy of Wang Daiyu. Liu Zhi encountered manifold challenges. Firstly, he took on Wang Daiyu's concept of the three Ones and improved it to unity in multiplicity and simultaneously also many-in-oneness. While Neo-Confucianism was traditionally weak on theism, Liu Zhi found a common ground exploiting the concept of the Great Ultimate as defined and developed by Zhu Xi. Secondly, he re-appropriated Neo-Confucian self-cultivation for

62. Murata, "Unity."
63. In Chinese 一念之動.

Islamic spirituality and contextualized the meanings of Islamic rituals. The practice of Islamic rituals shared common ground with Chinese self-cultivation. Thirdly, he integrated the concept of the Real and humanity with Sufi spirituality using the concept of return to the Real One. The return of Muslims to the Real is made possible because of who the prophet Muhammad is and what he has done. Liu Zhi always took care to emphasize the unique role of the Utmost Sage. Thus, integration was done perfectly and exemplarily by Muhammad, the holy sage as well as the ultimate prophet.

CONTEMPORARY SCHOLARSHIP ON LIU ZHI'S CONCEPT OF THE UNITY OF EXISTENCE AND DISCLOSURE

One of the major differences between Jin in China and Murata in America is their view of Liu Zhi's scheme of disclosure or structure of emanation. Jin Yijiu avers that Liu Zhi departed from monotheistic Islam. Jin argues that Liu Zhi's pantheism is most explicit in his divine disclosure and Sufi thought. Jin believes that the Chinese school of Sufism was always influenced by the works of Neo-Platonists from India and Persia. Jin asserts that Sufism in China absorbed the theory of disclosure from Neo-Platonism and the purification of souls from Gnosticism. For Jin, Liu Zhi readily accepted these foreign ideas in Chinese Sufism as long as these Sufi Islamic concepts agreed with Neo-Confucianism.[64] Jin believes that Liu Zhi absorbed Neo-Platonism most clearly in his concept of divine disclosure.[65] The disclosure of the Real as Real One, Numerical One and Embodied One means the fusion of real being with the created world. For Jin, then, theologically by the method of disclosure into various grades and philosophically through dialectical logic, the Real was manifested in the many.

One of the main supporting reasons is Jin's assertion that Liu Zhi differed from Ibn 'Arabi.[66] Liu Zhi did not posit the nature and principle of all created beings within the Real One.[67] Rather, Liu Zhi asserted that the root suchness of the Real was shared as communal root suchness. Since it is communal, it is also the root suchness of *manifested things*.[68] Based on such reasons, Jin then concludes that Liu Zhi's Islamic philosophy is fundamentally

---

64. Jin, *Exploring Chinese Islam*, 28.
65. Ibid., 42.
66. Hussaini, *Pantheistic Monism*.
67. Jin, *Exploring Chinese Islam*, 89.
68. Ibid., 88.

pantheistic. In his later edition of his study of Liu Zhi in 2010, his view remains unchanged.

Another point of view that supports Jin is the modern understanding of Sufism. It is known that Ibn 'Arabi's theoretical Sufism was spread through Naqshbandi masters into the Northwestern part of China by the seventeenth century as demonstrated by Joseph Fletcher.[69] By the beginning of the twentieth century, Sufism was accused of carrying heterodox elements especially by Muhammad Rashid Rida (1865–1935).[70] However, Murata in her earlier and recent works affirms that Liu Zhi's works which "provide theoretical explanations of the nature of things—God, the cosmos, the soul—belong to the Sufi tradition."[71] Liu Zhi's "inspiration derived in part from the specific strands of Muslim thought least beholden to the formal elements of the tradition, namely, theoretical Sufism (what in recent Persian history has typically been called '*irfan*, "gnosis") and philosophy."[72] Thus Murata believes that Liu Zhi's works are traditional and in accordance with the Ibn 'Arabi teaching. Liu Zhi got inspiration from this tradition and elaborated on them. Murata's works give no hint that Liu Zhi's Islam is pantheistic.

How Islamic are the texts written by Ibn 'Arabi's followers and the Sufi texts by Jami? Is Liu Zhi's Islam heterodox? Several responses may be given.

Firstly, we disagree with Jin's interpretation. Jin argues that since Liu Zhi's concept of the root suchness is inclusive of all the principles and manifestations of principles, Liu Zhi's Islam is pantheistic. As explained above, the unique Real Ruler has two aspects, namely transcendence and immanence. The unique panentheistic being is inclusive of all the principles and manifestations. This interpretation of the divine being is not pantheism at all. Liu Zhi attempted to give a balanced view of both the transcendence and immanence of the Real Ruler. If Jin had consulted in depth chapter 2 of *The Rules and Proprieties of Islam* he might have reached a different conclusion.

Additional support for Liu Zhi's panentheism is found in his interpretation of Jami's origin of transformation. In Jami's seventeenth Gleam, the transformation is described thus:

> The First Entification is an unmixed oneness and a sheer receptivity that comprises all receptivities . . .
>
> It is the level of Unity, and to it belong nonmanifestation, firstness, and beginninglessness . . .

69. Fletcher, *Studies*.
70. Sirriyeh, *Sufis*, 98–102.
71. Murata, *Gleams*, 26.
72. Murata et al., *Sage*, 21.

> It is the level of One-and-allness, and to it belong manifestation, lastness, and endlessness.[73]

Liu Zhi translated it as:

> [t]he First Movement is the upright one and the subtle conveyance that embraces and puts together...
>
> The level of the Only-One is the inward, the origin, and the beginning...
>
> The level of the First-One is the outward, the derivative, and the end.[74]

At the second grade of disclosure, the unique Real has two aspects that Jin fails to realize in Liu Zhi's translated text. Liu Zhi's translation and interpretation of disclosure is consistent with Jami and in accordance with the Ibn 'Arabi tradition.

Secondly, Liu Zhi consulted over sixty different titles in the first two works of his trilogy, fifteen of them of various Sufi works. Murata indicates that many titles did not cover the fields of *Kalam* and Islamic philosophy. She asserts that Sufi works provided the theological basis for Liu Zhi.[75] Liu Zhi's choice of and preference for such sources are significant and in accordance with the spirit of the Scripture Hall Education. The Scripture Hall Education emphasized classics which might be Sufi or non-Sufi works in Arabic or Persian and they were regarded as authoritative. While always upholding the theological significance of Islamic essential doctrines, Liu Zhi's program of contextualization was to integrate theology proper with ethical conduct. That is, while his works do not betray Islam, they should not be tied down by Islam.

It is beyond any reasonable doubt that Liu Zhi took the greatest care to obtain reliable Islamic sources available to him through his travel and network. The first two books of his trilogy recorded forty and forty five different sources respectively.[76] He was well aware of unreliable Islamic texts. With respect to his last work, *The True Record of the Utmost Sage of Islam*, Liu Zhi began translating it only when he felt sure his source was dependable. He began his translation in 1710. After over ten years of solitary work and three revisions, the first draft was ready around 1721. The gap between the first two books of his trilogy and the last one is about twenty years. The

---

73. Murata, *Gleams*, 160.
74. Ibid., 161.
75. Ibid., 26.
76. Ibid., 25.

True Record of the Utmost Sage of Islam was eventually printed in 1776 after his death.[77] It was also the longest work produced by Liu Zhi in his lifetime. By taking careful note the number of Islamic sources he consulted, the efficient network of the Muslim education halls known in Nanjing and other major cities, the common phenomenon of scholars travelling to Beijing and various parts of China, the care that Liu Zhi took to find a reliable source, and the time to carry out the work, one can safely conclude that these evidences point to the fact that Liu Zhi was prudent in finding a reliable source and translating the text. His translation, exposition and commentary works are a continuation of his received Islamic traditions in the common sense of the word *orthodoxy* (abiding with traditional view).

Thirdly, another issue is the question of the orthodoxy of Ibn 'Arabi thought. The following response is an indirect one that comes from Alexander Knysh's work. Knysh's research primarily focuses on the theological disputations between the supporters and opponents of the concept of the unity of existence championed by Ibn 'Arabi. Knysh asserts that orthodoxy and heresy is a distinctly Christian concept that should not be uncritically superimposed upon medieval Islam. For Knysh, one should take care to safeguard "the intrinsic pluralism and complex characteristic of the religious life of the Muslim community, leaving aside significant and sometimes critical nuances . . . to let it [Islamic tradition] communicate its own concerns, its own ways of articulation and interpretation of religious phenomena."[78] Knysh pleads that any Islamic researcher should not indiscriminately use the binary opposition orthodoxy/heresy with regard to Islamic history as a whole. Knysh's fair and realistic thesis is that in "each period and in each region of the Islamic world, one is likely to find a particular blend of orthodox ideas. This blend, however, often proves rather unstable and subject to a drastic change as a result of redressing the political and social balance of powers."[79] Knysh's cautious reminder is appropriate in responding to Jin's criticism and the larger issue of the orthodoxy of Ibn 'Arabi teachings. One should not indiscriminately judge Liu Zhi's Islamic tradition and his transmission without a careful analysis of his Islamic context. Thus, with the support from Knysh, we assert that Jin's comment on Liu Zhi's heterodoxy may not be accurate in the context of medieval Islam in pre-modern China because Liu Zhi's works are in accordance with the Ibn 'Arabi tradition. That is orthodoxy in the sense of abiding with Ibn 'Arabi tradition.

77. Jin, *Exploring Chinese Islam*, 19.
78. Knysh, "Orthodoxy," 62–63.
79. Ibid., 66–67.

Liu Zhi's Engagement with the Concept of the Unity of Existence 121

The question of orthodoxy or heterodoxy was not relevant in the era of pre-modern China and at a time when Ibn 'Arabi's theology was at its zenith in Chinese Islam. Scholars who have asserted that Liu Zhi's works were heterodox had to provide more substantial evidences by examining the Persian or Arabic source materials. It should be noted that freedom was needed because Liu Zhi attempted to define and translate often difficult and metaphysical Islamic concepts into Neo-Confucian terms with religious and metaphysical meanings. His approach to receiving and acquiring wisdom is through the person and works of the Utmost Sage Muhammad. That is, Liu Zhi's methodological approach is Muhammad-centric. It is undoubtedly a traditional approach in accordance with Murata's opinion of Liu Zhi's Islam.

Knysh expounds his insightful view further. Various categories may be used to describe a pure and impure form of religion. They are usually described as binary opposites, namely, straight and deviating, lettered religious and popular vulgarized, scriptural literal and symbolic hermeneutics, genuine and corrupted, mainstream and schismatic, conformist and free thinking, and most common of all orthodox and heterodox. Such categories reflect the theological polyphony of the great Islamic tradition.[80] This polyphony becomes an axiomatic fact as time progresses. Islamic thought in various parts of the Islamic world is developed by various creative thinkers in both Arabic and Persian. Such progressive development becomes a great Islamic tradition embracing a wide spectrum of Islamic thought. Furthermore, Islamic thoughts and practices need to take root in new cultural settings and cultures. Chinese Islam is necessarily different from Islam of Middle Eastern origin. Contextualized Islam which at first sight may be unrecognizable from the Middle East form is a necessary development.

Finally, Knysh opines that Ibn 'Arabi and his school can be used as a typical case to illustrate the problem of using the category of orthodoxy and heterodoxy. The great mystical thinker Ibn 'Arabi has massive collections of writings. His thinking is complex and difficult to understand even for trained reader of Ibn 'Arabi. For Ibn 'Arabi, his own vision of God is the orthodox view and all others are heretics. The highest degree of knowledge of spiritual attainment is achieved by the Sufi in a state of perpetual bewilderment. While Ibn 'Arabi is opposed by some who claim that he encourages an excessive esoteric approach, his opponent Ibn Taymiyya has also been repeatedly accused of excessive literalism. Such debate between two different approaches to the interpretation of Islam is a recurring pattern in the history of Muslim religious polemic.[81] Thus, Knysh concludes that the

80. Ibid., 49–50.
81. Ibid., 60.

use of orthodoxy and heterodoxy is a European interpretative category and not helpful. In the case of Liu Zhi's orthodoxy and his use of the Ibn 'Arabi tradition through Jami, Knysh has provided an indirect response which is convincing.

SUMMARY AND CONCLUSION

This chapter has discussed the concept of the unity of existence in both short and long works of Liu Zhi. Previous scholars have focused on either one part of his trilogy or a few sections of his works. This chapter has examined his source materials, translation and expository works, in particular his *Nature and Principle in Islam, Rules and Proprieties of Islam,* and *Displaying the Concealment of the Real Realm.* His source materials are writings from followers of the Ibn 'Arabi tradition, in particular Jami's *Lawa'ih*.

After examination of Liu Zhi's free translation of Jami's *Lawa'ih*, this chapter has shown that his effort of contextualization is to assist his readers to understand the difficult concept of the unity of existence. This translated work reveals quite clearly that Liu Zhi is faithful to Jami's text. Unlike Wang Daiyu and Jami, Liu Zhi puts more emphasis on the role of the heart.

5

Liu Zhi's Sufi Spirituality in Conversation with the Neo-Confucian Context in China

The last chapter has provided evidence that Liu Zhi's concept of the unity of existence, especially in his translated work, is in continuity with the Ibn 'Arabi tradition. Liu Zhi did not merely regurgitate the works of Wang Daiyu or Jami. He followed closely Jami's first grade of disclosure but adopted Wang's concept of the three Ones and interpreted the disclosure as creative transformation in Confucian terms. Unlike Jami and Wang, Liu Zhi emphasized more the role of the heart in return to the Real Ruler. The Ibn 'Arabi tradition usually locates the perfect human being at the last grade of disclosure, namely the fifth, sixth or seventh grade. However, in both Wang and Liu Zhi's scheme, even at the second grade of the Embodied One, the nature of humanity begins to manifest. Part of the reason may contribute to the strategy of contextualization initiated by Wang which Liu Zhi then continued to develop.

While the preceding chapter has demonstrated that Liu Zhi closely followed the Ibn 'Arabi tradition, this present chapter will demonstrate Liu Zhi's use of the Neo-Confucian context as conversation partner in his contextualization. He translated a *shari'a*-minded Sufi spirituality into Confucian self-cultivation. The first part of this chapter examines the form of popular literature intended to educate the Chinese about Confucian virtues in the early Qing dynasty. The second part is a detailed study of Liu Zhi's *Poem of the Five Sessions of the Moon,* which has been briefly studied in Chinese by Jin and hardly even mentioned by any other scholars in English.

This poem demonstrates that Liu Zhi's contextualization is carried out in dialogue with the Chinese contexts and with the goal that the Muslim readers can understand. The third part will explicate Liu Zhi's understanding of the pivotal role of the prophet Muhammad as the Utmost Sage. The final part will explain further his *Rules and Proprieties of Islam* in conversation with Confucian self-cultivation.

THEOLOGICAL CONVERSATION WITH THE CHINESE CULTURE: NEO-CONFUCIAN CLASSICS

Neo-Confucian Classics in the Early Qing Dynasty

While the writings of Liu Zhi are contextualized Islamic writings, the literary form of some of his works belongs to the popular Neo-Confucian classics in the Qing Dynasty in particular his shorter treatises, namely *The Three-character Classic* and *Poem of the Five Sessions of the Moon*. The *Three-character Classic* adopts a more rigid structure in that each phrase consists of three Chinese characters only as shown in the parallel translation of the last chapter. Three-character Neo-Confucian classics may even have rhymed structure and help beginners to memorize the content quickly. While Liu Zhi's *Three-character Classic* serves as an elementary text of the very basic beliefs of Islam for beginners, his *Poem of the Five Sessions of the Moon* serves to introduce both beginners, Muslims in general and even Han literati to the basics of Sufi thought emphasizing a Sufi spirituality of the *dao*. Although each phrase of Liu Zhi's poem is not three-character, the number of each phrase is either three- or seven-character.[1] It has a freer style than three-character classic but still is structured. An example of Confucian classics will be introduced, namely Zhu Zi's maxims (1627–1699). It was commonly used in primary education for centuries and is accessible today on the World Wide Web. The purpose of introducing this maxims is to show that Liu Zhi's *Poem of the Five Sessions of the Moon* conforms to the popular literary style of education in eighteenth-century China.

Three-, five-, and seven-character literary forms are commonly used in Chinese education. Zhu Zi's maxims is known as *The Chinese Code of Success*.[2] Only the first few phrases in the beginning of this classic are translated and in parallel format.

---

1. The literary form is illustrated in the full-text translation in Appendix I.
2. Many versions are available on the internet. Our version is based on the one in 360doc.com website.
http://www.360doc.com/content/12/0423/11/956246_205841851.shtml

Figure 5.1: The Chinese Code of Success

Get up at dawn and sweep the courtyard, so that the house is clean inside and outside.	黎明即起，灑掃庭除，要內外整潔，(4,4,5)¹
Rest early at night. Check personally that the doors and windows are properly shut.	既昏便息，關鎖門戶，必親自檢點。(4,4,5)
When you eat, remember that food is the product of hard work.	一粥一飯，當思來處不易；(4,6)
When you put on clothes, keep in mind that materials do not come by easily.	半絲半縷，恆念物力維艱。(4,6)
One should repair the house before it rains and not start digging a well when he already feels thirsty.	宜未雨而綢繆，毋臨渴而掘井。(6,6)
Be thrifty in satisfying your own needs, but generous in hosting a reception.	自奉必須儉約，宴客切勿流連。(6,6)

This classic was not written by the well-known Neo-Confucian Zhu Xi in thirteenth-century China but rather by the seventeenth-century scholar Zhu Zi. This poem was extremely popular during the Qing dynasty.³ This classic emphasizes moral development and holistic family in the context of educating and managing families. The strength of using such a literary style is the ease of memorization because the characters are simple and their meanings are easily understood. Another reason for its popularity is that a few catchy phrases can be selected, enlarged by Chinese calligraphy and posted in public places. One can notice from the above parallel translation that while the literary structure is not the rigid three-character or seven-character, there is still a pattern of structure. The number of characters is illustrated above in brackets and can be seen as follows: 4,4,5 is followed by another set of 4,4,5 characters. One set is mirrored by another subsequent set of character. Other sets of number of characters in brackets above are self-explanatory. It should be noted that Liu Zhi's *Poem of the Five Sessions of the Moon* resembles the literary form of Zhu Zi's maxims, a more flexible form and yet still structured. Most likely, Liu Zhi wanted to imitate

3. Chan, *New Exploration*, 283.

the success of such a literary device and contextualized his teaching of Sufi spirituality in accordance with this popular and well known literary style.

The Poem of the Five Sessions of the Moon

Contextualization of Liu Zhi's Poem using Neo-Confucianism, Buddhism, and Daoism

Only Jin has briefly studied the poem and is able to note its eclectic content. He concludes that, since this poem has borrowed plenty of Confucian, Buddhist, Daoist terms, and ethical concepts, one should not underestimate the erudition of Liu Zhi and his understanding of Chinese contexts in his time.[4] The following table will highlight some of the eclectic terms of this poem and give some remarks on his eclecticism. These remarks and comments have not been noted by any scholars in Chinese and English.

Table 5.1: Remarks and Comments of The Poem of the Five Sessions of the Moon

Session of the Moon	Eclectic Terms	Remarks and Comments
First	1.0 Comprehend	1.0 The verb has Buddhist origin and means to understand after examination and research.[A]
	2.0 Supreme Honored One	2.0 The term was commonly used by the Nestorian Christians in the sixth to seventh-century China to describe the Christian Lord.[B]
	3.0 Great and heavenly mandate	3.0 Mandate means destiny or the command of God. It is a Confucian term and used in the *Doctrine of the Mean*.[C]
	4.0 Vital-energy, Yin-yang, Non- and Great Ultimate	4.0 These are traditional Confucian terms usually used to describe the Confucian version of creative transformation.[D]
	5.0 Happy excursion	5.0 The term comes from chapter 1 of a well-known Daoist philosopher Zhuang Zi's book (c. 369–ßc. 286).[E]

---

4. Jin, *Exploring Chinese Islam*, 298.

Liu Zhi's Sufi Spirituality in Conversation

Second	1.0 Suffering world	1.0 Literally, this Buddhist term means bitter sea. It describes that the sorrow of this life is boundless and binding to all humanity.[F]
	2.0 Meaningless encounter	A Buddhist term: it describes this life in itself as meaningless and without permanence.
	3.0 Other side of *dao*	A Buddhist term: one is to stride forward and reach the realm of self-awareness.[G]
	4.0 Mysterious gate	4.0 For the Daoist, it refers to a mysterious gate before an entrance. For the Buddhist, the original meaning is the gate for the rite of passage.[H]
Third	1.0 Priceless pearl; seafaring	1.0 Buddhist terms to describe the Buddhist way to liberation.
	2.0 Ninth heaven	2.0 Daoist term to describe the highest level of heaven where the Immortals reside.[I]
	3.0 Subtle medicine, golden tablet	3.0 Common Daoist medicinal terms: Daoists attempt to use medicines to cure humanity and restore the balance of humanity with nature.[J]
Fourth	1.0 Mythical moon lady	A very popular mythical figure in Chinese folklore: she resides in the moon
	2.0 The world	Literally, it means the world of dust and may mean the world that inflicts hard work. The word is used by both Buddhists and Daoists.
	3.0 Jade Residence	3.0 A common term in Chinese folklore: it describes the residence of immortal rulers and other spirits.[K]
	4.0 Great Void	4.0 Zhuang Zi interpreted the Great Void as the realm of solitary mystery. Illusion and voidness are also common Buddhist terms to designate the realms of the phenomenal and the real.[L]
	5.0 Three vehicles	5.0 Vehicle is a traditional term used by Buddhists to seek the way to permanence and liberation.[M]
Fifth	1.0 Essence of meaning	The term originates from Buddhism. Such comprehension can explain the root of mystery.[N]
	2.0 Highest heaven	2.0 A Daoist term: it describes the highest level of heaven.

A. The word "comprehension" has the sense of enlightenment which is a common Buddhist term. Fung, *Short History*, 429.

B. When the Nestorian missionaries from Syria first arrived in Xian in sixth- to seventh-century China, they contextualized the name of the Christian Lord into the 'Supreme Honoured One' or 'Heavenly Honoured One.' Li, *Study of the History of Nestorian Christianity*, 129, 132.

C. Murataet al., *Sage*, 61–64.

D. Ibid., 60.

E. Fung, *Short History*, 168.

F. The technical term of Buddhist's understanding of suffering is *dukkha*. It also has the meaning of impermanence and imperfection. Irons, *Encyclopaedia*, 168.

G. Fung, *Short History*, 413.

H. http://www.zdic.net/c/4/10a/288256.htm/.

I. http://www.zdic.net/c/d/148/320750.htm/.

J. Kirkland, *Taoism*, 85.

K. http://www.zdic.net/c/9/13c/303635.htm/.

L. Fung, *History*, 239.

M. In China, the more popular Buddhist texts belong to the Mahayana (Greater Vehicle) Buddhism. Texts of the Hinayana (Lesser Vehicle) Buddhism are not common at all. Fung, *Short History*, 399. Fung, *History*, 347. A *vehicle* is like station, which is a term frequently used in Sufi discourse.

N. Fung, *Short History*, 403; Fung, *History*, 266.

The above table shows only some of the Buddhist, Daoist, and Confucian terms. Jin gives over forty five such terms. Several initial comments may be made on the eclectic character of this poem. Firstly, while the first and second parts of Liu Zhi's trilogy mainly employ Confucian terms to explain Islamic sciences and rites, the poem is definitely more eclectic and uses the Three Teachings of Chinese culture, namely Confucianism, Daoism, and Buddhism, to convey the meaning of Sufi thought.

Secondly, the first session of the poem still retains the major Confucian terms that Liu Zhi consistently used to explain the various grades of disclosure, namely the Ultimate, yin-yang, mandate, and others. However, the poem uses plentiful Daoist and Buddhist terms to describe the Sufi path, namely from the second to the fourth sessions of the moon. Liu Zhi contextualized his Sufi thoughts into Chinese thoughts by using all resources in the Three Teachings.

Thirdly, Buddhists conceptualize the liberation from the meaningless world as a seafaring journey. Their goal is the realm of permanence and escape from the ever-continuing wheel of life and death. While Liu Zhi disagreed with the Buddhist's negative view of the present world, he agreed with their search for enlightenment. He portrayed the Sufi path as a way towards enlightenment or union with the Real. Daoists search for harmony between humanity and nature. Their goal is the exalted human existence.

While Liu Zhi disagreed with the Daoist's abstract view of exalted human existence, he agreed with their worldview which was hierarchical and also comprised a belief in life after death. He selectively chose concepts in these teachings and used them for his own interpretation of Sufi thoughts.

Finally, the goal of the eclectic nature of this poem is that the readers can understand the basic message of Sufi thought. Simply put, Liu Zhi encouraged what he saw as orthodoxy, namely the right understanding of Islam. Theoretical Sufism as described in Jami's works and its corresponding Chinese translated works is not easily accessible and it is difficult for Muslims in general to understand it. This poem is a short Sufi work and readily available in the mosque and scripture hall. It uses very familiar Chinese eclectic terms and thus easy for readers to memorize. Liu Zhi was not afraid to employ various terms of the Three Teachings. Thus, Liu Zhi's contextualization is in active dialogue with his Chinese contexts and he regarded the Three Teachings as his conversation partners.

The Chiastic Structure of the Poem

The full English translation of the poem is provided in Appendix I.[5] The translation is in a parallel format to illustrate the literary form which shows a clear chiastic structure which has not been noted in any previous scholarship. Jin has discussed the poem briefly[6] but few Chinese and English scholars analyse it in depth. The first session (1.1, 1.2 and 1.3) of the moon is in clear contrast with the final session ('1.3, '1.2 and '1.1). The contrast is between the creative transformation of the Real Being and the return to the Real Being. The second session expounds the need to seek for the way, i.e. *dao*, and in contrast the fourth session emphasizes various methods of Islamic endeavor. The key to the poem is the mid-third session. Sufism begins with the heart and go on to manifest itself in action resembling a seafaring journey with the goal of homebound journey to the Real Being.

  1.1 Undifferential Being

  1.2 Ultimate Nonbeing and Great Ultimate

  1.3 Divine predestination and human religious endeavor

    2.1 The meaninglessness of life and daily activities

---

5. There are many versions with minor variations available in books and on the World Wide Web. Our version is based on Jin's work. See Jin, *Exploring Chinese Islam*, 323–24.

6. Ibid., 286–98.

2.2 The need for discipline and seeking of *dao*

2.3 The need for the Sufi master to direct the right way

3.1 The *dao* in the heart-mind

3.2 *The Sufi Seafaring Journey*

'3.1 Vision experience and life healing

'2.3 The possibility of heavenly and earthly union

'2.2 The need to eliminate any turbid substance

'2.1 The need for three vehicles and endeavors to achieve real humanity

'1.3 The eschatological ending by union of both divine and human

'1.2 Descent, ascent and the union of the arcs

'1.1 Return to the non-differential Real Being

Some preliminary observations can be made. In the first session of the moon, Liu Zhi expounded his concept of creative transformation. This provides the theological basis for humankind to strive for religious endeavor. He briefly discussed the characteristics of the Real Being and how it transformed the world of principle, the innate heaven, the world of guise/image, and the disclosure in the acquired heaven. In the state of non-differentiation, the Real Being is hidden and tranquil. There is no substance, function and act. Yet the Real Being is truly eternal, unlimited without beginning or end. The manifestation began when the Real Being began to differentiate. The use of Neo-Confucianized terms is clearly demonstrated by employing terms like the Great Ultimate, Ultimate Nonbeing, and the relationship between the two concepts. Such a familiar Chinese concept has the power of contextualizing the transformation using Neo-Confucian terms. Liu Zhi equated the Real Being with the Neo-Confucian concept of Ultimate Nonbeing. The first session ends forcibly with the need to pursue religious endeavor. Eventually, the ensuing eschatological event of judgment and reward will be the end.

The second session takes up the preceding argument of the last session by emphasizing the reality that one should take seriously the Sufi endeavor. For Liu Zhi, such an endeavor should be undertaken by every Muslim. The first part of this session explains the meaninglessness of the present life. The mid part emphasizes the importance of the *dao*. The end brings out the importance of the Sufi master for guidance in seeking the right endeavor.

In the third session, Liu Zhi moves from the external ritual observance to internal purity in pursuit of religious endeavor. At the ending of this session, Liu Zhi emphasized that the *dao* dwells inside humanity. This is also the part where Liu Zhi employed the Sufi wisdom. As illustrated from the chiastic diagram above, the central theme is clearly the seeking of the pearl treasure, starting off the seafaring journey, and ending with the return by ascent to the homeland.

The fourth session begins with a very popular Chinese moon lady myth but still continues to emphasize the Sufi pursuit, both external rituals and inner spirituality. This is a genuine contextualization of Islamic wisdom with Chinese folklore, not just a mere intellectual Neo-Confucianism in that the moon legend story has been deeply rooted in the Chinese seasonal mid-Autumn festival celebration. The fourth session has literary parallels with the second session in that it pours contempt on all the meaninglessness of this present life.

The fifth session begins with Islam's eschatological return emphasizing the concept of return to the Real Being. The theme of descent and ascent is like the descending and ascending arc. While the creative transformation begins with the Real Being, the return is by both divine and human and forms the eventual enclosed whole circle.

Comments and Analysis of the Poem

Firstly, it should be noted that Liu Zhi's *Poem of the Five Sessions of the Moon* is extremely popular even today not only within the Xi Dao Tang Scripture Hall Education System of the Hui Muslims in Northwest China but also in other branches of Chinese Islam. An abstract of the poem in two literary parallel stanzas may sometimes be hung on the side wall at the mosque entrance gate. Sometimes, the poem is sculptured onto a stele or hard wood e.g. in Yunnan province. In the province of Gansu, it is found that the whole poem was hung on a wall in a Hui community of Ningxia. Muslim children memorize the poem which they have learnt from their parents by oral tradition even though children may not know the meaning of the poem. Islamic themes are progressively developed from the first session to the end, i.e. the nature of Real Being, creative transformation, role of the heart, endeavor, seeking, revealing *dao*, teaching *dao*, sapientia in terms of upward path, nurturing inner nature, bearing fruits, and end time return to the Real Being. All these themes are expounded in greater depth in Liu Zhi's trilogy. While the prophet Muhammad is not explicitly mentioned, there is particular emphasis on seeking a Sufi master and being guided by him forward onto the mystical path.

Secondly, the literary format of the poem closely resembles the late Ming and early Qing Neo-Confucian or Daoist poem. The poem does not fall into the rigid literary and rhyming requirement of Neo-Confucian poetry which has strict literary structure and rhyming rules. Nevertheless, the literary form of Liu Zhi's poem is carefully crafted and tightly arranged. The usual format of Neo-Confucian poems has phrases consisting of three, five, six and seven characters as illustrated in the beginning of this chapter. However, the first, second and third stanza of each session of the moon is structured tightly. The following parallel translation of the first stanza of the first session of the moon is provided below to illustrate the literary form.

Figure 5.2: Translation of the First Stanza of the First Session of the Moon

In the beginning of the first session, the moon begins to appear. Comprehend the Real Ruler that has no form or image.	一更初,月正生,參悟真宰無影形。 (3, 3, 7)
Its subtlety is not known and is non-designated. It has no boundary and exists as the real reality.	妙難喻,無所稱。不落方所乃實真。 (3, 3, 7)
It is unique without beginning and end; the Supreme Honored one without any partner.	永活亙古無終始,獨一無偶唯至尊, (7, 7)
Creative transformation begins. Principle and image are completed. The great mandate is installed and there is an open door to other forms of creation.	開造化,理象成,大命立開眾妙門。 (3, 3, 7)

Liu Zhi's poem consists of a number of characters in the sequence of 3, 3, 7; 3, 3, 7; 7, 7; 3, 3, 7 in each of the three stanzas of each session. This is illustrated in numbers within the bracket in the table above. Each stanza of the poem has eleven phrases and has exactly a total of fifty-three Chinese characters; six phrases of three-character and five phrases of seven-character. This sequence of the number of Chinese characters is repeated for the rest of the whole poem, namely fifteen such stanzas (three stanzas in each session and five sessions in all). Undoubtedly, the poem can be sung in different catchy musical tunes for easy memorization. Phrases and sentences are short. The meaning of each Chinese character is concise but when putting three- or seven-characters together, the phrase has profound linguistic versatility. The three-character phrases are catchy and can be memorized easily. The seven-character phrases can convey more difficult theological concepts and expound metaphysical thoughts. It is due to Liu Zhi's mastery of literary devices that many preface writers of his works praised the artistic and literary achievement of Liu Zhi's writings.

Thirdly, Liu Zhi contextualized Sufi ideas in terms of three vehicles.[7] A vehicle bears a load. With the vehicle, the seekers can carry all manner of standards and morals. Thus, a vehicle embodies the law of rituals. According to Liu Zhi, the first vehicle is the ritual, second is the path and third is truth.

The first is called the vehicle of ritual (*shari'a*). It consists of both the way of heaven and the way of humanity. It is the regulation of every matter and act. This is the means of adopting the law for the one who is diligent in cultivating virtue and who respects his own vocation.[8] The vehicle of path (*tariqa*) is the second vehicle. It is the stage of the law that fully contains the universal principle of humankind and of all phenomena, as well as the completion of human potentiality in accordance with heaven. This is the means of adopting the law for the one who probes into principle and completes nature.[9] The third vehicle is the truth or principle (*haqiqa*). It fully contains the concept of "no-self" and "no-thing." It contains the subtle words and the symbolic language of the total integration of humankind and heaven. This is the means of adopting the law for the one who restrains his ego and fulfils the truth.[10] These three vehicles are under the totality of the law of vehicles which transcends even the highest of the spiritual levels. The law of three vehicles is the method of disciplining selfish desires. Yet, above the three vehicles there is the single law of a supreme, transcendent vehicle, by which heaven and man may be transformed and merged. At this level names and appearances are dissolved. This state cannot be communicated by spoken or written language. Only the individual himself can fully understand it, and

---

7. Jin asserts that the concept of three vehicles is often expressed in terms of boat, sea and treasure or seed, tree and fruit. Jin, *Sufism in China*, 167.
8. Frankel, "Liu's Journey," 180.
9. Ibid., 182.
10. Ibid., 183.

then only experientially.[11] This single law is used by Liu Zhi as a supreme vehicle, rather than the *shari'a* used by the Sufi master.

Frankel notes that Liu Zhi's law of three vehicles bears resemblance to Sufi discourse. "The hierarchy of spiritual progress as described in Sufi literature is generally divided into three ascending, interdependent levels."[12] As Jin puts it, the three vehicle law is often compared to different analogies e.g. firstly the analogy of an orange consisting of the peel, orange slice, and the seed; secondly the analogy of a tree consisting of the seed, the stem, and fruit; lastly the analogy of an egg consisting of the egg shell, egg white, and the yoke. Other scholars classify the three vehicles as the boat, sea, and the pearl treasure. The purpose of boarding the boat is to launch it into the sea. It symbolizes that the search involves hard work and strenuous striving with the need for courage in taking on risks.[13]

In Jin's study of Sufism in China, he avers that Islamic scholars in sixteenth to nineteenth-century China often affirmed three vehicles, occasionally even four vehicles.[14] These Muslim literati, including Liu Zhi, expounded the three vehicles idea in their own particular ways or expressions. The difference among them was minor and might be due to their respective sources or schools of Sufism. They agreed that the concept of three vehicles was an overarching principle of Sufism. Jin argues that "from low level striving for higher level, the ultimate purpose [of seekers] is to seek the pearl, the manifestation of real light and obtain what the holy sage has obtained."[15] While Liu Zhi's trilogy discusses generally Sufi thought and spirituality using the concept of the unity of existence and return to the Real Ruler through rules and proprieties of Islam, *The Poem of the Five Sessions of the Moon* clearly gives more emphasis on the characteristics of the Sufi way.

Fourthly, Liu Zhi's work emphasizes practical knowledge. Islamic wisdom is not so much about mystical paths. Rather, wisdom concerns daily Islamic living as a true Muslim. As a result of his editing work, Liu Zhi was able to present Chinese Islam in a way that was more easily acceptable by both the Qing ruling elites and the ubiquitous Hans. Simultaneously, he also convinced his own Hui Muslims that Islamic faith was creditable. On the one hand, Chinese Muslim literati like Wang Daiyu and Liu Zhi, reformed the Islamic tradition by transmitting texts into Chinese and that facilitated the propagation of the Islamic faith. On the other hand, Muslim

11. Ibid., 184.
12. Ibid., 179.
13. Jin, *Mysticism of Sufism*, 78–79.
14. Jin, *Sufism in China*, 165.
15. Ibid., 167.

literati who were competent in Neo-Confucianism also might excel in the Qing examination system. By directly competing with other Chinese literati and excelling, they could earn official posts in the government. Thus, Chinese Muslims could raise their social status, join the status quo, and simultaneously increase the acceptability of Islam in China. For survival and propagation, it was desirable for Liu Zhi and others to be both Muslims and Neo-Confucian literati.

Fifthly, an important and specific point of contextualization should be noted with reference to the key concept of seafaring journey in the chiastic structure of Liu Zhi's poem. Liu Zhi made modification and revision of a Buddhist concept. The middle stanza of the third session of the moon is translated as follows:

> In the mid third session, the moon is moving. A treasure pearl hides at the seabed. Stride quickly towards the journey and set sail for the sea. The turbulent waves keep coming as if you are being sucked into a dragon's den. You are tormented by limitless sufferings. Yet, the reward is to reap the priceless treasure pearl. Be alert and stand firm to defend. Don't fool around. For wealth and honor, seek to return back to the home country.[16]

The seafaring journey and attempt to land on the other shore are a common theme in Chinese Buddhism. The Buddhist way of living is to realize the meaningless value of materials in the transient world, practice regular meditation, cumulate merits of good work, and secure eternal permanence in this life or afterlife. This way of contemplative and non-competitive living is described figuratively as a seafaring journey. Landing on the other shore is described as the attachment to the realm of permanence. The Buddhist teacher Dao Sheng (c. 374–c. 434) in fifth-century China believed that sudden enlightenment and reaching the other shore of the sea journey were possible in this life. Fung explains Dao's teaching.

> The Buddhists use the metaphor of "reaching the other shore" to express the idea of achieving *Nirvana*. Tao-sheng [Dao Sheng] says: "As to reaching the other shore, if one reaches it, one is not reaching the other shore. Both not-reaching and not-not-reaching are really reaching. This shore here means birth and death; the other shore means *Nirvana*" . . . The world of Buddha is simply here in this present world.[17]

---

16. See Appendix I.
17. Fung, *Short History*, 412–14.

Dao's work asserts that humans have Buddha-nature originally within them. By learning and practicing the Buddhist way of living, humans can see their own Buddha-nature. This seeing may happen suddenly and is called sudden enlightenment. Alternatively, Buddhists may also have gradual enlightenment. That is, Buddhists' accumulation of learning serves as the proper way to free the mind from human ignorance of their Buddha-nature. So, Dao supported both sudden and gradual enlightenment.[18]

Murata notes a *hadith* of Hidden Treasure. She says that God replied to King David: "I was a Hidden Treasure, and I love to be recognized (*ahbabtu an u'raf*); so I created the creatures that I might be recognized."[19] In Liu Zhi's poem, the Sufi path is to seek the hidden treasure by a seafaring journey. The treasure is a priceless pearl and lays hidden in the deep seabed.

By comparing the teaching of the seafaring journey, hidden treasure, and the other shore as they appear in the Buddhist and Islamic exhortation to endeavors, one can note the similarities and differences. Both of them emphasize the importance of permanence. For Dao Sheng, liberation is the ultimate escape of the wheel of death and birth, namely *Nirvana*. For Liu Zhi, the final goal is the union with the Real Ruler. Both of them emphasize that humans have inner ability to reach the goal. For Dao, it is the inherent Buddha-nature in humans that enables them to reach the goal. For Liu Zhi, when God created the first human, he taught him all the names of God.[20] This means that the understanding of the unity of existence is innate to human nature.[21] Liu Zhi said at the end of second session that the *dao* included heaven and earth but humans also included the *dao*. Both of them emphasize reaching a goal. For Dao Sheng, the goal is to reach the other shore or to be enlightened. For Liu Zhi, the goal is to reach the treasure and return home.

The above specific example may give some clues to Liu Zhi's method of contextualization. He adopted this concept of seafaring journey from the Buddhist's idea of reaching the other shore. He revised and presented it as seeking a hidden treasure in the deep seabed. He further modified the Buddha-nature in Buddhists and the seafaring journey as a Sufi path with the goal of the self-realization and return to the Real. Liu Zhi adopted the similarities but rejected the differences between Islam and Buddhism. His contextualization is carried out skillfully by using the language of the Chinese contexts and communicating a Sufi concept.

18. Fung, *History*, 274–75.
19. Murata et al., *Sage*, 44.
20. Ibid., 45.
21. Ibid., 42.

A question may be asked. Should Liu Zhi adopt the Confucian spiritual cultivation rather than the Buddhist enlightenment to explain the Sufi path in his poem? This is a valid question as Liu Zhi contextualized Islamic rites primarily in Confucian terms in his *Rules and Proprieties of Islam*. Two possible answers may be given. Firstly, the linguistic power of a poem is to communicate powerfully a message with various images. The description of the roaring sea, the deep seabed, the hidden treasure, and a light ship in this part of the poem can add to the drama of the seafaring journey or the Sufi path. Liu Zhi's adoption of the Buddhist's concept may be due to the literary device of the poem. The second answer may even be more plausible. The concern of the poem is to teach the Sufi path and it is a poem of Sufism. Through the three vehicles (in the third stanza of the fourth session) or the rites of Islam, the Sufi can achieve self-realization. This is orthopraxis which is not merely intellectual or legalistic practice alone. This is right doing in the Sufi way. Liu Zhi adopted the Buddhist imagery of journey because it explained the Sufi way better than the Confucian spiritual cultivation. Fung explained the difference in spiritual practice between Buddhism and Neo-Confucianism: "while the Buddha must promote his spiritual cultivation outside of society and the human world, the Sage must do so within these bonds."[22] Basically, the goal of self-realization of Sufis is not sagehood that emphasizes harmonious relationship within human society and between humanity and the world. The goal of self-realization is union with the Real Ruler. Thus, the Sufi goal is similar to Buddhism in that it primarily focuses on the Sufis themselves and their realizations. This may explain another aspect of Liu Zhi's contextualization. He adopted a Chinese context that was most appropriate for his poem. While Liu Zhi explained Islamic concepts primarily in Confucian terms, he was erudite enough to choose other more appropriate Buddhist concept to interpret the Sufi path.

Finally, while the focus of the poem is on the Sufi path, the general teaching of Sufism is consistent with Liu Zhi's teaching in *The Nature and Principle in Islam* and *Rules and Proprieties of Islam*. From a general perspective, it is clear that the account of the first session of the moon is a very concise summary of various grades of disclosure in *The Nature and Principle in Islam*. The appearance of the perfect human being or ultimate human is the final grade of disclosure. However, the name of the prophet Muhammad is not mentioned but he is called the human ultimate or the perfect man.[23] While the second to fourth sessions primarily discuss the Sufi way in eclectic terms, the role of the heart in self-cultivation is once again emphasized

22. Fung, *Short History*, 444.
23. Little, "Perfect Man," 151–63.

in both the second and fourth session. So, mere intellectual understanding is not sufficient for the Sufi path. Orthopraxis begins with the heart. The fourth session highlights obedience to the Ruler and rites of Islam expressed as the three vehicles in *The Rules and Proprieties of Islam*. The fifth session shows explicit eighteenth-century Chinese Sufism as it discusses the arc of descent and ascent, return to the root suchness and differentiation becoming non-differentiation. Simply put, the basic teachings in Liu Zhi's major works are summarized in his poem.

The existence of the world is not merely an accident but it exists because of divine self-disclosure. Human existence without recognizing the Real Being is meaningless and futile. A seeker's path begins with a sincere and obedient heart. This seeker needs to seek guidance by the Sufi master and he starts with the five pillars of Islam, and other Islamic proprieties. The journey has the explicit characteristics of a Sufi path. The seeker practices good works and seeks control of his inner self, emphasizing both exoteric and esoteric aspects of Islam. He should empty himself and arrive at union with the Real Ruler. The above poem succinctly summarizes Liu Zhi's Sufi thought.

It is too simplistic and without sufficient evidence for anyone to assert that Liu Zhi's Islam is sinicized or Confucianized just by a mere observation of the plentiful use of Confucian, Daoist, and Buddhist terms in this poem or in any of Liu Zhi's works. Based on the analysis above, it is more appropriate to say that the framework of this poem has been demonstrated to be truly compliant with to Sufi thoughts and the eclectic terms are chosen carefully and selectively as interpretation tool. As a skillful translator and an erudite cultural agent, Liu Zhi was able to contextualize Sufi ideas in Chinese terms. The poem represents a simplified and poetic version of the basic message in Liu Zhi's *Nature and Principle in Islam* and *Rules and Proprieties of Islam*.

LIU ZHI'S THEOLOGICAL CONVERSATION WITH NEO-CONFUCIAN SAGEHOOD: *THE TRUE RECORD OF THE UTMOST SAGE OF ISLAM*

Examination of Liu Zhi's *True Record of the Utmost Sage of Islam*

This section will argue that Liu Zhi's *True Record of the Utmost Sage of Islam* is in accordance with the concept of the perfect man in the Ibn 'Arabi tradition. While Liu Zhi attempted to depict Muhammad as a contextualized Chinese sage for his Muslim readers, he clearly presented to them a unique sage, very different from all the holy sages in the Confucian tradition. Some sections of this work will be translated. An examination of his theological conversation with the Neo-Confucian sagehood will also be presented.

Isaac Mason translated and edited *The True Record of the Utmost Sage of Islam* nearly a century ago.[24] Both Murata and Leslie have briefly examined this work.[25] Liu Zhi's work is most probably based on the fourteenth-century Persian work, *Tarjama-yi mawlud-i Mustafa* by 'Afif ibn Muhammad Kaziruni. However, Liu Zhi "also condenses the text drastically and adds material from other sources."[26] Mason commented on Liu Zhi's work.

> It puts the best construction on all the acts of the Prophet, and credits him with virtues and powers which he himself never claimed, yet adds nothing heroic or noble to a character which has come down to us as a strange mixture of sincerity and inconsistency; of benevolence and cruelty; of self-restraint and self-indulgence; of faith, doubt, and superstition: these are some of the qualities associated with Mohammad, as found in this and other records of the Prophet of Arabia.[27]

Samuel M. Zwemer who wrote a foreword in Mason's book, asserted that from the critical standpoint, Liu Zhi's work was of little value because he had added to the story of Muhammad's life in order to whitewash it.[28] Murata comments that "Liu Chih [Zhi] retells many of the stories in 'Afif's work and follows the same general order . . . he freely adapts the stories to fit the needs of Chinese narrative; among other things, his version places a far greater stress on the supernatural elements than does the original."[29] However, Liu Zhi's contextualization of the life of Muhammad is carried out with great care. Zwemer was mistaken in saying that this work was of little value as it accorded with the Ibn 'Arabi tradition of the idea of the perfect man. Such work may contribute to a better understanding of the Ibn 'Arabi tradition in eighteenth-century China and the model of contextualization undertaken by Liu Zhi.

24. Liu Zhi's work has 20 chapters, but Mason only translated 18 chapters and deleted the rest because he said that sufficient account had been given of the life of the prophet Muhammad to give the English readers a fair view of Muhammad as known to Muslims in China. Mason, *Arabian Prophet*, 264. The chapter division in Mason's translation and that in Liu Zhi's differs slightly, but the main bulk concerns the life stories of Muhammad.
25. Murata, *Gleams*, 34.
26. Ibid., 34.
27. Mason, *Arabian Prophet*, 264.
28. Ibid., ii.
29. Murata, *Gleams*, 34.

Murata affirms the significance of the unique nature of Muhammad (nature of continuity, 繼性) in the works of Liu Zhi. Firstly, the concept of the perfect man in the Ibn 'Arabi tradition forms the background of Liu Zhi's understanding of humanity in his *Nature and Principle in Islam*.[30] In chapter 4 of *The Nature and Principle in Islam*, Liu Zhi used the term human ultimate. In Neo-Confucian thought, the human ultimate is one who unites with the Great Ultimate.[31]

Secondly, Murata also distinguishes between Muhammadan Reality and Spirit. What is Muhammadan Reality? Murata says that "In Ibn 'Arabi's terms, the Muhammadan Reality is the Logos as uncreated root of all things, embracing and comprising all the divine names and attributes in an undifferentiated, unitary manner; it is a prototype of the whole cosmos in divinis, and is no different from God himself."[32] What is the Muhammadan Spirit? The Muhammadan Reality gives rise to the Muhammadan Spirit.[33] The Muhammadan Spirit is the mandate which is neither God nor creation and stands between Real Being and absolute nothingness.[34] It also brings God and others together.[35] God began the process of creation by the Muhammadan Spirit which Liu Zhi called the nature of the Utmost Sage.[36] Thus, the significance of the person of Muhammad is his nature which is known as the nature of the continuity (繼性) of the Utmost Sage. This nature is related not directly to the Muhammadan Reality but the Muhammadan Spirit. This Spirit is often known as the mandate (literally, destiny) which is a common Confucian term.

Liu Zhi followed the tradition of Ibn 'Arabi through Razi's work and asserted the unique role of the nature of the continuity of Muhammad both in the innate and the acquired heaven. Liu Zhi's depiction of the life and record of Muhammad in his *True Record of the Utmost Sage of Islam* was consistent with his earlier teaching of the human ultimate in *The Nature and*

---

30. Murata, "Liu Zhi's View," 17.

31. Murata, "Unity of Cosmogony," 12. See also the comment by Tu Weiming in Murata's *Sage*, 613.

32. Murata et al., *Sage*, 216.

33. Ibid., 262. Murata says that "from the viewpoint of the Descending Arc, the seed of all principles and vital energies—the Muhammadan Reality or Logos—gives rise to the Ascribed or Muhammadan Spirit (Mandate), which embraces all natures and principles." The Mandate has two aspects, namely ontological and moral. "The Mandate is the means whereby Heaven bestows nature, and nature gives us our humanity . . . we need to cultivate our souls, polish our hearts, and clarify our root substance. The only way to do so is to follow the teaching of the sages." Ibid., 63.

34. Ibid., 216.

35. Ibid., 272.

36. Ibid., 58, 207.

Principle in Islam and *Rules and Proprieties of Islam* but in simpler narratives and short discourses.

The True Record of the Utmost Sage of Islam is divided into twenty chapters with chapter 1 as the introduction. This introduction is important as it highlights the unique importance of Muhammad in Islam. It provides explanations of his uniqueness, exaltation and the unique role of cosmic return to the Real. Most of his teachings on Muhammad have been covered in his earlier works but this introduction gives the reader a concise and simple summary of Liu Zhi's understanding of Muhammad with respect to the proprieties of Islam and the return to the Real. From chapter 3, Liu Zhi recorded the life history of Muhammad chronologically from birth to death at the end of chapter 15. The last four chapters are appendixes which Liu Zhi himself added. Firstly, selected sections of the introductory chapter 1 and 2 are translated to provide an insight into Liu Zhi's teachings on Muhammad. Secondly, a section of chapter 7 is translated about the beginning of Islam in China. Finally, a selected section chapter 18 will be translated and it shows clearly Liu Zhi's contextualization of Muhammad's teachings in Neo-Confucian terms.

In the introductory chapter, Liu Zhi introduced the foundational concept of the prophet Muhammad, emphasizing his exceptional characteristics. The translations below affirm the superiority of the prophet Muhammad from the land of Arabia and he is very different from any Chinese sage.

The introductory chapter gives an account of the honor and nobility of Muhammad.

> Humankind is honorable in heaven and earth. Among humankind, there are sages, worthies, wise and foolish. The sages are most honorable. Among sages, they are further classified into ordinary, ambassador, great and utmost. The Utmost Sage is the highest. Muhammad is the highest sage of all time and of all places and is called the Utmost Sage . . .
>
> At the beginning of creative transformation, humanity is classed by the principle (*li*) into nine groups. The Utmost Sage is the highest. After taking the form, humans take on nine groups of image. The image of the Utmost Sage is perfect. His principle is perfect . . .
>
> The principle and image of all things are to be found within the compass of the nine heavens and the seven earths. The heavens are superior to the earths and the *Aershi* surpasses the heavens. The nature and principle of the Utmost Sage were situated at

the *Aershi*.³⁷ Therefore, he is more honorable than any in all the heavens and the earths . . .

The ancestors of the Utmost Sage, going right back to Adam, never worshipped idols or prayed to heathen gods. This virtue of the ancestors nourished and cultivated generation after generation, culminating in the Utmost Sage. He is the most honorable in accumulated virtue.³⁸

Muhammad is also described to have existence in both the innate heaven and the acquired heaven.

From the time of the ancients, there have been many sages. Muhammad is the Utmost Sage. It is so called because he has all required virtues. His transformation is thorough. Through his whole body, the Real Ruler emanates to become the great function . . . the Spirit of the Utmost Sage existed before the heaven and the earth.³⁹ He is the fruit of all sages. While the heaven and earth are big, they are nurtured by the Utmost Sage. The spirits of ten thousand sages are under his shadow and they have life from him. Although he is the descendent of Adam with respect to form, his spirit is really before Adam. His teaching embraces ten thousand teachings. His rule collects and completes ten thousand rules. His way excels ten thousand ways and is upright, illuminates like the sun and moon, as long-lasting as the heaven and earth . . . With regard to his teaching, it has been attested by all later generations to be enduring. Its principle (*li* 理) is clear; meaning is articulate; literary artistry is excellent and above other literature. These prove that the Ruler reveals the sacred texts. Those who are obedient to the teaching, they are not tempted away by any riches and fame. Their ways are not blocked and this truth is proved by all who obey the way.⁴⁰

---

37. Murata avers that *Aershi* derives from the Arabic '*arsh*' which means the throne of God in Qur'an 20:5. Murata argues that Liu Zhi understood *Aershi* as the nature of the Utmost Sage. Alternatively, the term *Aershi* means the Ascribed Spirit blown into Adam, the Mandate. Murata et al., *Sage*, 58–59.

38. Appendix II.

39. The Muhammadan Spirit is interpreted as the Mandate which is a common Confucian term. Liu Zhi affirmed the spirit of the prophet Muhammad existed before heaven and earth. In this respect, the Utmost Sage is totally different from the Chinese sages. In the case of Razi in his *Path*, God began the process of creation by firstly creating the Muhammadan Spirit. Murata et al., *Sage*, 58–59.

40. Appendix II.

In chapter 2, Muhammad is described as the integrator of creative transformation from the beginning to the end.

> Transformation begins in the innate heaven, initiated by the great mandate. The great mandate is the act of all true principle (*li*). From the great mandate, there is the nature of continuity which is the root suchness of the Utmost Sage.[41] All other natures of the sages derive from him, including the nature of worthies. From the nature of worthies, all other natures like the ignorant . . . This is called exhausting the nature and principle and getting to the mandate. This is known as the descent and ascent of the great transformation. Likewise, this is also the way of humanity in the descent and ascent. Since the beginning of humankind, only the person Muhammad can achieve the ascent. He embraces the whole transformation from the beginning to the end. Thus, all return can benefit with Muhammad as the goal of return . . .
>
> Why Muhammad is called the Utmost Sage? How could the Utmost Sage include the great transformation? The great transformation stops at the Utmost Sage but this is not the end. The Utmost Sage continues the transformation to its completion. All individual transformation has its own aspect and is one-sided but the Utmost Sage's transformation covers all aspects. Thus, he can continue the work of the Real Ruler in the great transformation. He returns the transformation to the Real Ruler. He is the man from heaven and from the earth to heaven. He becomes the axis of transformation. Anyone who is not led by the sage's transformation, he will go astray and deviate from the way. He is lost from the real way.[42]

The above translations clearly demonstrate the superb honor, nobility, and existence of Muhammad. Above all, he is the axis of creative transformation and serves as the mediator between the heaven and earth.

In chapter 7, Liu Zhi recorded the story of first messenger sent by the prophet Muhammad to China.[43] This story has been intensely studied by both scholars in the West and some scholars in China.

> In the first year of the Prophethood of Muhammad, there was seen in the sky a strange star, the Chinese emperor Su Wei Ti

---

41. Root suchness can be paraphrased as "without beginning and already in existence." It can mean the root substance.

42. Appendix II.

43. Depending on edition and version of *The True Record of the Utmost Sage of Islam*, this story might be recorded in chapter 6.

> commanded his astronomer to tell him the meaning. He said, 'there would be an extraordinary person appearing in the West.' The emperor sent an envoy to investigate . . .
>
> The prophet sent his uncle Sa'ad ibn Abi Waqqas and three others to go with the envoy to China . . .
>
> The emperor Wen Ti hung up the portrait of the prophet and worshipped it, and when he arose, the scroll was there but the picture had vanished . . . The disappearance of the picture was due to the wonderful influence of the prophet. The emperor, alarmed, said, "It must really be that he is the Pure Emperor and the True Prince." . . .[44]
>
> The account of the entry of the religion . . . is given in detail in several Chinese histories, so it can be proved. The story of the worshipping of the portrait is not recorded in the histories; but it has been handed down by tradition, and may be seen recorded on stone tablets, so must not be rejected.[45]

The historicity and accuracy of Liu Zhi's record has been extensively debated and the consensus of opinion amongst contemporary scholars agrees that Liu Zhi's record above is not accurate. However, it seems that Liu Zhi does not intentionally falsify the record. Scholars in the West and China have given different interpretations according to their perspectives. From the perspective of Liu Zhi's contextualization, it may be enlightened to analyse this story in the light of this whole work. This will be done in the next section of analysis. Another interesting chapter from the perspective of contextualization is chapter 18.

Liu Zhi's *True Record of the Utmost Sage of Islam* has a chapter or really an appendix, namely the chapter 18, on Muhammad's deeds and teachings. This appendix was added by Liu Zhi himself to make this work more complete. Not only does it record the life history of Muhammad, but also his deeds and words are recorded in this additional chapter. This chapter offers thirty five concise discourses and includes demeanor, virtue, learning, bathing, worship, remembrance of the Lord, fasting, alms tax, pilgrimage, speech, moving and resting, father and mother, progeny, marriage, husband and wife, brothers, slaves and servants, interacting with people, dealing with things, banquets, dealing with disciples, making friends, harmonizing with neighbors, arts and career, pleading, travel, negotiation, healing, divination, interpreting dreams, dwelling, clothing, eating and drinking, and visiting

---

44. Mason, *Arabian Prophet*, 94.
45. Appendix *II*.

the sick.⁴⁶ One example of discourses deals with learning and it is a very common and important Neo-Confucian theme.

> Knowledge refers to the knowledge of the Real Ruler. One who seeks is not an ignorant and a seeker begins to learn. Seeking is indeed the beginning of learning. It is not shameful for a seeker to ask questions and a teacher should not withhold answers. It says, 'regardless of age or social class, anyone who can give benefit to learning is my teacher.' Day and night, ask the Lord to give you beneficial learning and avoid unhealthy habits. One rule of caution for the learner, it says, 'if one is close to learners, then one learns. If one works with greedy people, one is lost. Do not take in any unhealthy learning.' Befriend literati and honorable people. Do not let selfish desire blind you. Do not be poisoned by heresy . . .
>
> Myriad things are established in sincerity. Make your heart steady, your will upright. Then, things turn out pleasantly. It says, 'teaching is to clarify the way and for the service of the Lord. The way is manifested by learners' humility and carefulness. The principle of things is important as it can distinguish between understanding and misunderstanding. Do not give up even if you cannot understand just one principle. . . If you are diligent to learn Islam, you can broaden the horizon of benevolence and righteousness . . .⁴⁷

Comments and Analysis

Several comments on Liu Zhi's contextualization of the prophet Muhammad as the Utmost Sage in this work should be noted. Unlike other scholars who examine a few sections or paragraphs, this analysis is based on the whole of this work and also takes into consideration other works of Liu Zhi including shorter tracts and other longer works. The first two comments focus on the introductory and chapter 1. The third comment deals with the story of the beginning of Islam in China. The final comment will discuss the Confucianization of the prophet Muhammad's teaching on deeds.

Firstly, in terms of the layout of the work, Liu Zhi began with the honor, nobility, and superiority of the prophet Muhammad in the first few chapters. The prophet Muhammad is unique and superior to any holy

---

46. This eighteenth chapter is not translated by Isaac Mason in his work *The Arabian Prophet*.
47. Liu, *True Record*, 310–11.

sage. Thus, Islam with its Utmost Sage is a noble and honorable religion. In chapter 7, Liu Zhi's narrative of the beginning of Islam in China takes place at the imperial court and under the protection of the emperor. The spread of Islam into China was as early as the Sui dynasty (581–618). While he was not aware of the inaccuracy of his source materials, he emphasized that his sources and evidences were convincing enough. After the life history of Muhammad, Liu Zhi added several appendixes to this work. The reason for this addition is most likely his method of contextualization. In chapter 18, Liu Zhi discussed the deeds and actions of Muhammad. He explained them in full Confucian terms. The Confucian tradition fully complied with the deeds and teaching of the prophet Muhammad. It may be deduced from the general flow and development within this work that although Islam is a very different religion from the Middle East and Muhammad is the one and only Utmost Sage, the rules and proprieties of Islam are consistent with the Confucian tradition. Liu Zhi used the whole of this chapter to emphasize the compatibility. In addition, the approval and spread of Islam was carried out at the imperial level in China. This constitutes Islam as a valid and complementary alternative to the official Three Teachings in China. The narrative and teaching of *The True Record of the Utmost Sage of Islam* is itself an outward and clear presentation of Liu Zhi's method of contextualization. Islam with its Utmost Sage is uniquely distinctive and yet it is consistent with the Confucian tradition.

This is a long work of Liu Zhi. The narrative style, easy-to-follow chronological presentation of the life history of Muhammad, mythical stories of death and resurrection, stories of overcoming betrayal, treachery, seemingly supported by evidences, records, date of events and others have made this work very appealing for general readership. After reading this work, Muslims may be encouraged to obey faithfully the Real Ruler. They try to imitate the example of the Utmost Sage and eventually they also obey the rites of Islam, just like any literati who have followed the Confucian learning, not merely intellectually but with their hearts. The story and teaching in this work can reveal much about the goal of Liu Zhi's model of contextualization. He was faithful to the past tradition and yet he skillfully and actively conversed with the Chinese contexts.

Secondly, the role of Utmost Sage is unique and Liu Zhi connected his uniqueness with the ancient holy sages. Liu Zhi was emphatic and consistent in declaring that even the ancient most highly regarded sage like Confucius was not an utmost sage. This is a part of the strategy of Liu Zhi's adoption of the term Utmost Sage in all the works. However, the unique Muhammad as the Utmost Sage is not a stumbling block to Liu Zhi's contextualization. On the one hand, the utmost status of Muhammad resembles the human ultimate or the perfect man in the Ibn ʿArabi tradition. On the other hand, the concept of sagehood holds high esteem in Chinese society. At the time of Liu Zhi, only successful Confucian literati after official examinations were allowed to take government posts. Confucian literati aspired to be sages. Sagehood is an important status for Chinese culture.

Liu Zhi was not afraid to contextualize the prophet Muhammad as the Utmost Sage because he probably followed the argument that was put forward by a well-known Jesuit missionary Matteo Ricci (1552–1610) and his followers in the seventeenth and eighteenth-century China that the ancient emperors and sages in ancient China were monotheistic. Such ancient religion was later corrupted by generations of followers and became idol worship. The ancient sages did not regard themselves as divine. It was idolatry for their followers to worship their sages. Thus, the ancient holy sages neither worship idol nor teach any idolatry. Liu Zhi was comfortable in adopting the prophet Muhammad as the Utmost Sage as he set an example of worshipping no god but God. The concept of the Utmost Sage connects Islam with the foundational and unadulterated teaching of the ancient holy sages of China.

Thirdly, the beginning of Islam in China as recorded in chapter 7 is a topic of scholarly debate. Studies in Chinese are not as numerous as those in English by Ma Haiyun, Benite and others.[48] According to Liu Zhi's record, the beginning of Islam in China is during the lifetime of the prophet Muhammad. Similar claims and stories by different Muslim literati were common and generally accepted as historical accounts in the early period of the Qing dynasty. At the time of Liu Zhi, it was a common belief that Islam came to China at a very early time. However, the consensus of contemporary Chinese scholars puts the entry date of Islam at least one or two centuries later than these stories. Almost all of them do not support the stories by Liu Zhi and other Muslim literati. In the thematic study of Liu Zhi, Jin briefly describes Muhammad as the perfect man in Chinese Sufism.[49] He does not enter into any debate about the date and account of the beginning of Islam in China.

After studying the textual and contextual evidence of the mythical stories, Ma Haiyun speculates that such myths are created because of the expansion of the imperial Qing into Central Asia and Manchu interactions with Turkic Muslims in North-Western China.[50] Ma's textual analysis is weak and just based on a so called turban-wearing Muslim called Gess

---

48. Murata makes no comment about the beginning of Islam in China.
49. Jin, *Exploring Chinese Islam*, 246–52.
50. Ma, "Mythology," 445–52.

who was the companion of Saʿad ibn Abi Waqqas in China. Ma's contextual evidence is equally weak and not able to convince most readers of the claim that North-Western Turkic Muslims took side with the Qing army. "To reward the Hami Muslim allegiance, the Kangxi emperor granted Hami Muslims the right to live and safeguard Su Zhou of China proper and established Hami King . . . as the Manchu agent in Hami in the late seventeenth century."[51] For Ma, the mythical stories of Islam's entry into China are politically motivated.

A more thorough study based on different *Han Kitab* texts from seventeenth to eighteenth-century China is carried out by Benite. His focus is on the study of *Dao* and Muslim identity in the *Han Kitab*. He also specifically studies Liu Zhi's *True Record of the Utmost Sage of Islam* and the story of sending ambassadors by the prophet Muhammad to China. The key argument of Benite's work is that "in talking about Muhammad as a sage and about Islam as a *Dao*, Chinese Muslim scholars were talking about *themselves* and negotiating their identity as simultaneously Muslim and Chinese."[52] Benite's interpretation of the goal of Liu Zhi's story is the identity of Hui Muslims. "Liu Zhi would not have regarded his interpolation as a 'lie.' Rather, it was an expression of a meta-truth or a mythical truth, a truth that held that Islam had been in China since its very origins and that Muhammad had viewed China as an important site for the future of his calling."[53]

Ma's view is speculative and requires more pieces of evidence to prove that these stories were politically motivated by the imperial ruler. Benite's analysis demonstrates with primary texts of the *Han Kitab* that these stories serve to integrate Hui Muslims into Chinese culture. Since Liu Zhi's *True Record of the Utmost Sage of Islam* is the most well-known and detailed account of the life history of Muhammad in the *Han Kitab*, a more detailed study of this story within the context of the experience of Hui community at the time of Liu Zhi should give fresh insights in addition to Benite's point of view.

From the perspective of Liu Zhi's contextualization, Liu Zhi is both a translator of text and a cultural agent of his Chinese contexts. As a skillful cultural agent, he needs to take great care of the present experience of his personal and Hui community. He pays due regard to various aspects of culture, including secular and religious culture, social location, social change, and others. To determine an accurate understanding of the present experience, "one needs to juggle several things at one time, but it is not a

---

51. Ibid., 450. Hami is a region near Turfan in northwestern China.
52. Benite, *Dao*, 194.
53. Ibid., 210.

matter of just keeping everything moving smoothly. One needs, rather, to place emphasis on message at one point, while at another point one needs to emphasize cultural identity."[54] At the beginning of *True Record of the Utmost Sage*, Liu Zhi emphasized the message of Islam in the person of Muhammad. In chapter 7, he emphasized the cultural identity. Specifically, it was the Hui Muslims as a collective community in various parts of China for over a century that had traditionally identified the mythical stories as meta-truth during the time of Liu Zhi. In addition, Liu Zhi had consulted different apocryphal histories before he narrated the story.[55] Within that story, he admitted that a part was recorded in written form and other part was orally transmitted. Thus, Liu Zhi took great care to validate the accuracy of the story. Likewise, Liu Zhi began to write *The True Record of the Utmost Sage of Islam* at a time when he was fully confident that he had acquired a reliable source. With great care, then, Liu Zhi read and understood the present experience of the Hui Muslims.

Benite is sensible to assert that Liu Zhi did not believe the story was a "lie." Liu Zhi was emphatic that his evidence from both inside and outside the Hui community was sufficient to declare the story was accurate. The focus of the story is not so much whether it is historically accurate or even a fabrication in order to promote integration between Muslims and Chinese. If one takes that approach, one begins to devalue Liu Zhi's *True Record of the Utmost Sage of Islam*. Liu Zhi did not intend the last part of his trilogy to be devalued. The trilogy should be studied as one whole entity. In both chapter 7 and 18, Liu Zhi gave an account of the friendship between China and Arabia at an early stage of Islam and also affirmed various cultural similarities between Muslims and Chinese cultures. The story is better explained as a strategy of Liu Zhi's contextualization. While Liu Zhi emphasized Islam as distinctively unique especially in the role of the prophet Muhammad, Islamic rites and the origin of Islam in China may readily identify with the Chinese culture, including the approval of the imperial court, the customs of society, and local religious practice.

This explanation of Liu Zhi's contextualization is more convincing than other suggestions that argue for the Hui identity as simultaneously Chinese and Muslim, (e.g. Benite).[56] On the one hand, Liu Zhi's Islam is

---

54. Bevans, *Models*, 92.

55. Liu Zhi consulted five "historical" records. Since historical records were written by the Hans and approved by the imperial emperor, very little historical record of Hui Muslims and other ethnic minority groups is found in imperially approved records. They are found usually in the non-official history, namely apocryphal historical records.

56. Benite, *Dao*, 194, 209–13.

unique and different from Chinese culture when he speaks of the role of the prophet Muhammad as the Utmost Sage. On the other hand, Liu Zhi's Islam identifies with the Chinese culture when he narrates the story of the beginning of Islam in China and explains the rites of Islam in Confucian terms. Thus, Benite and others can explain partly Liu Zhi's works. From the perspective of contextualization, Liu Zhi's works are different and yet simultaneously identical with the Chinese contexts.

Finally, Neo-Confucian ideas are explicitly affirmed in chapter 18 which is one of the appendixes. According to the contemporary Confucian scholar Tu Weiming who has examined *The True Record of the Utmost Sage of Islam*, "Confucian motifs and themes are pervasive and conspicuous in several of these narratives."[57] Another well-known Confucian scholar, Fung Yu-lan points out that Confucius is an educator who emphasizes the way (the *dao*) and not just mere knowledge in learning.

> In the *Analects*, Confucius said: "Set your heart on the Tao." (VII, 6.) And again: "To hear the Tao in the morning and then die at night that would be all right." (IV, 9.) Here Tao [*Dao*] means the Way or Truth. It was this Tao which Confucius at fifteen set his heart upon learning. What we now call learning means the increase of our knowledge, but the Tao is that whereby we can elevate our mind.[58]

The teaching of the prophet Muhammad on learning is almost interpreted in Neo-Confucian terms above. The aim of Liu Zhi's *True Record of the Utmost Sage* is to ground the teachings of his two earlier works, namely, *The Nature and Principle in Islam* and *Rules and Proprieties of Islam* using the life, teaching and record of Muhammad. Liu Zhi chose his source materials carefully and edited them for his own purpose. The Muslim readers could learn from his account that the prophet Muhammad was both the pre-existent Muhammadan Spirit that existed before creation and the perfect man who set ethical rules as expressed in proprieties of Islam. In this work, Liu Zhi did not succeed in being an accurate historian of the record of Muhammad. However, he succeeded in integrating two of his earlier major works together into a consummate trilogy. That is, Liu Zhi's *Nature and Principle in Islam* clarifies the way. *The Rules and Proprieties of Islam* gives practical teaching of the way. Muhammad as recorded in this final work of the trilogy is the wondrous embodiment of both the teaching and way of Islam.

57. Murata et al., *Sage*, 593.
58. Fung, *Short History*, 74.

It can also be stated that through Muhammad, the Real Ruler begins the great transformation and also through him that the creation returns and unites with the Real Ruler eventually. While the Utmost Sage is similar to many holy Chinese sages in the teaching of self-realization and transformation, the Utmost Sage is totally unique. One may say that Liu Zhi made an attempt, namely chapter 18, to contextualize his Islamic practical teachings into Neo-Confucian ideas. However, his main effort in *The True Record of the Utmost Sage of Islam* was to do otherwise. Islam is superior and Muhammad is the one and only Utmost Sage. By taking a more serious consideration of this work and Liu Zhi's contextualization, one can conclude that Liu Zhi's contextualization is neither sinicization nor Confucianization.

LIU ZHI'S THEOLOGICAL CONVERSATION WITH NEO-CONFUCIAN SELF-CULTIVATION AND WISDOM: *THE RULES AND PROPRIETIES OF ISLAM*

It is necessary to elaborate and discuss the question of how *The Rules and Proprieties of Islam* actively makes dialogical engagements with Neo-Confucian culture. Comparatively, this second work of Liu Zhi's trilogy is easier to read and understand than his first book *The Nature and Principle in Islam* while both of the works may be scholarly enough to achieve the literary standard set by the imperial Qing court. The readership of *The Rules and Proprieties of Islam* is primarily ordinary Muslims and probably non-Muslims also. The work is intended for those Muslims who are not clear about the meanings of Islamic rituals while they may be keeping these rituals faithfully. For the non-Muslims, this work provides not only Islamic understanding but also rational and Neo-Confucian interpretations of the cultural and religious meanings of the proprieties of Islam.

While Liu Zhi explicated these proprieties within a Neo-Confucian framework, he also argued for the orthodoxy of Islamic proprieties against the heresies of Christian and Jewish rites. Furthermore, Liu Zhi asserted that the founders of Buddhism and Daoism, namely the Buddha[59] and Lao

---

59. Liu Zhi gave a brief account of the life of Buddha and his main teaching is concerned with the self-emptiness of worldly possessions and fleshly desires. Some later leaders emphasized the doctrine of reincarnation to deceive many ordinary followers. He was convinced that many Neo-Confucians had already condemned Buddhism. Appendix IV.

Zi,⁶⁰ respectively, were supporters of monotheistic religion.⁶¹ For Liu Zhi, it was some of the founders' followers and later supporters who corrupted the monotheistic teaching of the ancient sages. Thus, their religio-cultural proprieties were no longer the orthodox teaching of the founders. Clearly, Liu Zhi followed the successful argument of earlier Jesuits like Matteo Ricci in cross-cultural contextualization. Unlike the later conservative Jesuit missionaries, Liu Zhi refused to adopt the controversial and confrontational approach of cross-cultural dialogue. He opted for both civil obedience to the imperial rulers and simultaneous faithfulness to God.

Liu Zhi innovatively employed an ancient and Confucian concept of law, typically exemplified and embodied by Chinese ancient sages. Liu Zhi's law was the bridge between the way and teaching or between universal and relative aspects of Islam. He firmly linked the law with the religio-philosophical concept of the ancient Chinese sages.⁶² By the late Ming and early Qing dynasties, Chinese sages were regarded as occupying a special status in their tradition, sometimes, as the conduit of divine revelation. The sage was the bridge between the universal and relative, the divine and human.⁶³ Liu Zhi's originality lay in his emphases that firstly the ancient Chinese sages were monotheistic in their beliefs.⁶⁴ Secondly, for him the prophet Muhammad was a sage in the Arab world and also the prophet of Islam. Thirdly, the originally intended teachings and wisdom of Chinese ancient sages and the teachings of Muhammad and Islam derived from the same divine source.⁶⁵ In Neo-Confucian society, it was easily accepted by the public and Qing government that the sage was the one who acted as an agent of heaven, expressing its will, implementing the universal way by means of his teaching. Unlike Islam, the Neo-Confucian focus was not so much the divine will upon human social and religious affairs; rather its focus was social order, ethical conduct, and obedience to the imperial ruler. The Confucian sage was the infallible guide for human self-cultivation and acquiring wisdom of this world and for Daoists the world to come also. Liu Zhi exploited such precepts of the sage and argued that Muhammad's status belonged to the Utmost Sage.⁶⁶ Liu Zhi used the concept of law to underpin Islamic propri-

60. Liu Zhi provided a historical account of Lao Zi's life and his brief teachings. He sarcastically suggested that if Lao Zi was alive, he would have laughed at some of the deviations in the teachings of Daoism. Appendix IV.

61. Liu Zhi asserted that monotheism began at the very early stage.

62. Frankel, "Liu's Journey," 189.

63. Ibid., 192.

64. Ibid., 387.

65. Ibid., 197.

66. Liu Zhi asserted that Islamic prophets began from Adam and ended in the

eties and actions. Thus, his work became the authoritative guide on Islamic orthopraxy.

While Liu Zhi argued that Islamic proprieties were compatible with the idea of Neo-Confucian self-cultivation, he did not accept full compatibility. He made careful and selective uses of Neo-Confucian concepts. It must be emphasized that Liu Zhi rejected certain Chinese traditions and practices not only on the basis of Islamic rule but also on various rational grounds. He rejected certain Chinese clothing of the dead in special burial garments because there was no precedent and it was inconsistent with the teaching of the ancient sage. The wearing of headgear was not the rite of Muslims only. It was also taught in *Six Classics*.[67] While the prohibition of alcohol and pork were based on Islamic abstinence, he also argued the prohibition from rational, empirical and metaphysical grounds.[68] Thus, he was sensitive to the need for making a persuasive and rational argument, justifying his views to both non-Muslim and backslidden Muslims. When discussing the five pillars of Islam, he interpreted them as distinctively Chinese and yet in a very esoteric manner. He named the five pillars as the Neo-Confucian five meritorious works and they guided the seekers to return to the Real One.[69] Frankel argues that "[Liu Zhi] went on to discuss the specific details of the Five Pillars, Liu Zhi further drew inspiration from Neo-Confucian ideals of self-cultivation, which he effectively syncretized with Sufi notions of annihilation of the ego and subsumption in God."[70]

Two comments may be made. Firstly, it is fairly common to say that Liu Zhi's method in his *Rules and Proprieties of Islam* is acculturated and Liu Zhi often locates the rites of Islam, the concept of sage and law inside Neo-Confucian tradition, as opined by Benite[71] and Frankel.[72] However,

---

ultimate final prophet of Muhammad. Islamic prophethood had a long and ancient tradition. The role of the prophets is not only to reveal God and beliefs of Islam, it also confirms the traditional five relationships of Neo-Confucianism. See chapter 5 in Appendix IV.

67. Frankel, "Liu's Journey," 274.

68. With regard to the prohibition of eating pork, he quoted support from many classic teachings in Chinese medicinal manuals. Furthermore, pork was argued to be harmful because of the nature and habit of the animal. Abstinence from alcohol was due its hypnotic effect. He called alcohol the mother of all evils. Frankel, "Liu's Journey," 281–82.

69. Appendix IV.

70. Frankel, "Liu's Journey," 261.

71. Benite, *Dao*, 229.

72. Frankel argues that *Rules and Proprieties of Islam* is the most syncretic work in Liu Zhi's writings. The Muslims share with the Chinese understanding of rituals which are guides to human living. He calls Liu Zhi's assimilation 'unconscious.' Frankel, "Liu's

it is more accurate to assert that Liu Zhi's aim is to locate Islam both as an ancient western tradition and a valid complementary religio-cultural tradition alongside all the legitimate religio-cultural and philosophical Chinese traditions approved by the early Qing imperial courts. While both Benite and Frankel made contributions to this observation, they have not noted the Sufi background of Liu Zhi's teaching and more importantly, the method of Liu Zhi's contextualization.

The Neo-Confucian character of his work is due to his creatively dialogical engagement with Neo-Confucian culture in which all Muslims and non-Muslims are located. Liu Zhi is eclectic in that he accepts the contextualization of Islam as long as these various Chinese customs do not violate beliefs or practices of the basic tenets of Islam. It can be concluded that there is no syncretism in Liu's *Rules and Proprieties of Islam*. Rather, Liu Zhi makes a great effort at dialogical engagement with Neo-Confucian culture. As a result, his contextualized Islam is appropriate and intelligible to his readers.

Secondly, Liu Zhi's *Rules and Proprieties of Islam* is more than a mere exposition of Islamic law and legal obligations for Muslims. He expounded not only the five endeavors, but also family relationships, wealth, property, dress, wedding, funeral and other commonly practiced Chinese customs. He expounded a holistic and all-encompassing way of religious life. His substantial introduction and articulate explanation of the proprieties of Islam aimed at the Sufi notion of devotional piety, with emphasis on both heart and body, or attitude and action. For Muslim readers, it was the Real Ruler who established all the proprieties as moral imperatives as well as securing inward knowledge, similar to and yet different from Chinese literati who sought self-realization and transformation.

The goal of Liu Zhi's contextualization in *The Rules and Proprieties of Islam* is to affirm the unity of existence by following both the way of heaven and the way of humanity. The first half of the work deals with the way of heaven and the second half of the work deals with the way of humanity. The seeker's final destination is the Real and "his body and mind dissolve and merge with the Original essence of the True Lord."[73] The Chinese Neo-Confucians can do likewise in their self-realization by following the teachings of their ancient sages. Moreover, since Liu Zhi's teaching of the way of humanity is fully compatible with the teaching of the Confucian sages, the Neo-Confucians may be inspired to read Liu Zhi's *Rules and Proprieties of Islam*. Thus, this work can benefit both Muslims and non-Muslims. The

---

Journey," 206, 372.

73. Ibid., 336.

evidence of such understanding is the fact that *The Rules and Proprieties of Islam* is collected into the Qing imperial library catalogue, namely *Annotated General Catalogue of the Compendium of the Four Treasuries, Authorized by the Emperor.*

CONCLUSION

The first part of this chapter demonstrated that not only did Liu Zhi interpret Islamic concepts in Confucian terms; he also adopted a very popular Chinese literary writing style, namely, employing phrases often consisting of three, five or seven characters. Liu Zhi's *Three-character Classic* takes a strict three-character form.

This second part of this chapter translated and examined Liu Zhi's *Poem of the Five Sessions of the Moon*. The poem takes a literary form which can be memorized easily for beginners of Islam and is suitable even for children. It has many Sufi themes and a chiastic structure. The climax of the structure is the Sufi seafaring journey. We have shown that the poem has the ability to communicate difficult Sufi ideas in easy to understand cultural terms such as Buddhism's concept of vehicle, Confucianism's concept of self-cultivation and Daoism's concept of *dao*. As a result of Liu Zhi's contextualization of the poem, even Qing ruling elites and other Hans could find Chinese Islam acceptable and not too different from the Three Teachings in China. The poem emphasizes practical Muslim living more than the mystical path. It is "right doing" or orthopraxis in the Sufi way. Again, Liu Zhi emphasized the role of the heart. Seekers should seek control of their inner self, empty their self-centered desires and eventually arrive at union with the Real. The poem has a clear framework of Sufi thought and the eclectic terms are chosen carefully as an interpretative tool.

The final part of the chapter examined and analyzed Liu Zhi's *True Record of the Utmost Sage of Islam* which has not been previously studied by any contemporary scholars. The early part of this work emphasizes the honor, nobility, and uniqueness of the prophet Muhammad. Muhammad has existence in both the innate and the acquired heaven. He is also the integrator of creative transformation of the Real from the beginning to the end. Thus, Muhammad is unique and known as the Utmost Sage of Islam. Even though this work is primarily a life story of the Prophet Muhammad, Liu Zhi added an appendix at the end of this work on the moral teachings of Muhammad and contextualized them as Neo-Confucian ethics.

We also examined the scholarly controversy of Liu Zhi's record of the beginning of Islam in China. Liu Zhi did not fabricate mythical stories in his account. It is better to understand his record from the perspective of Liu Zhi's contextualization. That is, Liu Zhi emphasized the present experience of his Hui community. Hui Muslims had traditionally understood the beginning of Islam in China as the true record. His contextualization gives due regard to both the historical records and the present experience of his community.

It can be concluded that the strategy is to actively dialogue and engage with Chinese cultures in his contextualization. Liu adopted the literary Chinese writing style in his poem. He interpreted the poem by using concepts of the Three Teachings but maintained a distinctive Sufi framework. In his record of the beginning of Islam in China, he took seriously the present experience of his Hui community, which was supported by certain historical sources, to validate his account of the Prophet Muhammad. Clearly, Liu Zhi is a skillful cultural agent in his Chinese contexts.

6

Liu Zhi's Engagement with Islam and Neo-Confucian Culture in His *Rules and Proprieties of Islam*

An English Translation and Detailed Examination

In the last two chapters, we have discussed Liu Zhi's works in continuation with the Ibn 'Arabi tradition and in active conversation with the Chinese contexts. Liu Zhi's works are rooted in the teaching of the Ibn 'Arabi tradition. He faithfully translated the Islamic text. He also contextualized his Islamic texts by active dialogue and conversation with the Chinese contexts in order that his readers might understand them better.

Liu Zhi's *Rules and Proprieties of Islam* has been studied by both Chinese and English scholars. Liang and Jin have examined this work in their thematic study of Liu Zhi in Chinese. Frankel studies a few sections of the early chapters of this work and writes in English.

This chapter will focus on the first five foundational chapters of the second part of Liu Zhi's trilogy, namely *The Rules and Proprieties of Islam*. The goal of this chapter is to analyse Liu *Zhi's Rules and Proprieties of Islam*, chapter by chapter. It will confirm and demonstrate further his continuation of the Ibn 'Arabi tradition and proactive conversation with Neo-Confucianism. We offer for the first time a full translation of the first five chapters of Liu Zhi's *Rules and Proprieties of Islam* in English and also an analysis of each chapter. Thus, the originality of this chapter is based on a detailed analysis of these chapters of Liu Zhi's work from the perspective of his contextualization.

EXAMINATION OF FIRST FIVE CHAPTERS OF *THE RULES AND PROPRIETIES OF ISLAM*

Liu Zhi's *Rules and Proprieties of Islam* is one of the most important works in Islam's *Han Kitab*.[1] The work is divided into twenty volumes, more commonly known today as chapters. The content of the work may be summarized as follows:

- Chapter 1: It is foundational and gives an overview of Islamic theoretical teachings on divine unity, the creation of humankind and the role of prophets. Islamic prophets are usually called holy sages. It also briefly reviews the practical teachings of Islam, namely the five pillars of Islam (or endeavors) and five relationships (much used in Confucianism). Also, this chapter is an outline for all the remaining chapters.
- Chapters 2 and 3: These chapters discuss the theology of the Real Ruler who is superior to any concept of divine existence in Daoism, Buddhism, and Confucianism.
- Chapter 4: It explains the meaning of endeavor. To bear witness or the *Shahadah* is a verbal attestation of asserting the unity of God.
- Chapter 5: It discusses the various aspects of the five endeavors. It gives a general overview of the definition, content and meaning of the endeavors.
- Chapters 6 to 8: these chapters discuss more details of the other four endeavors. The five endeavors are regarded as the heavenly way of self-cultivation.
- Chapter 9: It is devoted to the ritual slaughter of animals.
- Chapters 10 to 13: the five endeavors are the way of heaven. The tenth chapter discusses the complementary way of humanity which is called the five relationships of Islamic ethics. The eleventh to thirteenth chapters contextualize the way of humanity into the Confucian concepts of five human relationships or ethical codes.
- Chapters 14 to 17: these delineate the four constants which are residence, property, clothes and food. Chapter 14 forbids any cohabitation

1. This work is collected into the Imperial library. The collection is known as '*Annotated General Catalogue of the Compendium of the Four Treasuries, Authorized by the Emperor.*'

of the mosque with other religions. Property and clothes occupy chapter 15. However, the discussion on food is longer and takes up chapters 16 and 17.

- Chapters 18 to 20: these are additional teachings on congregational prayer, marriage, and funeral rites, respectively.

Author's Preface: Personal Narrative[2]

Liu Zhi in his preface made several important points that could help contemporary scholars to interpret this work more accurately, allowing scholars to approach this work as Liu Zhi himself intended. Firstly, his work is meant to be understood and used. It is meant to be a pedagogical tool. Liu Zhi intended it to be a standard textbook on Islamic proprieties and used in various Islamic education networks. He formerly had written a very comprehensive version of *The Rules and Proprieties of Islam* but it was too difficult for general readership. It was at the request of his readers that Liu Zhi wrote the extant *Selected Explanation of the Rules and Proprieties of Islam* (abbreviated as *The Rules and Proprieties of Islam*). Not only does this present work contain the main discussion, it also has commentary, expanded annotation, a collected overview and even question and answer. It is designed to be a textbook suitable for most Muslims at different levels of learning.

Liu Zhi classified his readers into three categories and they should be helped by his extra commentaries and annotations. The first category was learners who were able to understand the work but found the meaning incomplete. Liu Zhi's extra commentary served to enhance understanding. The second category was learners who were able to understand but not able to grasp fluently the meaning of the work. Commentary and annotation should make their understanding more thorough and effective. The third category was the beginners who might know the meaning and reason but they still had doubts. Liu Zhi admitted using Confucian ideas primarily to help the last category of readers. His purpose for the section of questions and answers was to dispel confusion and misunderstanding for those who had distorted views on the original meaning of the text. Thus, one can say that this work is clearly intended primarily for a pedagogical purpose for all types of learners and secondarily an apologetic purpose.

Secondly, the real importance of this work is to teach the profound meaning of Islamic rites and proprieties. It aims to enable the reader's

---

2. The full text is translated into English in Appendix III.

inseparable union with the heavenly principle. Return to the Real Ruler is the ultimate aim of Islamic rites. Islamic rites are not meant to be legalistic.

Thirdly, Liu Zhi asserted that while one seemed to find Islamic truth difficult to understand, in fact Islamic truth was quite obvious. One should learn and understand Islamic books in a similar way to how one learned and understood Confucian books. Also, one who obeyed the rites of Islam was also similar to one who kept the rites as demanded by the holy Chinese ancient emperors. The point in this personal narrative really is that in the process of learning and understanding Islamic rites, beginners should not be frightened off.[3] Rather, they should be comforted and take the same learning attitude to both Chinese and Islamic literatures. Liu Zhi used Confucian ideas especially for the beginners to help them understand and they were tools of communication.

Finally, Liu Zhi highlighted the teaching of ancient sages and compared them with ancient worthies. He also highlighted the similarity between the holy sages of the East and the sages in the Arabia. While the sage from Arabia is not explicitly named, clearly it is the prophet Muhammad. Also, he is mentioned explicitly with regard to the teaching of propriety in the personal narrative. For Muhammad, propriety can establish humankind. For ancient worthies, humankind without propriety loses its humanness.

From the perspective of contextualization, this personal narrative by Liu Zhi confirms the discussion in the last chapter of this present study. Firstly, if one compares the personal narrative in his first work of trilogy, namely *The Nature and Principle in Islam* with his personal narrative in *The Rules and Proprieties of Islam*, one may note the overwhelming concern of Liu Zhi that the prime goal of his works is for the readers to understand. In the earlier first work, Liu Zhi "established explanations to transmit the meaning of the diagrams."[4] His method in *The Rules and Proprieties of Islam* is no longer diagrams but commentaries, annotations and other easier to read examples from daily living. He repeatedly emphasized that the beginners and the doubters may understand his trilogy. He made his works easy to understand by the use of diagrams in his first part of trilogy. He used commentaries and annotations in the second work and lastly in *The True Record of the Utmost Sage of Islam*, narrative with historical evidences from various sources to validate his records.

Liu Zhi in this personal narrative highlighted the reason for his use of Confucian terms. Primarily, he used Neo-Confucian terms for clearer explanation and to solve any doubt that one may have. He then continued

---

3. This point is explained in chapter 4 of Liu Zhi's work.
4. Murata et al., *Sage*, 95.

in his narrative to state his view of the similarities between Islam and Neo-Confucianism.

> In order to discuss the truth of Islam, we make our work easier to understand as it is no different to Neo-Confucian works. To learn and obey the Islamic propriety is likewise to learn and obey the teachings of the ancient sages and kings. The religion of holy sages, either in the East or the Arab world, either in ancient or modern times, is the same. However, people nowadays do not study and research this fact and gradually it disappears.[5]

The above quotation of Liu Zhi has led some scholars to believe that he simply asserted that Islam identified completely with Neo-Confucianism. Then, these scholars concluded that his Islam was sinicized. Such misinterpretation is due to the lack of deeper examination of the overall works of Liu Zhi and taking the above quotation out of the context of the whole personal narrative. He explained his view in greater detail in chapter 3 of his work later. It is emphasized that the above quotation should be understood and interpreted in the context of the whole work.

Chapter 1: Original Teaching

This chapter is the introductory and foundational chapter in understanding Liu Zhi's teaching of Islamic rules and proprieties. This particular chapter has been well known partly because it was adopted as compulsory reading in the Muslim education network soon after its publication.[6] It gives an overview of Liu Zhi's understanding of Islamic rites. It also serves as a useful resource to work out any unclear or ambiguous argument later in this or other of Liu Zhi's works.

Any first-time or even experienced reader of this chapter can easily detect Liu Zhi's emphasis on the superiority of Islam, very much like the first two chapters in *The True Record of the Utmost Sage of Islam*. Thus, one should be careful not to make the premature and unwarranted statement that Liu Zhi sinicized Islam into Neo-Confucianism. A careful reading of Liu Zhi's foundational first chapter may gain a better understanding of Liu Zhi's contextualization. Liu Zhi admitted that Islamic rites based on Islamic doctrine were not much different from Confucian ethics. However, Islam as a religion and a way to the knowledge of the divine being was superior to any Chinese thought systems including Daoism, Buddhism, and Confucianism.

5. Appendix III.
6. Liang, *Study of Liu Zhi*, 17–18.

Islam is superior because it is ancient, beginning from the creation of the world and humankind. It is superior not only because of its historicity and rapid global expansion, Islam has continued throughout all ages without any interruption. Several observations can be made. Firstly, the prophet Muhammad is significant at the beginning and end of this chapter. When Muhammad appeared, the Islamic way became clear and definitive. He revised all previous sacred texts into a final canon and formulated regulations. At the end of the chapter, the prophet Muhammad is implicitly mentioned and his role is also important for all Muslims. The role of the holy sages, including the seal of the prophets i.e. Muhammad, is to establish the religion of Islam so that humankind is not led astray. The way of these holy sages is the way of heaven. "The Sage is the personal agent of God's will."[7]

Secondly, the chapter continues to delineate the superior qualities of Islam from the historical perspective. The origin is geographically located in the central part of the world. The tradition has been continuous without interruption of sages and worthies. Liu Zhi also described the history of Islam, its continuation, and spread to various parts of the world throughout human history. While Muslims are scattered worldwide, they regularly come together in their localities and practice the same, unchanging rites. At the end of the chapter in his extended annotation, Liu Zhi gave an account using some Chinese historical records and asserted that Islam was more ancient than the Three Teachings of China. This expanded annotation is the longest section in this chapter. He attempted to demonstrate beyond any doubt that even the emperor Sui Mende (541–604)[8] admired the prophet Muhammad, sent an ambassador to the Middle East, and sought from him sacred texts. The above story is also repeated in the last part of his trilogy, namely *The True Record of the Utmost Sage of Islam*. This chapter may be regarded as a prelude to the final part of Liu Zhi's trilogy.

Thirdly, he creatively separated but did not divide the way of heaven and humankind. This chapter explains that both are aspects of Islamic rules and proprieties necessary for self-cultivation and return to the Real. The holy sages of Islam have set themselves up as examples of the way of heaven. Self-cultivation is the way of humankind, similar to the Confucian concept of realization. The usual Islamic concept of Five Pillars is the way of heaven. Both the way of heaven and humankind are integral in the process of ascending the path by continuously knowing the self, the Real, and eventual return to the Real. It should be noted that Jin identifies Liu

---

7. Frankel, *Liu's Journey*, 210.

8. Emperor Sui Wendi during the Sui dynasty (581–618). The accuracy of Liu Zi's dates between Islamic events and Chinese emperors has been doubtful. See Appendix II.

Zhi's understanding of the proprieties of Islam that his concept is based on a *shari'a*-minded Sufism.[9]

Fourthly, Liu Zhi cautioned that in applying the principle of Islamic rites in real contexts, Muslims must exercise the rites with care. Such caution opens a window to understand his contextualization. The following section summarizes his view.

> Theme: In all these regulations of activity and solitude, there is a principle that is unchanging and yet objectively adaptive, creatively in enforcing the rule of law.
>
> Explanation: Whatever can be seen, heard, spoken, intuited, or situations like eating and resting at home, large and small occasion, there is a historical law to regulate human behavior. So, Muslims are not to offend others and contravene propriety. At the same time, the law is objective and flexible enough to adapt appropriately, paying attention to the time and the context at that moment. This is to avoid holding firm to arid tradition with rigidity and stubbornly making no progress. In that way, the rule of the law continues to be complied with and yet it is exercised in a flexible manner without unfairness and with due respect to time and context. The rule of law remains the norm.[10]

Thus, the principle of Islamic proprieties remains unchanged but the application of the principle should be accommodating and flexible. How should one apply the principle? One must not be offending to one's local context at that time. Simply put, the revealed truth is eternally unchanging but the tradition within a specific context should be adaptive. A tradition that is adaptive in a local context is a living one. A rigid and stubborn tradition is soon obsolete. The tradition is always in the process of forming and re-forming responding to the ever-changing contexts. When one reads the above quotation, one should bear in mind that the Hui Muslims are an ethnic minority in China. Not surprisingly, Liu Zhi's caution makes real sense in that in exercising the rites of Islam, Muslims should not offend and be fair to the majority Han people in China. He strived at a harmonious relationship between the Muslims and non-Muslims. As Benite puts it, the Muslim literati sought to establish a dual identity of the Hui: both Chinese and Muslims. For Liu Zhi, the tradition of Islam makes progress and remains lively when the principle of the rites of Islam is applied with due respect to the cultural contexts.

---

9. Jin, *Exploring Chinese Islam*, 261.
10. Appendix IV.

Finally, an important point is made by Liu Zhi's contextualization of the Sufi path in Chinese terms. This introductory chapter gives a very clear goal of Islamic rules and proprieties. Liu Zhi used a Buddhist term, namely vehicle, which is commonly used by Buddhists in their search for enlightenment. The aim of Islamic rites is to know the Ruler and the goal is to return to the Real. Rules and proprieties are to serve humankind to achieve that goal. The path of return is through the way of heaven, namely the five endeavors or five pillars of Islam and the way of humankind, namely the five relationships. Again, it emphasizes the role of the Utmost Sage, namely the prophet Muhammad. "The Law is the non-human mechanism whereby this communication [human-divine] is achieved. As the living expression of the moral standard of the Way, it may even be said that the Sage is the embodiment of the Law."[11]

The law of proprieties is represented by the concept of three vehicles. These vehicles are carriers and are described in an ascending order. They correspond to the Sufi concept of law, mystical path and truth.[12] Liu Zhi explained the Sufi path in Confucian terms.

> Working hard for your virtues and honoring endeavors are for body realization. Understanding thoroughly the principle and knowing thoroughly the nature can enlighten the heart. With self-control and accomplishing the real, you can see nature. Without endeavor and cultivation, your heart is not illuminated. Such a heart cannot see nature. Without seeing nature, you cannot unite with heaven. Nature is not seen because the selfish 'I' has hidden it. Therefore, the rule of the three vehicles deals with the polishing up of the selfish 'I.' Above the rule of the three vehicles, a transcendent rule of vehicles exists. In it, both heaven and humans are transformed; with no name or trace left. There is no word to describe the experience except that you have to experience it.[13]

The following diagram by Liu Zhi may help to explain the practical aspect of the concept of three vehicles.

---

11. Frankel, "*Liu's Journey,*" 210.

12. Ibid., 178–84.

13. This argument in the introductory chapter is further explained in chapter 4 and 5 of *Rules and Proprieties of Islam.*

Liu Zhi's Engagement with Islam and Neo-Confucian Culture 165

Figure 6.1: Diagram of the True Practice of Sage Endeavor

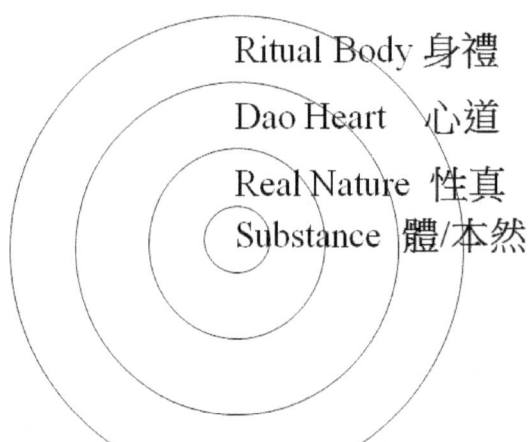

The above diagram is called "the True Practice of Sage Endeavour."[14] Liu Zhi expounded the relationship between the body, heart and nature which correspond to the propriety, way and real respectively. The function of the three vehicles is to remove all kinds of self-centeredness as the seeker makes progress in his path. At the centre is the root suchness. Liu Zhi used root suchness to describe the Real Being and the goal of the endeavor of the sage is the return to the Real. Murata explains the Islamic concept and the endeavor.

> Propriety (the *Shariah*) brings one's body and activities into harmony with the Self-so, the Way (the *Tariqah*) turns one's heart and consciousness away from the lower tendencies of the ego, and the Real (the *Haqiqah*) is the realization of the nature of continuity (the Muhammadan Spirit), which then spontaneously manifests itself in the body's observation of propriety and the heart's following the Way. At this stage, the individual endeavor has been reintegrated into the Self-so,[15] and the engendering and prescriptive commands coincide.[16]

14. The diagram is no. 4.6 of *Nature and Principle in Islam* and titled 'Diagram of the True Practice of Sage Endeavour. Murata et al., *Sage*, 448–9.

15. Self-so literally means nature (*ziran*). Murata translates Liu Zhi's *ziran* either into Self-so or Self-suchness. Murata says that it is a Daoist term. Murata et al., *Sage*, 200, 444.

16. Ibid., 452.

Thus, Liu Zhi's contextualization is to identify the Sufi path of law, path and truth as cultivated body, illuminated heart and unveiled nature respectively. While the law is able to cultivate the body or establish humanity, such mere outward compliance with the law is not sufficient. Islamic law and rites should not be regarded legalistically. Liu Zhi's contextualization emphasizes the transformation of the heart or the *dao* in the heart. Simply put, orthodoxy or mere right understanding is not sufficient for the complete Sufi path. The rite is the first vehicle and necessary beginning for any Sufi path and contributes towards the polishing up of the selfish I. This process is known as the illumination of the heart. Orthopraxis begins with hard work, honoring endeavors and continues polishing up the selfish I. It is right doing with emphasis on the inner transformation of the heart in addition to obedience to the rites of Islam. The second and third vehicle serves to enlighten the heart. Then, the enlightened heart can see the nature of the Sufi path. Such seeing is related to understanding the principle and knowing the nature of humanity.

Vehicle, body, heart, nature, principle, cultivation, enlightenment, and others are common Chinese terms in Liu Zhi's contextualization.[17] Liu Zhi used them skillfully to explain all the characteristics of a Sufi path with his own emphasis on the role of heart. The transformation must involve the heart without any negligence of outward compliance of the law. The goal of heart transformation is enlightenment and seeing. Alternatively put, this is unveiling in the context of Sufism.

Chapter 2: The Real Ruler

This is a recapitulation of Liu Zhi's first work, *The Nature and Principle in Islam*. In this chapter, Liu Zhi developed his understanding of the Real Ruler with respect to rules and proprieties of Islam. This chapter does not explicate the disclosure of the Real as in detailed a manner as his earlier work but the Confucian and commonly used concepts of substance, function, and act are concisely explained. Liu Zhi made a few emphases in this chapter but only two emphases are discussed because they are more relevant to the concept of unity of existence which is one of our objectives.

Firstly, he carefully highlighted the fact that the Real Ruler is both one and unique, notably at the beginning of the chapter and at the end when he unusually expounded the meaning of Qur'an Sura 112. "One and unique" means the Real Ruler is both a transcendent and immanent being.

---

17. This is an important point. Liu Zhi explained in greater detail in chapter 4 and 5 of *Rules and Proprieties of Islam*.

His transcendence is characterized by the pre-existent root suchness. His immanence is characterized by inclusivity and nothing is outside his manifestation. When he expounded Sura 112, he confirmed that there was only one Real Ruler. In addition, Liu Zhi offered two possible reasons for such affirmation in Sura 112. The first one was to refute other religions, possibly Christianity. Liu Zhi believed that in the Christian gospel, the father God begot a son. The second was to encourage the seeker to seek the way single-mindedly so that his body and heart could merge. Thus, the concept of oneness applies to the Real Ruler and also the seekers' union of the heart and body.

Secondly, Liu Zhi's understanding of the Real Ruler emphasizes integration. The Real is both transcendent and immanent. Transcendence is not in opposition to immanence. Rather, the two aspects complement each other. Taking them together, it gives a complete understanding of the Real Ruler. The substance and function of the Real Ruler should be distinguished and yet not separated. While the substance is distinguished from function in terms of being hidden and manifested, they belong to the same category.

Liu Zhi used two examples to illustrate his argument. Numerical numbers like one and ten are different numbers but they are related and belong to the category of number. Ice and coolness or fire and hotness have no chronological priority. Again, the concept of movement and stillness in the Real Ruler should be intertwined and integrated. The Real unceasingly moves and is eternally quiet. There is stillness in movement, movement in stillness. Liu Zhi used the examples of human breathing and the changing seasons to prove his point. Both movement and stillness belong to the ongoing cyclical event. Clearly, Liu Zhi's use of practical example is to help beginners to understand the relation between transcendence and immanence.

With regard to his strategy of contextualization, this chapter is easy to read and understand compared to his earlier work, namely *The Nature and Principle in Islam*. The intricacy of transcendence and immanence of the Real Ruler is clearly explained without the use of a complicated theosophical system. Emphatically, he denies the Christian doctrine that the divine father begot an incarnated son. He defends his understanding of the transcendence and immanence of the Real Ruler and upholds resolutely the oneness and uniqueness of the Real. His goal of contextualization is to help his beginner readers to understand and not to be misled. As for Muslims who have doubted they should cast away any doubt and overcome any heretical deviations.

Chapter 3: Epistemology

Liu Zhi began to explain epistemologically the connection between the ritual practice of a seeker's body, heart and nature with the Real Ruler who is both transcendent in its root suchness and immanent in its action in the acquired heaven. Here, our study will focus on the connection between the knowledge of the Real Ruler and the ritual practices of the seekers and Liu Zhi's contextualization of both knowledge and practice.

Firstly, the existence of a creator who is the Real Ruler is proved by the commonly known cosmological argument in monotheism. The existence of a creator God is the most appropriate explanation after observing not only the existence of the cosmos but also its design. However, the knowledge of this Real Ruler requires more than observations or speculations. Mere outward traits in this creation may not convince people of the existence and attributes of the Real Ruler. The seekers must exhaust the principle and ascertain the nature of all the traits or observable things. Heterodoxies arise because people misinterpret a human being who is a creature as the Real Ruler or an abstract principle as a divine being. Liu Zhi also encouraged his readers to observe one particular aspect of creation, namely the human soul.[18] Thus, observation should be done on both visible and invisible traits in creation. Knowledge of the Real Ruler is acquired through both the visible and invisible traits.

Secondly, it is vitally important to know the Real Ruler and return to him by the ritual practice initiated from the seeker's heart.[19] As noted before, Liu Zhi consistently emphasized the role of human heart. The Real Ruler belongs to the realm of invisibility and boundlessness. How can seekers who belong to the realm of visibility and finiteness make connection with the Real Ruler through ritual rules and proprieties? The key to answer-

---

18. Liu Zhi distinguished between the soul and heart in this chapter. "The heart and way cohere, the soul and subtlety unite." While the heart is related to the way, the soul is related to the subtlety. Murata helpfully explains the Islamic thought behind these two terms. The heart means the mind or the heart-and-mind. Liu Zhi's use of heart never refers to the physical heart. Rather, the heart is the locus of human awareness and consciousness. It embraces physical, psychical and spiritual dimensions. These dimensions are closely related to the Sufi path. The soul (literally as breath) has ambiguous meaning and usually means self. Murata asserts that the soul "is the locus of our individual awareness, our selfhood. Each of us represents a unique combination of spirit and body, light and darkness, intelligence and ignorance, remembrance and forgetfulness." Murata et al., *Sage*, 56. It is with such an understanding of the soul that Liu Zhi related the soul with the subtlety. Rather than the heart, the soul is a clear creation trait by which humanity can ascertain the existence of the creator.

19. When Liu Zhi discussed the Sufi path, the heart or mind played a very important role.

ing the question is Liu Zhi's integrative understanding of the Real Ruler who is both transcendent and immanent. Likewise, the humankind has both visible body and other invisible components like nature and souls. Liu Zhi explained clearly that while the Real Ruler's root suchness and substance were hidden, Ruler's actions were manifested in the innate and the acquired heaven.

This chapter explains that seekers can see the Real's traits in the world of image present in the acquired heaven. Mere compliance with the Islamic rite is not effective in interpreting the trait and experiencing the presence of the Real Ruler. The importance of the seeker's soul which is an invisible part of humankind is emphasized. Proprieties enable the seekers' body and heart to engage properly with the traits in the world. A clever and astute seeker is a trained spiritual person. He ponders the principle and vital energy of the Real Ruler and can see the Ruler in anything. Liu Zhi supported this argument by quoting Qur'an Sura 41:53 and a *Hadith* which says that understanding oneself is to understand the Lord. One should not misinterpret Liu Zhi's commentary of the sacred text. While Liu Zhi maintained the unbridgeable gulf between the human and divine, he also averred epistemologically that humankind had the innate capacity for a general knowledge of the existence of the Real Ruler. A specific knowledge of the Real Ruler must be carried out by unveiling through rules and proprieties with the inner transformation of the heart.

Finally, in the last section of the chapter, Liu Zhi briefly explained his adoption the Real Lord as the most common divine name of Islam. Lordship implies ownership and above all sovereignty. Real means it is the creator. The Real has full control from beginning to eternity and the power to order all things. Thus, Liu Zhi used the Real Lord/Ruler to denote a sovereign, invisible without any image, an all encompassing and pre-determining divine being. He reminded seekers that they should give up any desire to seek a visible image of the deity because it was false and not real. It should be clear in this chapter that while humankind resembles the Real Ruler, there is a significant ontological difference between them. Liu Zhi emphasized that the return to the Real should primarily focus on the practice of the heart although the practice of the body should not be ignored.

From the perspective of contextualization, the most important point is Liu Zhi's comparison between the Real Ruler of Islam and the divine being recorded in the *Analects* in the final paragraph of this chapter.

> My humble view: God as interpreted in the *Analects* as the heavenly Lord is similar to Islam that calls God by the name of the Lord Ruler. Look at the ancient historical records about the

five Emperors and three Kings. They had piety towards God and were sincere. The historical books record that God is called the heavenly Lord, other examples like, royal heaven, vast heaven, heavenly will, and heavenly wrath and so on. Here, we talk about heaven. It means God and does not mean the massive and visible sky...

The older generation of Confucian followers says, 'the evil of the heretics makes it impossible to explain the way.' I consider that the damage of the heresies is to stop the explanation of the way. Those who study the ancient texts, they understand the way. It is due to the words of the ancient emperors and the holy worthies. In this way, the heresy can be eliminated. As a result, the way of Islam can be clear and exposed.[20]

The above quotation gives the clearest answer that Liu Zhi found the Chinese contexts to be helpful conversation partners. He identified the Islamic Real Ruler with the deity taught in very ancient Chinese thought. This thought began around the period of Three Kings and Five Emperors. The estimated time of this period is around 2852–2070 BCE. There is little reliable written record. Liu Zhi believed that Confucius and his immediate followers also taught monotheistic faith but the later followers of Confucius corrupted it and turned the teaching into deviation. The successful earlier Jesuit missionaries in China adopted this argument and asserted that the ancient Kings and Emperors believed in monotheism similar to Christianity. Likewise, Liu Zhi possibly followed the strategy of the early Jesuits a century later. Thus, he intentionally adopted a specific strategy in his contextualization. The above quotation also confirms our interpretation of Liu Zhi's use of Confucianism in his personal narrative in the beginning of this work. Liu Zhi did not teach a sinicized Islam.

Chapter 4: Meaning and Witness

This chapter explains the meaning of endeavors. It focuses on the acquisition of the knowledge of the Real Ruler through nature and body with an emphasis on the role of the heart. Heart is emphasized in both this chapter and the next chapter. In order to explain endeavors in terms of the relationship between body, heart and nature, it is best to remember the earlier diagram of the "True Practice of the Sage Endeavour."

---

20. Appendix IV.

Liu Zhi's Engagement with Islam and Neo-Confucian Culture   171

> Endeavors involve both the body and nature with emphasis on the role of the heart. What do both body and nature prove? Within the body, there are visible, invisible components and also the movement and stillness of the whole body. This is ultimately due to nature. Humankind cannot continue its bodily function without its nature. Also, you cannot see nature outside the body. It is because nature comes first and then the body can function. Nature manifests through the function of the body. This is enough to prove that within this heaven and earth and ten thousand things, visible things and invisible spirit have their origin, namely, the one and real Lord. It is absolutely not that beside the real Lord there is a gap that can hold heaven and earth and ten thousand things. Also, they are not inside the Lord's root suchness that contains all these things. The subtle unity between the real Lord and all things is a mysterious principle similar to the union of heaven and humanity. It is not easy to explain. However, you may understand the mystery from both the body and nature. While it cannot be seen and heard, it can be completely heard and seen with body and nature. Originally, it is beyond our limits and without color and form. Yet you can see the encompassing flowing of substance and function. These are clearly revealed.[21]

In this chapter, Liu Zhi explained that endeavors are not for mere self-cultivation. Muslims use their endeavors to testify the unity of existence between the Real and other existents. While the Real is eternally hidden, both body and nature could manifest the Real in their endeavors.

The relationship between the nature and the heart is explained in the same chapter.

> Nature is invisible and it fully fills the person. Through the heart, the self can understand his nature and also the eyes can see. The thinking can perceive and see his nature but the ears cannot do so. Nevertheless, you have not had any difficulty in working out the form of nature, resulting in a nature that is uncertain and wavering.[22]

Two more quotations on the role of the heart in human endeavors appear in the next chapter, namely chapter 5.

> Why are there five endeavors? It is because the heart and nature of humanity are interconnected, similar to a lock and key. Ears,

21. Appendix IV.
22. Appendix IV.

eyes, mouth, nose and body are affected by sound, color, taste, smell and movement, respectively. These [physical images/ perception] may cause love and hatred toward fleshly feelings. Such feelings are like the spring of a lock, which triggers the lock, making perfect and faultless the union between the heart and nature. If you use the key to open the lock, the spring of the lock is released and thus the union is separated. The five senses of feelings, namely sound, color, taste, smell and movement are a burden and constrain humanity. Thus, five different methods are needed and they gradually can remove the burden. Human nature can be then manifested and the way [of cultivation] is clear. Thus, the five endeavors are necessary for cultivation. . .[23]

While humans may desire cultivating the way, they may not know the method and end in failure. Witnessing the Lord directs the heart to return and does not let the heart linger on aimlessly. Know that the real Lord is the origin of the great transformation and all mandates are derived from him. Anyone who desires to return to the mandate must then follow the real Lord as the reliable guide, achieving the return by constraining the body and heart. If humans give witness to other things, they fail both this life and the afterlife and are beyond any cure. How can it be possible for such humans to hope for any success?[24]

With reference to the diagram of the "True Practice of the Sage Endeavour" comprising four concentric circles, the entry outer circle of endeavor is the ritual body. Rites are carried out by the physical body. However, humanity is composed of both the visible body and invisible nature. Nature is interpreted as the control which governs the action and senses of the body. Thus, nature is inseparable from the body but needs to be distinguished from it. It is prior to the body and determines the body. Between the circle of ritual body and real nature, Liu Zhi put in the circle of *dao* heart. He averred that the real nature was interconnected with the *dao* heart. The relationship between nature and heart is similar to a lock and key. The *dao* heart could lock or open the real nature. When the real nature is locked, it can enter into the level of root suchness with the Real. Thus, the *dao* heart is located at a circle between the body ritual and the real nature. Simply put, the body that practices the rites is controlled by the real nature. However, the body can affect the *dao* heart and vice versa. The body experiences various external factors and this experience may affect the *dao* heart. Thus, the diagram of the True Practice of the Sage Endeavour is explained.

23. Appendix IV.
24. Appendix IV.

Liu Zhi's Engagement with Islam and Neo-Confucian Culture

The ritual body, *dao* heart and real nature are interconnected and inseparable although they are drawn in the diagram as concentric circles. It is the real nature that can unite with the Real but the role of ritual body cannot be ignored at all. The goal of Islamic rites is union with the Real. The role of the heart is that firstly it can affect the body by constant repetition of asserting the unity of God (*Shahadah*) and secondly, the self can then see the invisible nature and understand the mysterious unity of God. This explains Liu Zhi's constant emphasis on the role of the heart. It should be noted that a branch or school of Neo-Confucianism also emphasizes the heart. It is called the School of Mind.

A brief explanation of the School of Mind is now provided. This is needed because it explains the repeated emphases on the role of the heart in all Liu Zhi's works. Zhu Xi (1130–1200) is the leading thinker of the School of Principle and Wang Yangming (1472–1529) is the most important thinker of the School of Mind. At the time of Liu Zhi, the School of Mind is in decline but the School of Principle is gaining imperial recognition and support. Wang Yangming's most important concept of the mind (literally, heart) is related to Liu Zhi's concept of the heart. Wang's fundamental teaching is his interpretation of the Great Learning.[25]

> Wang understood the Great Learning as the learning of the great man. He wrote, 'The great man is an all-pervading unity, which is one with Heaven, Earth and all things.'[26] The great man is able to unite with all things 'because the human-heartedness is naturally so.'[27] The heart has natural instincts and knows that right is right and wrong is wrong. This is intuitive knowledge which is defined by Wang as 'the nature which Heaven has conferred on us, the original state of our mind, which is spontaneously intelligent and keenly conscious. Any ideas which arise are without fail automatically comprehended by this 'intuitive knowledge' of our mind. If they be good, the intuitive knowledge in our mind automatically comprehends this.'[28]

Wang's intuitive knowledge means that the heart in its original state is not obscured by selfishness.[29] This intuitive knowledge is always followed by a corresponding action. A selfish person would not follow the virtuous

---

25. Wang's major writing is *Questions on the Great Learning*. See, Fung, *History*, 598–603.
26. Fung, *Short History*, 508.
27. Ibid., 510.
28. Fung, *History*, 602.
29. Ibid., 604.

instinct of his heart because the heart is obscured. However, the "learning of the great man serves simply to clear away the obscuring and thus to manifest the illustrious virtue, so as thus to restore the original unity of Heaven, Earth and all things."[30] However, there is one major drawback in Wang's concept of intuitive knowledge. Although a pure heart knows right and wrong, it does not give a clear teaching of the practical know-how.

Chapter 4 of *The Rules and Proprieties of Islam* deals with the explanation, meanings and witness of the endeavors. In the beginning, Liu Zhi emphasized the need for exhaustive effort to understand the principle of endeavors and make all investigations of all aspects of endeavors. "Meaning is to know exhaustibly the principle and examine all things. Witness is to explore the mystery and explain the meaning."[31] He clearly adopted the School of Principle and Zhu Xi's concept of investigation of things and the extension of knowledge. The first sentence of this chapter is to emphasize orthodoxy, namely right understanding of Islamic rites, in terms of the School of Principle of Neo-Confucianism. For Liu Zhi, knowing the meaning of endeavors requires an on-going process of hard work. The knowledge needs to be continually expanded.

In the middle part of the chapter and the beginning of the next chapter, the role of heart is then emphasized. Through the heart, the self can understand his nature and also the eyes can see. The heart and nature are interconnected. Liu Zhi most likely adopted Wang Yangming's concept of the mind and explained that the heart must be pure and virtuous, free from any selfishness. While the School of Principle is seemingly in antithesis to the School of Mind in the interpretation of the world,[32] the order of things, and others, Liu Zhi employed both schools of Neo-Confucianism in his explanation of the endeavors. Thus, Liu Zhi's contextualization is to employ any aspect of Neo-Confucianism as long as he could explain the meaning of Islamic rites and also the need for the purity of heart. The School of Mind provides the insight for Liu Zhi to emphasize that the heart must not be obscured by selfish desires. With a pure and sincere heart, the Islamic rites are necessarily virtuous. Simply put, endeavors with right understanding and right doing involve both the body and heart.

In addition, the final goal of both right understanding and doing is unveiling. The prophet Muhammad provides not only the perfect example of endeavors but also assists Muslims' unveiling and their return to the Real.

30. Fung, *Short History*, 510.

31. Alternative translation: Testification.

32. The School of Principle asserts that the nature is principle but the School of Mind asserts that the nature is mind or heart. Fung, *Short History*, 504.

The context of this chapter makes it clear that while the sage in this chapter is not explicitly called the Utmost Sage, the holy sage can be interpreted as the prophet Muhammad.

> Imitate that which is visible and follow the way of the sage. Then, you can reach the realm that is conceived to be impossible to reach. The holy sage is indeed human but he is the representative of the way and also manifests the way. The real Lord is the origin of the holy way. Therefore, testifying to the sage is to testify to the Lord. If you testify thoroughly to the end, you also testify to the deeper mystery of the Lord. You can speak of two testimonies, one to the Lord and the other to the sage. In reality, it belongs to the same principle.[33]

Based on such analysis above, it may be concluded that Liu Zhi's contextualization is uniquely his own in that he selectively made choices from all aspects of Chinese contexts, both the School of Principle and Mind of Neo-Confucianism. He selected, edited and modified his Chinese contexts as necessary to communicate the meaning and witness of Islamic rites.

Chapter 5: Five Endeavors

This is one of the longest chapters in this work and it gives a clear and essential summary of the nature and meaning of the five pillars of Islam which are contextualized as the five endeavors. The Confucian basic meaning of endeavors has the connotation of merit. The word endeavor is a good translation because while the true practice is truly the hard work carried out by the seekers, it is fundamentally empowered by the Utmost Sage and preordered by the Real Ruler. Liu Zhi, the integrative thinker, consistently insisted that both aspects, divine and human, were necessary for humankind to return to the Real Ruler. The previous chapter emphasizes the spiritual or metaphysical meaning of true practice and the unique role of the prophet Muhammad. This chapter follows on from the previous chapter and discusses the complementary aspect of the true practice, namely the practical details for daily living of all Muslims. Liu Zhi emphasized the five endeavors because they were revealed in the sacred Qur'an as divine commands and exemplified by the prophet Muhammad.[34] After an overview in chapter 5, Liu Zhi used three subsequent chapters to expound the five endeavors in greater detail.

33. Appendix IV.
34. The opening prologue emphasizes that the five endeavors are divine commands.

Any reader who examines this chapter generally can get a good overview of the five endeavors. Firstly, one can clearly know that the aim of the five endeavors is more than mere self-cultivation of human character. It is to do ultimately with one's return to the Real or the unity of the human with heaven. The five endeavors are the means to the end. Secondly, one can notice that the major concern of Liu Zhi's discussion is on the first endeavor which is to bear witness, *Shahadah*. While he explained that there were ten extensive rules that governed the true practice of *Shahadah*, the other four endeavors were not given such detailed discussion. At the end of the chapter, he repeatedly emphasized the vital role of *Shahadah*. It is the foundation of the beginning of all things and the backbone of the five endeavors. The ten rules governed not only the external practice of audible and verbal recitation but also the internal practice of inaudible heart recitation. Not only Muslims should understand the meaning of their witness, they should readily without hesitation answer any queries about *Shahadah*.

A more detailed examination of this chapter can reveal Liu Zhi's systematic method in presenting the importance of five endeavors and his integration of outward and inward compliance of law by the true practice of the heart. Thus, the five endeavors are not interpreted legalistically. Also, there is a rational basis and yet the role of the heart is always emphasized. Liu Zhi further explained different aspects of the endeavors.

Firstly, Liu Zhi gave a rational account for the important roles of the five endeavors. While the five endeavors were external rites, they also resembled the five senses of humanity. He argued that physical senses were linked to the inner sentiments of the heart. For Liu Zhi, inner sentiments and feelings were burdens on the seekers, withholding, and constraining the seeker's progress. He used the example of a lock. This example is important and requires brief recapitulation. Sentiments are like the spring of a lock and enable the lock to be open position. The five endeavors are like the key to the lock. If the key is turned, the lock is closed, resulting in an ideal situation of union. The ideal role of the five endeavors is not to allow any inner sentiment to affect the locked position. After birth, human nature gradually becomes insensitive and falsehood grows daily. The five endeavors are to remove such hindrances to the seekers' path. While Liu Zhi occasionally used the Qur'anic source to assert the divine decree, he often resorted to rational argument and thus made his argument more convincing. Unlike *The Nature and Principle in Islam* which uses one diagram to discuss a theme, this chapter provides plentiful illustrations to make his arguments convincing and easier to understand. Obedience to the five endeavors is compared with the discovery of treasure. The seekers continue their endeavors because they are afraid of losing the treasure. The real Lord is the creator, controller, and manager of the cosmos. Liu Zhi illustrated this by saying that a knife must have a knife-maker; a racing chariot a rider in control and a garden a gardener to manage the garden. Thus, the importance of the five endeavors is argued rationally.

Secondly, the integration of the outward compliance of the five endeavors with the inward compliance by the true practice of the heart is emphasized. It is not the body but the heart that has contact with the way of heaven. The way of heaven works harmoniously with the human heart. When the five endeavors are accomplished, the seekers are at the end of the acquired heaven because their hearts are in the appropriate condition to perceive the substance and function in the innate heaven. That is, the seekers have accomplished the true practice of the bodily substance.[35] They may continue their paths or ways with their heart body and nature body. To a certain extent, the external compliance with the five endeavors concerns the true practice of the bodily substance but the internal compliance is equally important.

Another aspect of Liu Zhi's integration deals with the five endeavors. The first endeavor is witness (*Shahadah*). The witness is to direct the seeker towards the real Lord and the prophet Muhammad who was sent by God. This is the seeker's ultimate goal. The seeker should look at nothing in this world but out of this world for the real Lord because he is invisible. The second endeavor is ritual prayer which is the path of return. Seekers practice prayer and they are then on the path of return. It is because the seeker is aware of the final goal and he sets himself on the path towards that final goal. The third and fourth endeavors deal with self-centeredness. The third endeavor of fasting is to resist the temptation of material things and the seeker takes control of his desire. The fourth endeavor of alms-tax is even harder. It is to sacrifice the human self. It is not so much for one to let go of one's desire. More than that, one is dead to material things. The fifth pilgrimage means to return to the real Lord, forgoing the love of home and looking forward to a glorious union with the real Lord. The issue is not the temporary giving up of the visible home or to seek for a holy location. Rather, it is the fervent desire for the unity with the real Lord. Thus, the integration of the five endeavors is the union of humankind with the real Lord, contextualized as self-cultivation of body, heart and nature. Unsurprisingly, when discussing the first endeavor of bearing witness, Liu Zhi emphasized

---

35. Literally, bodily substance means the physical body (*shen ti*). Murata says that 'Liu commonly used *ti* for body, but he tended to use *shen* as a contrast for the heart.' Murata et al., *Sage*, 438. It should be noted that Liu Zhi asserted that humans have three substances, namely bodily substance, heart substance and nature substance. Murata et al., *Sage*, 519.

audible, inaudible, verbal and even nonverbal form of bearing witness from the heart. When discussing prayer, he emphasized set time, ritual and non-set time, and non-ritual prayers.

Finally, the seekers should pay careful attention to the prophet Muhammad who is their example in accomplishing the five endeavors. Liu Zhi laid down ten rules for the important first endeavor, *Shahadah*. In addition, he discussed the role of the Utmost Sage, the prophet Muhammad. The importance of Muhammad is due to both his nature and body. The significance of his nature or more correctly "nature of continuity" is due to its intermediary function. Without his nature of continuity, seekers are not able to actualize their full realization. The significance of his body is due to his receiving of the divine revelation, resulting in the gift of the Qur'an. His sensory and revelatory faculties are superbly miraculous. They are far superior to all previous holy sages. He possesses all the virtues. That is, the prophet Muhammad embodies Islam. To know Islam is also to know the Utmost Sage. In Liu Zhi's expanded annotation, he praised the glorious contributions of the prophet Muhammad.

> Great is the Utmost Sage! His mandate is before heaven and earth and yet he was born at the end of all holy sages.
>
> Great is the Utmost Sage! His way is the tradition of thousands of sages. He faithfully and utterly obeys the Lord of the cosmos.
>
> Great is the Utmost Sage! His endeavors are as huge as the heaven and earth. His way includes both the laws of divine and human.

It is clear and obvious that without the prophet Muhammad, the usefulness of the five endeavors is limited. Liu Zhi's clear and summarized narrative of the Utmost Sage in the final part of chapter 5 on the teaching of five endeavors gives a very clear emphasis that the role of the Utmost Sage is vital for the Muslims to return to the Real. The Utmost Sage has primordial existence in the innate heaven. He is the human ultimate. He is also a human being who has superior revelation and sensory power. Without knowing the Utmost Sage, there is no return to the Real. Any reader can hardly miss that such description of the prophet Muhammad belongs to the Sufi tradition. Like Ibn 'Arabi, Liu Zhi came perilously close to deifying the human ultimate.[36] Liu Zhi's Engagement with Islam and Neo-Confucian Culture

---

36. J. Little asserts that Ibn 'Arabi's concept of the perfect man came close to deifying the prophet. See Little, "Perfect Man," 54.

A CRITICAL ASSESSMENT OF CONTEMPORARY SCHOLARSHIP ON LIU ZHI'S *RULES AND PROPRIETIES OF ISLAM*

Before undertaking an overview of contemporary scholarship on Liu Zhi's *Rules and Proprieties of Islam*, it is necessary to explain Liu Zhi's understanding of the way of heaven and the way of humanity in chapter 10 of this so-called very Confucianized work. In chapter 5, there is an overview of the five endeavors and a brief description of each endeavor. Then, the first endeavor is explained in greater detail. More details of the other four endeavors are explained between chapters 6 and 8. It is in these chapters that the five endeavors are clearly stated as the way to heaven.

From chapter 10, Liu Zhi discussed the way of humanity which describes five Islamic ethics of human relationships (hereafter: five relationships) which bear strong resemblance to five Confucian ethical codes. The five Islamic ethics of relationships are the relationship between king and courtier, father and son, husband and wife, brother and sister and lastly a friend and another friend. These ethical rules for harmonious human relationship are a common code, the norm of nature and unchanging propriety.[37] However, they are more than mere harmonious human relationships. Liu Zhi imbued these relationships with Islamic content in his chapter 10.

> Islam establishes the five endeavors to achieve the way of heaven, also the five relationships to achieve the way of humanity. The way of heaven and humanity are not two ways but the external and internal aspect of just one way. To be on the way of humanity means eventually near to the way of heaven. The foundation of the way of heaven is the way of humanity. Being on the way of heaven is inclusive of the way of humanity. It is because the way of humanity is to put right the essential nature of humankind. At the end of both the way of heaven and humanity, humankind has accomplished things that ought to be done.[38]

Liu Zhi innovatively connected Liu Zhi's Engagement with Islam and Neo-Confucian Culture Liu Zhi's Engagement with Islam and Neo-Confucian Culture the five endeavors (i.e. five pillars of Islam) with the Confucian five ethical codes using both the concept of way of heaven and humanity. Thus, if one just reads chapters 10 to 20 of this work without any reference to all the previous chapters, one easily concludes that Liu Zhi's *Rules and Proprieties of Islam* sinicized Islamic ethics into Confucianism. However, if

37. Liu, *Rules*, 114.
38. Ibid., 116.

one just reads from chapters 1 to 9, one can easily conclude that Liu Zhi's Islamic five endeavors are superior religious proprieties and different from Confucianism. Also, if one focuses on the way of humanity and its parallel with the five Confucian codes, one will conclude Liu Zhi's work is totally sinicized. If one focuses on the way of heaven and its parallel with the five pillars of Islam, one will conclude that his work is very Islamic and yet contextualized. It should be noted that Liu Zhi himself refused to separate the two ways and interweave two aspects together. Thus, it is neither Confucianized nor a mere adaptation of the form of Confucianism. It is important to hold together the two aspects that Liu Zhi has integrated together. Thus, if one merely takes a section of Liu Zhi's work out of context, one can easily misinterpret Liu Zhi's works and his contextualization. We have persistently examined both the longer and shorter works and thus give a more balanced view of Liu Zhi's Islam in Confucian terms.

The common consensus of Chinese scholars on Liu Zhi's work is that *The Rules and Proprieties of Islam* is most Confucianized. A few careful and articulate Chinese scholars who study this work more thoroughly will take a minority view different from the consensus. From the West, there is only one scholar, namely James D. Frankel who investigates in detail some parts of *The Rules and Proprieties of Islam*. A critical assessment of scholarly opinions will be provided at the end of this chapter.

An Overview

With regard to Liu Zhi's Islamic works in general, some contemporary scholars argue that his *Han Kitab* is an articulate effort of Confucianization, Sinicization, indigenization, and even acclimatization[39] of Islam into Chinese culture in his times. Other scholars may assert that Liu Zhi's strategy is accommodation and adaptation. A few scholars may be more neutral in that Liu Zhi intended his works to be mutual cultural enrichment between Muslim and the Chinese. A typical slogan concerning Liu Zhi's works is that these works have tried to seek convergence with the Chinese culture and yet maintained the differences. The core issue is the degree and nature of such differences. Obviously, there is a spectrum of opinions. The majority of Chinese scholars assert that the difference is minor. Only a few scholars aver that the difference is irreconcilable. This consensus of scholarly opinions on the general works of Liu Zhi also carries forward to his *Rules and Proprieties of Islam*. The general consensus at this moment is that his *Rules and Proprieties of Islam* aligns the five relationships with the Confucian five ethical

---

39. Ding, "Issue," 77.

codes. This section will survey the contemporary scholarship and critically assess two contemporary scholarly opinions on this particular work of Liu Zhi.

Ma Duoyong investigates the localization of Islam in China. From a historical perspective, he studies the dialogue between Islam and Confucianism.[40] Ma asserts that Islamic writers, in particular Liu Zhi's *Rules and Principles of Islam*, absorb selectively and yet massively the five codes of Confucianism which are championed by Zhu Xi, the great pioneer of Neo-Confucianism. The basic contents of the five relationships are almost the same as the five codes and give the impression that the Islamic ethics are Confucian-like. Liu Zhi's work selectively avoids any discussion that may minimize the core teaching of Islam. Not only does he put the husband and wife relationship as the first order of his five Islamic ethics, unlike the five codes, Liu Zhi was silent about particular matters of details, such as Muslim widows who could remarry.[41] Re-marriage was despised by Neo-Confucians who considered any virtuous widow should not re-marry. While Liu Zhi emphasized the loyalty of the courtiers to the emperor, he also used Qur'anic teachings that the emperor should know the real Lord and uphold righteousness because the Lord himself symbolized righteousness.[42] Thus, the emperor was in fact under the rule of the real Lord and ruled his empire on behalf of the Real. The emperor should also imitate the sages who proclaimed the Lord's messages and be models and examples to others. Ma concludes that while the ethical systems of Islam and feudal Confucianism are different, they share the common and core concepts of piety and self-realization which closely integrate the two systems together. This integration transforms Islamic ethics into an Islamic ethical system with Chinese characteristics.[43] There is a difference between the two systems. In choosing his materials selectively, Liu Zhi has adapted Islamic ethics and expressed them in Confucian terms.

Ma's view is representative of many scholars in China who support the adaptation and integration of Islam so that Islam in China has its own unique Chinese characteristics. Zhu Xiaojun supports Ma. In his short essay, Zhu avers that Liu Zhi's transference and transformation of the five Islamic relationships into the five codes of Confucianism are mutually beneficial to both Chinese and Islamic traditions in China. Also, Zhu asserts that this is the only plausible way for Islam to continue its existence in China and also

40. Ma, "Dialogue between Islam and Confucianism."
41. Ibid. 26.
42. Ibid., 27.
43. Ibid., 28.

safeguard its interests.⁴⁴ After comparing the five relationships of Chinese Islam with the five codes of Confucianism, Shi Lili even declares that the writers of the *Han Kitab* proactively and strategically converge with the Chinese culture. Islam is thus almost sinicized by their tremendous effort of translation and transformation.⁴⁵

Another group of Chinese scholars are able to point out that while the Islamic rites in *The Rules and Proprieties of Islam* adapt to Neo-Confucianism, the two traditions have substantial differences and yet both benefit from the co-existence. Ji Fangtong examines the theory of self-cultivation between Islam and Confucianism in *The Nature and Principle in Islam*.⁴⁶ He argues with substantial evidence from some Neo-Confucian texts that Liu Zhi's understanding of self-realization has many resemblances and parallels with Neo-Confucianism with few insignificant differences in the true practice of the body, heart, and nature.⁴⁷ Ji acknowledges a major and essential difference. Liu Zhi's work emphasizes that the goal of self-realization is return to the Real and the method of eventual self-realization is annihilation.⁴⁸ Ji concludes that despite the religious difference, human self-realization is a universal phenomenon. Thus, the integration of Liu Zhi's ideas and Neo-Confucianism is an asset for humanity.⁴⁹

A similar view of adaptation and integration is presented by Hai Jing in his general study on filial piety and loyalty between Confucianism and Islam.⁵⁰ Hai says that although Liu Zhi's understanding of the five relationships has its source from the teaching of *Hadith*, the philosophy and the layout of his argument has massive parallels with Confucian ideas.⁵¹ Hai asserts that with respect to the issue of filial piety, Liu Zhi and other *Han Kitab* writers completely adopted the Confucian five codes. With respect to the issue of loyalty to the emperor, they articulately transformed into a dual loyalty to both the Real Ruler and the emperor. Hai Jing notes that to be loyal to the emperor is not necessarily to be disobedient to the Real Ruler. The two loyalties are not in antithesis. Such re-adjustment of the meaning of loyalty is able to reconcile the difference between the two ethical systems.⁵²

44. Zhu, "Briefly Exploring," 37–38.
45. Shi, "Comparison."
46. Ji, "Comparison."
47. Ibid., 139–40.
48. Ibid., 141.
49. Ibid., 142.
50. Hai, "Comparative Study."
51. Ibid., 40.
52. Ibid.

Another well-known scholar of Liu Zhi is Sha Zhongpin who examines specifically Liu Zhi's way of humanity.[53] Sha avers that both Liu Zhi and Neo-Confucians teach the way of heaven and the way of humanity. These two ways are not mutually exclusive but they are two aspects of the same self-realization. Sha concludes that in constructing an ethical thought system for the Hui Muslims, Liu Zhi's ethics have both outward form and inward spirit. The form is taken from Chinese culture and the spirit from Arabic Islam.

Thus, the general scholarly consensus from contemporary Chinese scholars asserts that Liu Zhi's ethical system, in particular his *Rules and Proprieties of Islam*, is Confucianized although he is articulate enough to maintain an Islamic framework or goal. Admittedly, there is a variable difference in degree of Confucianization among scholars.

It should be noted that there is a minority view which differs from the above majority view in China. After examining *The Rules and Proprieties of Islam*, Guo Suxing and Sun Zhenyu in their short essay modestly expound several key themes in Liu Zhi's work.[54] Their analytical exposition is based on a careful reading of the whole range of Liu Zhi's works. Firstly, Liu Zhi favors the heavenly principle, namely the way of the sages as required by the Real Ruler, though the way of humankind is not ignored. Secondly, the role of Islamic rites is to return to the Real and this aspect is silent in Neo-Confucianism. Thirdly, Muslims should have righteous deeds. Fourthly, while Islam emphasizes the religious teachings, it also integrates with the secular teachings of self-realization. The religious teachings are exemplified by the Islamic sages. The secular teachings are to emphasize strict morality in human relationships.[55]

While the work of Guo and Sun is not explicitly contrary to the common consensus, there is a scholar who explicitly disagrees with the majority view. Min Wenjie specifically examines and compares Liu Zhi's five relationships with the Confucian five codes in *The Rules and Proprieties of Islam*.[56] He says that the usual practice of investigating the dialogue between Islam and Confucianism tends to emphasize the common ground in both traditions. However, he emphasizes the qualitative differences.[57] He points out briefly five essential differences.

---

53. Sha, "Examining the Hui."
54. Guo and Sun, "On Liu Zhi's Islamic Thought," 108–15.
55. Ibid., 109–14.
56. Min, "Comparison," 32–36.
57. Ibid., 32.

Firstly, the five relationships are divinely ordained and commanded by the Islamic sacred scriptures. Confucianism has developed in its long history through alteration and enrichment by sages.

Secondly, the order of the five relationships is different from the five codes. Liu Zhi put the husband and wife relationship first because of the teaching of the Qur'an and *Hadith*. The creator created Adam and his wife. Their descendants multiplied and spread to become the whole humankind. Thus, the husband and wife relationship is first in the order of Liu Zhi's Islamic ethics.

Thirdly, it should be noted that the Qur'an and *Hadith* do not teach merely five Islamic ethics of human relationships. The Islamic sacred texts do teach a wide range of human relationships in minute detail. Thus, Min asserts that Liu Zhi selectively chose only five because of his strategic method of communicating Islamic teachings using well-established Confucian terms and practices.

Fourthly, Confucian codes are concerned with the order of human relationships in a feudal society. Islamic ethics are applicable for the sake of this life and the afterlife.

Finally, Islam has a strong view of the mandate or predestination of the Real Ruler and eventual return to him. The Real Ruler is to reward or punish humankind according to the deeds of this life on the Day of Judgment. There is no equivalent concept in Confucianism.[58] Min says that by popularizing the five relationships of Islam using the Confucian five codes among both the literati and the ordinary Han Chinese, other teachings of Islam are more easily accepted by Muslims and non-Muslims. He concludes that contemporary scholars who compare Islamic and Confucian ethical teachings should be cautious and avoid misinterpreting the basic spirit of Islamic ethical thought.[59] We stand with the minority view, namely Min's view and agrees with the reading and comments of Guo and Sun on Liu Zhi's works.

A CRITICAL ASSESSMENT OF CONTEMPORARY SCHOLARSHIP ON *RULES AND PROPRIETIES OF ISLAM*

Substantial monograph-level studies on *The Rules and Proprieties of Islam* have been completed by Liang Xiangming in China and James Frankel in America. There are two main reasons to choose Frankel and Liang. Firstly, this present work is more focused on Liu Zhi's *Rules and Proprieties of Islam*.

58. Ibid., 33–36.
59. Ibid., 36.

Only Frankel and Liang have done more substantial research on this work. Murata and Yin have studied very thoroughly Liu Zhi's *Nature and Principle in Islam*. They have focused more on cosmogony, divine disclosure and anthropology. Thus they are not chosen for assessment. Secondly, Frankel and Liang are chosen because they reflect two different perspectives on Liu Zhi's work. While Liang's analysis reflects his understanding of Liu Zhi in engagement more with his contemporary Chinese scholars, Frankel's work reflects his understanding of Liu Zhi in engagement more with contemporary Western scholarly research within the general Neo-Confucian context.

James Frankel's Works

Frankel's published book relates to Liu Zhi's *Rules and Proprieties of Islam*, in particular the first few chapters. Frankel has published a few essays on Chinese Islam.[60] Liang has published several academic articles in Chinese journals on Liu Zhi during the last fifteen years.[61] Two important book-length studies related to Liu Zhi's works have also been published.[62]

Frankel has made a great contribution to highlight the significance of *The Rules and Proprieties of Islam* in the *Han Kitab*. He also praises the literary erudition of this work. Frankel's substantial monograph asserts three main points. Firstly, in his support of Benite's thesis, he avers that the identity of Hui Muslims in late Ming and early Qing dynasties is Muslim and Chinese simultaneously. In other words, part of Liu Zhi's work is to raise the Hui Muslims' awareness of their Islamic and Chinese dual inheritance.

Secondly, he asserts that the concept of law or *shariʿa* in Liu Zhi's *Rules and Proprieties of Islam* is both to regulate behavior and prescribe a path for religious endeavor. In agreement with Murata, he says that Liu Zhi's concept of *shariʿa* is dependent heavily on Sufi thought.

Finally, Frankel explains that Liu Zhi carefully searches for Allah's Chinese name in the monotheistic antecedents in the Chinese tradition. Frankel believes that Liu Zhi's search is primarily influenced by the sixteenth-century Jesuits in China and Chinese Jews secondarily. The term *zhu* or lord is adopted eventually because "the fact that Nestorians had already established

60. Frankel, *Rectifying*. It should be noted that Frankel's PhD thesis often quotes the Chinese texts and the corresponding English translations. However, the Chinese texts are missing in his book, *Rectifying*. See also Frankel, "From Monolith to Mosaic," 249–58; Frankel, "Uncontrived Concord," 46–54; Frankel, "Apoliticization," 421–34.

61. Liang, 'On Political Ethic," 53–58; Liang, "On Traditional Ethics," 37–44; Liang, "View of the Hui Scholar Liu Zhi," 120–4; Liang, "Analysis," 86–92; Liang, "Liu Zhi: Using Confucianism," 88–91.

62. Liang, *Study on Ethics*. This is the published version of his PhD thesis in 2007.

this as a term suitable for monotheistic theology in the stele inscription of 781, followed later by the Jesuit coinage of the title *tianzhu*, 'Lord of Heaven,' set a precedent for Muslim writers to follow."[63] The central thesis of Frankel's monograph is that:

> [a]ccommodating his [Liu Zhi's] thought to the rational standard of contemporary Chinese thought, in his presentation of Islam Liu Zhi downplayed the role of revelation, expounding instead theological concepts, with frequent reference to natural law and sophisticated metaphysical arguments of Neo-Confucian lixue (lit. "study of principle"). In terms of Islamic orthopraxy, he harmonized Muslim religious practice with the Confucian principle of ritual (*li*), thus demonstrating that Islam is built upon the same central pillar of civilization as Confucian culture is.[64]

Frankel concludes his assessment and prefers the term accommodation to contextualization.

> Liu Zhi constructed effective arguments for the harmonization of Confucian and Islamic ideas of morality and ethics, hinging upon the concept of ritual. And while he did manage to syncretize certain important metaphysical concepts of the two traditions, he ultimately could not bridge the theological gap that divided them. Yet syncretism was Liu Zhi's method, not his goal—promoting better understanding of Islam was.[65]

Frankel's study on Liu Zhi in particular and *Han Kitab* in general gives a cautious and helpful insight for any contemporary study and scholarship of these Chinese Muslim literati whose existence was challenged by the hegemonic Chinese civilization in the late Ming and early Qing dynasties. Frankel's view is that

> It is not that conflict and concord are not prominent features of Chinese Muslim history; they certainly are ... The concord, or harmonization, that many observe in the writings of the Chinese Muslim literati elite ... was the organic product of individual minds, acting in a communal and generational context, in an effort to make sense of a hybrid intellectual, cultural and religious heritage.[66]

63. Frankel, *Rectifying*, 160.
64. Ibid., xix–xx.
65. Ibid., 180.
66. Frankel, 'Uncontrived Concord,' 46.

Thus, in terms of contextualization Frankel argues for a hybrid and organic relationship between Hui Muslim thought and Neo-Confucianism.

Liang Xiangming's Works

While Frankel's work involves both Chinese and Arabic sources, Liang's work focuses primarily on the Chinese sources and contexts. While Frankel's work focuses more on Liu Zhi's early chapters of *The Rules and Proprieties of Islam*, Liang's work examines more thoroughly many works of Liu Zhi including close reading of Islamic ethics in *The Rules and Proprieties of Islam*. Liang notes that Liu Zhi's task is difficult because Arabic religious and philological concepts are not easy to translate into Confucian terms. In *The Rules and Proprieties of Islam*, Liang notes that the content is concerned with fundamental Islamic doctrines, both theoretical and practical aspects. Liang also avers that Liu Zhi used Confucian concepts and ideologies merely to express his doctrinal teachings. Liang describes Liu Zhi's work as Islamic doctrinal teachings with Chinese characteristics.[67] In his study on Liu Zhi's Islamic ethics in *The Rules and Proprieties of Islam*, Liang agrees with the majority view that Liu Zhi intentionally contextualized the Islamic five relationships into the Confucian five ethical codes. However, Liang admits that such contextualization of Islam into Chinese culture is subtle and articulate.

Liang says that the first point of Liu Zhi's contextualization is flexibility. Confucian teaching insists on a courtier's obedience to the emperor to the extent that when the emperor orders him to die, the courtier should obey. While Liu Zhi followed the Confucian five ethical codes and insisted on the obedience of the courtier to the emperor, he also used Qur'anic verses (an example like the story of King David) and *Hadith* to command the emperor that he should rule righteously and under the sovereignty of the Real Ruler.[68] The second point of contextualization is Liu Zhi's insistence on both the way of heaven and way of humanity. While the five relationships are the way of humanity, it is the five endeavors that are the way of heaven. The way of heaven represents the distinctive Islamic worldview with its emphasis on afterlife and the spiritual aspects of Islamic rites. The Confucian worldview has more to say on human ethical relationships and very little on the afterlife.

Liang views Liu Zhi's works as a subtle, articulate and creative contextualization of Islam into the Chinese culture. With respect to cosmogony and epistemology, Liang says that Liu Zhi used Confucianism as his means

---

67. Liang, "Using Confucianism to Interpret Islam," 90.
68. Liang, *Study on Ethics*, 137.

to communicate Islamic teachings. However, with respect to an ethical system, Liang avers that Liu Zhi's Islamic ethics were enriched by Confucianism. Liang concludes that while the Islamic practices serve as the form, it is the Confucian five relationships that are the core contents of Liu Zhi's ethical system.[69]

In addition to a specific examination of Islamic ethics in *The Rules and Proprieties of Islam*, Liang also examines Liu Zhi's works in general. He has made several general observations. Firstly, Liang asserts that while Liu Zhi's cosmogony was primarily influenced by theoretical Sufism, his exposition was eclectic using philosophical ideas from Daoism, Buddhism and both the Principle and Mind School of Neo-Confucianism.[70] While his exposition was eclectic, Liu Zhi truly maintained his Islamic foundation and theology. Liang says that Liu Zhi held firm to the fundamental Islamic tenets that the real Lord is one and unique and also Muhammad is the ultimate prophet. There is no more Islamic prophet after him. Liang avers that this fundamental belief of Liu Zhi never disappears despite his contextualization of Islam to the Chinese culture.[71]

Secondly, Liang asserts that the doctrine of the unity of existence forms the overarching principle by which Liu Zhi integrated his various teachings of ontology, cosmogony, epistemology, and ethics.[72] His doctrine of the unity of existence is influenced clearly by mysticism.[73] The significance of this doctrine is primarily concerned with the knowledge of the Real Ruler. The Ruler reveals itself to creation by both invisible and visible manifestations. Humankind can know the Real Ruler by the way of heaven and the way of humanity paying careful attention to the true practice of the body and heart.[74] Liu Zhi's teaching on the true practice of the heart is explicitly influenced by Sufism.[75]

Thirdly, Liang argues that Liu Zhi made compromise in his political view. Liu Zhi taught that the emperor was a representative of the Real Ruler. That is, the emperor was the agent on behalf of the Ruler to govern the state. Anyone who prayed to the Ruler and ignored the emperor made no prayer

---

69. Ibid., 133–4.
70. Liang, *Study of Liu Zhi*, 32, 33, 44, 48.
71. Ibid., 52.
72. Ibid., 49, 57–62.
73. Ibid., 57.
74. Ibid., 62–73.
75. Ibid., 74.

to the Ruler at all. Liang concludes that in this particular view, Liu Zhi made compromise and his political view was explicitly Confucianzied.[76]

Finally, Liang supports the view that Liu Zhi's works primarily aim to expound Islamic doctrines and use Confucian concepts, logics, and thinking method as interpretative tools (以儒詮經).[77] Confucianism is just a means and not an end. The result is not merely a better understanding of Islam by Muslims and less misunderstanding of Islam by the majority Han Chinese. It also has the effect of mutual enrichment and complementarity between Islam and Chinese culture especially in the area of ethical thinking and human self-realization.[78] It achieves such a satisfactory effect because of Liu Zhi's flexible method and appropriate artifice in his interpretation.[79] Has Liu Zhi betrayed his Islamic original teaching? Liang asserts that a long period of continuous contextualization of Islam into Chinese culture has gone through a process of co-existence, exchange, and integration. Such a long process of contextualization has brought enrichment to the Chinese culture including astronomy, medicine, and architecture by the arrival and continual influence of Islam. This contextualization has thus exceeded the religious boundary.[80] Liang concludes that Liu Zhi's works are truly Islamic and have not betrayed at all the principle of beliefs in Islam.[81] In essence, Liang argues that Liu Zhi has Confucianized his Islamic ethics but not his basic tenets of Islamic belief.

A Critical Assessment of Frankel and Liang

Admittedly, the two scholars have made scholarly advances in the study of Liu Zhi's *Rules and Proprieties of Islam* and provided a better understanding of Islamic rites within the Confucian cultural background. Their contributions complement the recent research in the study of Liu Zhi's *Nature and Principle in Islam* by Murata and Jin. This critical assessment of the two contemporary scholars can cover various aspects from comparative religious studies to self-realization and return to the Real Ruler. However, we shall focus on the issue of unity of existence and Sufi spirituality by Liu Zhi. Several critical comments may be made.

76. Ibid., 85.
77. Liang makes helpful and general comments on various scholarly models about Lu Zhi's adaptations. Ibid., 161–62.
78. Ibid., 164.
79. Ibid., 165.
80. Ibid., 167.
81. Ibid., 198.

Firstly: while both Xiang and Frankel admit the influence of Sufism on Liu Zhi's works, their investigation is not detailed enough to provide an Islamic context to explicate Liu Zhi's explicit Ibn 'Arabi tradition. Other scholars, namely, Murata and Yin have paid careful attention to Liu Zhi's Islamic tradition. When Murata examines Liu Zhi's *Nature and Principle in Islam*, she often refers back to the Ibn 'Arabi tradition and Liu Zhi's quoted Sufi books in order to make sense of the meaning of various Chinese terms used by Liu Zhi. Moreover, she also refers to the later Arabic translation of *The Nature and Principle in Islam* by Ma Lianyuan, who is also known as Nur al-Haqq and Ma's Arabic translation has helped her to work out some of the difficult meanings of Liu Zhi's Chinese terms.[82] The strongest evidence that Liu Zhi is influenced by the Ibn 'Arabi tradition is his translation of Jami's *Lawa'ih* into *Displaying the Concealment of the Real Realm* in Chinese. Similarly, Yin also pays attention to Liu Zhi's Sufi sources and discusses their significance among Hui Muslims in their Scripture Hall Education System. Yin provides a detailed essay on Sufism in China and indirectly provides a detailed account of Liu Zhi's Sufi context.[83] Thus, the Islamic tradition of Liu Zhi has been carefully investigated by Murata and Yin. While both Frankel and Liang acknowledge that Liu Zhi was influenced by his tradition, both of them pay insufficient attention to Sufi influence in their interpretation.

Secondly, both Frankel and Liang have not sufficiently attended to the mystical role of the Utmost Sage, Muhammad in the Sufi tradition. This unique role of the prophet Muhammad has been discussed in the last chapter. The exemplary role of the Utmost Sage is vital and he is the perfect exemplar of all sages in Islam. He is also the sole vicegerent of humankind. He guides and enables all Muslims in their spiritual quests. The role of the Utmost Sage is important in both the innate heaven and the acquired heaven. In Liu Zhi's concept of the unity of existence, the Muhammadan Spirit (such as the concept of the nature of continuity of the Utmost Sage) gives rise to creation and humanity. Muslims are enabled by the Utmost Sage in their return to the Real Ruler. Both Frankel and Liang are willing to acknowledge the influence and significance of the Ibn 'Arabi tradition and its concept of the unity of existence. Again, both of them give insufficient attention to the role of the prophet Muhammad. Liang is able to give an account of Liu Zhi's Islamic worldview including the unity of existence and the role of Islamic ethics within such a worldview. However, Frankel gives more attention to the simultaneous Chinese-Muslim identity of the Hui and Liu Zhi's search for the Islamic name of God in Chinese. Frankel does not say much about

82. Murata et al., *Sage*, 15.
83. Jin, *Sufism in China*, 123–212.

the Utmost Sage but this is not the focus of his study. This second critique is in continuation of the first critique in that had Frankel and Liang paid sufficient attention to the Sufi context and the mystical tradition of the Utmost Sage in the writings of Liu Zhi, their studies would have greater insights.

Finally, we should consider their arguments about Liu Zhi's contextualization. Both Frankel and Liang have found it difficult to articulate a consistent strategy in Liu Zhi's contextualization. Frankel argues that Liu Zhi's method is syncretic but syncretism is not his goal. It is a means to an end. Also, Liu Zhi downplayed divine revelation and managed to harmonize Islamic practices with Confucian culture. In essence, Liu Zhi's Islam adapted merely the form of Confucianism. Thus, Frankel has not taken the side of the majority view. While Liang affirms that Liu Zhi's Islam is an adapted and subtle Islam with Chinese characteristics, in particular his political emphasis of Muslim loyalty to the imperial rulers, he also says that Liu Zhi adhered to the basic tenets of Islam. Thus, both of them find it difficult to give a neat, simple and direct statement of Liu Zhi's contextualization.

A brief recapitulation of the successful contextualization by the Jesuit missionary Ricci Matteo in seventeenth-century China is helpful. Matteo's contextualization can be similarly interpreted as a dialectical model of contextual theology. Later, the Jesuit mission in China faded away because of the rite controversy between the Qing Emperor Kangxi in China and the Pope in the Vatican. Liu Zhi employed a similar but not the same strategy of the Jesuit missionaries. Recent contemporary cross-cultural study emphasizes dialectical engagement.[84] Angie Pears avers that dialectical engagement is to avoid polarizing positions of continuity and discontinuity.[85] The two poles are really related to each other through creative interaction and also through critical affirmation and rejection of cultures. It means that the husk can synthesize with Chinese culture but the kernel is supracultural, namely context oriented and yet text-based.

Liu Zhi's model of contextualization has an irenic spirit. It is not confrontational, possibly avoiding the mistakes that later Jesuit missionaries made in eighteenth-century China. His model is definitely not setting the Hui Muslims up against other non-Muslims in China. His goal is to encourage Hui Muslims' right understanding, doing, and eventual unveiling without any alienation with the Chinese culture. Thus, his contextualization is strategically dialogical. His translation of Islamic texts has followed the similar strategy of his well-known predecessor Wang Daiyu in accordance

---

84. Contextual theology and dialectical engagement will be discussed in greater detail in chapter 7.

85. Pears, *Doing*, 1–49.

with the Ibn 'Arabi tradition. Liu Zhi's dialectical engagement is context-oriented, always in conversation with the Chinese culture but his content is supracultural and based on Islamic text. His model of contextualization is known as translation-conversation model.[86] The context and content are held dialectically in creative interaction. It is neither Confucianization nor mere adaptation of the form of Confucianism. His contextualization encapsulates the dialectical engagement, sensitive to the Confucian cultural context and faithful to the Islamic tradition. This model provides a neater and more coherent explanation than those arguments put forward by both Frankel and Liang.

CONCLUSION

This chapter translated and analyzed the first five chapters of *The Rules and Proprieties of Islam* with special reference to Liu Zhi's model of contextualization. The first part of the chapter examined each chapter of his work individually. The second part critically commented on contemporary scholarship on Liu Zhi's *Rules and Proprieties of Islam*. We have shown that while Liu Zhi claimed in his author's preface that his *Rules and Proprieties of Islam* was no different from Neo-Confucian works, this claim should be understood in the context of learning and understanding the rites of Islam. That is, the process of learning Islamic rites is no different from learning Neo-Confucian classical works. Scholars often quote this claim and erroneously assume that Liu Zhi's Islam is Confucianized.

In the first part of this chapter, we have shown that Liu Zhi interpreted the five endeavors or pillars of Islam in Islamic terms as the way of heaven and the five ethical human relationships in Confucian terms as the way of humanity. The two ways should be distinguished and yet not separated. The aim of Islamic rules and proprieties is to know the Real and the goal is to return to the Real. As noted, Liu Zhi emphasized the role of the heart in Islamic rites. Liu Zhi contextualized the role of the heart according to the School of Mind in Neo-Confucianism. In Liu Zhi's contextualization, he was willing to employ any school of thought in Neo-Confucianism as long as he could explain the meaning of Islamic rites and also the need for purity of heart.

The second part of this chapter discussed the scholarly debate between Frankel and Liang on Liu Zhi's *Rules and Proprieties of Islam*. Frankel avers that Liu Zhi might be influenced by the seventeenth- and eighteenth-century Jesuits in China and their strategy of accommodation or adaptation to

---

86. This model will be further discussed in the final chapter.

Chinese contexts. Frankel argues that syncretism was Liu Zhi's method but his goal was to promote better understanding of Islam. Liang asserts that Liu Zhi's contextualization of Islam into Chinese culture is subtle, articulate, and creative. Liang argues that Confucianism is just a means and not an end. Not only did Liu Zhi's contextualization promote better understanding of Islam, but he was also able to bring mutual enrichment and complementarity between Islamic and Chinese cultures especially in the area of ethical thinking and human self-realization. We have shown and argued that both Frankel and Liang have provided insights into Liu Zhi's contextualization but they find it difficult to give a neat, simple and direct statement of Liu Zhi's model of contextualization.

It is concluded that Liu Zhi's contextualization engages in active dialogue with Chinese contexts. His strategy is context oriented and yet text-based. This model should be called the translation-conversation model which will be further discussed in the next chapter.

7

Model of Contextualization, Contemporary Relevance and Final Conclusion

LIU ZHI'S TRANSLATION-CONVERSATION MODEL OF CONTEXTUALIZATION

In chapter 1 of this study, we discussed the six models of contextualization by Bevans. He notes that two or more models might be operating in a particular context. Based on the results of our investigation, we have selected a composite model. That is, Liu Zhi used the translation-conversation model in his contextualization of the Islamic tradition. He is an erudite Islamic scholar and a skilful cultural agent. Liu Zhi's contextualization presented a vital, transformative, and contemporary expression of Islam in the Neo-Confucian context.

Liu Zhi's translation-conversation model of contextualization has several characteristics. Firstly, Liu Zhi was in dialogue with several cultural frameworks: Buddhism, Daoism, and Neo-Confucianism. He was not merely interested in the School of Principle and the School of Mind in Neo-Confucianism. He was also in conversation with all aspects of the diverse Chinese cultures of his time. He was possibly aware of the Catholic missionary Matteo Ricci's approach of contextualization and might have read Jesuit books or their translated texts.

Secondly, Liu Zhi's contextualization adopted the various strengths of both translation and conversation models as discussed by Bevans and yet simultaneously reduced the built-in dangers of the two models. Bevans avers that the translation model persistently preserves the basic tenets of belief. Thus, the contextual situation ultimately is the vehicle of the basic message of religious faith. The context is always a secondary element. The major strength of the translation model is its safeguard of the integrity of the basic tenets of belief and the Islamic tradition. With respect to the conversation model, its major strength is its emphasis both on the uniqueness of Chinese culture and its complementarity with the basic Islamic tenets of belief. With such positive attitudes to culture and by the process of genuine conversation between the dialogical partners of Islam and diverse Chinese cultures, Liu Zhi seeks to create a reformed and renewed expression of Islam. The goal of conversation is that each partner can learn from the other, and each can profit from the other.

Liu Zhi's translation-conversation model of contextualization demonstrates that he upheld the basic tenets of Islam, including the unity of divine existence, return to the Real in the afterlife, and the basic five pillars of Islam. Without any sign of compromise in his contextualization, Liu Zhi emphasized the sole existence of the divine being, the unique role of the last prophet Muhammad, the ultimate authority of the Qur'an, and the divine revelation of the five pillars. Also, he readily employed both Neo-Platonic and Neo-Confucian concepts and terms to explain Islamic cosmogony. He used the idea of the innate and the acquired heaven to explain his Islamic worldview. Moreover, he employed well known concepts of Neo-Confucian self-cultivation to explain Islamic and Sufi spirituality. The most distinctive and creative expression of his contextualization was his affirmation of dual loyalty to both the divine being and the imperial non-Islamic rulers. Loyalty to the imperial ruler did not compromise any faithfulness to the divine being.

Finally, this model of contextualization can satisfactorily explain the modern opinions among both Chinese and English scholars. Many Chinese scholars note Liu Zhi's articulate contextualization by a careful and extensive use of Neo-Confucianism. Not surprisingly, some of them have commented that Liu Zhi's Islam was fully sinicized. Also, a few Chinese scholars note that Liu Zhi selectively used Neo-Confucianism. These few scholars assert that while Liu Zhi's five Islamic ethical relationships are very similar to the Neo-Confucian five merits, Liu Zhi's framework of such relationships was clearly based on a unique Islamic concept. In addition, Liu Zhi altered and re-arranged the order of the five relationships in accordance with Islamic values. Almost all the contemporary Chinese scholars agree that Liu Zhi's contextualization was able to enrich Neo-Confucianism with Islamic culture. All these comments bear the hallmark of the conversation model, namely a Hegelian sense of synthesis. On the other hand, the English speaking scholars are able to clearly illustrate Liu Zhi's faithful use of Persian and Arabic Islamic sources. Thus, Liu Zhi's translation and exposition of the Ibn 'Arabi tradition was conservative. Liu Zhi was an erudite scholar in his translation and exposition of difficult Islamic concepts. Simply put, his strategy is context oriented and yet text-based.

The following is a summary of the main characteristics of Liu Zhi's translation-conversation model of contextualization that we have demonstrated:

- Liu Zhi upholds the divine authority of the sacred texts, especially the Qu'ran, and highly valued his received tradition. Revelation is primarily propositional.

- His translation emphasizes both the exoteric and esoteric interpretations of Islamic texts. In his transmission of Islamic texts, Liu Zhi apparently chooses the Islamic texts selectively. He also expands the meaning of the texts in his interpretation and yet he is in accordance with the Ibn 'Arabi tradition of Islam.

- His exposition and explanation of Islamic thought are expressed mainly, but not exclusively, in Confucian terms.

- His engagement with Chinese culture is by active dialogue or conversation. He builds bridges between Islamic thought and the Confucian context, so that Muslims in their own Chinese contexts could understand the Islamic messages in the Chinese texts.

- His contextualization interplays the experience of the past (Scripture and tradition) with the experience of the presence (experience, culture, social location and social change).

- In his engagement with the Confucian concept of self-cultivation, he contextualizes it as Sufi spirituality.

- He upholds the teachings of ancient Chinese sages and understands Chinese culture as a partner of Islamic teaching. However, Liu Zhi insists that while the Prophet Muhammad was understood as the Utmost Sage, he was unique and superior to all other sages.

In view of the above characteristics of Liu Zhi's contextualization, it is best to describe Liu Zhi's model as translation-conversation. This model can also be understood as a movement of descent and ascent. His work of translation is to communicate the Islamic message in the language and culture of real people in their contexts. He seeks to build bridges between divine revelation and the human context. This is a movement from the revealed text to the context or descent. In addition, he engages and adapts the Confucian concept of self-cultivation as Sufi spirituality. This is a movement from below, or from the human context, back to the divine text or ascent, or where God wants humans to be. Both the concept of Confucian self-cultivation and the concept of Sufi return to the Real Ruler are understood as a single process of transformation. For Liu Zhi, this transformation includes individuals, as well as corporate and cultural systems. For the Muslim readers of Liu Zhi's works, their way or *dao* of Muslim living could be understood as Confucian self-cultivation.

TRIANGULATING THE TEXT, CULTURE, AND WISDOM IN THE NEO-CONFUCIAN CONTEXT

Liu Zhi was an erudite translator of Persian or Arabic text, well-versed in his own Islamic tradition. Also, he was a competent cultural reader, well-versed in his Neo-Confucian tradition. We have shown that Liu Zhi's contextualization has been effective because while he transmitted his Islamic tradition in Neo-Confucian culture, he contextualized it by triangulating text, culture, and wisdom together.[1] Thus, while the form of contextualization is translation-conversation, the content is triangulation of text translation, culture adaption, and spiritual wisdom.

The reasons for the appearance and common usage of *Han Kitab* (Islamic texts in Chinese) in Islamic education halls are many and should be carefully studied within the historical setting, philosophical thoughts and religious activities of that time. Firstly, in the case of the Nanjing Muslim literati of seventeenth- to eighteenth-century China, namely Wang Daiyu and Liu Zhi, the reasons for *Han Kitab* were as follows:

- defend the strange ritual practices;
- strengthen the Hui Islamic and cultural identity;
- achieve the balance of both exoteric and esoteric aspects of Islam;
- contextualize Chinese Sufism in the seventeenth century;
- adapt to the increasing imperial control in the Chinese language context; and

1. This view owes much to Kevin Vanhoozer's hermeneutical methodology. See Vanhoozer, "On the Very Idea," 125–82. While Vanhoozer triangulates between Scripture, church and the world or words, God's Word and the world, this study triangulates between text, culture and practical wisdom.

- provide some user-friendly textbooks, poems, tracts, and teaching aids for the Scripture Hall Education System.

Secondly, Liu Zhi sought to find an effective method of transmission embracing both translation of texts and dialogical engagement with the Chinese culture. He triangulated three aspects, namely creative translation of text, articulated interpretation of the Chinese culture and practical wisdom. Triangulation involves communicative interaction. It discards the subject/object dichotomy. That is, both the sacred text and Chinese culture interact with the world of practical wisdom. Putting this into Liu Zhi's context, both Islam and Neo-Confucianism are subjects and they communicatively interact with the world of wisdom in seventeenth-century China.

A SUMMARY OF LIU ZHI'S TRANSLATION-CONVERSATION MODEL OF CONTEXTUALIZATION

The following table is a summary of Liu Zhi's method of contextualization. None of the following points has been noted and discussed by scholars in English and Chinese with exceptions mentioned in the footnote.

Table 7.1: Various Aspects of Liu Zhi's Contextualization

Topics	Various Aspects of Liu Zhi's Contextualization
Liu Zhi's Use of Chinese Contexts	1.0 *The Poem of the Five Sessions of the Moon*: very eclectic and use Confucian, Buddhist, and to a lesser degree Daoist terms 2.0 *The Nature and Principle in Islam*: Mainly use Zhou Dunyi and Zhu Xi's cosmological terms i.e. Neo-Confucian terms[A] 3.0 *The Rules and Proprieties of Islam*: The Islamic concept in the second half of this work is interpreted in Confucianized term but the first half is not so obvious. 4.0 *The True Record of the Utmost Sage*: Muhammad is interpreted as the Utmost Sage. As a whole, use few Confucian terms except one appendix chapter at the end.
Liu Zhi's Pedagogical Method in his Works	*The Poem of the Five Sessions of the Moon*: Articulate Confucian literary style and ease of memorization *The Nature and Principle in Islam*: Diagram and explanation *The Rules and Proprieties of Islam*: Text, commentary, annotation and illustration *The True Record of the Utmost Sage*: Narrative, drama, mythical story and Chinese history

Text and Context	While the authoritative text remains unchanged, the application of the principle of rules and proprieties of Islam should be flexible and adaptive in various contexts. Progress is made when such application is fair and not offending to the community in the contexts at that time.
Sufi Wisdom	1.0 *Shari'a* law: Rites are based on the revealed text. 2.0 *Tariqa*: the Sufi path begins with a pure, sincere and virtuous *dao* heart without any obscuring. *Dao* heart works together with real nature and then can 'see' 3.0 *Haqiqa*: unveiling and return to the Real One; the vital role of the Utmost Sage[B]
Knowledge of Rites and the Real Ruler	Right understanding: the School of Principle; investigation of things and the extension of knowledge Right doing: the School of Mind; a pure *dao* heart without any obscuring leading to virtuous action Union with the Real Ruler: the goal of union is similar to other Chinese thoughts: That is firstly, treasure in the deep sea and Buddhist enlightenment; secondly, Daoist's exalted state of existence and the perfect man, and thirdly, School of Mind (the concept of the Great Man who unites Heaven and Earth).

  A. This point has been noted and discussed by Jin, Murata, and others.
  B. Murata et al., *Sage*, 71, 452.

We have shown that Liu Zhi's contextualization is by using the translation-conversation model. This conclusion is the result of research after translating, examining and critically commenting on Liu Zhi's major and some of his minor works. This model of contextualization provides a more convincingly explanation of existing arguments proposed by both Western and Chinese scholars on Liu Zhi's works. The following statements of his contextualization can be noted:

1. In general, all of Liu Zhi's works are contextualized and should be known as contextual Islamic theology.

2. With respect to his trilogy, the most contextualized work is his *Rules and Proprieties of Islam*. It is followed by *The Nature and Principle in Islam* and the least is *The True Record of the Utmost Sage of Islam*.

3. In *The Nature and Principle in Islam*, Liu Zhi used Neo-Confucian terms and concepts to explain the great transformation using the innate heaven and the acquired heaven. Human composition and social class divisions are also explained in Neo-Confucian terms. However, the theological framework is based on the worldview and tradition of the Ibn 'Arabi tradition.

4. In *The True Record of the Utmost Sage of Islam,* Liu Zhi made little effort to contextualize the prophet Muhammad except one chapter in the appendix.

5. In *The Rules and Proprieties of Islam,* Liu Zhi made use of the Neo-Confucian concept of self-realization to explain the five pillars of Islam. It is based on this work that many scholars argue that Liu Zhi adapted or inculturated Islam into Chinese culture.

6. In general, Liu Zhi was influenced by his Chinese Sufi tradition. He contextualized the Sufi spirituality of seekers as the way of return to the Real Ruler by using Neo-Confucian or other Chinese religious spirituality. This is clearly demonstrated by his poem, *The Five Sessions of the Moon* and can also be seen in other works, in particular *The Rules and Proprieties of Islam.*

THE CONTEMPORARY RELEVANCE: MUSLIMS AS MINORITIES

Liu Zhi translated and applied the Islamic texts which Muslim literati had received into their respective Chinese contexts. Liu Zhi had a daunting task because he argued that one could be both a Muslim and a Chinese under an increasingly oppressive Qing imperial rule. To do so, Liu Zhi endeavored to continue interpreting the received Ibn ʿArabi tradition within his own context in Chinese. On the one hand, he distinguished Islam from the Chinese culture by stating Islam belonged to the wisdom of the Arab world, founded by a western sage, Muhammad who received direct revelation from God. Thus, he separated Islam as a religion from Chinese social culture. On the other hand, he argued that Islamic rites and Chinese socio-religious culture were compatible and they would exist harmoniously.[2]

Liu Zhi's contextualization resonates with the contemporary Islamic scholar, Tariq Ramadan. Ramadan's works focus on Islamic theology and the position of the Muslim in the West and within Muslim minority countries.[3] Ramadan calls himself both a Muslim and a Swiss. He affirms that there is a difference in nature between the Islamic principles related to religious ritual and those that concern the affairs of the world and society.[4] In the realm

---

2. Any conflict between Islamic and traditional Neo-Confucian teachings is due to deviations and cults within Neo-Confucianism. Liu, *Nature,* 32–33.

3. Ramadan, *Western Muslims.*

4. Ramadan notes that while the scholastic traditionalism of Islam pays attention to

of religious rituals, detailed and precise instructions are laid down in the Qur'an and *Hadith*. In the realm of human affairs in the West, Qur'an and *Hadith* generally only give guidance and direction rather than a definitive framework.[5] According to Ramadan, the methodologies in these two realms are complete opposites. While ritual practice only relies on the Qur'an and *Hadith*, human affairs involve human reason and also allow creativity of interpretation. Ramadan asserts that in social human affairs, Islamic laws are interactive with reason. Also Islamic laws are interactive with the social context. Ramadan insists that reason should not be the sole responsibility of *ulama*. This reason is known as civil reason by a corporate body consisting of experts, social and natural scientists, intellectuals, and ordinary citizens.

As explicated by Andy Yu in his research, Ramadan puts civil reason at the centre of an interactive triangle.[6] It is the civil reason at the centre that can be interactive with three other points, influencing and being influenced by them.[7] The first triangular point is represented by the Qur'an and *Hadith*. Reasoning by such a civil corporate body should be based firmly in the explicit and implicit teachings of the Qur'an and *Hadith*. The second point in the triangle is the context of the society. The corporate body analyzes the social context by reasoning and then reflects upon the analysis after their experience. The third point is the need for critique. The corporate people analyze their critique and likewise reflect upon their criticisms. Ramadan argues that this ongoing reasoning, critique, and reflection upon the social context in the light of the Qur'an and *Hadith* are necessary in both western pluralistic and Muslim majority societies.

Similarly, Kemal Ataman also notes that the attitude of Muslims towards people of other religious traditions cannot be characterized as a definite, fixed doctrine in any given time and space in any multicultural society.[8] As one's context changes, so does the interpretation of the text that shapes one's consciousness, and therefore one's attitudes. Along similar lines of approach as Ramadan and Ataman, Hendrik M. Vroom opines that Muslim immigrants from Middle Eastern countries now living in Western

---

the revealed texts to elucidate Islamic principles, liberal reformism emphasizes reason as a means to work out the affairs of the world and society. For Ramadan, Sufism is more inclined towards the text than reason. Ramadan, *Western Muslims*, 29.

5. See Ataman, "Religion," 504.

6. Yu, "Framework," 74–75.

7. Ramadan interprets *shari'a* broadly incorporating the role of reason or thinking. It shows Muslims how to be and remain Muslim. The *shari'a* is not only the expression of the universal principles of Islam but the framework and thinking that makes for their actualization in human history. Ramadan, *Western Muslims*, 32.

8. Ataman, "Religion," 495.

Europe with a change in context need a process of deconstruction and reconstruction of Islam in their transition to a Western culture. Such a process involves reinterpretation in a different context of the principles of *fiqh* and the right understanding of the Qur'an and *Hadith*.[9]

Thus, Ramadan and others resonate with Liu Zhi's translation-conversation method of contextualization, in particular the realm of human affairs in the West where Muslims live as ethnic minorities. We conclude that Liu Zhi's model of translation-conversation contextualization with emphasis on triangulation between text translation, cultural adaptation and spiritual wisdom has relevance and may enlighten further understanding of Muslims in the West. That is, while Liu Zhi worked in the seventeenth- and eighteenth-century China, his ideas still have currency and current relevance.

In post-9/11 America, some American Muslims have made attempts to reclaim or re-state the true nature of their faith. Khaled Abou El Fadl laments that political discourses have displaced moral discourses.[10] In fact, Islam is concerned with building and creating life and thus is against violence. Furthermore, Taha Jabir Alalwani asserts that Islam summons Muslims to build a civilization, a community, with values, not a state.[11] A Sufi poet, Kabir Helminski says that "Islam is not a formulation, an ethical system, a practice, or even a revelation as much as it is a revelation to the divine."[12] Islam is a lifestyle that reflects tolerance and gentleness. Muslims should live in peaceful coexistence in a state of equality. These recent re-statements of faith by some American Muslims emphasize the experience of God and peaceful coexistence with other human beings. These teachings resonate with the key teachings in Liu Zhi's *Rules and Proprieties of Islam*.

THE LEGACY OF LIU ZHI IN CHINA

The legacy of Liu Zhi lasted into the mid twentieth-century China in Xi Dao Tang (西道堂) in Ningxia, China. The founder and leader of this group of Muslims was Ma Qixi who started the group in 1890. He adopted Liu Zhi's written works as his main sources of Islamic education and teaching. Ma was not a scholar but his poems on Islam were popular among his followers. A common understanding is that Liu Zhi is the seed and Xi Dao Tang is the fruit.[13] Jin Yijiu explains that the key point of this understanding is that Xi

9. Vroom, "Islam's Adaptation," 226.
10. Fadl, 'Peaceful Jihad' 35–36.
11. Masmoudi, "No More," 83.
12. Helminski, "Islam," 153.
13. Jin, *Exploring Chinese Islam*, 339.

Dao Tang persistently used Chinese cultural ideas to explain and expound Islam.[14] Not only did Xi Dao Tang adopt and embrace Chinese cultures to explain their beliefs, but also the Muslims of Xi Dao Tang used extensive networks of trade to engage and make friends with their neighbors, both Hans and non-Hans in nineteenth- and twentieth-century China. Ma followed Liu Zhi's teaching of harmonious co-existence between the minority Muslims and the majority Hans. Xi Dao Tang declined during the Second World War due to internal conflicts and other reasons. The co-existence between Muslims as ethnic minorities and other groups in that region of Ningxia, North China did not create any cultural, political, and religious animosity.

Muslims have been living in China for many centuries and there have been occasional rebellious uprisings and various governments have responded mercilessly. However, generally speaking, Muslims have co-existed with Han Chinese harmoniously for centuries. Contextualization and contextual theology are necessary for any Muslims living as ethnic minorities in the modern world. The contextualization of Liu Zhi is relevant in that the basic tenets of Islam can remain unchanged. The way forward for Islam in the modern world is to acknowledge the need for reform by contextualization into local culture.

FINAL CONCLUSION

This study was concerned with the issue of Liu Zhi's contextualization of Islam in seventeenth- and eighteenth-century China. The general consensus of most Chinese scholars is that Liu Zhi's Islam is Confucianized, but most English scholars aver that Confucianism in Liu Zhi's works is just a means and not an end. Chapter 1 explained the research questions and provided the methodological introduction. Various models of contextualization were explicated. Not only did Liu Zhi and other Muslim literati translate Islamic texts in Persian and Arabic into Chinese, they also interpreted Islamic concepts by primarily using Confucian terms. Liu Zhi's contextualization involved active engagement, dialogue and conversation with the Chinese contexts.

Chapter 2 gave an account of the historical, religious and philosophical contexts of Liu Zhi. The Three Teachings in China provided rich resources of philosophical and ethical materials for Liu Zhi to contextualize the Islamic message of divine being, rites, return to the Real and others.

---

14. Ibid., 330.

Chapter 3 gave an overview of almost all extant works of Liu Zhi and discussed the contemporary scholarship on Liu Zhi's works. Little study has been made by scholars, both English and Chinese, on the role of the Prophet Muhammad in Liu Zhi's overall teaching. Liu Zhi contextualized Muhammad as the Utmost Sage of Islam, superior to any Chinese sage.

Chapter 4 showed that unlike Jami, but in continuity with Wang Daiyu, Liu Zhi taught the concept of existence in terms of the three Ones, namely, the Real One, the Numerical One, and the Embodied One. Unlike both Jami and Wang, Liu Zhi put greater emphasis on the role of the heart in the practical aspect of the unity of existence. The goal of Liu Zhi's contextualization is to help his readers to understand the difficult philosophical concept of the unity of existence and to help them set their hearts on return to the Real.

In chapter 5, while Liu Zhi used plentiful Buddhist, Daoist, and Confucian terms and images in his poem of *The Five Sessions of the Moon*, the overall structure and themes complied with Sufi thoughts. His depiction of the Prophet of Muhammad in the early part of *The True Record of the Utmost Sage of Islam* was of a unique and extraordinary person with existence in both the innate and the acquired heaven. Liu Zhi contextualized Muhammad as the Utmost Sage who had a unique nature of continuity. Without Muhammad's nature, Sufi seekers could not actualize their full realization and return to the Real. Clearly, heaven, nature, and sagehood are common Confucian terms. Thus, Liu Zhi is a skillful cultural agent who contextualizes his Islamic message in active engagement, dialogue, and conversation with his Chinese cultural contexts.

Chapter 6 focused on only the first five chapters of Liu Zhi's *Rules and Proprieties of Islam*. Liu Zhi explicitly stated that he used Confucian terms to help his explanation, especially for those readers who might know the meaning and reason of the Islamic rites and yet still have doubts. While Liu Zhi's *Rules and Proprieties of Islam* has been claimed to be Confucianized, we conclude that only when Liu Zhi explained the way of humanity, did he identify the Islamic ethical relationships with Neo-Confucianism. When Liu Zhi explained the way of heaven in terms of the five endeavors of Islam, the Islamic concepts had distinctive meanings and the role of the Prophet Muhammad was vitally important for any seeker of Islam to return to the Real.

After examining the major and minor works of Liu Zhi, we conclude that Liu Zhi's Islam is in accordance with the Ibn 'Arabi tradition. Sufi ideas permeate all his works. Liu Zhi consistently contextualized his Islam into the Chinese contexts by using the translation-conversation model.

Appendix I

The Poem of the Five Sessions of the Moon[1] in English

In the beginning of the *first* session, the moon begins to appear. Comprehend the Real Ruler that has no form or image. His subtlety is not known and non-designated. He has no boundary and exists as the real reality.[2] He is unique without beginning and end; the Supreme Honored without any partner. Creative transformation begins. Principle and image are completed. The great mandate is installed and it opens door to various subtleties.

In the mid first session, the moon is new. There is a need to understand the intelligent Non-Ultimate as the root of nature and principle. The vital energy opens up. The ying-yang dissociates. When all the things are complete, the Human Ultimate[3] is begotten. The Non-Ultimate is the seed while the Great Ultimate is the tree.[4] The tree was once in the fruit which

---

1. The text follows the one published by Yin in 1999. See Yin, *Exploring Chinese Islam*, 323–24. The text and brief comments are also available on the internet: http://www.douban.com/group/topic/24083421/

2. The great transformation in the beginning session of the moon follows closely the initial stage of the great transformation of the Real in the first chapter of Liu Zhi's *Nature and Principle of Islam*. It is also in continuation with Wang Daiyu's concept of great transformation.

3. The Human Ultimate is Liu Zhi's term for the perfect man of the Ibn 'Arabi's tradition.

4. Non-Ultimate, Great Ultimate and Yin-Yang are often used Neo-Confucian cosmological terms. The three key movers in this great transformation are Non-Ultimate, Great Ultimate and Human Ultimate.

later gives rise to the root. There is a need to understand and distinguish the tree from fruit.[5] Avoid confusing the root with the one who plants the root.

At the end of first session, the moon is up high. There is a need to have firm belief in our teaching and reject other devious teachings. Seek endeavor in the acquired heaven, desire for forgiveness. Obey the heavenly mandate and holy rules. Obedience shall enjoy unlimited blessings in paradise. Disobedience leads to punishment in hell. I beseech you, dear children, waste no time in happy excursion. Otherwise, the afterlife will be in crying torment.

In the beginning of the *second* session, the moon is charming. This life on earth cannot give security to our mandate. Indulging in a glamorous life will reap all day labor and result in bitter torment in this suffering world. A hundred years have thirty six thousand days and humans rarely live over seventy years of age. I beseech you, dear children, think carefully. In a sudden moment, unexpected events may happen.

In the mid second session, the moon is round. Discipline your life and don't take a laid back life. Drink and eat less. Keep to your sleep. Always remember in your heart the *Shahadah*.[6] Hands should not let go the precious bronze green sword. Break away from indulgent love and abandon absurd relationships. From now on, strive forward step by step. Land onto the shore of *dao* and see the real vital-energy.

At the end of the second session, the moon is shining. When the heart is in danger, the *dao* is dim and weak in the heart. Monkey and horse are abominable. Dragon and tiger are threatening. Behind station after station stand tall and imposing mountain ranges.[7] Even though you have the green sword[8], you cannot cut open a way out into freedom. So, visit the spiritual master and seek to defend your *dao*.[9] Through the mysterious station,[10] then acquire real opportunity.

---

5. Liu Zhi used familiar Sufi analogy, namely the root, tree, and fruit.

6. Esoteric Sufi practices are rare in this poem. This is the only place where *dhikr* is mentioned with emphasis that such prayer is from the heart.

7. The Sufi path with station after station is clearly a confirmation of Liu Zhi's Sufi thought.

8. The bronze sword was known as a very sharp weapon in the Qin dynasty. Later it was superseded by an iron sword.

9. Liu Zhi clearly emphasized the Sufi master and seeker relationship. Again, this is one of the Sufi practices and only the seekers with the guidance and direction of the master can make further progress.

10. The word mysterious has Daoist connotations. It means not so much mystical but rather difficult to comprehend.

In the beginning of the *third* session, the moon is pure.[11] Seek the great *dao* from within yourself. While the cosmos is huge and things are difficult to name them, the *dao* has left its traits inside your heart.[12] The *dao* encloses the heaven and earth and yet humanity encloses the *dao*.[13] The *dao* penetrates both outside and inside; both coarse and fine. Learn this well and start your journey. When you understand yourself better, you also know the Lord.[14]

In the mid third session, the moon is moving. A treasure pearl hides on the seabed. Stride quickly for the journey and set sail for the sea. The turbulent waves keep coming as if you are being sucked into a dragon's den. You are tormented by limitless sufferings. Yet, the reward is to reap the priceless treasure pearl. Be alert and stand firm to defend. Don't fool around. For wealth and honor, seek to return back to the home country.[15]

At the end of the third session, the moon is high up. Be single minded and look forward to seeing the paradise in the jade garden.[16] Ascend to the heaven of Immortals and complete the jade ring. Be guided by the light of the Little Immortal and join the banquet. Pick some medicines and make some life-saving precious tables.[17] Meet the sick and give him the tablet for free. Heal the old and afflicted. Then, receive the reward of a long-lived life.

At the beginning of the *fourth* session, the moon is slanting. The legendary moon lady resides in the jade residence. She puts on her make up in front of the dressing table.[18] Her body is tenderly soft, her face with made-up

11. The third session takes up many Sufi themes but they are expressed eclectically.

12. Liu Zhi affirmed and argued rationally that the Lord has left many traits in the world. These traits may derive from the smallest details of humanity. The *dao* is ubiquitous and all embracing even within humans.

13. From the perspective of the world of images, the cosmos is huge and humanity is merely one of many creatures. From the perspective of the heart or spiritual world, the human heart can embrace the cosmos and is embraced by the *dao*.

14. Understanding oneself means also understanding the Lord. This theme is also explicit in the first introductory chapter of Liu's *Rules and Proprieties of Islam*.

15. This is the central and key section of the poem. Many characteristics of Sufi thought about seeking the *dao* and acquiring the wisdom of God are discussed. Seekers must be diligent and persistent in their pursuit of the Sufi path.

16. Literally, the words refer to the jade garden. It is paraphrased as paradise.

17. In Liu Zhi's *Rules and Proprieties of Islam,* he asserted that the five endeavors could have wonderful healing effects on human sickness and spiritual wholeness. The making of medicines and tables is a Daoist concern for good health and longevity.

18. The mythical lady is a popular figure in a Chinese ancient folk story. This beautiful lady lives on the planet moon. The use of this lady in this poem may have two meanings. Firstly, she refers to the wife of Adam. Secondly, she refers to the virtue and beauty of human spirituality. The possession of spiritual aspects in humanity beautifies the outlook of humankind.

powders. She moves softly and tenderly like a heavenly angel. Humankind was created from dust and yet possesses the spirit. Banish humankind into the world and humans have marriages. Man and woman enjoy. The yin and yang join together. Their intimate care and love last for thousands of years.

In the mid fourth session, the moon is towards the west. How can turbid substance return to the Real One? The method is refinement by the purifying furnace and burning by fire. This should do away with all the outer cosmetics. Then, collect the real sap after the purification. Endeavors need to be repeated hundreds and thousands of times.[19] This will produce the valuable tripod and golden tub. When the Lord calls, you do not disobey. Your whole self needs to return to the Real and ascend to the great void.[20]

At the end of the fourth session, the moon is full. Practice self-control, resume proprieties and then retain the nature. Practice three vehicles, pass through five elements[21] and accomplish the path to become the real "I"[22]; thus becoming real humanity. Inherently, I own the inner precious mirror.[23] I rank supreme among all in the creation. Steer forward the merciful sea journey and guide the lost. Then, reside with a sincere and compassionate heart.

In the beginning of the *fifth* session, the moon is shrinking. The heart embraces both the heaven and earth. The heaven folds up and the earth cleaves. The images of creation may decay but the principle is not to disappear.[24] Obstruction is overcome and non-differentiation begins. The two worlds of color and subtlety become transparent. It is difficult to communicate subtle sayings to ordinary people because it seems like a mouth that has no tongue.

In the mid fifth session, the moon is submerged. The pure heart manifests the nature and the *dao* is complete. When the ascent and descent unite,

19. The path of return is by extreme hard and disciplined work.

20. Literally, it means the great emptiness.

21. The concept of elements is based on Razi's Sufi path. These are foundational elements for the creation of the material world. The five elements refer to gold, wood, water, fire, and earth. Passing through the five elements means that the seeker is getting out of the realm of the material world and into the realm of transcendence.

22. Literally, accomplishing the path has four hidden aspects. These aspects may refer to the enlightenment of the heart, the realization of the nature, the transcendence of the material world, and finally union with the Real. At the end of the path, the seeker can acquire the realm of the "real" person.

23. This is an analogy. The Real is the real existence and humankind is the mirror which reflects the Real. It is because humankind can reflect the Real that humankind ranks supreme in creation.

24. The description is clearly of the final day of judgment. Although all the visible things are to be destroyed, the principle (*li*) of all things remains unchanged.

the circling is complete. Then, it completes the return to root suchness. Humanity and heaven unite. Images are transcended and the real essence of meaning manifests. At the end of three self-denials,[25] the root suchness shines. The invisible and visible disintegrate. The two arcs form a circle and eventually return to the original suchness.[26]

At the end of the fifth session, the moon is waning. Return to the Real and reach to the highest heaven.[27] There is neither color nor image, neither sound nor smell, only real quietude. A dust or grain may be small but its smallness embraces the greatness of the total substance. All things in the creation return to the origin and are no longer in time and space. The fruit is a union with the Real without any world of image. The afterlife is happiness and solitude.

---

25. The three denials refer to the denial of self, others and all visible things.
26. This is in accordance with the Ibn 'Arabi tradition.
27. The highest heaven (literal: huge heaven) is a Daoist concept. This shows Liu Zhi's extensive eclecticism.

Appendix II

Translation of Selected Texts of *The True Record of the Utmost Sage of Islam*[1]

INTRODUCTORY CHAPTER: EXPLANATION OF THE HONOR AND NOBILITY OF MUHAMMAD (AN OVERVIEW FROM VARIOUS CLASSICS)[2]

Humankind is honorable in heaven and earth. Among humankind, there are sages, worthies, wise, and foolish. The sages are most honorable. Among sages, they are further classified into ordinary, ambassador, great and utmost. The Utmost Sage is the highest. Muhammad is the highest sage of all time and of all places and is called the Utmost Sage.

At the beginning of creative transformation, humanity is classed by the principle (*li*) into nine groups. The Utmost Sage is the highest. After taking the form, humans take on nine groups of image. The image of the Utmost Sage is perfect. His principle is perfect.

The principle and image of all things are to be found within the compass of the nine heavens and the seven earths. The heavens are superior to the earths and the Aershi surpasses the heavens. The nature and principle of the Utmost Sage were situated at the Aershi. Therefore, he is the most honorable than any in all the heavens and the earths.

---

1. Liu, *True Record* (1984).
2. Ibid., 23–25.

The ancestors of the Utmost Sage, going right back to Adam, never worshipped idols or prayed to heathen gods. This virtue of the ancestors nourished and cultivated generation after generation, culminating in the Utmost Sage. He is the most honorable in accumulated virtue.

INTRODUCTORY CHAPTER: THE UTMOST SAGE[3]

From the time of the ancients, there have been many sages. Muhammad is the Utmost Sage. It is so called because he has all required virtues. His transformation is thorough. Through his whole body, the Real Ruler emanates to become the great function . . . the Spirit of the Utmost Sage existed before the heaven and the earth. He is the fruit of all sages. While the heaven and earth are big, they are nurtured by the Utmost Sage. The spirits of ten thousand sages are under his shadow and they have life from him. Although he is the descendent of Adam with respect to form, his spirit is really before Adam. His teaching embraces ten thousand teachings. His rule collects and completes ten thousand rules. His way excels ten thousand ways and is upright, illuminates like the sun and moon, as long-lasting as the heaven and earth . . . With regard to his teaching, it has been attested by all later generations to be enduring. Its principle (*li*) is clear; meaning is articulate; literary artistry is excellent and above beautiful literature. These prove that the Lord reveals the sacred texts. Those who are obedient to the teaching, they are not tempted away by any riches and fame. Their ways are not blocked and this truth is proved by all who obey the way.

CHAPTER 1: THE RECORD OF THE TRANSMISSION OF THE LIGHT OF MUHAMMAD THROUGH SUCCESSIVE GENERATIONS OF HIS ANCESTORS[4]

The Utmost Sage was established before the heaven and earth and began the transformation of all things. His designation then was named Ahmad. He was the progenitor of all creation. When he was born in the acquired heaven and earth as the seal of the all sages, he was named Muhammad.

The original form of an ordinary man is contained in the backbone of his ancestor. However, the Utmost Sage's original form was seen in the forehead of his ancestors. As the head is the noblest part of the body, and the forehead is the most honorable part of the head, we thus can see that

3. Ibid., 41–43.
4. Ibid., 46–47.

the place from which the Utmost Sage received his form was the most honorable.

The original form of the Utmost Sage was manifested on the forehead of Adam. His original principle was situated at the highest part of the ninth heaven; his exalted name was found in the foremost part of the *Aershi*; how could he be any other than the most honorable one?[5]

The sages are as numerous as the stars but the Utmost Sage is the sun among the stars. The tradition of teaching is like the baking of a cake. The former sages planted the wheat and made the flour and mixed it appropriately. The Utmost Sage completed the process of baking the cake. The Utmost Sage was the most cherished person of the whole creation. That is why the Lord said to Jesus, "had it not been for Muhammad, I would not have created heaven, earth, men and spirits." So there can be no doubt that the Utmost Sage had a special existence.

The roof of heaven bore his name. The gate of heaven was inscribed with his name on its door. The ancient books recorded his name. Angels and devils extolled it. The Utmost Sage's own body bore the stamp of his name. The heaven and earth and all things were created in accordance with his name. Who or what in heaven or on earth can surpass the Utmost Sage? Everything returns to him like all streams return to the sea. Those who return to him are the upright and those who do not return to him are the deceived people. Who can be compared to him?

CHAPTER 2: DIAGRAM OF TRANSFORMATION[6]

Transformation begins in the innate heaven, initiated by the great mandate. The great mandate is the act of all true principle (*li*). From the great mandate, there is the nature of continuity which is the root suchness of the Utmost Sage.[7] All other natures of the sages derive from him, including the nature of worthies. From the nature of worthies, all other natures like ignorant

---

5. Murata avers that *Aershi* derives from the Arabic *arsh* which means the throne of God in Qur'an 20:5. Murata argues that Liu Zhi understood Aershi as the nature of the Utmost Sage. Alternatively, the term Aershi means the Ascribed Spirit breathed into Adam, the Mandate. In the case of Razi in his *Path,* God began the process of creation by firstly creating the Muhammadan Spirit. Murata, *Sage,* 58–59.

6. Liu, *True Record,* 68–69.

7. Root suchness (*ren*) is a fundamental concept of Liu Zhi. Root suchness can be paraphrased as without beginning and already in existence. Murata uses the literal word 'suchness' and parallels it with the Arabic word *inniyya,* that-it-is-ness. In Islamic philosophy, *inniyya* is used as a synonym for existence (*wujud*). Murata further explicates root suchness as root substance which is the Real Being. Murata, *Sage,* 184.

... from the sage to the Utmost Sage, this return back to the root suchness of the nature of continuity. This is called exhausting the nature and principle and getting to the mandate. This is known as the descent and ascent of the great transformation. Likewise, this is also the way of humanity in the descent and ascent. Since the beginning of humankind, only the person Muhammad can achieve the ascent. He embraces the whole transformation from the beginning to the end. Thus, all return can benefit with Muhammad as the goal of return.[8]

THE UTMOST SAGE: THE INTEGRATION OF GREAT TRANSFORMATION

Why Muhammad is called the Utmost Sage? How could the Utmost Sage include the great transformation? The great transformation stops at the Utmost Sage but this is not the end. The Utmost Sage continues the transformation to its completion. All individual transformation has its own aspect and is one-sided but the Utmost Sage's transformation covers all aspects. Thus, he continues the work of the Real Ruler in the great transformation. He returns the transformation to the Real Lord. He is the man from heaven and from the earth to heaven. He becomes the axis of transformation. Anyone who is not led by the sage's transformation, he will go astray and deviate from the way. He is lost from the real way.[9]

CHAPTER 7: FIRST MESSENGER TO CHINA[10]

In the first year of the Prophethood of Muhammad, there was seen in the sky a strange star, the Chinese emperor Su Wen Ti commanded his astronomer to tell him the meaning. He said, "There would be an extraordinary person appearing in the West." The emperor sent an envoy to investigate . . . The prophet sent his uncle Sa'ad ibn Abi Waqqas and three others to go with the envoy to China . . .

The emperor Wen Ti hung up the portrait of the prophet and worshipped it, and when he arose, the scroll was there but the picture had vanished . . . The disappearance of the picture was due to the wonderful

---

8. This paragraph is a clear and concise summary of Liu Zhi's cosmogony in Confucian terms with emphasis on the important role of the prophet Muhammad.

9. The key role of the prophet Muhammad is mediating between humanity and the Real Ruler.

10. Liu, *True Record*, 120.

influence of the prophet. The emperor, alarmed, said, "It must really be that he is the Pure Emperor and the True King."[11]

The account of the entry of religion . . . is given in detail in several Chinese histories, so it can be proved. The story of worshipping of the portrait is not recorded in the histories; but it has been handed down by tradition, and may be seen recorded on stone tablets, so must not be rejected.[12]

THE LEARNING[13]

Knowledge refers to the knowledge of the Real Ruler. One who seeks is not ignorant and a seeker begins to learn. Seeking is indeed the beginning of learning. It is not shameful for a seeker to ask questions and a teacher should not withhold answers. It says, "regardless of age or social class, anyone who can give benefit to learning is my teacher." Day and night, ask the Lord to give you beneficial learning and avoid unhealthy habits. One rule of caution for the learner says, "If one is close to learners, then one learns. If one works with greedy people, one is lost. Do not take in any unhealthy learning." Befriend literati and honorable people. Do not let selfish desire blind you. Do not be poisoned by heresy.

The myriad things are established in sincerity. Make your heart steady, your will upright. Then, things turn out pleasantly. It says, "teaching is to clarify the way and for the service of the Lord. The way is manifested by learners' humility and carefulness. The principle of things is important as it can distinguish between understanding and misunderstanding." Do not give up even if you cannot understand just one principle . . . If you are diligent to learn Islam, you can broaden the horizon of benevolence and righteousness.

---

11. Mason, *Arabian Prophet*, 94. In Mason's work, this story is placed in the fifth chapter.

12. Liu Zhi quoted five historical records. Two of them are apocryphal historical records. The other three are more reliable records.

13. Liu, *True Record*, 310–11.

Appendix III

Personal Narrative of *Tianfan Dianli*
(*Selected Essential Explanations of the Proprieties of Islam*)[1]

In accordance with the wish of my deceased father, I translated the book *The Rituals and Rules of Islam*. The readers of the book responded that the work was so comprehensive and complicated that it was difficult for them to comprehend. They suggested a beginner's version with selected topics and commentaries. Therefore, I selected topics most important to practical living, edited it and called this work, *Selected Essential Explanations of the Proprieties of Islam*. However, the reader then found this work too concise and beginners could not understand properly. Therefore, after each topic, I added commentaries to ensure the beginners could understand the basic truths. The commentaries came from other places in this work and also external sources that I had collected and they dealt with the learning of Islam. In these commentaries, some comments deal with truths already understood but the explanation is not complete. Other comments serve to enrich. Some comments deal with meaning already explained but the truth conveyed is not straightforward. These extra comments serve to explain the meaning more completely and clearly. Some comments deal with meaning and truth already understood but the beginners still have doubt. Furthermore, some comments have been borrowed from Neo-Confucian sayings for clearer explanation. These comments are really common knowledge but some people with a narrow vision misunderstand the original meaning of

---

1. Liu, *Rules and Proprieties* (1988), 20–21.

the text and create disagreement. Thus, this work also contains questions and answers. They serve to discern the error and solve any puzzle.

Although we have explicated the propriety, which seems to be ordinary matter, the meaning of propriety is profound. If a person remembers it for the sake of his life and determines in his mind not to forget, then he achieves the unity of himself with the heavenly truth and there is no separation whatsoever. In this work, some may find the meanings concise and difficult but the reality is that they are quite obvious. In this work, some explanations have been borrowed from the imagery and examples of *Can Ran Wei Miao* 燦然微妙. In order to discuss the truth of Islam, we make our work easier to understand as it is no different to Neo-Confucian works. To learn and obey the Islamic propriety is likewise to learn and obey the teachings of the ancient sages and kings. The religion of holy sages, either in the East or the Arab world, either in ancient or modern time, is the same. However, people nowadays do not study and research this fact and gradually it disappears. Fortunately, it is only the Islamic propriety that still exists.

In this work, the opening part is a discussion of the fundamentals of the religion of Islam. The middle part talks about the rules and regulations. It deals with the heavenly five Endeavors and the five Relationships. It discusses the deepening of principle and nurturing nature. It talks about personal realization, forming family, serving the nation and various matters concerned with living and proper dressing. These issues are discussed concisely. Lastly, the work concludes with marriage and funeral.

This work has twenty chapters and twenty eight sections. The topics are not comprehensive but the content with various illustrations is very comprehensive. While this work does not discuss comprehensively every aspect of propriety, it contains principles and outlines for human living. The learner can enjoy their living accordingly. The prophet Muhammad said, "The propriety is the foundation of being human." The ancient sage has also made an analogy. "The relation between propriety and humanity is similar to the relation between sweet and honey. If honey is not sweet, the honey is not honey. How can humanity be humanity without propriety?" Therefore, it is said propriety is intimately related to humanity. It is indeed very intricately enwrapped!

My deceased father deeply felt that the Islamic propriety had not been explained and proclaimed. He was once committed to this work but he died without realizing his goal. Although my learning was shallow, I decided to carry on my father's wish. Now, in accordance with my limited knowledge, I wrote this work about the Islamic truth. If readers can receive it from the bottom of their hearts and put it into practice, they will not betray the vital meaning of the proclamation by the traditional sages through the ages.

This is also my purpose with this humble explanatory work. In terms of the selection of different contents, and the good and bad styles of my writing, I submit myself to correction and affirmation by all co-workers.

> A scholar of Islam,
> Liu Zhi of Jinling [Nanjing].

Appendix IV

The Rules and Proprieties of Islam[1]

CHAPTER 1: ORIGINAL TEACHING[2]

Theme: In the very beginning, before the formation of the ten thousand things[3], there is the Real Ruler. He is without limit[4] and likeness.

Explanation: In the very beginning, there is only the Real Ruler's root suchness, supremely pure and quiet, without limit and form, not controlled by light and darkness [yin/yang], not belonging to the creative transformation. The Real Ruler is really the root and source of heaven and earth, humans and things. All the principle and vital energy come from this root suchness. This is what is known as the ultimate union between heaven and humanity. This is also what is meant by returning to the root and back to the mandate. The Real Ruler is the home return of all principles and vital energies.

Theme: When the great mandate had accomplished the creation of heaven and earth, it also created all things therein.

Explanation: the Real Ruler is without any form. He manifested itself as the Great Ultimate that resolved into darkness and light [yin and yang]. When the darkness and light differentiated, the heaven and earth came into existence. When the heaven and earth had formed, the ten thousand things

---

1. The version used was printed in simplified Chinese in 1988.
2. Liu, *Rules and Proprieties*, 27–39.
3. Alternative translation is "myriads of creatures."
4. Alternative translation is "boundary."

were created. The heaven and earth are now ready and the subtlety of the Real Ruler embraces therein and threads through them.[5]

Theme: Humankind was created in the Muslim lands

Explanation: When the creation and all things are in order, then vital energy, water, fire and earth gather in their essences. In the Muslim lands, the forefather Adam was created in the wilderness of the Arab land.

Theme: In the Middle [East], the sages are begotten.

Explanation: the Middle East is the land of Muslims. It is the land in the midst of heaven, earth and the four directions of the world. Thus, it is called the Middle [East]. The holy sages congregated in this land and humankind had begun in the Middle [East].[6]

Theme: Comprehensive rules are set up and thus teaching has been established.

Explanation: Adam gave birth to sons and daughters. Generations of sages have been begotten. The practice of the way (*dao*), the establishing of the teachings, the principle of the transformation of cosmos and the meticulous function of all things, have been communicated to Adam from the Real Ruler who designs names, gives rules and declares them to later generations. Adam and the holy sages have not randomly formed their own ideas. Thus, the teaching of Adam is most ancient and not to be supplanted.

Theme: From that time on, humankind and creatures have multiplied from generations to generations and spread over all corners of the earth.

Explanation: According to the history of ancient Muslims, over a thousand years after Adam, there was a severe flood and many people lost their lives. After three months, the flood subsided. A great sage called Noah arose. He received the divine call to solve the problem of the flood. He sent people across the land to deal with the effects of the flood. Thus, humankind was scattered to all corners of the earth. Two thousand years had passed since the time of Adam.

Theme: If the teaching is not ancient, it should still exist. If it is ancient, the teaching should have been lost. Thus, most of the teachings in the modern world are not ancient.

Explanation: In the world, there are many countries and each country has its own unique culture. Therefore, scattered humankind has different languages and their writings are also different. Thus, is it possible for humankind to behave the same way? During the period of Three Kings and

---

5. Alternative translation is "Then, the subtle function of the true Lord fills all in all."

6. Liu Zhi used additional sections, about three hundred words long, known as verification, to discuss the central location of the Middle East. He used three geographical documents to affirm his view. This verification is not translated.

Five Emperors, their rules and regulations were of course also ancient. The Three Kingdoms era was more recent. After that era, hundreds of scholars emerged with their own distinctive and imaginative thoughts and ideas. They created many schools of thought, each one espousing their own particular theories. Each school developed its own religion and faith. This situation continued unabated. Eventually, not only were there different schools of thought but, even denominations within one school. The aims and doctrines of religious teaching no longer complied with the previous ancient teachings.

Theme: Islam is the only religion that passes down through generations of sages. The tradition of thoughts and systems has not been interrupted.

Explanation: From the time of Adam to Muhammad, there were many people who had been called to promulgate the teaching. These individuals were called the sages. However, there is a hierarchy of sages. In general, there are four levels. Anyone who is called to promulgate the teaching and has the gift of prophecy is known as the sage . . . Six hundred years after Jesus, Muhammad was born. Muhammad was called to eradicate evil words and illuminate the ancient teachings and inaugurate peace to all generations.[7]

Theme: From the time when Muhammad was called to sagehood, the teaching of Islam has been known widely to all, spreading across the world.

Explanation: Muhammad was a descendent of the royal family of the Muslim land. He was extremely clever and was a highly moral man with supreme moral ethics, a king of the world. He followed the rules of the ancient teachings. The teaching had stopped when Jesus died six hundred years ago. Muhammad was called The Seal, meaning that he was the last of all the prophets. The true Lord communicated to him six thousand six hundred and sixty six verses called Al-Furqan [the criteria].

Theme: Editing the sacred text

Explanation: Text means the revealed text given to holy sages before Muhammad. From the time of Adam to Jesus, there were one hundred and fourteen books. For example, the five books of Moses, the book of David and the gospel of Jesus are the major books. The Real Ruler appointed the prophet Muhammad to edit and revise the sacred texts. He revealed to Muhammad the Furqan [criteria] which contains all the meanings of previous sacred texts

Question: Someone may ask: "Since the sacred texts were given by the Real Ruler, all of them should be complied with. How come that they were edited and revised?" The answer is that the six hundred years after the death

---

7. Over two hundred words have not been translated. Liu Zhi's key point is to emphasize the continuity of Islamic prophethood.

of Jesus, various ridiculous views arose and confused the truth. The real sacred texts were corrupted and errors came into the texts. Many of them lost their original meaning and they lost their real value. Nevertheless, people still thought they were real and complied with their teachings. The errors continued to multiply. Eventually, texts were no longer the revealed text and people really rebelled against the truth. Therefore, the holy one[8] edited and revised the text. Original meanings were restored and errors were erased. The Furqan is set back onto the right track and covers a wide range of truth with accurate balance. It becomes the teaching and rule for living. The editing work stopped the downfall of the truth and restored the eternal shining light of the sacred text, like the sun and moon. This work has profound significance.

Theme: To set up the law.

Explanation: The law means the rules pertaining to fasting, worship, marriage, funeral rites and so on. Different situations require different ways to use the law. Major occasions mean Hajj and purification, minor means the food and daily living. The law covers all aspects of natural phenomena, propriety, culture, rules, medical treatment, prediction of success and failure and the rule of the nation. These are established by the text. These rules are like an eternal flame, giving eternal brightness which can never be extinguished. From generation to generation, humankind can clearly and unerringly comply with the law. Anyone who is clever and wise should not set himself above or contravene the law.

Theme: [Muhammad] summarized the essence of teachings of all the former sages and formed a system. From then on, the way of Islam was clear and complete.

Explanation: All the sages in human history resemble the moon in a long lasting night. Once the Utmost Sage appears, he resembles the sun in the mid-day. From Adam to Jesus all the sages in history, their propagation of the way resemble a plant that has roots, buds and branches with leaves and flowers. The way of the Utmost Sage resembles the fruits. On earth, there is no light brighter than the sun. In the growth of a tree, bearing fruit is the completion of growth. No one is as complete as the Utmost Sage in propagating the way in the history of the sages.

Selected key theme: [Muhammad] teaches the religion of Islam. The aim of Islam is to know the Lord.

Explanation: The Lord Ruler creatively transforms into all things. He is the root origin of our heart and nature. Owing to the manifestation of the Real Ruler, humans have their original nature. From nature, humans have

---

8. The context clearly indicates the holy one is the prophet Muhammad.

their heart. Then, "I" become the crown of creation which takes place in the realm of the innate heaven. Today, with the endeavor of their hearts, humans then know their nature. From knowing their own nature, humans can know the Real Ruler. This takes place in the realm of the acquired heaven. To know the Lord Ruler as the creative transformer is out from my heart and nature which should set upon a firm and right foundation, not able to be shaken by deviating views.

Theme: Our endeavor is to revere and serve.

Explanation: Reverence means with single-mindedness and solemnity, you devote yourself to the Lord. Service means each and every one of your acts is done with obedience to him. The single-minded and solemn reverence is concerned with the endeavor of the heart. The obedient action is concerned with the endeavor of the body. Thus, reverence is the origin of service. Service is the function of reverence. If the heart has reverence, then the service in this acquired world can succeed. If the service is without the reverence, then service is in vain.

Therefore, to serve the emperor with reverence in the heart means loyalty; to serve the parents with reverence in the heart means filial obedience. In all matters of seeing, hearing, speaking and acting, you should follow properly the rules and proprieties. With these in place, you are not without rules and not abandoning any proprieties. This endeavor is both profound and detailed; both strict and elaborate. By this, humans can achieve the union with heaven as exemplified by the sages and worthies. Therefore, you need to put reverence first in order to serve and obey the Real Ruler. With reverence, you can reap good fruit.

Theme: The eventual goal is to return and recover the mandate

Explanation: Returning to the root means returning to the beginning. Recovering the mandate means the completion of our heavenly duty. What is meant by the beginning? In the creation of humanity, there is the beginning of stillness, without any evil and without any adulteration of our root substance. What is meant by the heavenly duty of humanity? Humans are created so that by their hearing and seeing they are to understand the task of return. The Real Lord has transformed the heaven and the earth and manifested the basic meanings of all things and these are for the sake of their return.

You need to learn diligently, desire for realization and examine yourself. You need to examine things thoroughly, learn to understand the reality of these things and the way in which they develop. You need to work hard and accomplish realization, marriage and governance. Our work is for the sake of returning and recovering the mandate. Thus, Islam is to teach people to know the Lord and return to the root substance; to teach you to give reverence to the Lord and for the accomplishment of the first mandate. After that, you return to the root substance. This is the greatest achievement of Islam.

Theme: To obey with piety, the five endeavors are to accomplish all the way of heaven.

Explanation: The five endeavors are reciting the *Shahadah*, ritual prayer, fasting, alms-tax and pilgrimage. Always remember the Real Ruler. In quietness, remember him. In activity, observe things and remember him and do not distract yourself in meaningless thoughts. Say your prayers five times a day at the designated time with utmost diligence and purity of heart. Fast a month within a year. This is to control your fleshly desire. Give alms once a year to the poor, sharing materials in love and virtue with others. Once in a life time, do the pilgrimage and that will strengthen your sincerity of the heart to seek the Lord. When you obey the five endeavors, you have accomplished the way of heaven.

Theme: To hold the five relationships with sincere honor is to accomplish the way of humanity.

Explanation: The five relationships are the five ethical principles that are concerned with the relationship between the emperor and the courtier, the father and son, the husband and wife; brother and sister and between friends. In the Middle East, it is also called the five accomplishments. The Emperor and the courtier constitute the country; father and son the family, husband and wife the home; brother and sister constitute business; and friends together constitute [human] virtues. All the above mentioned relations have changeless propriety. If you obey the five relationships, then you have fulfilled the way of humanity.

Theme: The learning and achievement [five endeavors and relationships] may be elementary or profound. This depends on the individual.

Explanation: The way of Islam originates from one and is not complex. The wise person can understand its depth and profundity while the fool can understand its surface meaning. It depends on the person who may understand the superficial or the deep meaning of Islam. It also happens in any truth seeking that only the wise can come to the truth but the fool can hardly experience truth at all. It requires a courageous effort for anyone who wants to explore the truth.

Theme: The person may want to do one thing but not others. The principle of action depends on compliance with righteousness and fittingness.

Explanation: Righteousness means doing things justly and fittingly. A person who has thought carefully knows what is right. A person who is ignorant may lose the opportunity to do what is right. When we are encountering a situation, may it be proceeding with or backing off, the principle of action should be fittingness. We do not follow others who betray righteousness in order to achieve honor. We do not act improperly to achieve fame. We just hold fast to the true way, taking good care of our words and actions.

Theme: There is propriety for marriage and a rule for funerals.

Explanation: Marriage and funerals mark two important moments, the beginning and end of the way of humanity. The holy sage uses the way of heaven as the principle and fittingly regulates the rule of law for the whole world and for all further generations. Humankind is to comply diligently. It is enforced strictly without any regard for status, no matter if they are poor, rich, exalted or humble.

Theme: In all these regulations of activity and solitude, there is a principle that is unchanging and yet objectively adaptive, creatively enforcing the rule of law.

Explanation: Whatever can be seen, heard, spoken, intuited, or situations like eating and resting at home, large and small, there is a historical law to regulate human behavior. So, humans are not to offend others and contravene propriety. At the same time, the law is objective and flexible enough to adapt appropriately, paying attention to the time and the context at that moment. This is to avoid holding firm to arid tradition with rigidity and stubbornly making no progress. In that way, the rule of the law continues to be complied with and yet it is exercised in a flexible manner without unfairness and with due respect to time and context. The rule of law remains the norm.

Selected key theme: the rule [for realization] consists of three vehicles. However, it derives from the same principle.

Explanation: Vehicle is the means to carry. It carries different rules and meanings. It allows the seekers step by step to work at the rule. The first is said to be the propriety vehicle, which carries both the way of heaven and humanity and all rules of endeavor. You work to get virtues and honor your work also. This is the content of propriety vehicle. The next step is called the way [path] vehicle, which carries the human and material principles, fulfilling the rule in uniting heaven with humanity. You need to understand thoroughly the principle and know thoroughly the nature for the sake of satisfying the rules. The last step is called the principle vehicle, also called the real vehicle, which carries the non-self and non-thing, accomplishing the subtle union between heaven and humanity. Such rule means the self-control is complete and accomplishes the status of "Real."

Working hard for your virtues and honoring endeavors are for body realization. Understanding thoroughly the principle and knowing thoroughly the nature can enlighten the heart. With self-control and accomplishing the real, you can see nature. Without endeavor and cultivation, your heart is not illuminated. Such a heart cannot see nature. Without seeing nature, you cannot unite with heaven. Nature is not seen because the selfish "I" has hidden it. Therefore, the rule of the three vehicles deals with the polishing up of the selfish "I." Above the rule of the three vehicles, a transcendent rule of vehicles exists. In it, both heaven and humans are transformed; with no name or trace left. There is no word to describe the experience except that you have to experience it.

Selected key theme: Humanity is classified into nine levels but the principal aim derives from one vein.

Explanation: It is the same humanity but is classified into nine categories. The sage group has four, namely average, ambassador, great and Utmost Sage. Beneath the group of sage are the great worthies, the wise people, the pure and upright, the good people and the common people. While levels are different, they derive from the same vein. The sage founds the doctrinal content. The worthies assist the sage. The wise people are to spread the doctrine. The pure and upright, good and common people are to hold firm the doctrine.

If you do not attain the nature of the sage which is able to found the doctrine, you would attain that of the worthies who can assist. If not able to assist, you would attain the level of human nature to spread it. If not able to spread it, you would attain the level of human nature to receive it. Receiving and keeping the faith are the ways to return to the root. Then, your heart has no regret and you do not fail in this life.

Theme: The way of Islam is without any image. The Islamic teaching has law and no one is to contravene them.

Explanation: The way of Islam is to be understood by its teaching. Without teaching, laws cannot be established. The way is naturally to be the principle of heaven. The teaching is a guidance/regulation for humankind to follow. The law is to distinguish between the heavenly principle and human desire, discerning right from wrong, guiding everyone in the right direction.

To establish the teaching with an idol is ridiculous. To obey the teaching and rule with self-centered serenity and indulgence is greed. Indulgence will result in immorality. Immorality will forget the seeking of kindness. Without the kind, seeking heart, evil desire will arise. Therefore, the truth is veiled and the way to the real Lord is blocked. Therefore, the sages proclaim the truth in the world and establish Islam, without any pictorial images. Human beings who follow Islam and the sages should obey the law without any self-centered serenity and indulgence. Outwardly, human beings should not be tempted by idols. Inwardly, they should not be burdened by selfish desire. Therefore, the sages have established Islam that is superior to other religions.

Theme: The way of the holy sage envelops and penetrates everywhere whereas his teaching is both right and grand. Those who believe do not doubt and puzzle.

Explanation: The way of the holy sage is the way of heaven. The religion of the holy sage is the practice of the way of heaven. To believe in the holy sage's way is to obey the rules of the way of heaven and follow the tract of the way of heaven. Note that this is the way of heaven. It is broad and extensive, inclusive of all things, penetrating all things. Heaven and earth are within its bounds. Even minute dust particles cannot filter through. The way of heaven unifies and governs by making the sky clear, the earth peaceful, the sun and moon shining, summer and winter alternating without end, also the mountain stable, the water running, flower and tree blooming and decaying and bird flying.

Now that the real Lord decorated [the world with] the ten thousand things, how could they fit into their roles and develop their functions? If they were under bondage, how could they develop healthily? Therefore, according to the way of heaven, the holy sages founded the religion of Islam so that people would not be led astray and influenced by any devious views. People who are edified by the holy teaching are like grass and trees that are gently blown by the wind of the spring, like hibernating insects awaken by the thunder and like people with knowledge and wisdom. They are full of life and live according to their natures and within the boundary of the law. If they live and settle in the most right and ideal environment, how can they doubt Islam at all?

Theme: While Muslims have settled in all corners of the world, they meet [religiously] within a house. The Muslims have a long history and the teachings have remained unchanged.

Explanation: The way is the same regardless of time and location. Do the teachings change with time and location? Does humankind change with time and location? The holy teaching has lasted for centuries. Rules and proprieties remain unchanged. Followers have scattered to all corners of the world and their determination has remained unchanged. Thus, Islam has a long and lasting history.

Theme: Islam has been transmitted continuously and should be trusted as a magnificent way of living by the law. It has spread across the generations, remained unchanged and is prosperous.

Explanation: Continuity means there is no loss of momentum or pause. Trust is a belief. Our religion began from Adam, (and continued through) Noah, to Abraham and on for centuries. Sages emerged and continued until Muhammad who made the collection. The later worthies and learned persons then expounded the key meanings. Many people proclaimed the way and many people continuously received the way. So far, the history of the way is over seven thousand years old. The rules and regulations of the way have remained unchanged. The way has prospered continuously and spread far and wide. It is to be transmitted for generations to come and remain forever prosperous. Can this be doubted?

A Survey of Collected data:

... Ming dynasty historian Long Yin (朗英) and his 7th Revised Collections (a supplementary history of Yuen and Ming dynasty, 58 Volumes in total): The mosque came to China in the time of the Sui dynasty. Islamic teachings and rules cover many aspects of Muslim daily living. Our Confucianism is inferior to it. According to Islam, the wealth, poverty, life and death of any person are predestined. However, cults tempt people into believing in idols for their blessings. Muslims serve the Lord and emphasize filial piety and worship no other. Some Muslims are rich. In Confucianism, we do not practice righteousness to the poor even if they are close to us, let alone care for strangers. Muslims give alms each month to their neighbors. Even people who are not Muslim can also receive aid. Chinese Confucianism requires obedience to the teachings of the sages. Some positive traditions remain but others have been lost. However, Muslims worship the Lord and serve their parents. Their tradition of seeking righteousness and fostering assistance remains unchanged through history. Daoism and Buddhism are inferior to Confucianism and they are not worthy for any discussion ...[9]

CHAPTER 2: THE REAL RULER[10]

Theme: The magnificent Real Ruler is the one, the only one. He is without any image. He created heaven and earth, humankind and all things.

Explanation: In the massive cosmos, there is one and only one Real Ruler. He is without image and is most subtle. No words can express or capture the essence or the subtlety. He is the Lord of creation and un-creation. The Lord emanated all things that we may find in pairs or talk about. The Lord is prior to all heaven, earth, humankind and all creation.

Additional Explanation: One is unique and this uniqueness has two meanings. The first meaning of the unique one is that it transcends all things. The second meaning of the unique one is that it embraces all things.

---

9. This historical data is the most detailed discussion in this chapter. It consists of about one thousand and six hundred words. This account is reaffirmed in even greater detail in Liu Zhi's final work of his trilogy.

10. Liu, *Rules and Proprieties*, 40–46.

The transcendent One is beyond manifestations. Unlike the transcendent One, the heaven, earth and all things have manifestations. The vital energy then transforms to give out their forms. This is the number [function] of the acquired heaven. The root suchness of the Real Ruler does not have any manifestation. It does not participate in the vital energy's transformation and is not determined by the number of the acquired heaven. The Real Ruler does not have any boundary and physical form, he is most pure and subtle, and is difficult to describe. The unique one means he is transcendent over heaven, earth and all things.

With regard to the unique immanent one, he is unique because he is not to be separated from manifestation and thus become unique. He is not to separate from the many. He creates all matters from the beginning to now, both visible and invisible and governs their activities with its real principle. The substance is not separated from its function and it is undifferentiated from all materials. This One is unique because outside the One, there is no manifestation. Outside this One, there is no boundary. This is the meaning of the immanent one.

Guise has two levels of meaning. The first is the guise with visible form, the other is invisible. All things that the eye can see, the ear can hear, the nose can smell, the mouth can speak, the hand and legs can move and dance, are visible guises. All things that the heart can think and can reach are to be understood and belong to the invisible guise. Thus, the real substance is without manifestation, color, boundary, understanding, guessing and language. These are not the substance of the real Lord. If you search exhaustively the way, you should think. These thoughts are guise and may lead to awakening awareness. The Ruler makes transformation into various [outward/visible] guises and the Ruler is not these guises. He inspires all awakening awareness and is not the awakening awareness.

Theme: The substance exists before the division of the two vital energies [ying/yang]. The function manifests itself after the formation of the image of all things.

Explanation: The substance is concerned with the independence [of the Real Ruler]. Function is concerned with the original power. The function is not equated with the substance because the function derives from the substance. The substance is not the function but function can manifest the substance. The substance and function are not the same but they cannot be separated. It is similar to the relation between ten and one. One is not equal to ten but is not different from ten. Ten is not one but the whole of ten is one.[11]

---

11. Oneness may be divided into supra-numerical and numerical. Liu Zhi here talks

The substance [of the Real Ruler] is prior and the function later manifests. This is the way to describe the order of the hidden substance and the manifested function. It is not the way to say one has original priority over the other. Before the appearance of anything, the function [of the Real Ruler] is enclosed by the substance which is subtle or not apparent and the function cannot fathom. After the appearance of things, the substance is hidden within the function and seen in the function. The substance [is the Real Ruler, it is] not the [visible] substance. Thus, this substance cannot be understood analogically as the substance of all things. The function is [the function of the Real Ruler and] not the [visible] function. This function cannot be analogously described as the function of all.

Additional Explanation: The name of the substance is similar to the name of ten. The name of the function is similar to the name of one. Ten is not one. However, the whole of substance is one. As the substance, the ten consists of [many] one[s]. One is not ten. As the function, all the ones are acts of the ten. The substance and function of the Real Ruler is related similarly. The whole of substance [of the Real Ruler] is the function and all the functions are [acts of] the substance. Therefore, the two are not to separate. However, the two cannot be united because they have different meanings.

For everything that exists in this world, there is an assured suchness and there is also a causal suchness. Assured and causal suchness are not separable. When one thing exists, it follows that all that relates to this thing exists. It is not a chronological event. For example, it is like ice and coolness, fire and hotness. It is not ice first and then coolness comes afterwards, fire first and then hotness. The substance of the Real Ruler is like causal suchness. The function is like his assured suchness. However, the two have the difference of hidden and manifested and yet there is no chronological priority. In order to understand the Real Ruler in the future, you should note the perspective of hidden and manifested.

Theme: Prior to the existence of the Real Ruler, there was no other beginning. Posterior to it, there is no end. The size of its root substance is so massive there is no boundary. It is so small that nothing is within him.

Explanation: The Real Ruler exists before all things. So, there is nothing prior to him. He exists after all things end. So, there is nothing posterior to him. His substance is all inclusive and thus there is nothing outside him. His function is all penetrating and thus there is nothing smaller inside him.

He does not have any beginning but he initiated the beginning of all things. He does not end but govern the ending of all things. He is so

---

about supra-numerical one. The supra-numerical one can be interpreted and understood as the inclusive unique one. Murata, *Sage*, 504–06.

inclusive that he has no boundary. He is so penetrative and therefore very meticulous. Thus, he can be so tiny without limit. He is before the beginning and governs the ends of all things. Within him, there is no boundary and he is able to penetrate all boundaries. Outside him, there is no outer boundary and he includes all boundaries. This beginning, end, outside and inside phenomena may be accounted for by the emanation and penetration of the root suchness and the hiddenness and manifestation of the subtle function.

Theme: The true Lord has no image, takes no location, no nearness or farness. No other being is equal to him. It is not dependent on any other existence.

Explanation: Image, location, nearness and farness, equals are created by transformation. The Real Ruler is un-transformed and has no image, location, near or far and equal. Since no image is like him, he can then transform into image, location, near and far and equal. Since he does not take any location, he can allocate all locations. Since he is not nearness or farness, he can measure both near and far. Since there is no equal that can manage him, he can support and arrange all phenomena of equals.

Theme: [The Real Ruler] governs all the principles of all things and their developments. He controls the heaven and the destiny of humanity.

Explanation: The principle of all things is embedded in the subtle function. The numerical is the extension and expanding use of its function. Heaven is the biggest in the transformation; humanity is the most spiritual. All these derive from its subtle function. What can exceed its boundary? The entirety [of all things] derives from the transformation. What things are not under its control? Therefore, the Real Ruler controls and also transcends all things.

Theme: The Lord creatively transforms [into all things] but he [himself] does not transform. The real Lord himself has no trace but has left all subtle traces. However, is there not anything that is without its trace?

Explanation: The Lord masterminds the transformation and he does not transform. The fact that all things are transformed is due to the Lord's arrangement and adjustment. The subtle function of the Lord can penetrate the traces of all things but his own substance is without any trace. All traits of things were formed by his subtle function. The one who transforms others is necessarily not inside the transformation. From the arrangement of things, it is impossible to speculate on the cosmic arrangement of the Lord. Therefore, the root substance of the Lord is unchanging and yet it transformed into all things. It is not formed by the traits of all things. Also, it is impossible to speculate on the great transformation based on the traits. Therefore, that the Lord has no trait means that the transformation is indeed a miracle.

Additional Explanation: Transformation and traits are two but one entity. Both of them are manifestations of the function of the real Lord. Transformation is to awaken awareness of the subtle function of the real Lord. Trait is the concrete physical matter and can be observed from its subtle function. The function and substance are absolutely not two different entities. The transformation of all things manifests the change of the function of the real Lord. All things have their particular traits. This is really to prove the existence of the real Lord. Therefore, without transformation and trait, there is no other way to understand the real Lord. If you depart from the real Lord and erroneously understand transformation and trait, there is no way to understand transformation and trait.

Theme: The real Lord is omniscient, omnipotent, perfect and good in all.

Explanation: This is to say that the real substance of the Lord has no trace. His subtle function has all sufficiency. As for knowledge, it is omniscient. His knowledge is different from sensory knowledge. The spirit of the real Lord is omnipresent. He is insightful and illuminates all ancient and modern subtle principles. As for power, he is omnipotent. However, this power is different from the power of concrete action. The transformation of the real Lord spreads out into the whole creation. The beginning and return of all things is moved by the real Lord's transformation. Any material thing that develops is not outside its function. All that he has created, they are all self-contained. The transformation is complicated but it is done with precision and thus is most perfect. The root substance of the Real Ruler is pure and not contaminated. The created metal, wood, water, fire and earth are the elements of material things. The transformation of these elements nurtures to become all things. The eventual things are most subtle and good. These four virtues [knowledge, power, perfection and goodness] affirm that the real Ruler is the Lord. The Lord is also the cause for the transformation to take place.

Additional Explanation: The four virtues "knowledge, power, perfection, and goodness" are the cause for things to exist. They also penetrate into the images and substances of all things. Before the formation of the cosmos, nothing exists except the lofty Real Ruler. All things are formed in the real Lord because they are embedded in his knowledge. They are then seen in his power and they end up perfectly in the virtue of the Lord's goodness. If there is no knowledge of the Lord, there is no principle for any existence of things. If there is no power of the Lord, nothing is able to take on image and substance. If there is no perfection of the Lord, all things cannot continue their transformation and begetting. How can things be self-contained and fill the whole cosmos? If there is no goodness of the Lord, they cannot take various shapes and forms. Do not all things fit nicely for their advantage and in their good time?

Theme: the Lord created all things without depending on any precondition. The Lord has transformed all things and they continue to transform. With his mercy, the Lord enables life to multiply. All things have their needs without any shortage. The Lord eternally and endlessly gives life to all things.

Explanation: the subtle function is omnipresent. As for the transformation, it is naturally done without depending on any coinciding conditions. Talking about the transformation of the Lord into ten thousand things, it is about ten thousand things in their complexity that transform and develop without end and boundary. Talking about the transformation of the Lord into many lives, it is about ten thousand things that receive their needs without any neglect. Talking about the Lord's giving to ten thousand things, it is about the Lord who satisfies endlessly all the needs of nature. These four virtues are the reasons that the Real Ruler endlessly transforms into ten thousand things and they ceaselessly originate from him.[12]

Theme: The Lord has movement and stillness [hidden and manifested. He is not unchanging]. This is the reason for the ever changing [of all things].

Explanation: Here, it is about movement and stillness. It is a metaphorical way of saying the hidden and manifested Real Ruler. There is no such thing as movement and stillness in him. It is merely said here because the subject of transformation is discussed. The transformation of the Real Ruler begins in the movement of his principle in the stage of innate heaven. In the stage of acquired heaven, it begins from the movement of his vital energy. From the movement and stillness, the principle and vital energy figuratively explain the Real Ruler's hidden and manifested aspects. This also reflects the transformation of the Real Ruler, manifests the subtle function of the Real Ruler flowing out into the cosmos. The meaning of non-constancy is that there is movement and then follows by stillness. Also, stillness is followed by movement, like an eternal cycle without end. All things cannot exist. They exist because of the work of movement and stillness of the principle-vital energy. All things cannot transform. They are transformed because of the Lord's hidden and manifested aspects. Therefore, it is said that the Real Ruler is the root cause of all things.

Additional Explanation: The movement of [the Real Ruler] forever unceasingly moves. The stillness of the Real Ruler is eternally quiet. There is stillness in movement, movement in stillness. However, whether it is movement or stillness, it is manifested in material things. Whether in movement you do not know any movement or in stillness, you do not know any

---

12. An additional explanation of about seventy words have not been translated.

The Rules and Proprieties of Islam   233

stillness, this refers to the mechanism of transformation and flowing out of the subtlety. You need to explain the meaning of movement and stillness and cannot seek their form. The movement and stillness are not constant. It is not one moment of movement and then next moment of stillness, not movement of this side and stillness on the other side. Both poles have movement and stillness. In stillness, there is movement and in movement, there is stillness. This happens without end. When there is a break, it causes the destruction of the heaven and earth. A similar example is like human breathing. Breathing takes place all the time. How can there be a break in breathing? Another example is the coming spring. The tree develops branches because of the yang movement, causing the temperature to rise. When the autumn comes, the leaves wither because of the ying quietude, causing the temperature to lower and the drying up of leaves. The temperature reaches its climax and then drops to the bottom and return up again. Is there any moment of non-movement?

Theme: The hundred and twelfth chapter of the Qur'an says, "The Lord is the one and only one Lord. The Lord is the source of all things. It depends on no other. It does not reproduce and is not begotten. There is nothing that can compare with it."

Explanation: *Al-lkhlas* is the name of the one hundred and twelfth Sura of Qur'an. It specifies the real principle of the Real Ruler. "Say" means the Real Ruler decrees to the holy sages who proclaim to the people. "Is" is a verb that emphasizes the reality of the Ruler and summarizes the content of this chapter. The heart and way cohere, the soul and subtlety unite. Consequently, one can affirm that it is the true Lord. Apart from him, there is no Lord. One is the beginning of all numbers. It unites all the parts within a ten thousand and yet transcends the beginning and end of the ten thousand. Source means the return of all things. The Lord begets all things and also transcends all things inside out. When a woman gives birth, this is to reproduce. When material forms of life reproduce another form, this is to reproduce. The real Lord has nothing like that. There is no place for him to reproduce. It reproduces nothing and is not begotten. Other religions making such ridiculous claims, declares the Lord has a son and daughter. They are begotten by the Lord. Someone also says, "The Lord has a father. He is begotten by the father." The above "no one is comparable to Him" means the Lord is the most exalted one. No other can be equal with him. If there is one, the real Lord, then who is the second? How can one say that He is the only one? This is the meaning that the real Lord is the only one. The whole chapter of *Al-lkhlas* narrates the existence of the real Lord. His existence is concerned with the idea of one. The meaning of one and only has been fully explained. The real Lord is the source of all things, he does not reproduce. When one says no one is comparable to the real Lord, one really affirms the reality of one. When a learner is able to appreciate how the one is to be the one, he does not need more analysis and naturally will be able to understand.

Additional Explanation: From one, it gives rise to and completes the ten thousand. One penetrates the beginning and end of ten thousand. Ten thousand derives from one, governs by one. Ten thousand must have one. Therefore, within the ten thousand, every one of them is one. Without one, there is no ten thousand. The root substance of one is eternally unchanging and unmoving but as a number one can give rise to countless other numbers. If one is to disperse, it can become million. If one is to increase greatly, it becomes ten billion. No matter it is ten, hundred, thousand, and ten thousands and billion; it cannot do without one. Without one, no number may be formed. Once you know the meaning, you can work it out. That is the reason, the Lord is one and at the end of the chapter, none is like him. The relation between the Real Ruler and all things is like one and all the numbers. The original substance [root suchness] of one is all-inclusive, all-penetrating, without surplus and shortage and with all sufficiency. One can beget any number but it is not equal to any number which must begin with one. One is similar to any number but not equal to the number. One naturally penetrates into other numbers. The root substance of one is eternally unchanging and unmoving but one can change into ten thousand numbers. The root substance of the one is without increase or decrease but this one can naturally increase or decrease the ten thousand numbers. One has neither beginning nor attachment to any number. It becomes the beginning of any number which has to attach to the one. One is the beginning of any number but it is not attached to any number. Therefore, ten, hundred, thousand, ten thousand and countless other numbers have their source in one which is the beginning. Other numbers attach to one. All numbers including ten, hundred, thousand and ten thousand have their beginnings in one and are founded on one. The root substance of one is unparallel and none is like one. Any number is formed by addition, subtraction, multiplication, and division. If you take away this way of thinking, there is no existence of number. The result remains to be the same: one.

Explanation: Alternatively, the purpose of the one hundred and twelfth Sura is possibly to inform the seeker about the way. One is pure but two means contamination. Seekers with oneness of heart are without contaminated thoughts. From the heart, the seeker can give single-minded action. Then, the body and heart of the seeker merge and cannot be differentiated from the root suchness of the real Lord. Because of this, outside the real Lord there will be needless diversion [error], losing your concentration. So, you will not even ask where the one comes from. Such questions may shake your firm foundation, lose your single-mindedness and contaminate your purity.

CHAPTER 3: EPISTEMOLOGY[13]

Theme: Any craftwork must have a craftsman. The universe must require a Lord who has created it.

Explanation: In the world there are many things. A palace is a huge building. A plate is a small container. These things are created by their makers. Without the house builder, there will be no house. Without the craftsman, there will be no cookware. The sky is clear and high above. The earth is solid and broad. Since the sun, moon, stars, mountains and rivers, living creatures and plants exist and they are abundant and plentiful, surely the creator Lord Ruler exists. Is it possible that the sky, earth, moon, stars, mountains and living plants form themselves? If one lives all the time under the sky and ignorant of a Lord Ruler in the sky, then one really does not know the sky. If one lives all the time on earth and is ignorant of the Lord Ruler on earth, then one really does not know earth. Every day one can see the sun, moon, stars, mountains and living plants and yet one does not know who the Lord Ruler is. Is that person proficient enough to investigate and seek the true knowledge of heaven and earth? He is not proficient to know the heaven and earth. How can he then know his own heart and see his own nature? Without investigating and seeking the principles of a thing, resulting in true knowledge and according to his human nature, he is not able to interact with people or things. How can he then exalt his virtue and realization? This is a very important question. Humankind should really need to know the Lord Ruler of the universe.[14]

Theme: In the world, there are foolish, worthy and unworthy people. They all know the existence of the Lord Ruler. Whoever does not know him; he is then constrained in form and image and ends up in emptiness.

Explanation: Although a person may be aware of the existence of God, he does not know God really. By his meaningless imagination, he creates false knowledge and erroneous feelings. The fools stick to their forms and images instead of the Lord Ruler. Thus, they regard humans and things as the Lord Ruler. The Daoists and Buddhists seek the Lord Ruler outwardly in

---

13. Liu, *Rules and Proprieties*, 47–57.

14. An additional explanation of about two hundred words was provided by Liu Zhi but not translated. At the end of the section, he emphasized expanding knowledge of every detail of things before any self cultivation.

forms and images. Therefore, these are people who regard emptiness as the Lord Ruler. There are numerous examples that end in failure.

Theme: Some learners may seek Lao Zi.

Explanation: Lao Zi lived in the Zhou Dynasty. His teaching exalted abstraction and mysticism. He used his power to prepare medicines for immortality. Lao Zi sought to be elusive and tried to lose any trace. The Qin emperor sought immortality and popularized Daoism. Later, people regarded Lao Zi as the Lord.

Theme: Some learners may seek the Buddha.

Explanation: Buddha lived in the Shakya Republic and was an Indian. He pioneered Buddhism and exalted emptiness and meaninglessness. He was keen on spirits and attempted to rescue humankind from hardship. He taught others to become another Buddha. Buddhism teaches that Buddha is the most exalted being in the world. All things depend on and can succeed because of Buddha's emptiness. Buddha came to China during the reign of Emperor Han Mingdi. Therefore, people in the East regard Buddha as their lord.

Theme: Some may seek the heaven

Explanation: Some may understand heaven as the principle and others the form. With regard to the principle, the heaven means humankind can understand its subtlety and yet is unable to grasp its irresistible power. With regard to the form, the heaven means one can look up and see various movements in the sky. According to the *Analects* of Confucius, the heaven is known as God. This heaven really means the principle. However, foolish people do not understand the meaning of heaven and they just use any form as the Lord Ruler.

Theme: Concerning principle

Explanation: Principle is to explain the necessity of things. Heaven has its principle, humans have their principle and materials have their principle. It is like the relation between the meaning of an essay and the text. In the ancient five Chinese *Analects*, there is absolutely no statement saying that God is the principle. The later scholars speculatively tried to work out the nature of God. They tried to know God from image form but in vain. When they gave up the image form, they had no foundation to know God. Thus, they said that God was the principle. They regarded that in this world, there was no exaltation higher than the principle. Thus, they gave the principle the name of God. This is not appropriate.

Additional explanation: The principle relates to things and this relation is similar to the text and meaning of the text. This has been the ancient unchanging truth. Before you write, you need to form the meaning that becomes the central idea. When this meaning is written on paper, it becomes the story form with deciding content. No matter what the form or the content of this story is, there must be an author who firstly needs to determine the theme and work out the plot. He then develops it to become a story. No one should say that the central idea of the story is the author himself. The learner should understand the relation between the principle and its thing. This relation is similar to the meaning of the story and the way the text conveys the meaning. Should the learner understand such relation, he can avoid mistaking the principle as the author.

Theme: He who seeks speculatively does not know the real Lord.

Explanation: Lao Zi and Buddha are humans and they must be created. They could not escape life and death. Those who exalt them as lords are meaningless. Heaven is above the earth and both are created as a whole. Even if heaven merges with the earth, both are created and belong to the material world. Some fools call this the lord. The principle itself is an abstract concept that is embedded within the material world. The principle is not creative and it is ridiculous to call a principle the lord. Therefore, he who seeks to know the Lord speculatively does not know the Lord.[15]

Theme: The true Lord is without any form and image but he is real. The Lord created heaven and earth, humankind. It is the Lord of the principles and vital energies of all things.

Explanation: The Lord is without form and image. It is impossible to see him in form and color. If the Lord is real, it is impossible to seek him with abstraction and emptiness. Since the Lord is the creator, Lao Zi and Buddha are not lords at all. Since it is the Lord of principles and vital energies, the Lord can be understood by the process of analogy. Any scholar, who wants to know the Lord, must know its name and then the reality of the Lord.[16]

Theme: To know the Lord, you seek him heartily. This sets the seeker on a firm foundation. All deviations and incorrect views will not be able to confuse him.

Explanation: It is the Lord Ruler who gives me life; it also let me live. When I die, my life returns to the Lord Ruler. Thus, I can live in rest and peace without worry. If I live without knowing the Lord Ruler, what warrant do I have to return to the Real? Because of this, we should not be ignorant. It is serious that we need to know the Real.

We know the Lord and seek him obediently. We understand it in our hearts. In situations that we cannot hear or see, we still solemnly exalt him

---

15. An additional explanation in the form of a summary in about ninety words has not been translated.

16. An additional explanation of about forty words has not been translated.

with a fearful heart. It seems the Lord Ruler is very near and he watches quietly over us. Thus, our lives know him obediently. We need to be alert in our ritual relationship with the Lord Ruler who watches over us in all moments. Also, we must earnestly use our bodies to know him.

If I am obedient daily, I am not far from the Lord Ruler. Every moment I am obedient, and then the Lord Ruler is not far from me. When I live, there is no separation between us. Will I be far from the Lord if I die with the compliance of the Lord's way? Even when I live or die, I do not separate from the Lord Ruler. This is the right way to deal with life and death. I thus become a person of belonging to the root and returning to the Lord.

This is such an important idea that I really need to focus on it. Shall I spend my life and energy in meaninglessness? Is it worth it? Also, life is important that we should not waste time listening to heresies. Should our life be sorrowful and regretful?[17]

Theme: When you see the movement of grass and trees, you sense the coming wind. When you see the budding of seeds, you know the coming of the spring. Examine your soul and you see there is life. Examine the transformation of the world. You know there is Lord Master. This is a necessary principle.

Explanation: In the last section, I have discussed the real and false principles, trying to prove the existence of the Lord Ruler Here I discuss the ways and methods to seek the Lord Ruler and give some evidences for the seeker. Some may think that it is difficult to know the Lord but it is not that difficult. There are two categories. Firstly, the form can see other forms. Secondly, the other is formless that can discern and know from the traits of things. Thus, in this world, all things can be known.

For example, wind is without form and color. Humankind cannot get and know its essence. When the grass and trees move, we sense the coming wind. Another example, spring does not occupy space. Humankind cannot capture or know its essence. However, when we can see the budding of the seed, we know that spring has come. These two examples are of outward phenomena. Soul is a thing inside us. It is without form and space and yet it follows us daily. We do not see the root suchness of our souls. However, based on my sight, hearing, language, movement, daily living, we are able to know that the nature of the souls.

Looking at far away things and near things within us, we still cannot see many invisible things. While these things cannot be seen, we cannot cheat ourselves by saying that they are nothing. It is from their traits that

---

17. An appendix on the meaning of life in about three hundred words has not been translated.

we can discern that they exist. The Real Ruler exists in the universe, without form or color. Naturally, humankind cannot see his root suchness. If we see the transformation of world, the movement of the sun and moon, the orderliness of such movement, the fitting distribution of creatures, the passing of centuries, time unchanging and life without ceasing and continuing to multiply, we can know that the Lord Ruler is quietly in control. To say there is nothing and no Lord is cheating.

When the grass and trees move, the wind leaves its trait. When the seed starts budding, this is the sign of coming spring. The soul of humankind is the expression of his life function. The sign of the Lord Ruler's existence is revealed in the world's transformation and movement. Wind, spring and life are the transformation of the Lord Ruler. We cannot see the essences of wind, spring and life except their traits. Likewise, we can only know the traits of the Lord Ruler and do not see his root suchness.

Theme: The root suchness of the Lord Ruler is hidden in function, seen in acts, subtle in principle and formed in image. Before his subtlety manifests, we cannot see the substance. After the manifestations, are not all materials signs of his root suchness?

Explanation: This explains the reality of the real Lord so that seeker can find it. According to the real Lord's root suchness, it has substance, function and action. Its substance is hidden, quiet and difficult to be made known. The subtlety of its function is unpredictable. Its actions can scarcely be seen. Why is that? This is because the root suchness is hidden in function and seen in its action. The action of the true Lord is seen in the innate heaven and becomes the principle of all things. Its action is seen also in the acquired heaven and becomes the image of things.

The substance and function of the Real Ruler cannot be felt by us but we can feel the principle and image which is not the Real Ruler but they are his action in the innate and acquired heaven. When you see the principle and image, you are seeing the act of God, aren't you? The action of the Real Ruler is nothing other than the manifestation. When you see his action, don't you see the function of the Lord also? The subtle function is the original power. When you see the function of the Lord, don't you see the root suchness? From the manifested phenomena, we can understand complex philosophy. From what can be understood, we can see dimly the hidden subtlety. Gradually, our heart and spirit can engage properly. Therefore, things that may be difficult to explore can be grasped. Things that may be difficult to understand can be solved. Is this merely the problem of understanding and exploration? In reality, when we see all things, we also see the manifestations of the Lord's root suchness. Why should you bother to distinguish the substance, function and act of the real Lord? The subtle function of the Lord has already been manifested. We can see the real Lord every time and everywhere. Abdullah Ibn Umar once said: "Let it be if we cannot see. While we can see, we see the real Lord. This is the meaning as explained."

Theme: Qur'an (Sura 41:53) says: "I reveal my traits in all four corners and their locations of the world . . . How come that you cannot observe?"

Explanation: This Qur'anic verse explains what has been said previously, namely, all things are signs of the Lord Master. This verse is the evidence and the Lord's subtle function is manifested. It is because humankind observes things superficially that we are not able to understand deeply. Therefore, there is a distance between the Real Ruler and humankind. To us, it seems the Real Ruler is hidden. We do not know that all things are manifestations of the Real Ruler and we should be able to see him. The Real Ruler is not far away and not hidden. It is humankind whose eyes are blind and ears are deaf. We ourselves are far from it and have hidden from the Lord.

The clever and astute people can observe the real Lord in anything. They ponder the principle and vital energy and know the hidden real Lord. They observe the day and night [ying and yang] and understand the endless great transformation. They then know the magnificence and exaltation of the real Lord. They look up to the sun and moon and can imagine the clairvoyance of the real Lord. They search ceaselessly the mountains and oceans and see his plentiful immanence and endless nurture in all. They see the mountains and rivers. Then they can experience the ever-flowing abundant grace of the real Lord. They watch the flowers and plants and can discover the wideness of his transformation. They observe the birds and animals and can see the universal love of the real Lord. They appraise the spirit and god and can know the wonder and omniscience of the real Lord. They observe the seasons and the weather and know the Lord's regulation of all natural cycles. They study the metabolism of creation and can know the Lord's control of the up and down of all things. All the true facts above are the manifestation of his subtle function and the lodging residence of the root suchness of the real Lord. Where materials exist, the real Lord is also present. Therefore, a text says: "only when you are near to things, you are able to know the real Lord. What is the point of seeking the true Lord in a far place?"

Theme: The holy sage says: "understanding oneself is to understand the Lord." That is, you need to understand yourself first before you understand the Lord.

Explanation: In the section above, from the things far way, you can see the proof of the Lord. Here in this section, the holy sage speaks from a nearer [with respect to humanity] perspective. You can know the reality of the real Lord. As your humanity is the microcosm, the nature of this person is also the Real Ruler. As you do not know the necessity of your root suchness, neither do you know the Real Ruler's root suchness. However, if you seek yourself and know the necessity of your nature, then even the necessity of the Real Ruler's root suchness is also known because it is not outside your nature.

For humans to be human there are four conditions that should be needed. Humans have their root suchness, which is the true nature. They have their subtle function, which gives intellectual power. Also, they have innate ability to see, hear, speak and act. Finally, they can act creatively in art and craft writing.

For the Real Ruler to be the Real Ruler, likewise there are four conditions that should be needed. The root suchness is the real substance. The subtle function is intellectual ability. Its root ability includes root seeing, hearing, speaking and acting. [Lastly], it has [splendid] acts. It governs the time of things by perpetual begetting and return. Thus, if you know the causal suchness of your substance and function, you also know the causal suchness of the Real Ruler. Is this a very appropriate comparison? This is the key meaning of the statement above that to know yourself is to know the Real Ruler.

True meaning: the meaning of the Lord Ruler is similar to the head in a family. The ruler is the highest position and received respect and reverence from the family members. He manages all family affairs and no one can supplant him. While the usual interpretation is of extreme exaltation, it is used because the Lord Ruler in reality holds sovereignty over certain things, similar to a landlord and an emperor. It is from this sovereignty that the name Lord Ruler originates. This Lord Ruler is one who holds sovereignty over others and the Lord Ruler is thus called.

Our teaching believes that the transformation is concerned with the root suchness. The Lord is the convergence of both the world of image and principle. It governs the transformation. Nothing is more exalted than the Lord. Nothing can really describe him. It is similar to the lordship of the landlord and emperor. Based on this sovereign idea, it is then called the Lord. While the Lord is sovereign over creation, human sovereignty over other things cannot compare to it. Although the use of the word Lord may be similar, this usage is only a metaphor, using the metaphorical argument to illustrate the principle. The visible is metaphorical to the invisible. In reality, the two lords have basic qualitative difference.

The Lord is prefixed by the word "real." It is because the meaning of Lord is different to different people. The lord may mean that it may control one thing, one moment or even the ignorant may illegally occupy and control a location. There is no fixed rule to use the word lord. Such lordship is very different from the creator Lord. The Lord thoroughly controls the world of image and principle, from beginning to now, without any disorder. This is the real Lord. Some people may misunderstand this meaning. They think that the creator Lord is the same as the emperor. They give the Lord a visible image. Most important, the real Lord means that it is the creator of all things and this is to show the meaning of Lord. Any seeker needs to know the meaning. He should not stop and try to seek the visible image of the Lord.

Additional Explanation: Zhu Xi says that "according to the *Analects*, in the universe, there is a heaven Lord . . . He is known as the principle.[18] He also says that the magnificent Lord bestows grace upon humankind." The will of the heavenly Lord predetermines the blessings and disasters of humankind. This proves the existence of the Lord Ruler. Someone asks: "While we call the Lord Ruler by the name of the heaven Lord, who is this Lord Ruler?" Zhu Xi answers, "The Lord Ruler exists naturally. Since the sky is solid and strong material and moves endlessly, then there must be a Lord Ruler who causes the natural movement of the sky." He also say, " . . . Today, people call the heaven Lord by the name of Lord Ruler who is without form. This is not an appropriate way. Even worse, some people in society call the Lord Ruler by the name of the mythical emperor."

My humble view: God as interpreted in the *Analects* as the heavenly Lord is similar to Islam that calls God by the name of Lord Ruler. Look at the ancient historical records about the Five Emperors and Three Kings. They had a piety for God and were sincere. The historical books record that God is called the heavenly Lord, other example like, royal heaven, vast heaven, heavenly will, and heavenly wrath and so on. Here, we talk about heaven. It means God and does not mean the massive and visible sky. The historical record does not explain the reason of naming the heaven as God. From the time of Confucius and Mencius, it is common to name God as heaven and not sovereign emperor. Fools do not know the profound meaning and consider the heaven as the visible sky. Other people may also become speculative. They create many unfounded theories. Therefore, many deviations begin to creep in . . . As mentioned by Zhu Xi. He says, "Heaven is used to describe the Lord Ruler that transforms all things. This heaven is known as the principle. There is nothing in the world that is nobler than the principle. Thus, the principle is called [heaven] emperor." He also says, "This principle is a pure, inclusive and abstract concept. It cannot create. Through

---

18. This is a detailed historical data section and translation is only for the section on Zhu Xi. About three hundred words are not translated.

movements, the vital energy can attend to and cohere to form many things . . ." According to the above three arguments, sometimes it is due to the principle, or sometimes due to the vital energy or sometimes due to no principle or vital energy. Therefore, if someone asks about the truth of return, which way should they go? What evidence can they get in order to get back to the root and return to the mandate? Or rather than answering the question, let the heretics speak. They then become popular day by day. Should they be allowed to be unceasingly popular? The older generation Confucian followers say, "The evil of the heretics makes it impossible to explain the way." I consider that the damage of the heresies is to stop the explanation of the way. Those who study the ancient texts, they understand the way. It is due to the words of the ancient emperors and the holy worthies. In this way, the deviation can be eliminated. As a result, the way of Islam can be clear and exposed.

CHAPTER 4: MEANING AND WITNESS[19]

Prologue: Meaning is to know exhaustibly the principle and examine all things. Witness[20] is to explore the mystery and explain the meaning. In Islam, the "meaning and witness" is a method for the heart to pass on knowledge. This is a unique and singular way to know the Real Ruler. This chapter consists of five subchapters.

Subchapter 1 Theme: I testify there is no god except one, not two, God. It is the only real Lord. I testify the prophet Muhammad is the messenger sent by the Lord.

Explanation: The witness is to prove the reality of the real Lord and to know the root suchness of the real Lord. My witness is to use the self as proof without seeking any proof from outside the self. The fact is that the human self is composed of body and nature. That may be the body proof or may be the nature proof or may be the unified body nature proof. These may be sufficient to prove the real principle of the real Lord.

What does the body prove? The body of humanity has form and also invisible nature. The body including the inner hundreds of body parts is the visible part of nature. Vision, hearing, speech and movements are deeds under the control of nature. Nature enables the body to act and generate senses. This is sufficient to prove that the heaven and earth and ten thousand things do not have any self-government. They are all determined by the Real Lord and Ruler.

19. Liu, *Rules and Proprieties*, 58–61.
20. Alternative translation is "testification."

What does nature prove? Nature is invisible and it fully fills the person. Through the heart, the self can understand his nature and also the eyes can see. The thinking can perceive and see his nature but the ears cannot do so. Nevertheless, you have not heard any difficulty in working out the form of nature, resulting in a nature that is uncertain and wavering. From this argument, the real Lord has invisible originality. However, he embraces all forms of visible things and yet you cannot use word, concept, analogy and debate to seek him.

What do both body and nature prove? Within the body, there are visible, invisible components and also the movement and stillness of the whole body. This is ultimately due to nature. Humankind cannot continue its bodily function without its nature. Also, you cannot see nature outside the body. It is because nature comes first and then the body can function. Nature manifests through the function of the body. This is enough to prove that within this heaven and earth and ten thousand things, visible things and invisible spirit have their origin, namely, the one and real Lord. It is absolutely not that beside the real Lord there is a gap that can hold heaven and earth and ten thousand things. Also, they are not inside the Lord's root suchness that contains all these things. The subtle unity between the real Lord and all things is a mysterious principle similar to the union of heaven and humanity. It is not easy to explain. However, you may understand the mystery from both the body and nature. While it cannot be seen and heard, it can be completely heard and seen with body and nature. Originally, it is beyond our limits and without color and form. Yet you can see the encompassing and flowing of substance and function. These are clearly revealed. This is the meaning of personal proof. You may seek proof external to the self. Can that external proof be as clear?

Explanation: The [ultimate] sage is also another proof[21]. He further explains and expounds what is said above. The real Lord is invisible and controls the transformation in the innate heaven. The holy sage is the visible vicegerent of ten thousand things in the acquired heavenly realm. It is impossible for the invisible Lord to make any description to humankind but the visible sage can explain it. Therefore, you are able to understand the difficult truth that is impossible to understand otherwise.

Imitate that which is visible and follow the way of the sage. Then, you can reach the realm that is conceived to be impossible to reach. The holy sage is indeed human but he is the representative of the way and also manifests the way. The real Lord is the origin of the holy way. Therefore,

---

21. Although the text does not clearly indicate the sage is the prophet Muhammad, the subchapter title clearly indicates the concerned sage is the prophet Muhammad.

testifying to the sage is to testify to the Lord. If you testify thoroughly to the end, you also testify to the deeper mystery of the Lord. You can speak of two testimonies, one to the Lord and the other to the sage. In reality, it belongs to the same principle.

Translation: Witnessing the word and understanding the text of the Lord have a single core idea. It has two words, namely, "not two," only one single idea. The seeker who works hard needs to witness the reality of "not two." Such work completes the whole of witness. It is because the beginning and end of the heaven and earth, [that is] all things are operating intricately and that is merely the real Lord's manifestation of his subtle function. Such manifestation of the function and the subtle function of root suchness are different and yet not separable. They have different categories and are known by different names. Both of them eventually return to the one Lord. Those who are foolish and confused are not able to understand. They hold on to their own senses, erroneously exploring things beyond the real Lord. They are mistaken to hold firm to images. They are wrong to seek the real Lord from the created things that are outside the Lord or to seek it from the outside of the created things. Then, they conclude that the transformation of all things is a constancy of reality. How can they understand the subtle truth of the return to the real Lord? It is no wonder that many have not understood and are doubtful of the "not two." It is really disheartening!

Subchapter 2 Theme: All things are not the Lord, there is only the real Lord; Muhammad is the Lord's messenger.

Explanation: The witness, namely *Shahada*, is to do without the need of the proof of trace. There exists one Real Ruler. It is without boundary and has no body. However, the seeker can examine self and then he can witness the Lord, resulting in the meeting of the human with the heaven. The method is unavoidably based on the trait, namely, human self. The human self is not antithetical to the Real Ruler.

Explanation (continued): This chapter does not have to do with any proof by word nor with the existence of one Real Ruler. In its undifferentiated heavenly principle, it transforms and leaves traces. All things that have names are embedded in the unnamed. Thus, those named things are really unnamed things. All things that belong to the acquired heaven are undifferentiated in the innate heaven. Hence, the acquired heaven is also the innate heaven. Named things and unnamed things do not have boundaries. The innate and acquired heaven have no difference. Because of this, what is the point in insisting on proof? If the seeker can know this realm of understanding, then, he has reached the highest end point of exploring the Real Ruler. There is no knowledge that the seeker cannot get!

Subchapter 3 Theme: I believe in the Lord's root suchness [no beginning and original existence]. The subtle function reveals his exalted name. I confess that the real Lord reveals all laws.

Explanation: To summarize the meaning of witness, it concerns the subtlety of the Lord's substance and function. The real Lord's original substance has no trace; in the beginning it has no name. When the function manifests, his exalted name is then revealed. As an illustration, the real Lord sees, hears, knows and empowers all things, begetting and transforming. These are due to the principle of root suchness and the name of subtle function. When the subtle function is not manifested, the principle is concealed. When his subtle function manifests, the principle is then revealed. Therefore, there is no place or thing that does not exhibit the trace of the Lord's root suchness and subtle function. Those who are not focused to examine, do not understand this fact in their heart.

After witness then you can know un-differentiation and transformation. Because of this, the complete substance and great function of the real Lord are revealed thoroughly in the human self who seeks witness. If the seeker is sincere, the result will certainly be real. Once you have the certain reality, you accept and obey all the laws of the real Lord. Naturally, you do not relax yourself and withhold progress. Therefore, you seek to unify with the substance and function [of the real Lord], faithfully obey the Lord, wholly practice the Lord's law and work them out.

Subchapter 4 Theme: I believe in the real Lord. I believe in all heavenly spirits, and the sacred texts. I believe in the holy sages and the afterlife. I believe in the predestination of good and evil, that humankind has the choice of good and evil and believe in resurrection of life after death.

Explanation: the particulars of faith express specifically the subtlety of function and action.[22] The Lord Ruler transforms all things. The highest of all is the spirit and sage. The sacred text is to teach humankind, distinguishing right and wrong, confirming good and evil. The Lord transforms the visible world which is this life. It also arranges the life after. Once there is life after, there will be return. You can clearly know and understand the subtlety of the real Lord as if it manifests clearly before you. Then, you can unceasingly and anywhere meet with the Lord. Likewise, you can unite unceasingly and anywhere with the substance and function of the Lord Ruler.

Subchapter 5 Theme: the real Lord is lofty! All praises belong to the Lord. Ten thousand things are not the lord, but only the real Lord. The Lord is greatest. We are powerless and dependent on the exalted Lord.

---

22. Frankel, "Liu's Journey," 367.

Explanation: The big praise is the ultimate act of witness.[23] Such witness is at the realm of true reality. You believe and obtain the complete substance and function [of the Lord]. This means your endeavor is pure; your heart is focused; not external to the Real Ruler and able to see again one thing. Not external to the Real Ruler, your heart has one thought. Then, when you see with your eyes, you can see the Lord. When your heart desires, you desire the Lord. When this happens, you should not hold on to your cleverness and ability. You should un-differentiate and yourself transform into the subtlety of the root suchness. There is no need to say praises external to the whole substance and great function of the Real Ruler, is there?

A humble conclusion: These five subchapters are really one chapter; five contents, but really one content. The five chapters have their titles. This is to show clearly the development of content. The previous chapter gives a hint of the following chapter and the subsequent chapter supplements the content of the previous chapter. The order is not to be reversed, added or subtracted. If the learner is serious about knowing, then he can reap the reward. Learners can continue to discover from each chapter, the more they study, the more they are impressed.

CHAPTER 5: FIVE ENDEAVORS[24]

The five endeavors are the way of cultivation, realizing the rule of uniting humanity with the heaven. The first endeavor is the witness of *Shahadah*; the second ritual prayer; the third fasting; the fourth alms-tax and the fifth pilgrimage. All five endeavors are the Lord's commands. The holy sage has shown himself as the example to all others.

Prologue: When the humans begin to form within the mother's body, the way of heaven is hidden. Then, the vital energy grows daily but real truth grows dim. Both reality and falsehood grow daily and yet human nature becomes insensitive. The understanding has become obscure and purity is contaminated. The way is then blocked. Humans do not know the way of return. The five endeavors of Islam, namely witness, ritual prayer, fasting, alms-tax and pilgrimage, are the ways of cultivation and return to human origin.

Explanation: The way of heaven works harmoniously with the human heart. The Lord gives one principle to humanity but each human receives the principle differently. Thus, there is a difference between the sage and

---

23. This is the corporate celebration among Muslims who memorize the *Shahadah* vocally at the end of Ramadan.

24. Liu, *Rules and Proprieties*, 62–74.

ordinary humans. The holy sage uses the way to explain things [the physical images] and he understands clearly the truth. The ordinary humans use things [physical images] to explain the formation of things and the truth is concealed. How can humans understand? How can humans return to their origin? Then, the real Lord gives the five endeavors. This is the way of cultivation, clearing the blockage, pointing out the way and guiding the path of return.

Why are there five endeavors? It is because the heart and nature of humanity are interconnected, similar to a lock and key. Ears, eyes, mouth, nose and body are affected by sound, color, taste, smell and movement, respectively. These [physical images/ perception] may cause love and hatred toward fleshly feelings. Such feelings are like the spring of a lock, which triggers the lock, making perfect and faultless the union between the heart and nature. If you use the key to open the lock, the spring of the lock is released and thus the union is separated. The five senses of feelings, namely sound, color, taste, smell and movement are a burden and constrain humanity. Thus, five different methods are needed and they gradually can remove the burden. Human nature can be then manifested and the way [of cultivation] is clear. Thus, the five endeavors are necessary for cultivation.

Theme: Witness is to know clearly the return.

Explanation: While humans may desire cultivating the way, they may not know the method and end in failure. Witnessing the Lord directs the heart to return and does not let the heart linger on aimlessly. Know that the real Lord is the origin of the great transformation and all mandates are derived from it. Anyone who desires to return to the mandate must then follow the real Lord as the reliable guide, achieving the return by constraining the body and heart. If humans give witness to other things, they fail both this life and the afterlife and are beyond any cure. How can it be possible for such humans to hope for any success?

Theme: Ritual prayer is to practice the way of return

Explanation: If humans desire to practice the way, they must first know the way. They can then speedily and directly arrive at the destination. Otherwise, they may divert to another way and have no chance of arriving at the destination at all. It should be noted that the Lord gives life at the beginning. Humans pass from the fetus stage to adulthood and their experiences are different. By such different experiences, humans are further away from their beginnings. More experiences mean further away, making a return to the beginnings more difficult. Humans have passed through various stations, one after another. Is it possible for humans to return just by one step? Propriety means humans walking through their previous experiences, making their way back to the start. Since the Lord has given humans lives, so they can step by step, station by station, experience their lives. Thus, humans can now return to the mandate of the Lord station after station. This is the meaning of propriety.²⁵

Theme: Fasting is to abstain from material things.

Explanation: Humans desire material things and that may constrain humanity. Humans cannot easily give up this desire because they need such materials. Fasting is to abstain from the need for materials. Human nature is originally good but the desire for materials means constraint. Constraint results in the unavoidable need for materials. Fasting is the endeavor of abstinence from materials. Through the exercise of abstinence, humans have no desires for materials. Abstinence from materials means that human nature is not interfered with and thus nature can return to the Lord without any second thought.

Theme: Alms-tax is to sacrifice human selfishness.

Explanation: Humans do not align with the way [of the Lord] because of their self-centeredness. The endeavor of the alms-tax is in practical terms the giving up of personal possessions. In reality, it is the self that needs to be given up. Humans may possess many things but it is money that means the most. While you may not know how to give up the self, alms-tax is indeed the giving up of the self. To give alms means the self is to die. When you are dead, you are suitable to unite with the way of the Lord. Thus, if you are seeking the way, outwardly you are dead to material things. Inwardly, you are also dead to the self. Hence, strings of desires completely disappear. Contaminated things are then purified. You no longer need to seek the way diligently because the way unconsciously undifferentiates with you subtly.

Selected key theme: Pilgrimage means the return to the Real.

Explanation: The more you desire to stay in your home, the less you long for the way. The Lord commands pilgrimage and wants you to give up your selfish desires, be on the way and near the origin. Pilgrims give up their love for their home. They travel precariously and then arrive at their destination. Therefore, those who seek cultivation need to give up their self, practice asceticism and eventually arrive at the Real. This is to use visible practice to reveal the meaning of the invisible pilgrimage.

Theme: The cultivation of these five endeavors is to end the way of acquired heaven.

Translation: These five endeavors are the method of cultivating of the way and keeping humans close [to the Real]. This way embraces heaven and earth. It reveals concealment. Nothing can exist outside the way. Also,

---

25. Then, Liu Zhi continued to provide a broader meaning of proprieties in about five hundred words. This section is not translated.

humans cannot exist without the way. The way transforms all things and all things return back to the way. If humans come from the transformation of the way and cannot return to the way, does it mean that the way is far away from humans? No, it is humans who are distant from the way. Humans can use these endeavors to cultivate the way. Frequent witness enables human return. Frequent ritual prayer enables humans to know the journey. Fasting enables humans to give up materials and directs them to the way. Alms-tax is the giving up of the human self and to control their own self. Pilgrimage means that humans are to move from far to near, from outward to inward and return to their place in the original substance. Outward pilgrimage means that humans still leave behind their walking trace, but inward pilgrimage means to be undifferentiated and be one with the Real Ruler. This is the purpose of cultivating the way. Is there any purpose more superior to this?

Theme: Witness is to set your heart to the Real Ruler. Witness can be heart (unspoken) and mouth (spoken) witness.

Explanation: Heart witness means single-mindedly thinking of and remembering the Lord, as if you are returning to your origin. It is inaudible and invisible also. Mouth witness means adoration and praise, not forgetting the Real Ruler has no beginning. This has form and is audible. When the mouth praises, the heart must go along with it. Such prayer is not superficial and able to enlighten the mind. It can generate a heart sincere to the Lord. The ritual law requires mouth witness. To be close to the Real Ruler, you need heart witness. Therefore, witness is the first step towards realization.

Theme: The mouth witness has a set time but heart witness does not have a fixed time.

Explanation: Mouth witness has form and sound but form and sound are disturbing. Say for example, you cannot do mouth witness when you are busy and not free. However, heart witness is invisible and inaudible. Form and voice are not a hindrance to heart witness. Another example, when you hear and see movement, eat and work, you can still single-mindedly focus on the Lord and dare not forget him. In this way, you always remember the Lord. There is really no set time to regulate your remembrance of the Lord. Thus, there is no set time for heart witness. This is the situation for people below the middle class who hope for realization. As for the people of the higher level and their realization, it is their whole body and mind that unite together. Return to the Lord must be done with the coherence of both the inside and outside person. In your daily living and dealing with people, you need to remember the Lord. This is the superior wisdom. Only the wise people can understand and do it. Those who have yet to achieve this level are difficult to understand.

Theme: The endeavor and function of witness is great.

Explanation: The function of witness is important. When all things have not yet been formed, the heart of humankind has moved. This is the beginning of good and evil, and the source of principle and desire. Every moment remember the Lord. In the midst of seeing and hearing, consider the uprightness of the Lord and do not fall into the danger of desire. In every event you tirelessly remember the Lord. In your daily work, seek diligently and sincerely with reverence. Do not be lazy and fall into falsehood. Pray in all things lest your body suffers worry. If you don't pray in all things, this may lead to a life of disaster. Thus, the function of witness is important. This witness is the core of self-realization and an affirmation of the teaching.

Theme: In witnesses, there are ten rules.

Explanation: Rule means the main rules. In each of the five endeavors, there are main rules, holy rules, propriety and secondary endeavor. The main rule is the rule of the Lord. Holy rule is the act of sages. Propriety is the combination of holy rule and ritual. This has to be practiced from the ancient to the present time and is regarded as normal practice. Secondary endeavor means that the individual can seek his resource for realization. Witness includes both heart and mouth witness and has ten rules. Learners need to pay careful attention and experience intimately so that their witness is not meaningless.

Theme: Recite the witness

Explanation: The first of the ten rules is to recite the witness. This witness is discussed in chapter four on meaning and witness. Here, to recite means mouth witness. You recite the witness. Before you pray, you need to know the Lord. To know him intimately, there is no better way than to recite the witness. It is to affirm the truth without error. When the sages teach the way, they require accurate recitation. The rule of sequence of regulations can judge the evil of acts and deeds and the judgment is also in accordance to this recitation.

Theme: Know the meaning of the witness

Explanation: The second rule is to know the meaning of witness. This is to know the meaning of the recitation. Since you recite the witness, you need to know the meaning. If it is merely mouth recitation and not knowing the meaning, you really have not recited at all. Thus, while knowing the meaning is number two in the sequence of regulations; it is number one and most important in the way of realization. This is because to come close to the Lord, the basic requirement is the heart witness which is most important and mouth recitation comes second.

Theme: To believe the principle of witness.

Explanation: The third rule is to believe the principle of witness. It is to believe what you have recited and witnessed. The correct way is to recite verbally, know the meaning and the heart believes truly the principle. Ordinary people can merely recite verbally and know the witness. The heretics can do likewise. If the heart does not have sincerity, how do you differentiate from the ordinary people? The reason that ordinary people are ordinary is that they do not understand the principle of witness. Heretics are heretics because they do not believe the principle of witness. The knower is the person who knows the witness. The believer is the person who believes the witness. Therefore, we are called Muslims and this term does not apply to any other people.

Theme: To obey the way permanently.

Explanation: Permanency means to keep the way all the time. You know the principle of witness is right and should always remember it in your heart and never forget it. For example, a traveler needs to follow the path in his journey. He may lose his path and not be able to return home. Another example, a person picks up a treasure. He needs to keep it carefully as if it were treasure and fears losing it. If you face towards the Lord, you have achieved the principle of witness. You need to be vigilant daily and always pious to the Lord. In any movement, do not forget the Lord. In any quietude, remember him. You are afraid to make a mistake, losing your way and unable to return to him. You believe him sincerely; firmly keep your right way. If your whole life does not forget him, you do not need to worry about your life and death. This is the fourth of the ten rules.

Theme: If questioned, do not avoid your answer. If asked, do not be slow to teach.

Explanation: Someone might ask about the principle of witness. You should answer clearly and without hesitation. This shows that you already believe. Also, it helps the other towards their belief. Some might ask to be taught about the principle of witness. You should use correct recitation to teach them, without any delay and do not pass on the responsibility to anyone else. Thus, we have the principle and pass it on to others who also receive the principle. The first four rules are concerned with you and your understanding. The fifth and sixth rules are about your passing on from you to others so that others can fully understand. The last four rules are concerned with the affirmation of belief without doubt. This can give weight to the argument and get rid of any heresy.

Theme: To know clearly the principle that the Lord really exists.

Explanation: Three reasons for the principle that the Lord exists. Firstly, it is the principle of creating all things. Another principle is the control of all things and lastly the management of all things. What is the principle of creation of all things? There is a maker of every container or thing. For example, a small cup or container must have a craftsman; a knife made by a knife-maker; a house by a builder. There is nothing in this world that naturally exists without being made. The world has visible form and how can there not be a creator? Therefore, it is doubtless to ascertain the existence of a creator Lord Master.

What is the principle of the control of all things? It is humankind that makes the first move. Any ship that sails has a sailor. A racing chariot has a rider. The flying kite has a person that controls the wire. The arrow that hits the bullseye has an archer. Without the person, a ship, chariot, kite, the arrow cannot work. Look, the world turns in an orderly fashion and all things continue endlessly. How come there is no one in control if the world continues to turn and things endlessly continue? Therefore, it is impossible to deny the existence of the Lord Master who is in control.

What is the principle of management of all things? No matter whether the property is occupied or abandoned, someone does the management. For example, a house has an owner, a garden has a gardener. This applies to all containers and things without exception. Now that the world is enormously complex, how can it exist without the existence of a Lord Master who manages all things? Therefore, it is doubtless to ascertain the existence of a Lord Master who manages all things.

Theme: To know that the Lord is one.

Explanation: Three reasons that we know the Lord is one. Firstly, it is the proof of one; secondly, the proof of family governance and lastly the proof of principle. What is the proof of one? It is from one that you get all other numbers. Number one does not come from two. The Lord initiates the beginning and end of the world. How can there be two? From this point, it is obvious that the Lord is one and not two. What is the proof of family governance? In a family, there must be a head and the family prospers. In a country, there must be one ruler to rule it. No one has seen two parents having the same status and also two emperors governing the same country, resulting in harmonious ruling. Even more, is it possible that the Lord is two as he is and the source of all things? From this you can see the Lord is one and not two.

What is the proof of principle? Assuming there are two lords, can the two lords have the same power? Alternatively, can the two lords have different powers? If they have the same power, it is enough just to have one and the second one is superfluous. If there are different powers, it means there is an opposition of powers. When there is opposition, the appearance of the world is not unitary. The stronger one will lord it over the weaker who should not be the lord after all. From this principle, you can see the Lord is one and not two.

Theme: The proof that nothing can be comparable to the real Lord

Explanation: Comparison means there is something similar. Things can always find other matching things. The true Lord is incomparable. All things have their form, color, sound and taste and one thing can be distinguished from another. The principle, vital energy and image of things can also find their match. The Lord is unlike any form, image, sound, taste. It does not belong to any principle, and vital energy. What can you compare it with? The root suchness of the Lord is pure without any contamination and outside any human mind and thinking. Not only is its substance incomparable but his subtle function is also incomparable. Not only is his function incomparable but his act is also incomparable.

Let's take a look at the creation of the Lord. His creation is lively. Humankind cannot create. For example, an ant, a mosquito, grass, seeds are all full of life. Can humankind create ants, mosquitoes, grass and seeds that have life? In all things, what is more exalted than humankind? Who is cleverer than humankind? From this, we know there is no one similar or comparable to the Lord. Summarizing the argument above, we prove by using things that are outside us. This is not the most relevant proof. The most relevant proof comes from within us. Humankind has nature and that can prove the existence of the real Lord who is one. This is the most superior and firm proof. Is there any human body merely without nature in the world? Are there two natures in one human body? What can someone say about the form of this nature and how comparable is this nature with the other? If the scholars can learn and explore from within the human self to know the real Lord, they have come over half way.

Theme: Know the prophet Muhammad as the sage, the Utmost Sage.

Explanation: From the ancient times, there have been many sages. Only Muhammad is the Utmost Sage. He possesses all the virtues and his transformation is clear. He perfectly practices the will of the Lord. He has a long ancestral tradition and exceptional sensitivity. His spirit begins superbly before the foundation of the world. He is the master of all principles and natures. The body of the Sage emerges as the heaven and earth are formed. He is the fruit of all the sages throughout the ages. As an illustration, the heaven and earth symbolize a tree. The Utmost Sage is the seed and also the fruit of the tree. Seed and fruit are "not two." Therefore, while heaven and earth are huge, they are formed into reality by the nurture of the Utmost Sage. The spirits of all sages have begun under the shelter of the Utmost Sage. The form of the Utmost Sage belongs to the heir of Adam but his spirit is the ancestor of Adam. His religious tradition unifies all other religions and his collected laws fulfill all other laws. His way is superior to other ways with unbiased accuracy, shining like the sun and moon and as long-lasting as the heaven and earth. According to ancient texts, if humans want to know the Utmost Sage, they need to know the Utmost Sage's religion as described above.

The sensory and revelatory faculties[26] of the Utmost Sage are superb and he is far superior to all the sages. These include, for example, the seed of the Utmost Sage's shadow appearing on the foreheads of his ancestors. Also, the chest of the Utmost Sage bears a seal which has words written by the angel in his flesh. The light of Muhammad appears on the forehead of Adam. When the ancient Chinese emperor tried to worship a painting of the Utmost Sage, his image in the painting disappeared. The other sages have experienced none of Muhammad's faculties. His sensory and revelatory faculties have long lasting effect and all later generations can confirm that. He received from the Lord the gift of Qur'an and all followers of Islam . . . Islam is adaptable to all particular situations and it is passed on from generation to generation without any change to another faith. The way has been prosperous and without any hindrance. Therefore, such [growth] can be a proof of the sensory and revelatory faculties of the Utmost Sage. After examination, humankind can say that his religion has a long tradition, his sensory faculties are miraculous, and his proclamation is accurate and great. Since the beginning of humanity, there has been no other person comparable to the Utmost Sage. Thus, it is obvious that he is known as the Utmost Sage.[27]

Theme: The witness endeavor is accomplished when the ten rules are completed

Explanation: If you do not recite the witness, there is no proof of the Lord. Without the meaning of the witness, you do not understand. Without any understanding, the witness has no foundation. Without any faith, there is no solid action. Without perseverance, there is no sincerity. Without any action and sincerity, witness has no effect. When questioned, do not give any answer and thus become a cheat. When asked, do not teach the knowledge and thus become a miser. Cheating and miserliness are the two worst defects in your witness. If you do not know the reality of the Lord, your witness is meaningless. If you do not know the uniqueness of the Lord, your witness is unfocused. The result of meaninglessness and lack of focus is a shaky and even doubting faith. If you do not know the superiority of the

---

26. Literal translation is telepathy.

27. Liu Zhi gave another detailed account in about nine hundred words based on Chinese historical record to expand his view on the prophet Muhammad. This account is not translated.

Lord, your witness is not pure. Impurity can lead to the rise of superstition and evil thinking. If you do not know the Utmost Sage, Muhammad, you lose direction in your way. Therefore, there is no way for you to return. You enter into deviations. Therefore, if you can complete the ten rules, you can accomplish the endeavor of witness.

Theme: The holy sage says, "Witness is the core of all endeavor. It is the source of all goodness. Benevolent people perpetually witness and are free from any worry. People who emphasize realization will not forget the endeavor of witness."

Explanation: The core is the backbone of the matter. Source is the beginning of things. All endeavors are achieved through witness. It is like the body that needs a backbone in order to perform normal functions. All good works require the witness endeavor to begin. It is like the primordial energy that creates all things. Witness is the fountainhead, leading all the endeavors. If you always keep your witness endeavor, your endeavor is perfect and your virtues plentiful. You are naturally free from worry and anxiety. In all your daily living, your basic practice is to witness to the Lord. If you are serious about realization and seeking human divine unity, should we not emphasize witness as the most important element?

Bibliography

'Abduh, Muhammad. *The Theology of Unity*. New York: Humanities Press, 1966.
Affifi, Abu al-Ala. *The Mystical Philosophy of Muhyid Din-Ibnul Arabi* Lahore: SH. Muhammad Ashraf, 1939.
Ai, Yuejie. "The Three-character Classic of Liu Zhi." *http://blog.sina.com.cn/s/blog_5ef66f4bo100j6rs.html*.
Akkach, Samer. "The World of Imagination in Ibn 'Arabi's Ontology." *British Journal of Middle Eastern Studies* 24.1 (1997) 97–113.
Al-Faruqi, Isma'il Raji. "On the Nature of Islamic *Da'wah*." *International Review of Mission* 65 (1976) 391–409.
Algar, Hamid. "The Naqshbandiya Order: A Preliminary Survey of its History and Significance." *Studia Islamica* 44 (1976) 123–52.
Alles, Elisabeth. "Chinese Islam: Unity and Fragmentation." *Religion, State and Society* 31.1 (2003) 7–35.
Al-Massri, Angelika. "Imagination and the Qur'an in the Theology of Oneness of Being." *Arabica* 47 (2000) 523–35.
Almond, Ian. "The Meaning of Infinity in Sufi and Deconstructive Hermeneutics: When Is an Empty Text an Infinite One?" *Journal of the American Academy of Religion* 72 (2004) 97–117.
———. *The New Orientalist: Postmodern Representations of Islam from Foucault to Baudrillard*. London: Tauris, 2007.
———. "The Shackles of Reason: Sufi/Deconstructive Opposition to Rational Thought." *Philosophy East & West* 53 (2003) 22–38.
———. *Sufism and Deconstruction: a Comparative Study of Derrida and Ibn 'Arabi*. London: Routledge, 2004.
Al-Tustari, Sahl. *Tafsir al-Tustari: Great Commentaries of the Holy Qur'an*. Translated by Annabel Keeler and Ali Keeler. Amman: Royal Aal al-Bayt Institute for Islamic Thought, 2011.
Ansari, Muhammad Abdul H. *Sufism and Shar'ah: a Study of Shaykh Ahmad Sirhindi's Effort to Reform Sufism*. Leicester, UK: Islamic Foundation, 1986
Arberry, Arthur J. *Classical Persian Literature*. Richmond: Curzon, 1994.
Armijo-Hussein, Jaqueline. "Sayyid 'Ajall Shams al-Din: A Muslim from Central Asia, Serving the Mongols in China, and Bringing Civilization to Yunnan." PhD diss., Harvard University, 1997.
Asin Palacios, Miguel. *Islam and the Divine Comedy*. Translated by Harold Sutherland. London: Murray, 1926.

Ataman, Kemal. "Religion, Culture and the Shaping of Religious Attitudes: The Case of Islam." *Islam and Christian-Muslim Relations* 18 (2007) 495–508.
Atwill, David G. *The Chinese Sultanate: Islam, Ethnicity, and the Panthay Rebellion in Southwest China, 1856–1873*. Stanford: Stanford University Press, 2005.
Aubin, Françoise. "Chinese Islam: In Pursuit of Its Sources." *Central Asian Survey* 5.2 (1986) 73–80.
———. "En Islam Chinois: Quels Naqshbandis? " In *Naqshbandis: Cheminements et Situation Actuelle d'un Ordre Mystique Musulman*, edited by Marc Gaborieau et al., 492–572. Istanbul: Isis, 1990.
———. "A Glimpse of Chinese Islam." *Journal of Muslim Minority Affairs* 12 (1991) 335–45.
———. "Les Ordres Mystiques Dans la Chine." In *Les Voies d'Allah, Les Ordres Mystiques Dans le Monde Musulman des Origines à Aujourd'hui*, edited by Alexandre Popovic et al., 262–67. Paris: Fayard, 1996.
———. "Tasawwuf in Chinese Islam." In *Encyclopaedia of Islam*, 8:337–39. New ed. Leiden: Brill, 2000.
Awn, Peter J. "The Ethical Concerns of Classical Sufism." *The Journal of Religious Ethics* 11 (1983) 240–63.
Bai, Shouyi. *History of Chinese Hui Ethnic Minority*. Vols. I and II. Beijing: Chung Hwa, 2003.
Bakar, Osman, ed. *Islam and Confucianism: A Civilizational Dialogue*. Kuala Lumpur: University of Malaysia Press, 1997.
———. "Sufism in the Malay-Indonesian World." In *Islamic Spirituality II: Manifestations*. Edited by Seyyed H. Nasr, 259–89. London: SCM, 1991.
Bektovic, Safet. "The Double Movement of Infinity in Kierkegaard and in Sufism." *Islam and Christian-Muslim Relations* 10.3 (1999) 325–37.
Ben-Dor, Zvi Aziz. "Even Unto China: Displacement and Chinese Muslim Myths of Origin." *Bulletin of the Royal Institute for Inter-Faith Studies* 4.2 (2002) 93–114.
Benite, Zvi Ben-Dor. *The Dao of Muhammad: A Cultural History of Muslims in Late Imperial China*. Cambridge: Harvard University Press, 2005.
Berg, Herbert. *The Development of Exegesis in Early Islam. The Authenticity of Muslim Literature from the Formative Period*. Richmond: Curzon, 2000.
Bergmann, Siguard. *God in Context: a Survey of Contextual Theology*. Aldershot, UK: Ashgate, 2003.
Berkson, Mark A. "Conceptions of Self/No-Self and Modes of Connection. Comparative Soteriological Structures in Classical Chinese Thought." *Journal of Religious Ethics* 33 (2005) 293–331.
Berlie, Jean A. *Islam in China: Hui and Uyghurs Between Modernization and Sinicization*. Bangkok: White Lotus, 2004.
Berthrong, John. *Concerning Creativity: A Comparison of Whitehead, Neville, and Chu Hsi*. Albany: State University of New York Press, 1998.
Bevans, Stephen B. *Models of Contextual Theology*. Expanded ed. Maryknoll, NY: Orbis, 2002.
———. "Models of Contextual Theology." *Missiology: An International Review* 13.2 (1985) 185–202.
Bousfield, John. "Good, Evil and Spiritual Power: Reflections on Sufi Teachings." In *The Anthropology of Evil*, edited by David Parkin, 194–208. Oxford: Blackwell, 1985.

Brainard, F. Samuel. "Defining Mystical Experience." *Journal of the American Academy of Religion* 64 (1996) 359–93.
Brook, Timothy. "Rethinking Syncretism: The Unity of the Three Teachings and their Joint Worship in Late-Imperial China." *Journal of Chinese Religions* 21 (1993) 13–44.
Broomhall, Marshall M. *Islam in China. A Neglected Problem.* London: Darf, 1987.
Burckhardt, Titus. *An Introduction to Sufi Doctrine.* San Bernardino, CA: Borgo, 1990.
Burrell, David B. "Creator/creatures Relation: 'the Distinction vs. Onto-theology.'" *Faith and Philosophy* 25 (2008) 177–89.
Cai, Degui. "The Adaptation of Liu Zhi's Islamic Philosophy into the Chinese Traditional Philosophy." *History of Chinese Philosophy* 1 (1997) 108–15.
———. "The Fusion of Liu Zhi's Islamic Philosophy and Chinese Traditional Philosophy." *History of Chinese Philosophy* 1 (1997) 108–115
Chan, Wing-Tsit. *Chu Hsi: Life and Thought.* Hong Kong: The Chinese University Press, 1987.
———. *Chu Hsi New Studies.* Honolulu: University of Hawai'i Press, 1989.
———. *New Exploration of Zhu Xi.* Beijing: East China Normal University Press, 2007.
———. *A Source Book in Chinese Philosophy.* Princeton: Princeton University Press, 1963.
Chan, Wing-Tsit, ed. *Chu Hsi and Neo-Confucianism.* Honolulu: University of Hawaii Press, 1986.
Chang, Haji Yusuf. "The Ming Empire: Patron of Islam in China and Southeast and West Asia." *Journal of Malaysian Branch of the Royal Asiatic Society* LXI Part 2 (1988) 1–44.
———. "Muslim Minorities in China: An Historical Note." *Journal of Muslim Minority Affairs* 3 (1981) 3–34.
Cheng, Chungying. "Li and Qi in the Yijing: a Reconstruction of Being and Nonbeing in Chinese Philosophy." *Journal of Chinese Philosophy* 36 (2009) 73–100.
———. "On Harmony as Transformation: Paradigms from the Yijing." *Journal of Chinese Philosophy* 36 (2009) 11–36.
——— "Philosophy of Yijing: Insights into Taiji and Dao as Wisdom of Life." *Journal of Chinese Philosophy* 33 (2006) 323–33.
Chi, Hsiao-la, et al. *Annotated General Catalogue of the Compendium of the Four Treasuries, Authorized by the Emperor* Reprinted. Taipei: Commercial Press Reprint, 1971.
Ching, Julia. *To Acquire Wisdom: the Way of Wang Yang-ming.* New York: Columbia University Press, 1976.
———. *Chinese Religions.* Basingstoke, UK: Macmillan, 1993.
———. *The Religious Thought of Chu Hsi.* New York: Oxford University Press, 2000.
Chittick, William C. "Anthropocosmic Vision in Islamic Thought." In *God, Life and the Cosmos: Christian and Islamic Perspectives,* edited by Ted Peters et al., 125–52. Aldershot: Ashgate 2002)
———. "Between the Yes and No: Ibn al-'Arabi on Wujud and the Innate Capacity." In *The Innate Capacity: Mysticism, Psychology, and Philosophy,* edited by Robert K.C. Forman, 95–110. Oxford: Oxford University Press, 1998.
———. "The Circle of Spiritual Ascent according to al-Qunawi." In *NeoPlatonism and Islamic Thought,* edited by Parviz Morewedge, 179–209. Albany: State University of New York Press, 1992.

———. "On the Cosmology of *Dhikr.*" In *Paths to the Heart: Sufism and the Christian East*, edited by James Cutsinger, 48–63. Bloomington, IN: World Wisdom, 2002.

———. "Death and the World of Imagination: Ibn al-'Arabi's Eschatology." *The Muslim World* 78 (1988) 51–82.

———. "The Five Presences: from Al-Qunawi to Al-Qaysari." *The Muslim World* 72 (1982) 107–28.

———. "Ibn 'Arabi." In *Islamic Philosophy and Theology*, edited by Ian Richard Netton, vol. 4, 122–34. London: Routledge.

———. *Ibn 'Arabi: Heir to the Prophets*. Oxford: Oneworld, 2005.

———. "Ibn 'Arabi and His School." In *Islamic Spirituality: Manifestations*, edited by Seyyed Hossein Nasr, 49–79. World Spirituality 20. London: SCM, 1991.

———. "Ibn al-'Arabi's Hermeneutics of Mercy." In *Mysticism and Sacred Scripture*, edited by Steven T. Katz, 153–68. Oxford: Oxford University Press, 2000.

———. *Imaginal Worlds: Ibn al-'Arabi and the Problem of Religious Diversity*. Albany: State University of New York Press, 1994.

———. "The Islamic Concept of Human Perfection." In *Jung and the Monotheisms*, edited by Joel Ryce-Menuhuin, 154–64. London: Routledge, 1994.

———. "Muslim Eschatology." In *Oxford Handbook of Eschatology*, edited by Jerry L. Walls, 132–50. New York: Oxford University Press, 2008.

———. "Mysticism versus Philosophy in Earlier Islam History: the Al-Tusi, Al-Qunawi Correspondence." *Religious Studies* 17 (1981) 87–104.

———. "The Perfect Man as the Prototype of the Self in the Sufism of Jami." *Studia Islamica* 49 (1979) 135–57.

———. "The Pluralistic Vision of Persian Sufi Poetry." *Islam and Christian-Islam Relations* 14 (2003) 423–28.

———. "Presence with God." The Muhyiddin Ibn 'Arabi Society web site *http://www.ibnarabisociety.org/articles/presence.html*.

———. "The Role of Liu Zhi's *Philosophy of Islam* in the Islamic Tradition." *Journal of Nanjing University (Philosophy, Humanities and Social Science)* 3 (2006) 50–53.

———. "Rumi and *wahdat al-wujud.*" In *Poetry and Mysticism in Islam: The Heritage of Rumi*, edited by Amin Banani, Richard Hovannisian, and Georges Sabagh, 70–111. Cambridge: Cambridge University Press, 1994.

———. *The Self-Disclosure of God: Principles of Ibn al-'Arabi's Cosmology*. Albany: State University of New York Press, 1998.

———. "Spectrums of Islamic Thought: Sa'id al-Din Farghani on the Implication of Oneness and Manyness." In *The Heritage of Sufism*, edited by Leonard Lewisohn, vol. 2, 203–18. Oxford: Oneworld, 1999.

———. *The Sufi Path of Knowledge: Ibn al-'Arabi's Metaphysics of Imagination*. Albany: State University of New York Press, 1989.

———. *Sufism: A Short Introduction*. Oxford: Oneworld, 2000.

———. "*Wahdat al-Shuhud* and *Wahdat al-Wujud.*" In *Encyclopaedia of Islam*, 37–39. New ed. Leiden: Brill, 2002.

Chodkiewicz, Michel. *Seal of the Saints—Prophethood and Sainthood in the Doctrine of Ibn Ibn 'Arabi*. Translated by Liadain Sherrard. Cambridge: The Islamic Text Society, 1993.

Corbin, Henry. *Creative Imagination in the Sufism of Ibn 'Arabi*. Translated by Ralph Manheim. Princeton: Princeton University Press, 1969.

———. *History of Islamic Philosophy*. London: Kegan Paul International, 2006.

Dagli, Caner K. "On Beginning a New System of Islamic Philosophy." *The Muslim World* 94 (2004) 1–27.

———. "From Mysticism to Philosophy (and Back): an Ontological History of the School of the Oneness of Being." PhD diss., Princeton University, 2006.

Dillon, Michael. *China's Muslim Hui Community: Migration, Settlement and Sects.* Richmond: Curzon, 1999.

Ding, Hong. "About the Issue of Islam's Acclimatizing Itself to China's Society: From the Angle of Cultural Identification of Hui." *N.W. Ethno-National Studies* No.2, 45 (2005) 69–77.

Ding, Ke-jia. "Cultures Expressed in Chinese Language Context and the Philosophical Communication between China and Iran." *Journal of Hui Muslim Minority Study* 59.3 (2005) 25–30.

Ding, Minjun. "Anatta—the King of Anxi Region in Yuan Dynasty Conversion to Islam and His Influence." *Studies in World Religions* 43 (1991) 68–76.

———."Study on the Marginal Chinese Muslim." *Journal of Hui Muslim Minority Study* 56 (2004) 38–47.

Ernst, Carl W. *The Shambhala Guide to Sufism*. Boston: Shambhala, 1997.

Esposito, John L., ed. *Islam in Asia. Religion, Politics & Society*. Oxford: Oxford University Press, 1987.

Fadl, Khaled Abou El. "Peaceful Jihad." In *Taking Back Islam*, edited by Michael Wolfe, 33–39. Emmaus, PA: Rodale, 2002.

Fakhry, Majid. *A History of Islamic Philosophy* 3rd ed. New York: Columbia University Press, 2004.

Faruqi, Maysam J. "*Umma*: The Orientalists and the Qur'anic Concept of Identity." *Journal of Islamic Studies* 16 (2005) 1–34.

Feng, Huaixin. "An Exploration on the Contemporary Adaptation of Chinese Islam in Communism." *N.W. Minorities Research* 20 (2001) 79–85.

Fletcher, Joseph F. *Studies on Chinese and Islamic Inner Asia*. Aldershot, UK: Variorum, 1995).

Ford, Joseph F. "Some Chinese Muslims of the Seventeenth and Eighteenth Centuries." *Asian Affairs* 61 (1974) 144–56.

Frank, Tamar. "'Tasawwuf is . . .': On a Type of Mystical Aphorism." *Journal of the American Oriental Society* 104 (1984) 73–80.

Frankel, James D. "Apoliticization: One Facet of Chinese Islam." *Journal of Muslim Minority Affairs* 28.3 (2008) 421–34.

———. "Liu's Journey Through Ritual Law to Allah's Chinese Name: Conceptual Antecedents and Theological Obstacles to the Confucian-Islamic Harmonization of the *Tianfang Dianli*." PhD diss., Columbia University, 2005.

———. "From Monolith to Mosaic: A Decade of Twenty-First Century Studies of Muslims and Islam in China." *Religious Studies Review* 37.4 (2011) 249–58.

———. *Rectifying God's Name: Liu Zhi's Confucian Translation of Monotheism and Islamic Law*. Honolulu: University of Hawai'i Press, 2011.

———. "Uncontrived Concord: the Eclectic Sources and Syncretic Theories of Liu Zhi, a Chinese Muslim Scholar." *Journal of Islamic Studies* 20 (2009) 46–54.

Fung, Yulan. *A History of Chinese Philosophy*. Vol. 2: *The Period of Classical Learning*. Translated by Derk Bodde. Princeton: Princeton University Press, 1953.

———. *A Short History of Chinese History*. Tianjin: Tianjin Academy of Social Sciences, 2007.

Gao, Zhanfu. "The Problem of Religion and the Modernization of China seen from the Perspective of Xi Dao Tang." *Studies in World Religions* 68 (1997) 93–98.
Gardet, Louis. "Dhikr." In *The Encyclopaedia of Islam*, 223–27. New ed. Leiden: Brill, 1965.
Gardner, Daniel K. *Zhu Xi's Reading of the "Analects": Canon, Commentary and the Classical Tradition*. New York, Columbia University Press, 2003.
Gätje, Helmut. *The Qur'an and its Exegesis: Selected Texts with Classical and Modern Muslim Interpretation*. Oxford: Oneworld, 1996.
Geels, Antoon. "A Note on the Psychology of *Dhikr*: The Halveti-Jerrahi Orders of Dervishes in Istanbul." *The International Journal for the Psychology of Religion* 6 (1996) 229–51.
Geertz, Clifford. *The Religion of Java*. New York: Free Press, 1960.
Gladney, Dru C. *Dislocating China: Muslims, Minorities and Other Subaltern Subjects*. London: C. Hurst & Co., 2004.
———. "Islam." *Journal of Asian Studies* 54.2 (1995) 371–77.
———. "Islam in China: Accommodation or Separatism?" *The China Quarterly* 174 (2003) 451–67.
———. *Muslim Chinese: Ethnic Nationalism in the People's Republic*. 2nd ed. London: Council of East Asian Studies, Harvard University, 1996.
Gladney, Dru C. and Shouqian Man. "Interpretations of Islam in China: A Hui Scholar's Perspective." *Journal Institute of Muslim Minority Affairs*, 10.2 (1989) 475–85.
Graham, William A. "Traditionalism in Islam: An Essay in Interpretation." *Journal of Interdisciplinary History* 23 (1993) 495–522.
Guo, Suming and Sun Zhenyu. "On Liu Zhi's Islamic Thought." *Yin Shan Academic Journal* 24.6 (2011) 108–15.
Haar, Ter Johan G.J. *Follower and Heir of the Prophet: Shaykh Ahmad Sirhind (1564–1624) as Mystic*. Leiden: Het Oosters Instituut, 1992.
Hai, Jing. "A Comparative Study on Attitude toward 'Filial Piety' and Conscientiousness between Confucianism and Islam." MPhil diss., Lanzhou: Northwest University for Nationalities, 2011.
Haque, Serajul. "Ibn Taimiyyah." In *Islamic Philosophy and Theology Vol. IV*, edited by Ian Richard Netton, 97–121. Oxford: Routledge, 2007.
Heath, P. "Creative Hermeneutics: A Comparative Analysis of Three Islamic Approaches." *Arabica* 36 (1989) 173–210.
Heck, Paul L. "Mysticism as Morality: The Case of Sufism." *Journal of Religious Ethics* 34.2 (2006) 253–86.
Heer, Nicholas. 'Al-Jami's Treatise on Existence.' In *Islamic Philosophical Theology*, edited by Parviz Morewedge, 223–56. Albany: State University of New York Press, 1979.
Heffening, Willi and Joseph Schacht. "Hanafiyya." In *The Encyclopaedia of Islam*, 162–64. 2nd ed. Leiden: Brill, 1979.
Helminski, Kabir. "Islam: a Broad Perspective on Other Faiths." In *Taking Back Islam* edited by Michael Wolfe, 153–57. Emmaus, PA: Rodale, 2002.
Henderson, John B. *The Construction of Orthodoxy and Heresy: Neo-Confucian, Islamic, Jewish and Early Christian Patterns*. New York: State University of New York Press, 1998.
Hesselgrave, David J., and Edward Rommen. *Contextualization: Meanings, Methods and Models*. Grand Rapids: Baker, 1989.

Hirtenstein, Stephen. *The Unlimited Mercifer: the Spiritual Life and Thoughts of Ibn 'Arabi*. Oxford: Anqa, 1999.
Ho, Wai-Yip. *Islam and China's Hong Kong: Ethnic Identity, Muslim Networks and the New Silk Road*. Abingdon, UK: Routledge, 2013.
———. "The Search for *Qing Zhen* in the Islamic Literary History of the Soul: A Christian Interpretation of the Chinese Sufi *Tariqa—Jahriyya*." *China Graduate School of Theology Journal* 40 (2006) 137–76.
Hoffman, Valerie J. "Annihilation in the Messenger of God: the Development of a Sufi Practice." *International Journal of Middle East Studies* 31 (1999) 351–69.
Huart, Clement. "Djami." In *Encyclopaedia of Islam*, 421–22. New ed. Leiden: Brill, 1965.
Hussaini, Abdul Qadir. *The Pantheistic Monism of Ibn Al-'Arabi*. Lahore: Ashraf, 1970.
Ibn 'Arabi. *The Bezels of Wisdom*. Translated by Ralph W. J. Austin. New York: Paulist, 1980.
Irons, Edward A. *Encyclopaedia of Buddhism*. New York: Facts on File, 2008.
Isaacson, Jason F., and Colin Rubenstein, eds. *Islam in Asia. Changing Political Realities*. London: Transaction, 2002.
Israeli, Raphael. "Ahung and Literatus: A Muslim Elite in Confucian China." *Die Welt des Islams* 19 (1979) 212–19.
———. "The Cross Battles the Crescent, One Century of Missionary Work among Chinese Muslims (1850–1950)." *Modern Asian Studies* 29.1 (1995) 203–21.
———. *Muslims in China: A Study in Cultural Confrontation*. London: Curzon, 1980.
———. "Myth as Memory: Muslims in China Between Myth and History." *Muslim World* 91 (2001) 185–209.
Israeli, Raphael, ed. *The Crescent in the East. Islam in Asia Major*. London: Curzon, 1982.
Israeli, Raphael, and Anthony H. Johns, eds. *Islam in Asia*. vol. 2, *Southeast and East Asia*. Jerusalem: Magnes, 1984.
Israeli, Raphael, and Adam Gardner-Rush. "Sectarian Islam and Sino-Muslim Identity in China." *Muslim World* 90 (2000) 439–57.
Izutsu, Toshihiko. *Sufism and Taoism: A Comparative Study of Key Philosophical Concepts*. Berkeley: University of California Press, 1983.
Jami, Abd al-Rahman. *Al-Lama'at*. Translated by Bin Ruan. Beijing: Commercial, 2001.
Jensen, Lionel M. *Manufacturing Confucianism: Chinese Traditions and Universal Civilization*. Durham: Duke University Press, 1997.
Ji, Fangtong. "A Comparison of Life Self-Cultivation between Hui and Confucianism. A Study based on Early Qing Hui Thinker Liu Zhi and his Work." *Philosophy of Islam,' N.W. Ethno-National Studies* 46.3 (2005) 134–42.
Jin, Gang, and Minghua Liu. "Sinicization: Adaptation Models of Foreign Religion to Chinese Society." *N.W. Minorities Research* 29 (2011) 73–78.
Jin, Yijiu. *Exploring Chinese Islam: a Study of Liu Zhi*. Beijing: Oriental Press, 1999.
———. *Exploring Chinese Islam: a Study of Liu Zhi* New ed. Beijing: China Renmin University Press, 2010.
———. "On the Idea of the Divine Light in Early Islamic Writings in Chinese." *Studies in World Religions* 22 (1985) 1–11.
———. "Ideological Structure of Wang Daiyu's Works." *Researches on the Hui* 4 (2002) 14–19.

———. "Liu Zhi's Explanation of the Meaning of Arabic Alphabets." *Studies of the Arabic World* 4 (1996) 22–29.
———. "The Localization and Nationalization of Islam in China." *Studies in World Religions* 59 (1995) 1–8.
———. *The Mysticism of Sufism in Islam*. Beijing: Chinese Academy of Social Sciences, 1995.
———. "The Qur'an in China." *Contributions to Asian Studies* 17 (1982) 95–101.
———. "Reading the *Al-Lama'at* in Chinese. *Studies in World Religions* 4 (2012) 1–8.
———."On the San Yi Doctrine of Chinese Islamic Spirituality." *Studies in World Religions* 47 (1992) 6–17.
———. *A Study on Wang Daiyu's Thoughts*. Beijing: Ethnic Publishing House, 2008.
———. *Sufism in China* . Beijing: Social Sciences Academic Press China, 2012.
———. "Sufism and Chinese Madrassa Education." *Studies in World Religions* (1994) 64–76.
———."Sufism and the Islamic Writings in Chinese." *Studies in World Religions* 16 (1983) 100–9.
Jong, Frederick de and Bernd Radtke, eds. *Islamic Mysticism Contested: Thirteen Centuries of Controversies and Polemics*. Leiden: Brill, 1999.
Johns, Anthony H. "Perspectives of Islamic Spirituality in Southeast Asia: Reflections and Encounters." *Islam and Christian-Muslim Relations* 12 (2001) 5–21.
Kalin, Ibrahim. "Mulla Sadra's Realist Ontology of the Intelligibles and Theory of Knowledge.' *The Muslim World* 94 (2004) 81–106.
Kamada, Shigeru. "Mulla Sadra Between Mystical Philosophy and Qur'an Interpretation: Through His Commentary on the 'Chapter of Earthquake." *International Journal of Asian Studies* 2 (2005) 275–89.
Kamal, Muhammad. "The Self and the Other in Sufi Thought." *Religion East & West* 6 (2006) 21–32.
Ke, Fan. "Ups and Downs: Local Muslim History in South China." *Journal of Muslim Minority Affairs* 23 (2003) 63–87.
Keeler, Annabel. "Sufi *Tafir* as a Mirror: al-Qushayri the *Murshid* in his *Lata'if al-isharat*." *Journal of Qur'anic Studies* 8 (2006) 1–21.
Kim, Hodong, *Holy War in China: the Muslim Rebellion and State in Chinese Central Asia, 1864–1877*. Stanford: Stanford University Press, 2004.
Kim, Kirsteen. "Missiology as Global Conversation of (Contextual) Theologies." *Mission Studies* 21.1 (2004) 39–53.
Kirkland, Russell. *Taoism: The Enduring Tradition*. London: Routledge, 2004.
Knysh, Alexander. *Ibn 'Arabi in the Later Islamic Tradition: The Making of a Polemical Image in Medieval Islam*. New York: State University of New York Press, 1999.
———. *Islamic Mysticism: A Short History*. Leiden: Brill, 2000.
———. "Multiple Areas of Influence." In *The Cambridge Companion to the Qur'an*, edited by Jane D. McAuliffe, 211–34. Cambridge Companions to Religion. Cambridge: Cambridge University Press, 2006.
———. "Orthodoxy and Heresy in Medieval Islam: An Essay in Reassessment." *Muslim World* 83 (1993) 48–67.
———."Sufism and the Qur'an." In *Encyclopaedia of Qur'an Vol. V*, edited by Jane D. McAuliffe, 137–59. Leiden: Brill, 2006.

———. "Sufism as an Explanatory Paradigm: The Issue of the Motivations of Sufi Resistance Movements in Western and Russian Scholarship." *Die Welt des Islams* 42 (2002) 139–73.

Kovelant, Kevin. "Peering through the Veil: Death, Dreams and the Afterlife in Sufi Thought." *Academy of Spirituality and Paranormal Studies, Inc. Annual Conference Proceedings* (2007) 148–56.

Kucuk, Hulya. "A Brief History of Western Sufism." *Asian Journal of Social Science* 36 (2008) 292–320.

Landau, Rom. *The Philosophy of Ibn 'Arabi*. New York: Macmillan, 1959.

———. "Philosophy of Ibn 'Arabi." *Muslim World* 472 (1957) I. 46–61 and II. 146–60.

Levenson, Michael R., and Abdul Hayy Khilwati. "Mystical Self-Annihilation: Method and Meaning." *International Journal for the Psychology of Religion* 9 (1999) 251–57.

Leslie, Donald D. *The Integration of Religious Minorities in China: the Case of Chinese Muslims*. The Fifty-ninth George Ernest Morrison Lecture in Ethnology 1998. Canberra: Australian National University, 1998.

———. "Islam in China to 1800: A Bibliographical Guide." *Abr Nahrain* 16 (1976) 16–48.

———. *Islam in Traditional China: A Short History to 1800*. Canberra: Canberra College of Advanced Education, 1986.

———. *Islamic Literature in Chinese: Late Ming and Early Ch'ing*. Canberra: Canberra College of Advanced Education, 1981.

———. "Living with the Chinese: the Muslim Experience in China, T'ang and Ming." In *Chinese Ideas about Nature and Society*, edited by Charles Le Blanc and Susan Blader, 175–93. Hong Kong: Hong Kong University Press, 1987.

Leslie, Donald D. and Ludmilla Panskaya. *Introduction to Palladi's Chinese Literature of Muslim*. Canberra: Australian National Press, 1977.

Leslie, Donald D. and Mohamed Wassel. "Arabic and Persian Sources used by Liu Chih." *Central Asiatic Journal* 26 (1982) 78–104.

Leslie, Donald et al. "Arabic Works Presented to *Qianlong* Emperor in 1782." *Central Asiatic Journal* 45 (2000) 7–27.

———. *Islam in Traditional China: a Bibliographical Guide*. Sankt Augustin: Monumenta Serica Monograph Series LIV, 2006.

Li, Bin. "On the Origin of Liu Zhi's Concept of Religion and its Morality." *Journal of Northwest Normal University (Social Sciences)* 41 (2004) 22–27.

Li, Shujiang and Karl W. Luckert. *Mythology and Folklore of the Hui, A Muslim Chinese People*. New York: State University of New York, 1994.

Li, Tang. *A Study of the History of Nestorian Christianity in China and Its Literature in Chinese*. Frankfurt: Peter Lang, 2002.

Li, Xinghua, Huibin Qin, Jinyuan Feng and Qiuzhen Sha. *History of Islam in China*. Beijing: Chinese Academy of Social Sciences, 1998.

Li, Zhenzhong. "Wang Daiyu and Sino Arabic Cultural Exchange." *Researches on the Hui* (1999) 58–62.

Liang, Shaohui. *A Critical Biography of Zhou Dunyi*. Nanjiang: Nanjing University Press, 1994.

Liang, Xiangming. "An Analysis of the Epistemology of "Harmony of God and Man" by Liu Zhi." *N.W. Minorities Research* 29 (2001) 86–92.

———. "Liu Zhi: Using Confucianism to Interpret Islam or Discarding Scripture and Tradition." *Researches on the Hui* 41 (2001) 88–91.

———. "On Political Ethics of Hui Nationality of Being Obedient to Allah and Loyal to the King." *Nationalities Research in Qinghai* 20.3 (2009) 53–58.

———. "The Study on Ethics of Three Chinese Translators during the Late Ming Dynasty to the Early Qing Dynasty." PhD diss., Central University for Nationalities, China, 2007.

———. *The Study on Ethics of Three Chinese Translators during the Late Ming Dynasty to the Early Qing Dynasty*. Beijing: Guangming Daily, 2010.

———. *A Study of Liu Zhi and His Islamic Thought*. Lanzhou: Lanzhou University Press, 2004.

———. "On Traditional Ethics of the Hui Family." *Journal of Hui Muslim Minority Studies* 65.1 (2007) 37–44.

———. "The View of the Hui Scholar Liu Zhi on Islam." *Heilongjiang National Series* 76 (2003) 120–24.

Liao, Dake. "To Survey the Early Dissemination of Islamism in Indonesia from Chinese Annals of Semarang." *Studies in World Religions* 109 (2007) 98–108.

Lin, Chang-Kuan. "Three Eminent Chinese 'Ulama' of Yunnan." *Journal of Muslim Minority Affairs* Part 2 (1990) 101–17.

Lipman, Jonathan N. "The Border World of Gansu, 1895–1935." PhD diss., Stanford University, 1981.

———. *Familiar Strangers: A History of Muslims in Northwest China*. Seattle: University of Washington Press, 1997.

———. "Hui-Hui: An Ethnohistory of the Chinese-Speaking Muslims." *Journal of South Asian and Middle Eastern Studies* 11 (1987) 112–30.

———. "Sufism in the Chinese Courts: Islam and Qing Law in the Eighteenth and Nineteenth Centuries.'" In *Islamic Mysticism Contested: Thirteen Centuries of Controversies and Polemics*, edited by Frederick De Jong and Bernd Radtke, 553–75. Isalmic History and Civilization 29. Leiden: Brill, 1999.

Little, John. "Al-Insan al-Kamil: the Perfect Man according to Ibn al-'Arabi." *Muslim World* 77 (1987) 43–54.

Liu, James T. "The Classical Chinese Primer: its Three-character Style and Authorship" *Journal of the American Oriental Society* 105 (1985) 191–96.

Liu, Yihong. "*Dialogue between Islam and Confucianism: The Islamic Belief and the Confucius' Dao*." Beijing: Religion and Culture, 2000.

Liu, Zhi. "*Displaying the Concealment of the Real Realm*." Beijing: n.p., 1923.

———. *The Explanation of the Five Endeavours*. Beijing: n.p., 1924.

———. *The Explanation of the Meaning of Arabic Letter*. Reprinted. N.p., 1879.

———. *The Nature and Principle in Islam*. Shanghai: n.p., 1863, 1928.

———. *The Nature and Principle in Islam*. Reprinted. Shanghai: Shanghai Classic, 1995.

———. *The Poem of the Five Sessions of the Moon*. http://www.douban.com/group/topic/24083421/.

———. *The Rules and Proprieties of Islam*. Annotated by Wenbo Na. Yunnan: Yunnan Nationalities Publishing House, 1990.

———. *The Rules and Proprieties of Islam*. Tianjin: Tianjin Ancient Books House, 1988.

———. "*The Three Character Classic for Moslems* by Lieo Kai Lien of Nanjing." Translated by Francis J. M. Cotter and Karl L. Reichelt, *Moslem World* 8 (1918) 10–15.

———. *The True Record of the Utmost Sage of Islam*. Beijing: China Islamic Association, 1984.

———. *The True Record of the Utmost Sage of Islam*. Reprinted. Shanghai: Shanghai Classic, 1995.

Lo, Yuetkeung. "Change Beyond Syncretism: Ouyi Zhixu's Buddhist Hermeneutics of the *Yijing*." *Journal of Chinese Philosophy* 35 (2008) 273–95.

Loewenthal, Rudolf. "Sino-Islamica: Bibliographical Notes on the Chinese Muslims." *Monumenta Serica* 22 (1963) 209–12.

———. "Russian Materials on Islam in China: a Preliminary Bibliography." *Monumenta Serica* 16 (1957) 449–79.

Lombard, Denys and Claudine Salmon. "Islam and Chineseness." *Indonesia* 57 (1994) 115–31.

Loutfy, Nour and George Berguno. "The Existential Thoughts of the Sufis." *Existential Analysis* 16 (2005) 144–55.

Ma, Deliang and Qian Ding. "Preliminary Analysis of the Influence of Liu Zhi upon Xi Dao Tang." *Studies in World Religions* (1995) 16–23.

Ma, Dexin (Fuchu). "The Three-Character Rhymed Classic on the Ka'bah." Translated by Peter Hobson, *Studies in Comparative Religion* 14 (1980) 181–94.

Ma, Duoyong. "The Dialogue between Islam and Confucianism and Cultural Self Consciousness in Chinese History." MA diss., Nanjing: Cadre Institute of CPC Jiangsu Provincial Commission Party School, n.d.

Ma, Haiyun. "The Mythology of Prophet's Ambassadors in China: Histories of Sa'd Waqqas and Gess in Chinese Sources." *Journal of Muslim Minority Affairs* 26 (2006) 445–52.

Ma, Tong. *A Short History of Islamic Religious Sects and Tariqat in China*. Yinchuan: Ningxia People's Publishing House, 2000.

Ma, Xiumei. "Islam Creed and its Imparting System in China." *Journal of the Hui Muslim Minority Study* 55 (2004) 18–24.

———. "Islamic Folklore Standardized by Classics." *Journal of Hui Muslim Minority Study* 54 (2004) 106–12.

Ma Zhu. *The Compass of Islam*. Reprint. Tianjin: Huizu Zhongguo Yisilanjiao, 1987.

Ma, Zongbao. "A Discussion on Cultural Adaptation of the Hui in History." *Journal of Hui Muslim Minority Study* 43 (2001) 15–18.

Malamud, Margaret "Gender and Spiritual Self-Fashioning: the Master-Disciple Relationship in Classical Sufism." *Journal of the American Academy of Religion* 64 (1996) 89–117.

Masmoudi, Radwan A. "No More Simplistic Answers." In *Taking Back Islam,* edited by Michael Wolfe, 82–88. Emmaus, PA: Rodale, 2002.

Massignon, Louis. *The Passion of al-Hallaj: Mystic and Martyr of Islam*. Vols. I–IV. Translated by Herbert Mason. Princeton: Princeton University Press, 1982.

———. *The Passion of al-Hallaj: Mystic and Martyr of Islam*. Translated by Herbert Mason. Abridged ed. Princeton: Princeton University Press, 1994.

Mason, Isaac. *The Arabian Prophet: A Life of Mohammed from Chinese and Arabic Sources, a Chinese-Moslem Work by Liu Chia-lien*. Shanghai: Commercial Press, 1921.

———. "The Mohammedans of China: When, and How, They First Came." *Journal of the North China Branch of the Royal Asiatic Society* 60 (1929) 1–54.

———. "Notes on Chinese Mohammedan Literature." *Journal of the North China Branch of the Royal Asiatic Society* 56 (1925) 172–215.

Matsumoto, Akiro. "Discussion of Ma Lian-yuan's *Lataf* and His Philosophy of Being." *Journal of Hui Muslim Minority Study* 54 (2004) 14–18.

———. "The Sufi Intellectual Tradition among Sino-Muslims." In *Sufism: Critical Concepts in Islamic Study*, edited by Lloyd Rigeon, 101–19. London: Routledge, 2008).

Mayer, Toby. "Theology and Sufism." in *The Cambridge Companion to Classical Islamic Theology*, edited by Tim Winter, 258–87. Cambridge Companions to Religion. Cambridge: Cambridge University Press, 2008.

McAmis, Robert Day. *Malay Muslims: The History and Challenge of Resurgent Islam in Southeast Asia*. Grand Rapids: Eerdmans, 2002.

McAuliffe, Jane D. "The Tasks and Traditions of Interpretation." In *The Cambridge Companion to the Qur'an*, edited by Jane D. McAuliffe, 181–210. Cambridge Companions to Religion. Cambridge: Cambridge University Press, 2006.

Merriman, Hannah Bigelow. "The Paradox of Proximity to the Infinite: An Exploration of *sidrat al-muntaha*, "the Lote Tree beyond Which None May Pass."" *Religion and the Arts* 12 (2008) 329–42.

Mi, Shoujiang and Ma Duoyong. "The Islamic Jinling School and the Confucian Civilization." In *Dialogue between Civilizations*, edited by Yang Huaizhong, 268–75. Yinchuan: Ningxia People's Publishing House, 2006.

Min, Wenjie. "The Comparison between Five Ethics of Confucianism and Five Ethics of Liu Zhi's Thought." *Journal of Hui Muslim Minority Studies* 65 (2007) 32–36.

Mojaddedi, Jawid A. "Getting Drunk with Abu Yazid or Staying Sober with Junayd: The Creation of a Popular Typology of Sufism." *Bulletin of the School of Oriental and African Studies* 66 (2003) 1–13.

Moeller, Han-Georg. *Philosophy of the Daodejing*. New York: Columbia University Press, 2006.

Morewedge, Parviz. "Greek Sources of Some Near Eastern Philosophies of Being and Existence." In *Philosophies of Existence Ancient and Medieval*, edited by Parviz Morewedge, 285–336. New York: Fordham University Press, 1982.

Mungello, David E. *The Great Encounter of China and the West, 1500–1800*. Lanham, MD: Rowman & Littlefield, 2005.

Murata, Sachiko. *Chinese Gleams of Sufi Light: Wang Tai-yu's Great Learning of the Pure and Real and Liu Chih's Displaying the Concealment of the Real Realm*. New York: State University of New York Press, 2000.

———. "Former Heaven and Latter Heaven in Liu Chih's T'ien-fang,' Hsing-li." *Journal of Hui Muslim Minorities Studies* 74 (2009) 100–102.

———. "Liu Zhi's View on Perfect Manhood." *Journal of Hui Muslim Minority Studies* 62 (2006) 16–18.

———. "Reading Islamic Texts from the Standpoint of Yin and Yang." In *Islam and Confucianism*, edited by Osman Bakar, 95–117. Kuala Lumpur: University of Malaysia Press, 1997.

———. "Sufi Texts in Chinese." In *The Heritage of Sufism Late Classical Persianate Sufism*, edited by Leonard Lewisohn and David Morgan, vol. 3, 376–88. Oxford: Oneworld, 1999.

———. "The Synthesis of Islamic and Neo-Confucian Cosmology in Liu Chih's T'ien-fang hsing-li." *Researches on the Hui* 4 (2002) 9–13.

———. *The Tao of Islam: A Sourcebook on Gender Relationships in Islamic Thought*. New York: State University of New York Press, 1992.

———. "The Unity of Being in Liu Chih's Islamic Neo-Confucianism." The Muhyiddin Ibn 'Arabi Society web site. http://www.ibnarabisociety.org/articles/islamiceoconfucianism.html.

———. "Unity of Cosmogony between Islam and Neo-Confucianism in Liu Zhi's *Nature and Principle in Islam.*' *Researches on the Hui* 48 (2002) 9–s13.

Murata, Sachiko, and William C. Chittick. *The Vision of Islam*. St. Paul: Paragon, 1994.

Murata, Sachiko, et al. *The Sage Learning of Liu Zhi: Islamic Thought in Confucian Terms.* Cambridge: Harvard University Press, 2009.

Nasr, Seyyed Hossein. *The Garden of Truth: The Vision and Promise of Sufism, Islam's Mystical Tradition.* New York: HarperOne, 2007.

———. *An Introduction to Islamic Cosmological Doctrines* Revised ed. London: Thames & Hudson, 1978.

———. *Islamic Philosophy from Its Origin to the Present. Philosophy in the Land of Prophecy.* New York: State University of New York Press, 2006.

———. ed., *Islamic Spirituality I: Foundations.* London: Routledge & Kegan Paul, 1987.

———. ed., *Islamic Spirituality II: Manifestations.* New York: Crossroad, 1997.

———. "The Meaning and Role of "Philosophy" in Islam." *Studia Islamica* 37 (1973) 57–80.

———. "Reply to Huston Smith." In *The Philosophy of Seyyed Hossein Nasr,* edited by Lewis E. Hahn, Randall E. Auxier, and Lucian W. Stone, Jr. 159–67. Chicago: Open Court, 2000.

Nasr, Seyyed Hossein, and Oliver Leaman. *History of Islamic Philosophy*. London: Routledge, 1996.

Nizami, Haliq Ahmad. "The Impact of Ibn Taimiyya on South Asia." *Journal of Islamic Studies* 1 (1990) 120–49.

Nurbakhsh, Javad. "Two Approaches to the Principle of the Unity of Being." In *The Heritage of Sufism: The Legacy of Medieval Persian Sufism,* edited by Leonard Lewisohn, vol. 2, xv–xviii. Oxford: Oneworld, 1999.

O'Fahey, Rex S., and Bernd Radtke. "Neo-Sufism Reconsidered." *Der Islam* 70 (1993) 52–87.

Paracka Jr., Daniel J. "China's Three Teachings and the Relationship of Heaven, Earth and Humanity." *Worldviews* 16 (2012) 73–98.

Pattison, Stephen "Some Straw for the Bricks: A Basic Introduction to Theological Reflection." In *The Blackwell Reader in Pastoral and Practical Theology,* edited by James Woodward and Stephen Pattison, 135–45. Blackwell Readings in Modern Theology. Oxford: Wiley-Blackwell, 2000.

Pears, Angie. *Doing Contextual Theology.* London: Routledge, 2009

Petersen, Kristian. "The Heart of the Islamic-Chinese Dialogue: Wang Daiyu and the Creation of a Chinese Muslim Discourse." MA thesis, University of Colorado, 2006.

Radtke, Bernd. "Sufism in the 18th Century: An Attempt at a Provisional Appraisal." *Die Welt des Islams* 36 (1996) 326–64.

Ramadan, Tariq. *Western Muslims and the Future of Islam.* New York: Oxford University Press, 2004.

Rastogi, Tara C. *Islamic Mysticism and Sufism.* New Delhi: Sterling, 1982.

Rauf, Imam Feisal Abdul. "Asceticism in Islam." *Cross Currents* 57 (2008) 591–602.

Razi, Najm al-Din. *Mirsad al-ibad The Path of God's Bondsmen from Origin to Return.* Translated by Hamid Algar. New York: Caravan, 1982.

Riddell, Peter G. *Islam and the Malay-Indonesian World*. London: Hurst, 2001.
Ridgeon, Lloyd. *Aziz Nasafi*. Richmond: Curzon, 2002.
———. *Persian Metaphysics and Mysticism: Selected Treatises of Aziz Nasafi*. Richmond, UK: Curzon, 2002.
Ridgeon, Lloyd, ed. *Sufism: Critical Concepts in Islamic Studies*. Vols. 1–4. New York: Routledge, 2008.
Rippin, Andrew, ed. *Approaches to the History of the Interpretation of the Qur'an*. Oxford: Clarendon, 1988.
———. *The Quran and its Interpretative Tradition*. Aldershot, UK: Ashgate, 2001.
———. *World Islam: Critical Concepts in Islamic Studies*. Vols. 1–4. New York: Routledge, 2008.
Rizvi, Sajjad H. "The Existential Breath of *al-Rahman* and the Munificent Grace of *al-Rahim*: The *Tafir Surat al-Fatiha* of Jami and the School of Ibn 'Arabi." *Journal of Qur'anic Studies* 8 (2006) 58–87.
———. "Mulla Sadra and Causation: Rethinking a Problem in Later Islamic Philosophy." *Philosophy East and West* 55 (2005) 570–83.
———. "Mysticism and Philosophy: Ibn 'Arabi and Mulla Sadra." In *Cambridge Companion to Arabic Philosophy*, edited by Peter Adamson, Richard C. Taylor, 224–46. Cambridge Companions to Philosophy. Cambridge: Cambridge University Press, 2006.
Rosenthal, Franz. "Ibn 'Arabi between 'Philosophy' and 'Mysticism': Sufism and Philosophy are Neighbours and Visit Each Other." *Oriens* 31 (1988) 1–35.
Rossabi, Morris. "Islam in China." In *Encyclopaedia of Religion*, edited by Mircea Eliade et.al., vol. 8, 377–90. New York: Macmillan, 1987.
———. "The Muslims in the Early Yuan Dynasty." In *China under Mongol Rule*, edited by John Langlois Jr., 257–95. Princeton: Princeton University Press, 1981.
Royster James, E. "Configurations of *Tawhid* in Islam." *Muslim World* 77 (1987) 28–42.
Rustom, Mohammed. "Approaches to Proximity and Distance in Early Sufism." *Mystics Quarterly* 33 (2007) 1–25.
Saeed, Abdullah *Approaches to the Qur'an in Contemporary Indonesia*. London: Oxford University Press, 2005).
———. *Interpreting the Qur'an: Towards a Contemporary Approach*. Abingdon, UK: Routledge, 2006.
Schimmel, Annemarie. *And Muhammad is His Messenger The Veneration of the Prophet in Islamic Piety*. Lahore: Vanguard, 1987.
———. *Mystical Dimensions of Islam*. Chapel Hill, NC: University of North Carolina Press, 1975.
———. "Some Aspects of Mystical Prayer in Islam." *Die Welt des Islams* 2 (1952) 112–25.
Schreiter, Robert. *Constructing Local Theologies*. Maryknoll, NY: Orbis, 1985.
Scott, David. "Buddhism and Islam: Past to Present Encounters and Interfaith Lessons." *Numens* 42 (1995) 141–55.
Sells, Michael A. *Early Islamic Mysticism: Sufi, Qur'an, Mi'raj, Poetic and Theological Writings*. New York: Paulist, 1996.
Sha, Zongping. *Chinese Islam: a Study of Liu Zhi's Philosophy*. Beijing: Beijing University Press, 2004.
———. "The Concept of Real One in Islam and the Ancient Chinese Idea of Heavenly Lord." *Journal of Hui Muslim Minority Studies* 61.1 (2006) 78–84.

———. "Confucianism and Islam Fused into One in the Context of 'Zhen-Yi' Theory." *Journal of Nanjing University (Social Sciences)* 40.1 (2003) 52–9.
———. "Examining the Hui Islamic Ethics from Liu Zhi's Five Relationships of the Way of Humanity." Lecture notes. Shihezi: Shihezi University Xinjiang, 2004.
———. "The Orthodox Religion and Orthodox Knowledge: the Concepts about Religion and Knowledge of Wang Daiyu in the 'Real Hermeneutics of Orthodox Religion." *Researches on the Hui* 53.1 (2004) 87–91.
———. "A Study of the Transformation and Return Philosophy of Liu Zhi: the Hui Thinker in Early Qing Dynasty." *Researches on the Hui* 46.2 (2002) 78–87.
Shah-Kazemi, Reza. "The Notion and Significance of *Ma'rifa* in Sufism." *Journal of Islamic Studies* 13 (2002) 155–81.
———. *Paths to Transcendence: According to Shankara, Ibn 'Arabi, and Meister Eckhart.* Bloomington, IN: World Wisdom, 2006.
Shen, Yiming. "A Famous Sufi Classic across Space and Time: A Preliminary Comparison between Jami's *Lava'ih* and Liu Zhi's *Zhen Jing Zhao Wei*." *Journal of Hui Muslim Minority Studies* 69 (2008) 106–112.
Shepherd, Robert J. "Perpetual Unease or Being at Ease? Derrida, Daoism, and the Metaphysics of Presence." *Philosophy East & West* 57 (2007) 227–43.
Shi, Lili. "The Comparison between Five Ethics Thought of Confucianism and Five Ethics Thoughts of Chinese Islam." MPhil diss., Lanzhou: Northwest University for Nationalities, 2010.
Singh, David E. "Ayu' Sh-shams Wa'L-Baha (Nizam) in Ibn Al-'Arabi's *Tarjuman Al-Ashwaq* and her Significance for World Affirmation." *Asia Journal of Theology* 12.2 (1998) 311–37.
———. "Heart: The Way to Knowing Reality." *Bulletin of the Martyn Institute of Islamic Studies* 15.1/2 (1996) 20–40.
———. "An Onto-epistemological Model: Adam-Muhammad as the Traditional Symbols of Humanity's All-Comprehending Epistemic Potential." *Muslim World* 94.2 (2004) 275–301.
———. "The Possibility of Having Knowledge of *al-wujud al-mahd* 'Sheer Being' according to Ibn 'Arabi's *Kitab al-jalal wa-al-jamal*." *Islam and Christian-Muslim Relations* 10.3 (1999) 295–306.
———. "Rethinking Jesus and the Cross in Islam." *Mission Studies* 23.2 (2006) 239–60.
———. *Sainthood and Revelatory Discourse: an Examination of the Basis for the Authority of Bayan in Mahdawi Islam.* Oxford: Regnum, 2003.
Sirriyeh, Elizabeth. *Sufis and Anti-Sufis: The Defence, Rethinking and Rejection of Sufism in the Modern World.* London: Curzon, 1999.
Smith, Jane Idleman and Yvonne Yazbeck Haddad. *The Islamic Understanding of Death and Resurrection.* Albany: State University of New York Press, 1981.
Smith, Huston. "Chinese Religion in World Perspective." *Dialogue & Alliance* 4.2 (1990) 4–14.
Stöcker-Parnian, Barbara. *Jingtang Jiaoyu—die Bücherhallen Erziehung: Entstehung und Entwicklung der islamischen Erziehung in den chinesischen Hui-Gemeinden vom 17.-19. Jahrhundert.* Frankfurt: Peter Lang, 2003.
Sun, Junping, and Su Baogui. "Introductory Exploration of *Rites of Islam*." *Philosophical Researches* 11 (1993) 63–66.
Sun, Zhenyu. *A Critical Biography of Wang Dai Yu, Liu Zhi.* Nanjing: Nanjing University Press, 2006.

Tan, Tan. "A New Exploration into the Motive of the Voyage to the South Asia and the East Africa Made by Zheng He." *Studies in World Religions* 101 (2005) 95–103.

Tang, Li. *A Study of the History of Nestorian Christianity in China and its Literature in Chinese: Together with a New English Translation of the Dunhuang Nestorian Documents.* European University Studies. Series XXVII: Asian and African Studies 87. Frankfurt: Lang, 2002.

Thomas, David. "Receiving and Acquiring Wisdom in Islam." *Journal of Chinese Philosophy* 33 (2006) 439–52.

Thompson, Kirill, O. "The Archery of "Wisdom in the Stream of Life: Wisdom in the Four Books with Zhu Xi's Reflections." *Philosophy East and West* 57 (2007) 330–44.

Thomson, Alan. "Bevans and Bediako: Reconsidering Text-Based Models of Contextual Theologizing." *Evangelical Review of Theology* 33:4 (2009) 347–58.

———. "Learning from the African Experience: Bediako and Critical Contextualisation." *Evangelical Review of Theology* 30:1 (2006) 31–48.

Treiger, Alexander. "Monism and Monotheism in al-Ghazali's *Mishkat al-anwar*." *Journal of Qur'anic Studies* 9 (2007) 1–27.

Trimingham, J. Spencer. *The Sufi Orders in Islam* 2nd ed. Oxford: Clarendon Press, 1998.

Tsai, Yuan-Lin. "The Construction of the Religious "Other" in Liu Zhi's *Tianfang Xingli*." *Taiwan Journal of East Asian Studies* 4.2 (2007) 55–84.

Tu, Weiming. "The Development of Civilization Dialogue and its World Significance." *Researches on the Hui* 51.3 (2003) 5–13.

———. *Humanity and Self-Cultivation: Essays in Confucian Thought.* Berkeley: Asian Humanities Press, 1979.

Tucker, Mary Evelyn. "Religious Dimensions of Confucianism: Cosmology and Cultivation." *Philosophy East and West* 48 (1998) 5–45.

Tuoheti, Alim. "A Study of Wang Daiyu and Liu Zhiyu's Concept of the Universe." *Journal of Yunnan Nationalities University (Social Sciences)* 27.6 (2010) 105–8.

———. "On Wang Daiyu's and Liu Zhi's Contributions to Islamic Philosophy." *Journal of Xinjiang University (Philosophy, Humanities & Social Science)* 35.6 (2007) 104–7.

Turner, Colin, ed. *The Koran: Critical Concepts in Islamic Studies.* Vols. 1–4. New York: Routledge Curzon, 2004.

Vanhoozer, Kevin. "On the Very Idea of a Theological System: An Essay in Aid of Triangulating Scripture, Church and World." In *Always Reforming: Explorations in Systematic Theology,* edited by Andrew T. B. McGowan, 125–82. Downers Grove, IL: InterVarsity, 2006.

Vroom, Hendrik M. "Islam's Adaptation to the West: on the Deconstruction and Reconstruction of Religion." *Scottish Journal of Theology* 60 (2007) 226–41.

Wang, Daiyu. *Collected Classical Writings of the Chinese Hui Nationality: True Explanation of the Right Religion; The Great Learning of the Pure and Real; Orthodox Answers of the Precious True.* Yinchuan: Ningxia People's Press, 1988.

Wang, Genping. "Explanation and Comments on the Arabic Sources in Liu Zhi's Works." *N.W. Ethno-National Studies* 56 (2008) 37–47.

Wang, Gungwu. "The Opening of Relations Between China and Malacca 1403–5." In *Malayan and Indonesian Studies,* edited by John Bastin and R. Roolvink, 131–46. Oxford: Clarendon, 1964.

Wang, Jianping. *Glossary of Chinese Islamic Terms.* Richmond, UK: Curzon, 2001.

Wang, Junrong. *The Unity of Heaven and Man, the Return of Material Beings to Reality: Exploring the Ontology of Ibn 'Arabi*. Beijing: Religion and Culture, 2006.
Wei, Qi. "Zhu Xi's Philosophy and Religion." *Studies in World Religions* 38 (1989) 31–43.
Welch, Alford T. "Kur'an, al-." In *The Encyclopaedia of Islam*, 400–429. Leiden: Brill, 1986.
Whittingham, Martin. *Al-Ghazali and the Qur'an One Book, Many Meanings*. Abingdon, UK: Routledge, 2007.
Wild, Stefan, ed. *The Qur'an as Text*. Islamic Philosophy, Theology, and Science 27. Leiden: Brill, 1996.
Wolfe, Michael. *Taking Back Islam*. Emmaus, PA: Rodale, 20023.
Wu, Haiying, ed. *Zhenghe and Hui Islamic Culture*. Yinchuan: Ningxia People's Publishing House, 2005.
Yan, Tao. "A Critique of Liu Zhi's Philosophy—Islamic Philosophy in Confucian Culture." *Wen Shi Zhe Journal of Literature and Philosophy* 2 (1991) 54–59.
Yang, Guiping. *A Study of Ma Dexin's Thought*. Beijing: Religion and Culture, 2004.
Yang, Huaizhong. "Do not Betray Islam and Do not be Tied Down by Islam: Hui Intellectuals' Attitude toward the Cultural Exchange between the Hui Scholars and Confucians." *Researches on the Hui* 48 (2002) 5–8.
Yang, Huaizhong and Zhengui Yu, eds. *Islam and Chinese Culture*. Yinchuan: Ningxia People's Publishing House, 1995.
Yang, Zhijiu. *A Study of the Hui Nationality in the Yuan Dynasty: its Formation and Humanics*. Tianjin: Nankai University Press, 2003.
Yang, Zhongdong. "Arabian Principles of Nature and Sufis Mysticism." *Journal of Xinjiang University (Social Science Ed.)* 30.1 (2002) 86–90.
———. "A Comparative Study between *Mirsad* and Liu Zhi's Cosmogony." *Journal of Ningxia University (Social Science Edition)* 105 (2002) 26–28.
———. "Pilot Study of Liu Zhi's Idealism in Life and Difference between Liu Zhi and Zhu Xi." *Journal of Xinjiang University (Social Science Ed.)* 29.1 (2001) 55–56.
——— "Similarity in Forms and Dissimilarity in Content: A Comparative Study of Liu Zhi and Zhu Xi." *Journal of Xinjiang University (Social Science Ed.)* 31.1 (2003) 48–51.
Yao, Xinzhong. "From 'What is Below' to 'What is Above': A Confucian Discourse on Wisdom." *Journal of Chinese Philosophy* 33 (2006) 349–63.
Yao, Xinzhong, and Yanxia Zhao. *Chinese Religion: A Contextual Approach*. London: Continuum, 2010.
Yu, Andy. "A Framework of Positioning Islam in a Pluralistic Society: A Study of the Thought of Tariq Ramadan." In *Confluence of Civilizations: Prospect of Dialogue between Christianity and Islam*, edited by Lau Yee-cheung and Li Lin, 51–89. Hong Kong: Alliance Bible Seminary, 2012.
Yu, Jiyuan. "Yi: Practical Wisdom in Confucius's Analects." *Journal of Chinese Philosophy* 33 (2006) 335–48.
Yu, Ting. "Interaction between Sacredness and Secularity in Hui Culture." *Researches on the Hui* 45 (2002) 97–100.
Zhang Qianhong. "From Judaism to Confucianism: Studies on the Internal Causes for the Assimilation of the Kaifeng Jewish Community." *Studies in World Religions* 109 (2007) 109–24.
Zheng, Wenquan. "Islamic Philosophy in China." http://www.arts.cuhk.edu.hk/~hkshp.

———. "Southeast Asian Confucianism from the Perspective of Islamic Study." *Studies on Confucian Culture* 10 (2008) 41–68.
———. "A Study on the Islamic Nature of Liu Zhi's Philosophy." MA diss., National Central University, Taiwan, 1998.
Zhixu, Ouyi. "Pi Xie Ji: Collected Refutations of Heterodoxy." Translated by Charles B. Jones. *Pacific World* 11 (2009) 351–407.
Zhou, Chuanbin. "A Survey of Western Studies of Islam in China." *N.W. Ethno-National Studies* 44 (2005) 97–106.
Zhou, Xiefan, ed. "The Great Classics of the Pure and Real Vol. 19." In *The Chinese Religious History Collection*. Hefei: Huang Shan, 2005.
Zhou, Xijuan "Review Article Islamic Theology in Chinese Culture: Translation and Transmission." *Edebiyat* 13.2 (2003) 245–49.
Zhou Yaoming. "On the Ideologies of the Eulogizing of Muhammad in *Tiangangshijing*." MA Diss., NingXia University, 2003.
Zhu, Xiaojun. "Briefly Exploring the Five Rituals of Liu Zhi." *Journal of Chongqing University of Science and Technology (Social Sciences Edition)* 8 (2009) 37–38.
Zhu, Zi. *The Chinese Code of Success*. http://www.360doc.com/content/12/0423/11/956246_205841851.shtml

Index

A

Adam, Muhammad and creation of, 51
Aershi, Muslim concept of, 142n37
'Afif ibn Muhammad Kaziruni, 69n11, 139
Africa, Christian liberation theology in, 4
Alalwani, Taha Jabir, 202
al-Busiri, 33
al-Ghazali, hermeneutics of, 5–7
Allah, perfect man concept and, 50–53
Allah, zhu as Chinese name for, 185–87
al-Lama'at (Jami), 104, 114–15
Alphabet Classic, 72
Analects of Confucius, 56, 62–63, 169–70
Annotated General Catalogue of the Compendium of the Four Treasuries, Authorized by the Emperor, 68–69, 155
anthropological model of contextual theology, 9–15
anti-Sufism, 48n115
'Aqaid text, 31
Arab-Chinese contacts, history of, 20
Arabic alphabets, 71–72
Arabic Islamic texts
  Chinese transmission of, 27–33
  contemporary scholarship on Liu Zhi's sources, 74, 81, 82–87
  Hui translations of, 22, 26–27
  Liu Zhi's translations of, 1–2, 30–32, 71–72
  Ma Dexin's translations of, 32–33
ascent and descent
  in Liu Zhi's theosophy, 41–42
  in *Poem of the Five Sesssions of the Moon*, 131
Ashi'at al-Lama'at (*Rays of the Flashes*) (Jami), 39, 41–42, 99n19
Ataman, Kemal, 201–2
Aubin, Françoise, 24

B

Baydawi, Qur'anic commentary by, 39
being, study of. *See wujud* (existence or being)
belief systems, translation model of contextualization and, 11–15
Benite, Zvi Ben-Dor, 22, 75, 78–81, 147–49, 154
  Frankel and, 185
  Rules and Properties of Islam and, 163–66
Berthrong, John, 56n154
Bevans, Stephen, 9–15, 194–95
Book of Changes, 37
The Book of Propriety: The Explanation of the Five Endeavors. See *The Explanation of the Five Endeavors* (Liu Zhi)
Broomhall, Marshall, 24, 73
Buddhism
  Chinese religion and culture and, 59–62

Buddhism *(continued)*
  contemporary Chinese scholarship on, 82–88
  contextualization of *Poem of the Five Sessions of the Moon* and, 126–29, 135–36
  Liu Shi's discussion of, 30–32, 65, 72, 151–52, 188–92
  in pre-modern China, 35–37
  Rules and Properties of Islam and, 161–66
  translation-conversation contextualization model and, 194–204
  Wang Daiyu's Islamic interpretations and, 28–30

C

Chang Wing-Tsit, 55n152, 58–59
Chanist Explanation of the Changes, 35–36
Chen Tuan, 57n157
chi (ultimate), 37–38
chiastic literary structure, of *Poem of the Five Sessions of the Moon* (Liu Zhi), 1 35, 129–31
China. *See also* People's Republic of China
  context of Islamic texts in culture of, 4–8, 62–64, 78–81
  Ibn 'Arabi tradition and Muslims in, 50–55
  intolerance of Islam in, 15–16
  Muslim ethnic nationalities in, 19n1
  pre-modern Islam in, 19–24, 64–65, 75–78
  religion and self-cultivation in culture of, 59–62
The Chinese Code of Success (Zhu Zi), 124–26
Chinese culture
  Chinese education system and, 124–26
  Confucianism and, 59–62, 77–78
  contextualization of Islamic texts and, 4–8, 62–65, 78–81, 87–88, 120–22
  Liu Zhi's legacy in, 202–4
  Liu Zhi's rejection of traditions and practices in, 153–55, 180–84
  Neo-Confucianism and, 7–8, 124–38
  popularity of *Poem of the Five Sessions of the Moon* in, 131–38
  religion and self-cultivation in China and, 59–62
  three-, five-, and seven-character literary forms and, 124–26
  translation-conversation contextualization model and, 194–204
  triangulation of text, culture, and wisdom in, 197–98
  in *True Record of the Utmost Sage*, 149–51
Chinese language
  contemporary scholarship on Islam in, 75–78, 81–87
  early Islamic texts in, 1–2, 39–43, 184–85
  transmission of Islamic texts to, 27–33
Chinese philosophy
  Confucian law and, 152–55
  Liu Shi's Islamic scholarship and, 3
Chinese Sufism, early influences in, 1–2
Ching, Julia, 7–8, 56, 59
Chittick, William, 7, 43–55
Chodkiewicz, Michel, 51
Christianity. *See also* missionaries
  in Africa, 4
  Liu Zhi's discussion of, 167
  praxis model of contextualization and, 11
civil reason, Islamic principles and, 201–2
Collected Essays Refuting Heterodoxy (Ouyi Zhixu), 35n68
colonialism, Christian liberation theology and, 4
Confucianism
  Chinese religion and culture and, 59–62, 77–78
  contemporary scholarship on, 81–88

contextualization of *Poem of the Five Sessions of the Moon* and, 126–29, 137–38
contextualization of *True Record of the Utmost Sage* and, 146–51
five endeavors and, 175–78
five ethical codes and, 179–80
Han Kitab and, 180–84
Ibn 'Arabi tradition and, 91n3
Islam in context of, 2–3
literary classics in, 124
in Liu Zhi's Islamic scholarship, 72, 104–8, 191–92
Ma Dexin's Islamic scholarship and, 33
Neo-Confucianism and, 8
in pre-modern China, 33, 37
Rules and Properties of Islam and, 161–66, 179–80, 182–84, 187–92
self-cultivation and, 62–64
translation-conversation model and, 196
Zhu Xi's scholarship on, 55–56, 65
contemporary scholarship. *See* specific authors
in Chinese language, 75–78, 81–87
English-language texts, 73–75, 78–81
history of Islam in China and, 147–51
Ibn 'Arabi tradition in, 54–55
Islamic scholarship in People's Republic of China, 70
on modern relevance of Liu Zhi, 200–202
mysticism in, 53
on *Rules and Properties of Islam*, 179–92
translation-conversation model of contextualization and, 195–204
on unity of existence and disclosure, 117–22
on Wang Daiyu, 48
contextualization of Islam
Chinese culture and, 4–8, 64–65, 87–88, 120–22
exoteric and esoteric interpretations and, 5–7

Frankel and Liang analysis of, 191–92
by Jesuits in China, 191–92
models of, 8–15, 194
Neo-Confucianism and, 7–8
in *Poem of the Five Sessions of the Moon*, 126–29, 135
Real Ruler in Islam and, 168–70
religious message of Islam and, 4
in *Rules and Properties of Islam*, 151–55, 161–66, 187–93
translation-conversation model of, 194–204
triangulation of text, culture, and wisdom in Neo-Confucian context, 197–98
in *True Record of the Utmost Sage of Islam*, 143–51
Corbin, Henry, 49
cosmogony
ascent and descent in, 41–42
contemporary scholarship on Liu Zhi and, 78, 187–92
Liu Zhi's teachings on, 72
Cotter, Francis, 74, 97
countercultural model of contextual theology, 9–15
creation narrative, perfect man in, 51–53
creative transformation, in *Poem of the Five Sesssions of the Moon*, 130–31
creativity of God, 56n154

D

Dagli, Caner K., 45n102
daily life, in *Poem of the Five Sesssions of the Moon*, 129–31
dao
in Chinese Islam, 67–68
heart's relationship to nature and, 172–75
in *Poem of the Five Sesssions of the Moon*, 129–31, 136–38
Daodejing (*Classic of the Way and Power*) (Lao Zi), 34–35

Daoism
  Chinese culture, religion and self-cultivation and, 60–62
  contemporary Chinese scholarship on, 82–88
  contextualization of *Poem of the Five Sessions of the Moon* and, 126–29
  Han Kitab texts and, 148
  Liu Shi's work and influence of, 30–32, 72, 151–52, 188–92
  in pre-modern China, 33–35
  Rules and Properties of Islam and, 161–66
  Sufi spriprituality and, 124
  translation-conversation contextualization model and, 194–204
  unity of existence and, 65
  Wang Daiyu's Islamic interpretations and, 28–30
Daosheng, 36
Dao Sheng, 135–36
"Diagram of the Limitless or Infinite," 57–59
dialectical engagement, Liu Zhi's use of, 191–92
Ding Kejia, 82
disclosure, 46–47, 91–95, 106–8
  contemporary scholarship on, 117–22
  divine self-disclosure, 138
  grade of, 111–14, 123
  unity of existence and and, 115–17
Displaying the Concealment of the True Realm (Liu Zhi translation), 67, 71–72, 74, 80, 82
  divine disclosure in, 111–14
  as translation of Jami's *Lawa'ih*, 48, 65, 99–108, 190
  unity of existence concept in, 90
divine being, Liu Zhi's doctrine of, 84, 161–66
divine emanation, Neo-Platonic concept of, 104
dualism, Neo-Confucianism and, 8

E
education system in China. See also Scripture Hall Education system
  cultural influences in, 126–27
  Muslim education network and, 161–66
Embodied One concept, 30, 84, 91, 94–95, 109–11
  sub-grades of, 115–17
endeavors
  five endeavors, in *Rules and Properties of Islam*, 175–78
  Liu Zhi's teachings on five endeavors, 70–71, 154–55
  meaning and witness of, 170–75
  in *Poem of the Five Sesssions of the Moon*, 129–31, 135–38
English-language texts on Liu Zhi, contemporary scholarship on, 73–75, 78–81
enlightenment, Buddhist search for, in *Poem of the Five Sesssions of the Moon*, 128–29, 135–36
epistemology, in Liu Zhi's texts, 168–70, 187–92
esoteric interpretation
  of Islamic texts, 5–7, 121–22
  translation-conversation model and, 196
exoteric interpretation
  of Islamic texts, 5–7
  translation-conversation model and, 196
An Explanation of the Arabic Alphabets, 67
An Explanation of the Meaning of Islamic Letters (Liu Zhi), 71–72
The Explanation of Four Classics (Ma Dexin), 32–33
The Explanation of the Five Endeavors (Liu Zhi), 16, 67, 70–71, 85

F
Fadl, Khaled Abou El, 202
Fansuri, Hamzah, 94n12
Farghani, Sa'id al-Din, 45–48, 54, 112n55

The Final Return of the Great Transformation (Ma Dexin), 32–33
fiqh, principle of, 202
five-character literary form
    Chinese education and, 124–26
    in Neo-Confucian tradition, 132
five endeavors, in *Rules and Properties of Islam*, 175–78, 187–92
five ethical codes, in *Rules and Properties of Islam*, 179–80, 187–92
Five Pillars, Islamic concept of, 162–63
    five endeavors and, 175–78
    translation-conversation model and, 195–204
Five Sessions of the Moon (Liu Zhi), 40–41
Fletcher, Joseph, 118
Ford, Joseph, 73
Frankel, James, 3, 75, 78–81, 87
    on contextualization by Liu Zhi, 134, 153n72, 154
    on *Rules and Properties of Islam*, 157, 184–87, 189–93
Fung Yulan, 7n25, 33, 35–37, 135
furkan (separation), in Ibn 'Arabi tradition, 43–44

G

Gess (early Chinese Islamic figure), 147–48
Gladney, Dru, 23–24
Gleams. See Lawa'ih (Gleams) (Jami)
Gnosticism, Sufism and, 117–22
God, multiplicity and unity of, Liu Zhi on, 68
Great Learning, Wang Yangming on, 173–75
Great Learning of the Pure and Real (Wang Daiyu), 74, 93–95
The Great Learning of the Pure and Real (Wang Daiyu), 29–30
Great Ultimate (*taiji*), 56–59, 65, 67–68
    Neo-Confucian sagehood and, 140
    in *Poem of the Five Sesssions of the Moon*, 129–31
Guo Suxing, 183–84

H

Hadith
    five relationships and, 182–84, 187–92
    literature of, 47, 53
    Muslim minorities in modern era and, 201–2
    in *Poem of the Five Sesssions of the Moon*, 136
Hai Jing, 182
Hanafi School of Law, 31
Han Chinese
    Liu Zhi's scholarship and, 134–35
    Muslims and, 20–22, 23n20, 189–92
Han Kitab, 68–69, 74, 77, 80, 87
    Confuciansm and, 180–84
    contemporary scholarship on, 148
    Frankel on Liu Zhi and, 185–87
    Rules and Properties of Islam as part of, 157–58
The Happy Excursion (Zhang Zi), 34–35
haqiqa (truth), in *Poem of the Five Sessions of the Moon*, 133–38
heart
    five endeavors and, 175–78, 192
    knowledge of Real Ruler and, 170–75
    in *Rules and Properties of Islam*, 165–66, 168–70
    Wuang Daiyu's discussion of, 95
heaven, way of, in *Rules and Properties of Islam*, 179–80, 183–84, 187–92
Helminski, Kabir, 202
Hesselgrave, David, 8–9
heterodoxy, in Chinese Islam, 120–22
historiography, Chinese cultural religion and, 60–62
history
    in *Rules and Properties of Islam*, 162–66
    translation-conversation model and, 196
Hu Dengzhou, 25

Hui Muslims
  Chinese scripture language of, 27n42
  contemporary scholarship on, 23–24, 75, 78–79, 81–88, 148–51
  contextualization of Islam and, 4, 16, 64–65, 191–92
  Frankel's discussion of, 185–87
  missionary scholarship on, 73
  Nanjing School and, 25–27
  Poem of the Five Sessions of the Moon and, 131, 134–35
  in pre-modern China, 20–24
  Rules and Properties of Islam and, 163–66
  scholarly Muslim literature of, 26–27
  statistics on, 19n1
  Sufism and, 190
humanity
  in Liu Zhi's scholarship, 96–99, 164–66, 183–84
  in *Rules and Properties of Islam*, 179–80, 182–84, 187–92
  in Wang Daiyu's scholarship, 91–95

I

Ibn 'Arabi
  contemporary scholarship on, 81, 86
  foundational principles in writing of, 43–44
  interpretation of Islamic texts by, 6–7
  Jami and, 41–42, 99–108
  Liu Zhi's scholarship and, 48, 65, 99–108, 111–14, 117–20, 140
  in modern scholarship, 54–55
  Naqshbandi Sufism and, 118–22
  Nasafi's work and, 39, 42–43
  orthodoxy in philosophy of, 120–22
  perfect man concept and, 50–53
  spirituality of Sufism and, 48–55
  Sufism and, 1–3, 49–50, 120–22, 190–92
  translation-conversation model and, 196–204
  translations of, 50n124
  unity of existence concept and, 43–48, 90–122
  Wang Daiyu and influence of, 90–95
Ibn Sab'in, 46
Ibn Taymiyya, 121–22
Ibu Battutah, 20
immanence (*bao*)
  divine disclosure and, 111–14
  of Real Ruler, 109–11
  Real Ruler and, 167
imperial rule, Liu Zhi's support for, 63n180, 188–92
Integration of Islamic theory
  contemporary scholarship on, 181–84
  five endeavors and, 177–78
  Liu Zhi and, 114–17
An Introduction of Collected Islamic Books in 1780, 78n53
Islam
  historical context in China for, 19–33, 146–51
  Liu Zhi on origin and history of, 1–2, 96–99
  philosophical context in China of, 33–39, 64–65
  in *Rules and Properties of Islam*, 157–93
Islamic texts
  in Chinese, 39–43
  Chinese transmission of, 27–33
  context in Chinese culture of, 4–8, 39–64
  exoteric and esoteric interpretations of, 5–7
  Wang Daiyu's transmission of, 90–95
Israeli, Raphael, 24

J

Jahriyya Sufism, 31
Jami, Abd al-Rahman, 54
  contemporary Chinese scholarship on, 82
  contemporary English scholarship on, 80–81
  Islamic texts by, 3, 39, 41–42, 50

Liu Zhi's translation of, 99–108,
111–14, 123, 190
origins of transformation and,
118–22
perfect man concept and, 51–52
Poem of the Five Sesssions of the Moon and influence of, 129
tawhid in work of, 105, 114–15
wahdat al-wujud theology and, 45
Jesuits in China, 9, 35n68, 152,
185–86, 191–92
translation-conversation contextualization model and, 194
Jews in China
in Frankel's research, 185–87
Liu Zhi and, 185–86
Ji Fangtong, 182
Jin Yijiu, 24n33, 48, 50, 72
analysis of *Poem of the Five Sessions of the Moon* by, 126–31
on disclosure and emanation,
117–22
on Liu Zhi, 76–77, 87–88, 103–4
on *Nature and Principle in Islam*,
189
on perfect man in Chinese Sufism,
147–48
on *Rules and Properties of Islam*,
157, 162–63
Sufism studied by, 133–34
on Wang Daiyu, 91–92
on Xi Dao Tang Muslim community, 202–4
Johns, Anthony, 2

K

Kalam, 119
Kalin, Ibrahim, 47–48
Kamal, Muhammad, 5–7
Kangxi (Emperor), 191–92
Kant, Immanuel, 11
karma, in Chinese religious culture,
62
Khuilai Khan, 20
Knysh, Alexander, 5–7, 49–50,
52n142, 120–22
Koranic exegesis, 47
Koyama, Kosuke, 14

kur'an (togetherness), in Ibn 'Arabi tradition, 43–44

L

Lao Zi, 34–35, 151–52
Latin America, Christian liberation theology in, 4
Lawa'ih (Jami), *tawhid* in, 105,
114–15
Lawa'ih (*Gleams*) (Jami), 3, 39, 41–42,
50, 80–82
divine disclosure in, 111–14
Liu Zhi's translation of, 99–108
law of properties. *See also shi'a*
Liu Zhi's use of Confucian concepts in, 152–55
in *Rules and Properties of Islam*,
164–66, 185–87
learning, in *True Record of the Utmost Sage of Islam*, 145, 150–51
Leslie, David (same as Donald?), 24
Leslie, Donald, 22, 31, 69n11, 74
on *True Record of the Utmost Sage of Islam*, 139
li (principle), 8, 37–39. *See also* School of Principle
contemporary Chinese scholarship on, 86
in *True Record of the Utmost Sage of Islam*, 143–44
in Zhu Xi's teachings, 56–59
Liang Xiangming, 3, 76–77, 82–87
on *Rules and Properties of Islam*,
157, 184, 187–93
Lipman, Jonathan, 24
Liu Sanjie, 78–79
Liu Yihong, 28–29, 76, 82–83
on Sufi spirituality, 48
Liu Zhi, 1
Chinese contemporary scholarship on, 75–78, 81–88
Chinese cultural religion and,
60–62
contemporary scholarship on, 48,
73–89, 180–84
contextualization of Islam by, 4,
64–65
Daoism and scholarship of, 35

Liu Zhi *(continued)*
　divine disclosure and, 111–14
　English-language contemporary scholarship on, 73–75, 78–81, 87–88
　Frankel's analysis of, 181–87
　Hui Muslims and, 26
　imperal status of works by, 68–69
　imperial rule in teachings of, 63n180, 188–92
　intolerance of Islam in China and, 15–16
　Islamic texts discussed by, 39–64
　law of three vehicles of, 133–38
　legacy in China of, 202–4
　on life of Buddha, 151n59
　models of contextualization and work of, 9–15
　modern relevance for Muslim ethnic nationalities in China, 200–202
　on Muhammad, 53, 95
　Nasafi's work and, 42–43
　Neo-Confucianism and, 7–8, 55–64, 95–99, 123–56
　Neo-Platonism and, 117–22
　overview of trilogy by, 66–67
　Qing dynasty and, 22
　on Razi's *Mirsad al-'ibad*, 40–41
　sagehood in Neo-Confucianism and work of, 138–51
　Scripture Hall Education System and, 26–27
　Sufi spirituality in works of, 31–32, 39, 50, 55–64, 123–56
　translation-conversation model of contextualization, 194–204
　translation of Jami's *Lawa'ih* (*Gleams*), 99–108
　transmission of Islamic texts by, 30–32
　unity of existence concept and, 48, 65, 90–122
　Western scholarship on, 24n31
　Zhu Xi's interpretations and, 56–59
Loewenthal, Rudolf, 24
Long Yin, 190

M

Ma Dexin, 32–33
　contemporary Chinese scholarship on, 76, 83
Madrasah education system, 91n5, 99n19
Ma Duoyong, 181
Ma Haiyun, 147–48
Mahayana Buddhism, 36
Ma Hualung, 23
Ma Lianyuan, 31, 32, 108, 190
Ma Mingxin, 22–23
Manchu invasion, 56
mandate
　Islamic concept of, 71
　in Liu Zhi's writing, 128, 140–45, 184
Ma Qixi, 3, 31–32
Maqsad-i aqsa (*The Furthest Goal*) (Nasafi), 39, 42–43
Mason, Isaac, 24, 32, 69, 73, 139
Massignon, Louis, 46
Matsumoto, Akiro, 40–41, 99n19
Ma Zhu, 4, 28–29, 70
　contemporary scholarship on, 76, 78–79
meditation, in Razi's *Mirsad al-'ibad*, 40–41
Ming dynasty
　Buddhism in, 35–37
　Chinese sages in, 152
　contemporary scholarship on, 85–86
　literary format during, 132
　Muslims in, 21–22, 186–87
　Nanjing School and, 25–27
　Neo-Confucianism and, 38–39, 56
　philosophical traditions in, 33–39
Min Wenjie, 85, 183–84
Mirsad al-'ibad (*The Path of God's Bondsmen from Origin to Return*) (Razi), 39–41
missionaries, Chinese Muslims and, 24, 73
Models of Contextual Theology (Bevans), 9–15
modern Islamic scholarship
　Hui Muslims and, 23–24

on Liu Zhi, 48
Sufism in, 48–49, 53–55
Mongol Yuan dynasty, 20
monism, Neo-Confucianism and, 8
monotheism
  cosmological argument in, 168–70
  in early China, 147, 185–87
  Liu Shi's discussion of, 151–52
moon lady, myth of, in *Poem of the Five Sesssions of the Moon*, 131
moral cultivation, perfect man concept and, 62
Muhammad
  five endeavors and, 177–78
  Liu Zhi's teaching on, 32, 65, 68–70, 78, 96, 146–51, 190–92
  Ma Dexin's Islamic scholarship on, 33
  Ma Zhu's discussion of, 70
  perfect man concept and, 50–53, 138–51
  in *Rules and Properties of Islam*, 162–66, 175
  in *True Record of the Utmost Sage of Islam*, 140–45
Murata, Sachiko, 3, 8, 39, 41n84, 69n11
  on disclosure and emanation, 117–22
  on heart and soul, 168n18
  on Islamic endeavor, 165–66
  on Jami, 99–104
  on Liu Zhi, 74–75, 78–81, 87–88, 103–4, 107–9, 111–14
  on *Nature and Principle in Islam*, 189–90
  on *Poem of the Five Sesssions of the Moon*, 136
  on root substance, 112–14
  on *True Record of the Utmost Sage of Islam*, 139–40
  on Wang Daiyu, 91–95
Muslim ethnic minorities. *See also* Uyghur Muslims; specific Muslim groups, e.g. Hui Muslims
  in modern era, 23–24, 202–4
  modern relevance of Liu Zhi and, 200–202
  in pre-modern era, 19–24
  Rules and Properties of Islam and, 163–66
  Scripture Hall education system and, 25–27
  Sinicization of, 77–78, 81–87
  statistics on, 19n1
Muslim litreati in China
  Confucianism and, 22
  contemporary scholarship on, 73–75, 78–87, 186–87
  contextualization of Islam by, 4–5, 134–35
  Ibn 'Arabi tradition and, 92–95
  ministerial offices held by, 33–34, 135
  Rules and Properties of Islam and, 163–66
  scholarship on, 26–27, 29
  schools established by, 26
  three vehicles metaphor of, 134
Muslim rights, in *Rules and Properties of Islam*, 163
mutakallimun, wujud theology and, 44
mysticism
  contemporary scholarship on Sufism and, 53, 86–87, 190–92
  in Liu Zhi's scholarship, 50, 72
  Razi's interpretation of, 39–41
  Sufism and, 2
mythical stories, Islam in China and, 147–48

N

Nanjing School, Chinese Muslims and, 25, 75, 78–79
Na Qi, 81
Naqshbandi Sufism, 41–42, 99–108, 118–22
Nasafi, Aziz al-Din, 39, 42–43, 54
Nasr, Seyyed Hossein, 54n149
nature, heart's relationship to, 171–75
The Nature and Principle in Islam (Liu Zhi), 3, 30, 31, 32, 39, 66–68, 103
  contemporary scholarship on, 78, 83–87, 150–51, 182–84, 189–92

The Nature and Principle in Islam (Liu Zhi) *(continued)*
   contextualization in, 199–200
   cosmogony in, 72
   humanity analyzed in, 140
   Islamic sciences in, 114–17
   Rules and Properties of Islam compared with, 151–55, 160–61, 166–67
   Sufism and, 137–38
   unity of existence in, 90, 108–17
neo-Confucianism, Liu Zhi and, 1–2
Neo-Confucian tradition
   Chinese culture, religion and self-cultivation and, 60–62, 124–38
   contemporary Chinese scholarship on, 75–78, 82–88
   contemporary English scholarship on, 80–81, 88
   contextualization of *Poem of the Five Sessions of the Moon* and, 126–29
   deviations and cults within, 63n181
   Hui translations of Islamic texts and, 22–23
   humanity in, 183–84
   literary classics in Quing dynasty and, 124–38
   Liu Shi's scholarship and, 3, 15–17, 30–32, 64–65, 71–72, 160–61, 188–92
   Muslim litrerati and, 134–35
   poetry in, 132
   practical wisdom in, 62–64
   in pre-modern China, 33, 37–39
   in *Rules and Properties of Islam*, 151–55, 157–93
   sagehood in, 138–51
   School of Mind and, 174–75
   School of Principle and, 174–75
   Sufi spirituality and, 55–64, 123–56
   theism and, 7–8
   translation-conversation contextualization model and, 194–204
   translation-conversation model and, 195–204
   triangulation of text, culture, and wisdom in, 197–98
   in *True Record of the Utmost Sage*, 148–51
   unity of existence and, 116–17
   Wang Daiyu's transmission of Islamic texts and, 28–30
   Zhu Xi and, 55–59
Neo-Daoism, 33
Neo-Platonism, 104
   Sufism and, 117–22
   translation-conversation model and, 195
Neville, Richard, 56n154
Nirvana, Buddhist concept of, 136
Numerical One concept, 30, 84, 91, 94–95, 109–11
Nur al-Haqq. *See* Ma Lianyuan

O

oneness, concept of, 45n102
orthodoxy, in Chinese Islam, 120–22, 151–55
orthopraxis
   of al-Ghazali and Ibn 'Arabi, 7
   in Liu Zhi's work, 105–6, 137–38
   in *Rules and Properties of Islam,* 166
   Schimmel's work on, 53

P

panentheism, 110–11
   divine disclosure and, 111–14, 118–22
pantheism
   disclosure and, 117–22
   immanence and, 110–11
Pears, Angie, 4, 191–92
People's Republic of China. *See also* China
   contemporary Islamic scholarship in, 75–78, 81–87
   Liu Zhi's legacy in, 202–4
   marginalization of Sufism in, 48–49
   modern Islamic scholarship in, 70, 73–74
   Muslims in, 23–24
perfect man concept
   Chinese self-cultivation and, 62
   in Ibn 'Arabi tradition, 50–53

in *True Record of the Utmost Sage of Islam* (Liu Zhi), 138–51
Peripatetic philosophy, 46
Persian-Chinese contacts, pre-modern trade and diplomatic relations, 19–20
Persian texts
    Chinese transmission of, 27–33
    contemporary scholarship on Liu Zhi's sources, 74, 81–83
    Hui translations of, 22, 26–27
    of Jami's work, 99n19
    Liu Zhi's translations of, 1–2, 30–32
    Ma Dexin's translations of, 32–33
Petersen, Kristian, 75
philosophy
    Chinese cultural religion and, 60–62
    Chinese Islam in context of, 33–39
The Poem of Eulogizing the Prophet Muhammad, Ma Dexin's translation of, 33
The Poem of the Five Sessions of the Moon (Liu Zhi), 16, 40–41, 67, 71–72, 88, 123–24
    basic elements of Sufism and Sufi spirituality in, 124–26, 133–34
    chiastic structure of, 129–31
    commentary and analysis of, 131–38
    contextualiztion of using Neo-Confucianism, Buddhism, and Daoism, 126–29
    English translation of, 205–9
    literary form of, 125–26, 131–33
political activism, Sufism and, 48n115
portraying (*yu*), Liu Zhi's usage of, 106
practical knowledge, in *Poem of the Five Sessions of the Moon*, 134–38
praxis model of contextual theology, 9–15
predestination, in *Poem of the Five Sesssions of the Moon*, 129–31
preserving (*cun*), Liu Zhi's usage of, 106
The Proper Meaning of Islam (Xu Lan), 72

Q

Qasida al-Burda (*Poem of the Mantle*), 33
qi (vital energy), 8
    in Zhu Xi's teachings, 56–59
Qing dynasty
    Buddhism in, 36–37
    Chinese sages in, 152
    Hui literati in, 4
    Islamic scholarship in, 22–23, 63
    Jesuits in China and, 191–92
    literary format during, 132
    Liu Zhi's scholarship and, 22, 63n180, 68–69, 134–38
    Muslims in, 1, 186–87
    Neo-Confucianism and, 38–39, 56, 124–38
    philosophical traditions in, 33–39
    religious and cultural traditions in, 153–55
    Turkic Muslims and, 148
Qunawi, Sadr al-Din, 45–48, 54–55
Qur'an and Qur'anic materials
    Baydawi's commentary on, 39
    exoteric and esoteric interpretations of, 5–7
    five endeavors and, 175–78, 187–92
    Liu Zhi's translations of, 1–2
    in modern scholarship, 53–55
    Muslim minorities in modern era and, 201–2
    Sufism and, 49–50
    translation-conversation model and, 196

R

Ramadan, Tariq, 200–202
Razi, Najm al-Din, 39–41, 140
Real One (Real Being) concept, 30, 67, 72, 84–85, 91, 94–95, 109
    in *Poem of the Five Sessions of the Moon* (Liu Zhi), 128–31
    translation-conversation model and, 195–204
    unity of existence and, 114–17
Real Ruler principle
    epistemology and, 168–70

Real Ruler principle *(continued)*
   five endeavors and, 175–78
   knowledge of, 170–75
   in Liu Zhi's scholarship, 65, 72, 84–87, 96–99, 117–22, 136–38
   in *Rules and Properties of Islam*, 166–67, 187–92
   support for emperor and, 63n180, 188–92
   transcendence and immanence, 109–11
   in Wang Daiyu's teachings, 90–95
The Real Commentary on the True Teaching (Wang Daiyu), 29–30
   unity of existence in, 90–95
Register of Lineage and Transmission of Classical Learning, 78n53
Reichelt, Karl L., 74, 97
religion
   Chinese culture and self-cultivation and, 59–62, 153–55
   definitions of, 7n25
   Neo-Confucian practical wisdom and, 62–64
   orthodoxy and heterodoxy in, 120–22
religious message of Islam, context in Chinese culture of, 4
re-marriage, Liu Zhi on, 181
Ricci, Matteo, 9, 147, 151–52, 191–92, 194
Rida, Muhammad Rashid, 118
righteousness (*Yi*), 62–64
ritual prayer, five endeavors and, 177–78
Rizvi, Sajjad H., 46–48, 54
root suchness
   Liu Zhi's concept of, 112–14, 118–22, 143
   Real Ruler in *Rules and Properties of Islam* and, 166–67
   in "True Practice of Sage Endeavor" diagram, 165–66
Ruan Bin, 41–42, 104n28
The Rules and Properties of Islam (Liu Zhi), 3, 16, 30, 39, 66–69
   author's preface and personal narrative in, 159–61

   Confucian spirituality in, 137–38
   contemporary scholarship on, 75, 78, 80–81, 87, 179–93
   contextualization in, 151–55, 161–66, 191–92, 199–200
   divine disclosure in, 111–14
   English translation of, 157–58, 192–93, 218–56
   epistemology in, 168–70
   Explanation of the Five Endeavors and, 71
   five endeavors in, 175–78
   Frankel's analysis of, 181–87
   Islamic theory and practice in, 114–17, 157–93
   legitimacy of Qing government in, 41
   Liang Xiangming's analysis of, 187–92
   meaning and witness in, 170–75
   Muhammad in, 150–51
   Neo-Confucian culture in, 151–55, 157–93
   original teaching of Liu Zhi in, 161–66
   outline of chapters in, 157–58
   Real Ruler in, 109–11, 166–67
   substance discussed in, 106
   unity of existence in, 90, 108–17

S

Sa'ad ibn Abi Waqqas, 148
Sadra, Mulla, 46–48
sages
   Neo-Confucian concept of, 62, 138–55
   Rules and Properties of Islam and, 162–66
   translation-conversation model and, 196
The Sage Learning of Liu Zhi: Thought in Confucian Terms (Murata), 74–75
Sayyid 'Ajal Shams al-Din, 20
Schimmel, Annemarie, 48–49, 53
School of Mind, 37–39, 188–92
   heart's relationship to nature and, 173–75, 192

School of Principle, 37–39, 55–59, 173–75, 188–92
Scripture Hall Education system, 25–27
  contemporary scholarship on, 75, 77–78
  Jami's texts in, 41–42, 45, 104, 114–15
  Mirsad al-'ibad (Razi) required in, 39–41
  Nasafi's work in, 39, 42–43
  Poem of the Five Sessions of the Moon in, 131
  Sufi literature in, 50, 119–22, 190
  textbooks included in, 39
seafaring journey metaphor, in *Poem of the Five Sessions of the Moon*, 126–29, 135–36
Selected Examination of the Rules and Properties of Islam (Liu Zhi), 159–61
  English translation of, 215–17
self-cultivation
  Chinese culture and religion and, 59–62
  contemporary scholarship on, 182
  endeavor and, 171–75
  five endeavors and, 175–78
  Neo-Confucian wisdom as, 62–65
  in *Rules and Properties of Islam*, 151–55, 162–63
  translation-conversation model and, 196
senses, five endeavors and, 176–78
seven-character literary form
  Chinese education and, 124–26
  in Neo-Confucian tradition, 132
Shams al-Din al-Samatra'i, 94n12
shari'a. *See also* law of properties
  in *Poem of the Five Sessions of the Moon* in, 133–34
  Ramadan's interpretation of, 201n7
  in *Rules and Properties of Islam*, 162–63, 185–87
  Sufism and, 43, 50, 65
Sha Zhongping, 76–77, 82–87
  on humanity in Liu Zhi, 183–84
Shen (wonder or god), 36

She Yunshan, 41–42
Shi'a Islam
  hadith literature of, 47
  Liu Shi's Islamic scholarship and, 31–32, 43, 50, 65, 105–8, 123–24
Shi Lili, 182
Silk trade
  Muslim minorities in China and, 25–27
  spread of Islam and, 20
Singh, David, 51n134
Sinicization of Islam
  contemporary scholarship on, 77–78, 81–87, 195–96
  Liu Zhi's teachings on Islam and, 161–66
Siriyeh, Elizabeth, 48n115
Six Classics, 153
Smith, Huston, 7n25
Song Dynasty, 37, 96
soul, Liu Zhi on heart and, 165–66, 168n18
spirituality in Sufism, 2
  Chinese cultural religion and, 60–62
  Ibn 'Arabi tradition and, 48–55
  Liu Zhi's analysis in Neo-Confucian context, 123–56
  Neo-Confucian practical wisdom and, 62–64
  translation-conversation model and, 196
Stöcker-Parnian, Barbara, 75
substance, Liu Zhi's discussion of, 106
Subtle Analogy Classic, 72
suchness (*ren*), Liu Zhi's concept of, 109n48
Sufism in China
  contemporary scholarship on, 53–55, 77–78, 82–88, 190–92
  contextualization of *Poem of the Five Sesssions of the Moon* and, 128–38
  as contextualized Neo-Confucian wisdom, 62–64
  Frankel on Liu Zhi and, 190–92
  history of, 91n5
  Ibn 'Arabi tradition in, 43–55

Sufism in China *(continued)*
  Jami's interpretations of, 41–42, 99–108
  Knysh's discussion of, 49–50
  Liang Ziangming on Liu Zhi and, 188–92
  in Liu Shi's Islamic scholarship, 31–32, 39, 65, 72, 82, 119–22
  Liu Zhi's law of three vehicles and, 133–38
  moderation in interpretations of, 7
  in modern era, 48–49
  mysticism *vs.* spirituality in, 2
  Neo-Platonism and, 117–22
  perfect man concept in, 50–53, 147–51
  Razi's interpretation of, 39–41
  Rules and Properties of Islam and, 164–66
  shari'a and, 43, 50, 65
  spirituality in, 48–55, 60–64, 123–56
  translation-conversation model and, 195
  wahdat al-wujud theology and, 44–48
Sui dynasty, 146
Sui Mende (Emperor), 162
Sunni Islam, 31
Sun Zhenyu, 76, 183–84
syncretism
  Chinese Islam and, 87
  in *Rules and Properties of Islam*, 153n72
synthetic (conversation) model of contextual theology, 9–15, 194–204

T

tai chi (Great Ultimate), 37–38
Tajik ethnic minority, 23n20
Tang dynasty, Neo-Confucian tradition in, 37
Tang Xiaoping, 23
tanzih (incomparability), in Ibn 'Arabi tradition, 43–44
tariaqa (path), in *Poem of the Five Sessions of the Moon*, 133–38

Tarjama-yi mawlud-i Mustafa ('Afif ibn Muhammad Kaziruni), 69n11, 139
tashbih (similarity), in Ibn 'Arabi tradition, 43–44
tawhid
  in Ibn 'Arabi tradition, 43–44, 46
  in Jami's work, 105, 114–15
  in Wang Daiyu's teachings, 90–95
theism
  Neo-Confucianism and, 7–8
  in Zhu Xi's teachings, 56–59
Thomas, David, 52–53
Thompson, Kirill, 62
three-character literary form
  Chinese education and, 124–26
  Liu Zhi's use of, 95–99
  in Neo-Confucian tradition, 132
three Ones of Wang Daiyu, 109–11, 115–17, 123. *See also* Embodied One, Numerical One and Real One concepts
Three Teachings in Chinese culture, 33–39, 60–62, 162
  contextualization of *Poem of the Five Sesssions of the Moon* and, 128–29
  contextualization of *True Record of the Utmost Sage* and, 146–51
The Three-Character Classic (Liu Zhi), 67, 71–72, 104
  contemporary scholarship on, 74
  as elementary text on Islam, 124–26, 155
  Neo-Confucianism and, 95–99
  unity of existence concept in, 90
Tianfan Dianli personal narrative, 215–17
tianzhu ("Lord of Heaven"), 186
Tillich, Paul, 7n25, 110n53
transcendence
  of Real Ruler, 109–11
  Real Ruler and, 167
transcendent model of contextual theology, 9–15
translation-conversation model of contextualization, analysis of, 194–204

translation model of contextual theology, 9–15, 194–204
triad of interconnected relationships, 61–62
"True Practice of Sage Endeavor" diagram, 165–66, 170–75
five endeavors and, 175–78
True Record of the Utmost Sage of Islam (Liu Zhi), 16
The True Answers of the Very Real (Wang Daiyu), 29–30
The True Record of the Utmost Sage of Islam (Liu Zhi), 53, 67, 69–70
absence of current scholarship on, 78
commentary and analysis on, 145–51
contextualization in, 199–200
English translation of, 210–214
Mason's translation of, 73
Muhammad in, 140–45, 162
Neo-Confucian sagehood and, 138–51, 155–56
sources for, 119–22
unity of existence, 108–17
Turkic Muslims, in pre-modern China, 22, 147–48
Tustari, Sahl al-, 50–51
Tu Weiming, 91n3, 150

U

Ultimate of Nonbeing (*Wuji*), 58
in *Poem of the Five Sesssions of the Moon*, 128–31
unboundedness, Liu Zhi's translation of Jami's concept of, 107–8
unity of existence
contemporary scholarship on, 117–22
in Ibn 'Arabi tradition, 43–48
in Jami's *Lawa'ih*, 99–108
Liang Xiangming's discussion of, 37–39, 188–92
Liu Zhi's concept of, 48, 65, 90–122, 190–92
in *Poem of the Five Sesssions of the Moon*, 136–38
return to the Real and, 114–17
translation-conversation model and, 195–204
Wang Daiyu and, 90–95
unveiling in Islamic theology, modern scholarship on, 53–55
Utmost Sage
Confucian tradition and, 146–51
contemporary scholarship on, 190–92
five endeavors and, 177–78
Liu Zhi's discussion of, 53, 65, 67, 69–71, 96–99, 138–55
Neo-Confucian sagehood and, 62, 138–51
in *Rules and Properties of Islam*, 164–66
Uyghurs
contemporary scholarship on, 75, 86–87
Islamic reforms and, 27n41
missionary scholarship on, 73
in modern China, 23–24
in pre-modern China, 20, 22–24
statistics on, 19n1

V

vehicle metaphor
in *Poem of the Five Sessions of the Moon*, 133–38
in *Rules and Properties of Islam*, 164–66
veils, in Islamic tradition, 53–55
Vroom, Hendrik M., 201–2

W

wahdat al-shuhdud, 46, 52n142
wahdat al-wujud
Ibn 'Arabi's understanding of, 43–48
Jami's popularization of, 99–108
unity of existence and, 116–17
Wang Daiyu, 4, 22, 26
contemporary Chinese scholarship on, 76–77, 82–84, 87–88
contemporary English scholarship on, 48, 74–75, 87–88

Wang Daiyu *(continued)*
  Ibn 'Arabi tradition in China and, 90–95
  influence on Liu Zhi of, 123, 191–92
  on Muhammad, 68
  three Ones of, 109–11, 115–17, 123
  transmission of Islamic texts by, 28–30
  unity of existence and, 115–17
Wang Fuzhi, 56
Wang Junrong, 50, 76, 92–95
Wang Yangming, 38, 56, 173–75
Wassel, Mohamed, 31, 74
Western society, Muslim minorities in, 200–202
Whitehead, Alfred N., 56n154
Whittingham, Martin, 5
Wiqaya text, 31
wisdom
  Neo-Confucian concept of, 62–64
  in *Poem of the Five Sessions of the Moon*, 134–38
  in *Rules and Properties of Islam*, 151–55
  triangulation of text, culture, and wisdom in Neo-Confucian context, 197–98
witness (*Shahadah*)
  in *Rules and Properties of Islam*, 170–75
  tradition of, 55, 176–77
wujud (existence or being), 44–48. *See also wahdat al-wujud*
Wu Zunqi, 76

X

Xi Dao Tang Muslim community, 31–32, 202–4
Xu Lan, 72

Y

Yang Huiazhong, 85–86
Yang Zhijiu, 21
Yang Zhongdong, 86–87
Yao, 60
Yao Xinzhong, 62
Yijing (Classic of Change), 35–36
Yin/Yang thought, 34–35, 37, 57–59, 65
  contextualization of *Poem of the Five Sesssions of the Moon* and, 128–29
Yongle, 25
Yongzheng, 36
Yu, Andy, 201
Yuan dynasty, philosophical tradition in, 33
Yuan Guozuo, 78n53
Yuan Ruqi, 78
Yuet Keunt Lo, 36
Yu Jiyuan, 62–63

Z

Zhao, 60
Zhao Can, 78n53
Zheng He, 21
Zheng Wenquan, 3, 85–86
Zhixu Ouyi, 35
Zhou Dunyi, 37
  Great Ultimate concept and, 56–58
Zhuang Zi, 34–35
Zhu Xi, 8
  contemporary Chinese scholarship on, 77, 86
  Neo-Confucian tradition and, 37–39, 55–59
  School of Principle, 173–75
  Thompson's analysis of, 62
  Wang Fuzhi's rejection of, 56
Zhu Xiaojun, 181–82
Zhu Yuanzhang, 21, 25
Zhu Zi, maxims of, 124–26
Zwemer, Samuel M., 139

www.ingramcontent.com/pod-product-compliance
Lightning Source LLC
Chambersburg PA
CBHW061431300426
44114CB00014B/1633